20ᴛʜ Cᴇɴᴛᴜʀʏ Rᴏᴄᴋ ᴀɴᴅ Rᴏʟʟ

ALTERNATIVE ROCK

Alan Cross

Watch For The Rest Of The Series

A GUIDE TO THE ARTISTS WHO MADE THE CENTURY'S GREATEST ROCK MUSIC

20th CENTURY ROCK AND ROLL

A COLLECTOR'S GUIDE PUBLISHING SERIES

For ordering information see our web site at
www.cgpublishing.com

We acknowledge the financial support of the Government of Canada through
the Book Publishing Industry Development Program for our publishing activities.
Published by Collector's Guide Publishing Inc., Box 62034, Burlington, Ontario, Canada, L7R 4K2
Printed and bound in Canada
20th Century Rock and Roll - ALTERNATIVE MUSIC
by Alan Cross
ISBN 1-896522-19-X

20TH CENTURY ROCK AND ROLL

ALTERNATIVE ROCK

Alan Cross

TABLE OF CONTENTS

Preface

In its purest form, rock and roll is a snapshot of the present — a moment, a feeling, a vision — that's forever captured in time. Music has the ability to suck you in, creating powerful emotional and physical reactions, and often leaves behind an indelible time and date stamp on your brain. Think about it — how many times has a specific song triggered a memory, an emotion, a sensation? All it takes is a few notes and part of you is instantly transported back to the time in your life that's subconsciously associated with that song.

But, inevitably and inexorably, the music of our present becomes the music of our past. In the process, much of it is forgotten or rendered irrelevant, left to die on some dusty shelf. That's the way it is with most pop and rock; music that is made for moment often doesn't age that well. (Who remembers the name of the second Buggles album? Whatever happened to the Hoodoo Gurus? Did Adorable really have to break up?) It's not a stretch to say that 99.9% of all rock and roll is ultimately as disposable as your last Starbucks coffee cup.

However, there is that remaining one tenth of one percent. This is the music that becomes part of the foundation upon which the future is built. Its performers were pioneers, artists who were able to push things to the limit by making music that colored outside the lines. As this music slowly bubbled up from the underground, it created new trails for others to follow. Through their risks, experiments and mistakes, they were the ones who dragged the rest of the rock and roll universe to the next level. Had it not been for the contributions and sacrifices of these men and women, the music of this moment would sound very, very different.

This book is dedicated to the elite few from the 20th century who, by accident or design, showed us the future — whether or not we were ready to hear it.

Alan Cross
Waterdown, Ontario
August 1999

Acknowledgments

Once again, the Official Support Team came through. Without them, I would never be able to write these damn books.

Special thanks to my friends and co-workers at Edge 102 / Toronto, especially Hal and Stu who indulge me and my writing projects.

Then there's Carmen, Sarah and all the Internet folk (like Larry, David, Anthony and Christophe) who were always quick with an answer. Diane, Rob, Tony and Ivar all helped with photos.

My love to my wife who understands why I spend all those hours alone in the den. She also works as an unofficial editor, secretary and research assistant during these frantic periods of writing and rewriting.

And once again, the Strange Little Dog came through, keeping watch and offering perspective from her spot next to the desk. All writers need to go on a nice, quiet walk with a dog from time to time. It clears your head.

Introduction

You should know that this book is the product of equal parts anxiety and fiery debate. With all the new rock and alternative music we've heard over the last four decades, how could anyone possibly distill everything down to a definitive list of the Greatest of All Time that could satisfy all music fans?

The answer is: you can't.

Up close, music, like every other form of art, is a very subjective thing. Every fan has his or her own preferences, biases, prejudices, agendas and emotional attachments. These factors are further skewed by such things as age, race, geography, education, income level and any other demographic and psychographic element you care to name. Alt-rock has the added complication of being so diverse in sound and scope that it can be infinitely customized, allowing each individual fan to find a niche all his own.

For example, when I solicited opinions from fans about who should be covered in this book, many people made impassioned pleas that the Psychedelic Furs be included. Songs like *The Ghost in You* and *Love My Way* was the music of their youth, making the Furs one of those bands that made a huge emotional impact as they became musically aware in their teens and early twenties. The Furs were thus understandably enshrined in their memories as being *truly important* — and it's from this emotionally charged perspective that they nominated the Furs as one of the best alt-rock groups of all time. Meanwhile, upon hearing of this suggestion, other fans were quick to heap scorn on the Furs, dismissing them as inconsequential pop fluff and demanding that they be dropped from the list and replaced with a *real* band like My Bloody Valentine. Arguments such as this merely point to the fact that it would require a tremendous act of arrogance for someone to publish a book declaring that these twenty five acts are unquestionably the *best* alt-rock performers of all time. "The Best" is fightin' words, an unnecessary provocation.

Happily, there is a way around this.

All history — including the history of music — is a moving target. Our perceptions of the past are limited by our exposure to it — what we've seen, what we've heard, what we've been told. But as we grow older, our perspective on the past will inevitably begin to change. People, concepts and events that seemed boring, stupid or inconsequential at the time may eventually come to be regarded in a different light. Who, for example, could have predicted the eventual impact of the Velvet Underground when they started playing for Andy Warhol in 1966? When R.E.M. was being dismissed as another frat-boy party band in the early 1980's, who could have guessed that they would become one of the most important bands in the world?

The only way to construct a proper historical evaluation of new rock and alternative music is from a perch that is emotionally detached and untainted with personal biases. Instead of entering a dangerous and doomed debate over the musical talent of specific artists, you focus on *historical significance* and *subsequent impact on music as a whole*. The question thus becomes "Which performers have had the greatest effect on the music of today?"

The nub of this proposal is simple: whether you care for their music or not, certain performers have had a greater long term effect on the alt-rock universe than others. While Nirvana may not be your style, there's no question that once they showed up on the rock and roll radar, they altered the future of music. The Smiths may have been before your time (or you, like me, may find Morrissey a little too whiny at times), but music historians will tell you that the Smiths' effect on pop and indie rock in the UK is legendary. For many people, this book may be the first time they've ever heard of Jonathan Richman, a guy who's never sold that many records, but — take it from the experts — this guy is very important to the story of alt-rock.

Here, then, are some of the things that I tried to use when narrowing things down to this list of what turned out to be the twenty five most important alt-rock / new rock bands of the 20th century.

History is important: Each act must have made an important and profound contribution to the evolution and mutation of our music. These contributions may have been in the form of musical innovation, attitude, image, technology or social change. It's also necessary for the impact of these contributions to last not for weeks or months but for decades and generations.

Record sales don't count: It's not how many records you sell, but who buys them. For example, R.E.M. wouldn't exist if it weren't for Patti Smith, who, for the most part, remains a cult figure to this day. Trent Reznor's life was changed by Skinny Puppy, a band so uncompromising in terms of sound that no one ever suggested that they were candidates for a platinum album. Kraftwerk, while making it possible for bands such as the Prodigy to exist, were never considered to be much of a commercial success.

Keep emotions in check: When reading this book, try to maintain a dispassionate viewpoint. The object is to assess *impact* and *influence* without letting your personal musical tastes color your judgment. If this were a textbook dealing with the most important political figures of the last one hundred years, it would be irresponsible to leave out Hitler or Stalin just because they happened to be grotesquely evil.

The further you go back, the easier it gets: Picking candidates from the 1960's and 1970's was easy. The passage of time allows us to gain perspective making it easier to evaluate the influence and contributions of these artists. But by the time you get to the mid-80's, and the entire decade of the 90's, it starts to get weird. How, for example, can you assess the long term influence of Marilyn Manson when the group has only been around for a couple of years? Is Manson going to be viable and relevant in the year ahead or is he just a momentary distraction? Conversely, it's quite possible that some unknown band may be a few months or years away from doing something so profound that the history of alt-rock will have to be rewritten. In any event, we won't know until ten or fifteen years after this book is published. That's why there are there are ten acts from the 60's and 70's, ten from the 80's and only five from the 90's.

All opinions are valid: To ensure that this list was as complete and comprehensive as possible, I posted it several times on a web site (www.edge102.com) and asked for suggestions on how it could be improved. For those who contributed, thank you — your input proved to be extremely valuable. And please don't be offended if your favorite band didn't make it into the book. No one is casting aspersions on your musical tastes or the viability of your band; it's just that some cold, hard choices had to be made in order to get this list down to a manageable size.

Well, what about some of the bands that didn't make the list? It doesn't take a brain surgeon to realize that the 1990's gave us a bunch of acts that show potential for being very influential in the long term. These performers may very well end up altering the world of music forever in the same way the Pixies did. That's why they're included in an appendix entitled Hope for the Future.

My favorite isn't on that list, either! What gives? Hang on. Look in Appendix 2 for a long list of Honorable Mentions. These acts have all contributed something important to the evolution of alt-rock. While their influence wasn't quite of the magnitude of the Velvet Underground or Nirvana, they did fill in all the blanks by providing essential nuances and subtleties.

There are no "right" answers: Feel free to argue about the choices made for this book. That's all part of the fun. Just because I wrote a book doesn't mean I have all the answers. *Please* don't take my word as gospel. Read as many other books, magazines and web site postings as you can, starting with some of the recommended readings and web site addresses. Your research may turn up a few different conclusions.

Ready? Let's begin . . .

> Music is a language by whose means messages are elaborated. That such messages can be understood by the many but sent out only by few, and that [music] alone among all the languages unites the contradictory character of being at once intelligible and untranslatable — these facts make the creator of music a being like the gods.
> — French anthropologist Claude Levi-Strauss

THE 1960'S

~ 1 ~
THE VELVET UNDERGROUND
The first alternative band ?

There is an old music industry saying that goes "the Velvet Underground didn't sell many records, but everyone who bought one of their albums formed a band." Whoever first uttered those words wasn't just being glib — virtually every alternative band formed over the last thirty years owes some debt to the original Velvets. If you need to put some sort of number on things, consider this: close to one thousand different bands from around the world (from Nirvana to Jane's Addiction to R.E.M.) have recorded versions of Velvet Underground songs.

The Velvets' style was intentionally crude and obnoxious. Peppered with sex, drugs and tales of deviant behavior, the music offered a paranoid, self-destructive vision of life on the streets of New York. It was bleak, in-your-face rock and roll that challenged (and ultimately destroyed) the wide-eyed innocence of rock and roll. While the enormity of their accomplishments wasn't apparent until years after they broke up, no other band from the 1960's had a greater influence on post-punk music.

Lou Reed was born Lewis Alan Firbank on March 2, 1942 in Brooklyn and was the eldest of two children. Raised in Freeport, Long Island, he was sent to a psychiatrist at age 17 when his parents (a wealthy accountant and ex-beauty queen) became alarmed at his wild mood swings and violent outbursts. Other accounts suggest that they were concerned that their son had homosexual tendencies, something that needed to be discouraged. After threatening an ROTC instructor and punching a hole through a wall, young Lou was subjected to eight weeks of shock treatments in the summer of 1959 — an experience later recounted in a song called *Kill Your Sons* on his 1974 solo album SALLY CAN'T DANCE.

Despite his parents' objections, Reed formed several rock combos in his teens. The earliest seems to have been the Jades, a group named after Reed's birthstone. In 1958, when he was 15, the Jades recorded a single called *So Blue*, a song that Reed had written in his bedroom. However, just before the record came out on November 28, the Jades realized that there were too many other bands using that name. This is why all copies of the 45 list the group as The Shades. Reed hand delivered a copy to New York DJ Murray the K who liked the song's do-wop / Buddy Holly sound and featured it on his program. This led to a quickie deal with a label called Dot.

After graduation in 1961, Reed enrolled in Syracuse University where he studied creative writing and poetry under Delmore Schwartz, the streetwise New York poet whom Reed would later describe as his "spiritual godfather." Thanks to these classes (and more likely, Schwartz's frequent spontaneous lectures in the campus bar), he not only became a major influence on Reed's future song writing style, but also on his general outlook on life. Reed eventually dedicated the song *European Son* from the first Velvet Underground album to Schwartz's memory.

Between classes, Reed worked as a DJ at the campus radio station, spinning an esoteric variety of R&B, do-wop and jazz on a program he called "Excursion on a Wobbly Rail." In his spare time, he read the works of James Joyce, William Burroughs and Raymond Chandler. Several evenings per week were spent jamming in a series of bands. These noisy, unstructured rehearsals attracted a guitarist named Sterling Morrison (born Holmes Sterling Morrison, August 29, 1942) who was intrigued by the guitar noise drifting from Reed's room. Although Morrison wasn't officially student at Syracuse — he couldn't get the scholarship he needed but went to classes anyway — he still managed to find space in the dorm next door. He stayed at Syracuse for two semesters before enrolling at City College in New York.

Once Reed graduated in 1964, he moved back in with his parents where they once again kept him on a tight leash with the help of a tranquilizer called Placidyl. Even though his parents did their best to keep their son from visiting the city, Reed soon found a job at the headquarters of Pickwick Records on Staten Island. Pickwick specialized in low budget albums of big hits recorded by anonymous studio groups which were then sold at supermarket check-outs and low-end department stores. Reed's position was essentially that of a hack songwriter, a guy who was paid to crank out forgettable formulaic pop songs for the masses. Despite the assembly line nature of the work, it was here that Reed wrote a near hit in 1964. *Do The Ostrich* was a send-up of the dance crazes that were sweeping America at the time (think of the Twist and the Mashed Potato), something that Pickwick was only too happy to exploit. They quickly issued the single under the name The Primitives. When *American Bandstand* called and asked if this fictitious group was available for an appearance on the show, Pickwick scrambled to put together some kind of band. Enter John Cale.

Cale was a Welsh born (March 9, 1940) avant-garde classical musician who had been working as a viola player in the Dream Syndicate, part of La Monte Young's Theatre of Eternal Music in New York. Cale then had a chance meeting with Terry Phillips, a producer with Pickwick (who assumed that Cale was a rock musician because of his long hair.) It was Phillips who convinced Cale and another musician named Tony Conrad to participate in the Primitives masquerade in exchange for a few fast bucks. After being introduced to Reed at a party, the project was given the go ahead. But even though everyone gave it their best shot, the record bombed and the Primitives evaporated into history.

The effort, however, did give Reed and Cale a chance to connect. After the Primitives charade ended, Reed played Cale *Heroin* and *Waiting for the Man*, just two of the Delmore Schwartz inspired songs he had written on his own time. Although Cale hated folky acoustic music, he immediately recognized that Reed's lyrics were different from anything he'd ever heard — quite simply, they were different from anything that any rock and roller had ever written. Impressed with the literary and straight-from-the-heart qualities of Reed's music, Cale began to share some of his avant-garde approaches to music. The two of them started applying weird ideas to basic rock — detuned string instruments, one chord improvisations and atonal arrangements.

Since these initial collaborations went well, Reed moved into Cale's apartment at 56 Ludlow Street in New York and the two of them began to play in a series of bands. The first was the Falling Spikes, a name derived from the time Reed and Cale both caught hepatitis from the heroin syringes they shared. Several women were part of these early projects, including an unemployed actress into S&M and a single mother / nymphomaniac. In early 1965, they issued a single called *Why Don't You Smile Now* as the All Night Workers, a group that sounded vaguely like the Everly Brothers crossed with Motown. Both Reed and Cale supported these groups — and their new drug habits — by selling blood to blood banks and by posing for pictures as murderers and rapists in cheap "true crime" magazines.

In April 1965, they met Sterling Morisson on the subway and asked if he was interested in joining their new band, the Warlocks. Together with drummer Angus MacLise (a neighbor and occasional participant in La Monte Young's projects), they finally began to get serious about music as a career. Gigs were few and far between, but they did find work providing music at screenings of experimental films.

The turning point came several weeks later when Tony Conrad dropped in on a rehearsal carrying a trashy paperback he had found in the gutter along Broadway. The name of the book was *The Velvet Underground*, a study of weird suburban sex habits and fetishes written by Michael Leigh. That was certainly a better name than the Warlocks (which, by the way, had already been taken by the San Francisco group that was about to become the Grateful Dead.) With a permanent name finally in place, the group was encouraged to send out very rough sounding demo tapes to record labels across the country. These tapes, recorded in the Ludlow Street apartment, featured early versions of future the VU classics *Black Angel's Death Song* and *Venus in Furs*, and show the first signs of Kinks and Who inspired guitar feedback. No one took the bait.

In mid-1965, over Maclise's objections, the group finally decided to hire a proper manager and chose pop writer and club promoter Al Aronowitz. He got the band their first paying gig — they received $75 for a show at Summit High School in Summit, New Jersey. This, however, created a crisis. Fed up with what he saw as Reed and Cale's increasingly capitalistic motivations, MacLise quit on the grounds that accepting money for creating art was against his principles. He then suddenly left for Nepal, where he would eventually die of malnutrition in Katmandu in 1979.

Desperate for a replacement, they contacted Jim Tucker, an old buddy from Syracuse, who set them up with his sister, Moe (born Maureen Tucker, 1945.) Although her drumming style was rather unorthodox (she says her main influence was Nigerian drum virtuoso Babatunde Olatunji, which is why she eschewed cymbals and laid the kick drum on its side, playing it with mallets instead of with a foot pedal), she fit in well with what Cale called the VU's "demonic invocations" and was hired. [1]

With the lineup complete, the Velvet Underground played their first paying gig at the high school dance on November 11, 1965. They were sandwiched between a group called 40 Fingers and a local garage band called the Myddle Class. By some accounts, the VU set was so loud that it nearly emptied the gym of both students and teachers — but they managed to collect their $75 fee.

The following month, Aronowitz set up a two week residency at a scummy bar on MacDougal Street in Greenwich Village called Café Bizarre. They played six nights a week, six sets a night (40 minutes on, 20 minutes off) for five dollars each. They were fired at least once for insisting on performing *Black Angel's Death Song*, a song that tended to send audiences running for the door. Fortunately, before they were fired for good, Andy Warhol and his entourage swooped in to have a look at this fierce sounding band that sang about things like scoring dope in Harlem. He was so impressed with this barrage of sound and fury that he immediately invited the group into his special circle of artists, freaks and parasites. They were granted admission to The Factory, Warhol's infamous studio and hangout at 231 East 47th Street.

The Factory was heaven for Reed. The endless parade of characters provided a continuous supply of lyrical ideas. He would eavesdrop on conversations, scribbling phrases and descriptions in the notebook he carried wherever he went. Many of those scraps were recycled into song lyrics. The free sex and drugs provided additional inspiration.

Warhol soon made a proposition: in exchange for twenty five per cent of their earnings, he would buy the VU new instruments, act as their manager, get them shows and secure them a recording contract. This would, Warhol assured the band, allow them the freedom to work on their music without having to worry about the financial end of things. There was, however, one catch: the group had to take on a new member, a recent Warhol "discovery."

Her name was Nico (born Crista Päffgen, October 16, 1938), a six foot, tone deaf, bisexual German actress. Believing that the Velvet's stage presence lacked charisma — and intrigued by Nico's icy cool persona — Warhol wanted her to be the band's singer. This, naturally, did not sit well with Reed and Cale because it reduced everyone else to the status of backup band. In the end, a compromise was reached. Nico would sing a few songs then step back to play the tambourine and dance, surrendering the microphone to Reed. At first, this arrangement seemed to work — perhaps even too well. Shortly after Nico was thrust upon the band, she found herself embroiled in affairs with both Reed and Cale.

As the official house band for The Factory, the VU was called upon to provide the music for "The Plastic Exploding Inevitable," Warhol's touring multimedia presentations. This consisted of little more than the band playing in front of or behind a screen that was showing various experimental films. The group was sometimes joined on stage by a parade of Factory sycophants who would act out S&M whippings and mock crucifixions. Nico, meanwhile, would sing her three songs and then stand off to the side like some kind of statue. It was all very strange.

In the spring of 1966, Warhol declared that it was time for the Velvets to make an album. Since funds were tight, the group was booked into Cameo-Parkway Studios on Broadway, a terrible facility with torn up floors, rickety walls and only four working microphones. Despite the fact Warhol had never produced an album before, he nevertheless declared he would supervise the recording of the album. In effect, his "producing" consisted of letting the band do whatever they wanted without any outside interference. On the other hand, there's little doubt that a real producer would have diluted and sanitized the VU's cacophonous fury. Warhol's non-involvement in these recording sessions meant that the band's live sound was captured on tape. The total cost of the one or two days spent in the studio (perhaps eight

---

1. The hiring of Moe Tucker was an important gender breakthrough. Not only was it rare for a rock group to feature a female instrumentalist in 1965, but a girl *drummer?* Conventional wisdom to that point was that drumming was a man's job. Oddly enough, no one paid much attention at the time. Only in retrospect was Tucker given her due as a pioneer.

hours in total) is estimated at around $1,500.

Once the album was completed (*Heroin, Venus in Furs* and *I'm Waiting for the Man* were subsequently re-recorded in Los Angeles with producer Tom Wilson), the group played a series of Warhol sponsored events all over North America, including a week long engagement at Expo 67 in Montreal. Meanwhile, a contract had been secured with Verve, an American label that had little experience with rock and roll. They released *All Tomorrow's Parties* (a mono radio edit issued in July 1966), but the rest of the album was nowhere to be seen. The release date was pushed back and then pushed back again. The label was having trouble producing the Warhol designed "peeling banana" cover; the master tapes were lost; the label's attention was diverted by their other new signing, Frank Zappa. The truth was that Verve didn't know what they were going to do with something this avant-garde. Finally, THE VELVET UNDERGROUND AND NICO was released in March 1967.

Today, the VU's debut album is considered to be one of the most influential recordings of all time. But back in 1967, no one knew what to think. Raw and abrasive, it was unlike any other pop and rock record of the era. Compared to most albums of its day (the big sellers were from the Monkees, Herb Alpert and Bobby Gentry), it stood out like an abscessed thumb. While everyone else — including the Beatles — had been seduced by psychedelia or the "peace and love" mantra of the hippie era, the VU was singing about junkies, transvestites and S&M (in the first person!) over a drone of feedback, noise and detuned instruments. The mesmerizing piano chop of *All Tomorrow's Parties* (derived from Cale's personal warm-up exercise) is especially interesting — how many bands would later loop and sequence keyboard lines and samples in this way? In the context of the music of the mid-60's, the VU was in essence the first *anti-rock* band in history, an alternative to what the rest of the rock world was doing. They became the template for countless "alternative" bands that were to follow over the decades.

The world, however, was not prepared to accept a band that sang about sex, drugs and leather. The music industry was still pretty conservative in those days. Radio stations (save for a few brave "underground" FM's) were unwilling to expose themselves by playing such controversial material for mainstream America. It's no wonder album peaked at No. 171 on the *Billboard* album charts. There were, however, other extenuating circumstances. By the time the record was released, the VU had severed their ties with Warhol (Reed fired him as manager in the summer of 1967) after disagreements over that 25 / 75 financial arrangement struck a year earlier. Without the notoriety and cache that came with an association with Warhol, the album didn't receive the publicity it would have had it been released in 1966. There was an added complication in the spring of 1967 when someone lodged a complaint about the artwork. The back of the album featured a Warhol hanger-on named Eric Emerson. According the VU, he had just been arrested on drug charges and needed money to pay for a lawyer. Demanding payment for being included in this photo without his permission, Verve instead elected to recall the album and then reissue it without the offending photo. By the time this new version of THE VELVET UNDERGROUND AND NICO appeared in the stores, all momentum had been lost.

This didn't seem to phase the group. Now officially exiled from the mainstream, they were free to proceed as they pleased. They were also quite happy to jettison Nico. That was fine with her because she had grown bored in her role within the band.

The second Velvet Underground album was recorded in September 1967 at Mayfield Sound Studios in New York. As noisy as the first record was, WHITE LIGHT / WHITE HEAT made it look pale by comparison for two reasons. First, since Cale no longer had to write gentle songs for Nico, everyone was free to be as loud and as aggressive as they wished. Secondly, the Velvets were determined to capture the essence of their live performance on tape. That meant cranking all the amps up as far as they could go and if that meant all the dials in the control room were pegged in the red, so what? There was a conscious effort to make the album as loud and abrasive as possible. Reed called this combination of fuzz and fury "power cubed."

Sister Ray, the album's signature piece about some blow job-hungry sailors visiting a drag queen, was recorded in one long take lasting nearly eighteen minutes. Legend has it that when the song was being recorded, Gary Kellgren, the engineer, walked out of the studio, saying "Let me know when it's over."

Another standout track was a spoken-word piece entitled *The Gift*. Cale came up with the idea; why didn't they use one of Reed's old short stories from college? Rummaging around through some old creative writing assignments, Reed found his tale of Waldo Jeffers, which Cale then read over an old VU instrumental jam called *The Booker T*. Since stereo was still something of a novelty, it was decided that Cale should be recorded telling the story on one channel and while the music occupied the other. The thinking was that the listener could chose to listen to either the narration or the music or both by just adjusting the balance control.

Other songs relied on different effects. John Cale remembers that one song (*Stephanie Says*, which didn't make the final cut) was recorded under the influence of heroin. The only Warhol contribution on the album can be found in the artwork — it was Warhol who suggested the stark white-on-black motif and image of the skull tattoo.

WHITE LIGHT / WHITE HEAT was released on January 20, 1968 — and flopped. Its highest chart position was No. 199 on the Top 200 chart for a single week in March. It received no radio airplay. It was so far off the scale that it's a miracle that Verve agreed to release it at all.

The Reed / Cale partnership began to unravel in April when Cale married fashion designer Betsey Johnson. Even though Reed, Cale and Morrison had grown used to competing with each other for things like women and drugs, Reed was especially uncomfortable with Cale's relationship with Johnson, a strong women who demanded certain loyalties from her new husband. As the acrimony began to build, the music began to suffer. Cale's determination to push the band in an even more experimental direction clashed with Reed's desire to add more formal pop structure to the songs. By September, the clash of egos reached a crescendo and at a meeting with Morrison and Tucker at the Riviera Café in the West Village, Reed laid out an ultimatum: unless Cale was fired, he would quit. The coup d'état was successful and Cale was ousted from the group.

On October 2, 1968, a new version of the Velvet Underground debuted at La Cave in Cleveland. On bass was Doug Yule, a former member of a group called the Glass Menagerie who had met the band during a residency at The Tea Party, one of the VU's favorite Boston haunts. Although he lacked Cale's creative flair, Yule proved to be very competent, which gave the band the confidence to begin work on their next album in Los Angeles just one month later. It was their first under a new deal with MGM Records.

The sound of THE VELVET UNDERGROUND was completely different from WHITE LIGHT / WHITE HEAT. Since he no longer had to deal with Cale's experimental predilections, Reed ensured that the songs were shorter and cleaner. There was more structure to the arrangements, fewer technical glitches caused by high recording volumes and a strong thematic cohesiveness to the entire album. This is the direction Reed was looking for — but that's not the whole story. When the band arrived in LA to start work on this album, they discovered that a good portion of their gear — including all their effect boxes and distortion pedals — had been stolen. Rather than replace all this equipment, the band went into the studio believing that they could do without it. The result was a quieter, more gentle VU.

Reed's new attention to detail extended to the final mix of the performances, which is why THE VELVET UNDERGROUND was mixed twice. The first was a well-balanced stereo mix by Val Valentin, the MGM house engineer assigned the project. Reed, however, was unhappy with this version and remixed the album himself, bringing up the vocals and pushing the music into the background, almost obliterating the entire bottom end. This "closet" mix (after Sterling Morrison suggested it now sounded like an album that was recorded in a closet) is the one that appeared on every US edition of the album issued before 1985. The versions of THE VELVET UNDERGROUND sent to Canada and the UK featured Valentin's original mix.

The album was released in March 1969 and, like the previous two releases, it was a sales disaster. Part of the blame can be put on Reed's muffled remix. Despite the fact that the group had never played and sung this well before, the performances were lost in the muddy sonics of the final mix. MGM dumped them that fall.

In early 1970, a strange savior in the form of Atlantic Records came the rescue. Atlantic had been interested in the band as early as 1966, but chairman Ahmet Ertegun was against any band recording drug songs for his label. However, four years later, he had a minor change of heart. Believing that the VU had developed some excellent rock sensibilities, Atlantic came knocking with an offer of a two-album deal. Even though all the members of the VU were burned out and on the verge of collapse, they were temporarily heartened by this show of good faith and began work on a new album. The enthusiasm proved to be short-lived.

LOADED was recorded between April and July 1970 under enormous tension. Tucker, having become pregnant and needing an extended leave of absence, was replaced by Yule's brother, Billy. Sterling Morisson had enrolled in literature classes at City College and found it tougher and tougher to make it to rehearsals and studio sessions. Meanwhile, a long residency as the house band at Max's Kansas City took its toll on Lou Reed. In between fights with VU manager Steve Sesnick (who wanted Reed to be more animated on stage), the effort of performing night after night led to a serious case of exhaustion. With Reed often sick and unable to sing, Doug Yule was forced to take more and more control. By early August, he was the de facto focus of the band on stage. Naturally, this became a point of contention with Lou Reed.

The result was a repeat of the confrontation Reed had with John Cale two years earlier — only this time, it was Reed who left. After one final performance with the Velvet Underground at Max's on August 23, Reed quit. He moved back into his parents' home in long island and took a part time job as a typist with his father's accounting firm. He was paid forty dollars a week for the next two years.

By the time LOADED was finally released in September 1970, it was obvious that the VU had lost its way. In a doomed effort to replace Reed, Yule brought in a Boston musician named Walter Powers to play guitar. As the band was preparing to fly back to New York from Houston in March 1971, Sterling Morrison suddenly gave his notice, giving up the life of rock and roll for an academic career at the University of Austin, rather than continuing in a band that he believed had no future. Although Moe Tucker did return as drummer in late 1970, she only lasted for another year before moving to Phoenix to raise a family. On the behest of VU manager Steve Sesnick (a man reviled by just about everyone who played in the band), Yule did his best to keep the VU name alive. Together with Deep Purple drummer Ian Paice, Yule recorded an album in 1973 called SQUEEZE that was released under the VU name. It's a record that hardcore VU fans avoid like the plague. After an aborted and ill-advised attempt to tour Europe in 1973, Yule finally pulled the plug.

Over the next thirteen years, each of the original Velvets had vastly different experiences. Lou Reed was able launch a successful solo career, thanks in large part to his new friend, and VU fan, David Bowie. Cale became a respected record producer, working with everyone from Nico (who became a cult recording figure on her own) to Patti Smith and Squeeze. Sterling Morrison gave up a life in rock and roll entirely and finally received a Ph.D. in medieval literature in 1986. Moe Tucker drifted into obscurity for years and at one point worked at a Wal-Mart in Douglas, Georgia to make ends meet for her five children.

Meanwhile — much to the surprise of almost everyone — the legends and musical legacy associated with the Velvet Underground grew ever stronger. A new generation of musicians was coming to a slow appreciation of the original group's body of work. As this rediscovery continued, hundreds of bands began covering VU material. And in the ultimate act of fealty, some groups (such as the Psychedelic Furs) adopt names inspired by VU songs. This reassessment gathered steam in 1985 when Polydor released a collection of previously unreleased material called V.U., along with a boxed-set entitled ANOTHER LOOK. Insiders believed that it was only a matter of time before this renewed interest drove the band back together.

The first reunion took place on June 15, 1990, at an Andy Warhol exhibit at Jouy en Josas outside of Paris. The highlight of the event (sponsored by Cartier) was a rendition of Heroin, which marked the first time the original Velvets had performed together in about twenty years. The ten minute appearance led to more mini-reunions over the next few years, culminating with a much-hyped series of European shows, beginning with a concert at Wembly Arena on June 6, 1993. The Paris show on that tour was captured on the double CD entitled LIVE MCMXCIII. On November 18, 1994, the band reunited for one last time at the opening of the Warhol museum in Pittsburgh.

Sterling Morrison died of non-Hodgkin's lymphoma on August 30, 1995 in Poughkeepsie NY. The Velvet Underground was finally inducted into the Rock and Roll Hall of Fame on January 17, 1996.

Fast Facts

o Since 1972, Lou Reed has released more than twenty solo albums.

o In a meeting with Reed, Czech president Vaclav Havel once joked that his country's "Velvet Revolution" was inspired by (and named after) the Velvet Underground. (Havel was a huge fan of the VU and Frank Zappa in his youth.) Meanwhile, Reed has hinted he's a fan of the Barenaked Ladies.

o Along with producing albums for a variety of artists, John Cale has released in the neighborhood of two dozen albums of his own, including collaborations with Lou Reed and Brian Eno.

o The government of the Netherlands once commissioned Cale to set some of the poetry of Dylan Thomas to music.

o In addition to being a professor at the University of Austin, Sterling Morrison also once served as the captain of a tugboat.

o In the 80's, Moe Tucker was rediscovered by a new generation of indie musicians (most notably Jad Fair and the members of Sonic Youth.) She then switched to guitar and has been able to make a full-time living as a musician ever since, releasing a series of albums that became cult favorites.

o Moe's big break as a solo performer came when she was signed by an indie label called 50 Skidillion Watts, which is owned by long-time VU fan Penn Gillette (of the comedy / magic team, Penn and Teller.)

o Nico was given that name at age 15 by a photographer on Ibiza. He took to calling her by the name of a recently departed boyfriend named Nico Papatakis.

o Nico had a child in 1962 with a French actor named Alain Delon. His name is Ari.

o After leaving the Velvet Underground, Nico recorded nine solo albums that attracted the attention of a small but fiercely loyal audience. Her music continues to be revered by some members of the goth community.

o Nico died at 8 PM July 18, 1988, of a brain hemorrhage after falling from her bike on the island of Ibiza off the coast of Spain. Her ashes are buried next to her mother in Berlin in a small cemetery in the Grunewald Forest at the edge of Wannsee.

o One of the major reasons Doug Yule was hired to replace John Cale was because he, like Cale, was a Pisces. This maintained the astrological balance in the band with Reed (Pisces), Morrison (Virgo) and Tucker (Virgo.)

o After retiring the VU name in 1973, Yule joined a group called American Flyer. He was also occasionally seen in Lou Reed's touring band in the mid-70's.

o Yule eventually retreated to Brooklyn where he became a wood worker and carpenter.

o When *All Tomorrow's Parties* was released as a single in 1966, one copy featured a picture sleeve hand-painted by Andy Warhol. With an *minimum* value of $5,000 US, this may be the rarest and most valuable alternative record in the world.

Recommended Listening

o THE VELVET UNDERGROUND AND NICO (MGM / Verve, 1967)

o WHITE LIGHT / WHITE HEAT (MGM / Verve, 1968)

o THE VELVET UNDERGROUND (MGM / Verve, 1969)

o LOADED (Atlantic, 1970)

o If you can afford it, buy the five-CD boxed set PEEL SLOWLY AND SEE (Polydor, 1995.) It features all four of the above albums plus a fine collection of unreleased material, outtakes and live tracks. Some of the material is from the "missing" VU album that was recorded between THE VELVET UNDERGROUND and LOADED.

Internet Resources

o www.loureed.org

o www.polygram.com/VU/

o www.angelfire.com/ny/vu1/

Recommended Reading

o Heylin, Clinton. *From the Velvets to the Voidoids: A Pre-Punk History for a Post-Punk World*. New York, New York: Penguin Books, 1993.

o Kostek, M.C. *The Velvet Underground Handbook*. London: Black Spring Press, 1992.

o McNeil, Legs and McCain, Gillian. *Please Kill Me: The Uncensored Oral History of Punk*. New York, New York: Grove Press, 1996.

Related Listening

o   Lou Reed's solo albums, especially TRANSFORMER (RCA, 1972), BERLIN (RCA, 1973) and NEW YORK (Sire, 1989.) A good anthology is BETWEEN THOUGHT AND EXPRESSION (three CD's, RCA, 1992.)

o   A good introduction to John Cale's solo career is an album entitled CLOSE WATCH: AN INTRODUCTION TO ... (Island, 1999.) His reunion with Lou Reed on SONGS FOR DRELLA (an elegy for Andy Warhol, Sire 1989) is compelling listening.

o   Moe Tucker has become something of a cult phenomenon among certain segments of the alt-rock underground. Try I SPENT A WEEK THERE THE OTHER NIGHT (Rough Trade, 1991 and Sky, 1994) and DOGS UNDER STRESS (Sky, 1994.)

The Story Thus Far ...

Starting in the mid-1960's, the Velvet Underground changed the course of rock and roll by presenting deliberately harsh, sleazy and obnoxious music as an art statement. They sell almost zero records but light a spark in a few like-minded souls.

~ 2 ~
IGGY POP
The Godfather of Punk

Iggy Pop spent so much of his career teetering on the edge of the abyss that it's amazing he's still alive. When Iggy first appeared in 1967, no one had ever seen a performer pursue physical and chemical self-destruction with such energy and zeal. For years, Iggy approached each performance — in fact, each day — as a dare, a kind of stare-down with the Grim Reaper that said "Go on! Try and take me!" His survival, redemption and subsequent rebirth as a punk icon has only enhanced his position as one of the greatest rock and roll legends of all time.

James Jewel Osterberg was born on April 21, 1947, in Ypsilanti, Michigan, which is a forty minute drive west of Detroit. His father, Newell, was a highly strung, uptight English teacher and former minor-league baseball player; his mother, Louella, worked as a secretary. "Home" was a 50-by-20 foot Vagabond trailer on Lot 96 of the Coachville Mobile Home Park at 3423 Carpenter Road. At the nearby Pioneer High School, Jimmy served as president of the student council and vice-president of the debating team. He didn't smoke, didn't drink, didn't do drugs and was often seen wearing cashmere sweaters and penny loafers. In grade nine, his classmates voted him as the student most likely to succeed. As good and as virginal as he seemed to be, he still somehow managed to earn the nickname "Horse Dick."[1]

In 1962, Jimmy started playing drums for a local group called the Iguanas, an arrow-straight pop band that favored short haircuts and matching sport coats. They were, however, reasonably accomplished — they were respected enough to land some opening slots for the Marvellettes and for a few of the other major Motown acts of the day. Jimmy's playing impressed one of the staff producers at Motown who offered him the occasional bit of studio work. Although it can't be verified, it's quite possible that Jimmy is heard playing drums on *Leader of the Pack*, the 1964 hit by the Shangri-Las. (The second half of this story suggests that the piano parts were played by a young Billy Joel. However, because the drums and the piano were recorded on separate days, Iggy and Billy were never in the same studio together.) In 1965, The Iguanas managed to release one single, a track called *Mona* (a Bo Diddley cover), but it had little impact outside the group's immediate circle of friends and fans.

In 1966, Jimmy moved to a group called the Prime Movers before dropping out of the University of Michigan and quitting his job at a store called Discount Records. He hitchhiked a ride to Chicago with a couple of coworkers and spent the next eight months sitting in with a variety of blues musicians on the city's south side. Impressed by the simplicity and emotion of this music, Jimmy began to appropriate some

---

1. If you believe Iggy, it's eleven inches.

---

of these blues stylings for himself. He also had his first drug experiences in Chicago, beginning with the discovery that smoking marijuana didn't seem to bother his asthma at all.

Having successfully avoided the Vietnam draft (legend has it that Iggy flashed his genitals at the recruiter, proclaiming himself to be gay, giving the U.S. Army pause about handing him a loaded weapon), Iggy began to enjoy being weird for the sake of being weird — anything to shock people. His strange haircuts and propensity for wearing big, poorly fitted overalls periodically caught the attention of the local police, who often stopped him on the street, mistaking him for an escaped mental patient.

Inspired by his musical experiences in Chicago, Jimmy moved back in with this parents to contemplate his future. After seeing a Velvet Underground gig in April 1967, and a show by the Doors that summer (events that he later claimed changed his life), he phoned up Ron Asheton, one of his bandmates in the Prime Movers and someone who he knew was looking to form another group after his last one (the Dirty Shames) had disintegrated. The initial plan was to have Jimmy play organ (his mother helped him buy one on the condition that he cut his long hair), but as this new group came together, it became clear that Jimmy's role was to be lead singer. Jimmy taught Ron's brother, Scotty, what he knew about the drums, freeing himself to step out front.[1] This new outfit, founded over a bag of dope while watching a Three Stooges marathon on TV, became known as the Psychedelic Stooges.

This is when Jimmy Osterberg became Iggy Pop. The "Iggy" was a natural derivation from his association with the Iguanas. The "Pop" was borrowed from a friend named Jim Pop, a local junkie who had lost all his hair — including his eyebrows — due to a nervous condition. When Iggy decided to shave off his eyebrows (an act of solidarity perhaps?), he was immediately tagged as Iggy Pop.

The Psychedelic Stooges (who, in all honestly were more of a fun-loving, drug-taking gang of delinquent slobs than a group of musicians with any serious pretensions) played their first show at a private party in Ann Arbor on October 31, 1967. Even by the standards of Halloween, it was a frightening event. Their performance was so crazy that after the set, some of the friends who hadn't fled in embarrassment asked Iggy if he was having mental problems. At the same time, their manager quit in disgust and returned to his job as a schoolteacher.

The Stooges' first public performance was held in March 1967 at the Grande Ballroom in Ann Arbor. The opening act was a food processor — a blender with a little bit of water in it — that roared through the PA for about fifteen minutes before the band took the stage. When the Stooges finally appeared, Iggy strode on stage wearing a full-length nightshirt, golf shoes, white mime makeup and an Afro wig made out of tinfoil. Behind him, drummer Scott Asheton kept time by banging on a pair of fifty-gallon oil drums with hammers instead of drumsticks. Any heckling from the audience was met with threats of violence and spews of spit from the stage.[2]

As the Stooges began playing regular shows, they were attracting a following of what could best be described as "anti-hippies." They came to hear angry, violent, primitive rock and roll that was totally free of love beads and flower power; it had nothing in common with psychedelia of the Haight-Ashbury scene in San Francisco, and it certainly wasn't the sugarcoated pop that dominated AM radio. It was brutal, ragged and high-energy, unbound by any dreary social or political agenda — music made *by* misfits and outsiders *for* misfits and outsiders.

An even more compelling reason to buy a ticket to a Stooges show was to see what Iggy would do next. Going to a gig became like getting a ringside seat at a car accident. Iggy's antics grew more outrageous and extreme with each show. Having seen how far Jim Morrison of the Doors was willing to take things on stage, Iggy was hell-bent on not only pushing the edge of that envelope, but ripping it up entirely.

1. Since Jimmy was tapped out financially (he already held two jobs: stockroom clerk at Discount Records and a cook at a hamburger stand), he couldn't afford to buy Scott a full set of drums. Instead, he improvised with a couple of 55-gallon oil drums scavenged from a local junkyard. Drumsticks were large, semi-plastic hammers. For an added decorative touch, the drums were then scrawled with both obscenities and Indian symbols for "love" and "regeneration."

2. In his autobiography, *I Need More*, Iggy suggests that the Stooges subsequent effect on music began with a simple misunderstanding. The day before their first show, Ron Asheton painted Iggy's Hawaiian guitar in day-glow colors. Unfortunately, he also painted over the pickups, ruining them completely. Although Iggy's instrument was now useless, he decided to take it with him on stage anyway. Normally, he would play it sitting down, but since the guitar was now nothing more than a prop, he stood up. That's when his pants started falling down. Realizing the audience thought that this was all part of the show (and not burdened with playing an instrument), Iggy made the best of the situation, doffing his clothes and doing crazy things.

Before each show, Iggy ensured that any inhibitions were destroyed with a buffet of crank, LSD (usually "orange sunshine") and pot. Most of his clothes came off during the first few songs. After smashing himself in the mouth a few times, he would rub raw meat and peanut butter (usually Skippy) over his bare chest, throwing the remains into the crowd. If the audience threw bottles at the stage, Iggy picked up the broken glass and carved long wounds into his chest and arms. If there was no glass, Iggy would simply pull out the steak knife that he kept for such emergencies. At other points in the show, Iggy would climb up the PA stacks or the lighting rigs. If he believed that a certain member of the audience deserved to be attacked physically, Iggy would launch himself into the crowd. In the absence of hecklers (or gang members that Iggy happened to piss off), he would literally walk *on* the audience, supported by willing hands and shoulders.

As the maelstrom unfolded, the rest of the band, often decorated with Nazi regalia, generated a swirling drone of power chords and feedback while stepping gingerly through the broken glass and blood that washed across the stage. Occasionally Ron Asheton would step forward brandishing a bullwhip to peel a few strips of flesh from Iggy's back.

No one knew what to make of this. Was this the future of rock? Or were Iggy and the Stooges just obscenely bad? Local police weren't amused and they were often only too happy to bust Iggy for indecent exposure and lewd behavior. (Remember, too, that this is the late 60's. Imagine the public outcry if someone tried to do these things today!)

By 1968, the Stooges shared a management team with the MC5 (another notorious anti-mainstream band from Detroit.) When Elektra Records came to have a look at the MC5, they also decided to take a chance on the Stooges after seeing them play a benefit for a local children's school at the University of Michigan. One of the many apocryphal tales about the Stooges states that the group had never written a complete song before they signed that first recording contract. Armed with three chords, a bad attitude and a satchel full of narcotics, the group took all of four days to make THE STOOGES (the "Psychedelic" part of their name having been dropped by this time) with John Cale of the Velvet Underground as producer. Two songs from this record, *No Fun* and *I Wanna Be Your Dog*, later became staples in the Sex Pistols' repertoire. The album peaked at No. 106 on the American charts.

Offstage, the Stooges made no effort to appear as model citizens. Taking their advance money from Elektra, they rented a large house on the corner of Packard and Eisenhower Street in Detroit where they'd sleep all day and party all night. Any female visitor who dared enter the foul Stooge Manor (sometimes called Fun House) was asked to donate her panties, which were then stapled to the kitchen counter. Iggy married Wendy Weisberg,[1] a groupie nicknamed the Potato Girl (the marriage lasted one month), before returning to a regular diet of sex and drugs. This included a torrid affair with Nico, who was still with the Velvet Underground. She allegedly gave Iggy his first case of VD.

1. They were married on the front lawn of Fun House with Ron Asheton acting as best man. Instead of a tuxedo, he wore a real Nazi SS uniform. All the guests took bets on how long the marriage would last.

Iggy Pop

Elektra decided that the second Stooges album should be recorded in Los Angeles and hired Don Gallucci (ex-keyboardist for the Kingsmen) to produce. FUN HOUSE was even more frightening than THE STOOGES. It was aggressive and primal, a chunky, thudding pre-cursor to several types of heavy / hard rock that were to take shape later in the decade. But this was 1970 and few people (with the exception of a few critics like Lester Bangs), were interested in what the Stooges had to offer and FUN HOUSE was declared a commercial disaster.

Had the Stooges sold a few more records, Elektra might have been inclined to overlook some of the group's personal shortcomings. But by the summer of 1971, angered by the number of canceled shows, the stories of drug use, Iggy's indiscretions with an underage fan and $500,000 in unexplained expenses over six months, Elektra decided that it was time to bail out. By August, torn apart by debt, various addictions and under investigation by the IRS for non-payment of taxes — not to mention the medical bills that piled up after Scott Asheton tried to drive the band's fourteen foot truck under a thirteen foot bridge — the Stooges split. It was just as well — the instruments not destroyed in the accident had been pawned in order to buy more heroin. Iggy spent the next six months in Florida where he was reduced to cutting the lawns for retirees before voluntarily spending time in a Detroit mental ward in an attempt to curb his heroin habit.

Iggy's savior arrived in the form of David Bowie. In 1971, Bowie met Iggy at a party thrown by RCA in the infamous back room at Max's Kansas City party in New York. He was quite anxious to meet Iggy. Bowie was impressed by the decadent depths of Iggy's American rock and roll lifestyle, something that was very foreign to Bowie's British art school sensibilities. (In early 1972, Bowie wrote The Jean Genie, a song said to be inspired by that first meeting.) At Bowie's urging, his manager, Tony DeFries, secured a recording contract with CBS worth in the range of $100,000, selling the label on the fact that Iggy could be CBS's answer to Warner Brothers' Alice Cooper. By April 1972, Iggy and a reorganized version of the Stooges were working on a new album in London. The result was RAW POWER.

Released in May 1973, RAW POWER was probably the most nihilistic album ever recorded to that point. With songs like Search and Destroy, Death Trip and the title track, it was a truly fearsome listening experience. At the same time, Bowie's tutelage showed itself in the form of songs with more structure and discipline. The only unfortunate Bowie contribution was the final mix of the album, a soggy, muddy master tape that took some of the urgency out of the performances. Nevertheless, Iggy was back, crazier than ever.

Naturally, it couldn't last. In February 1974, after RAW POWER peaked at No. 184 on the US album charts, the Stooges ended their crash-and-burn cycle with one final performance at the Michigan Palace in Detroit. This six song performance was captured on a legendary bootleg entitled METALLIC KO. In between Iggy's baitings of the crowd,[1] you can actually hear the beer and whiskey bottles shattering on the stage. Less than a month later, the Stooges broke up for good. They had blown their last chance at redemption.

Iggy had nowhere to go. Plans for a UK tour were shelved almost as soon as they were announced. Most of that $100,000 advance from CBS had been spent on a suite at the Beverly Hills Hotel and an ever-deepening coke and heroin addiction. He had become a babbling, strung-out junkie, prone to blackouts and random acts of violence. When LA police found him under the counter of a hamburger joint, he was given a choice — jail or a stint in an institution.[2]

Once again, it was Bowie to the rescue. During the time Iggy was committed to the Neuropsychiatric Institute in Los Angeles, Bowie was his only visitor. When he was approved for weekend leaves, Iggy found that Bowie had arranged for him to record some new songs at the home of songwriter Jimmy Webb, thanks in part to a sponsorship by a rock writer named Bob Edmonds. Although the sessions collapsed (Iggy just wasn't up to the rigors of recording), these tracks were eventually released in 1978 under the

1. The target of his heckling was a local street gang called the Scorpions. Having lost a fight to one of their members earlier, Iggy went on the radio before the gig and challenged the entire gang to come to the show and beat him senseless.
2. The bizarre "Elton John Incident" occurred at around this time. Having just set up Rocket Records, Elton flew to Atlanta to get a first-hand look at look at Iggy with an eye on perhaps signing the Stooges. For some reason, he decided to make an unannounced appearance in mid-set dressed in a gorilla costume. Iggy, wired on a cocktail of PCP, speed and coke, freaked out at the sight of what he thought was a real gorilla. The set was ruined and Elton left without offering the band a contract.

title KILL CITY.

After a setback in March 1976 (Iggy and Bowie were arrested in a Rochester, New York, hotel room with six ounces of marijuana), they began work on what would become Iggy's first solo album. Eager to get away from the decadence and temptations of Los Angeles (Bowie's intake of alcohol and cocaine was at legendary highs), the two moved to a recording studio in Chateau d'Herouville, France in June 1976. In October, they relocated to the Schöneberg district of West Berlin, which became their home base for the next three years.

This period proved to be one of the most productive and prolific times in the careers of both musicians. In a remarkable burst of creative energy and clear thinking, Bowie not only recorded his famous "Berlin Trilogy" of albums during this time (LOW, HEROES, LODGER — see the separate chapter on Bowie), but he was also instrumental in helping Iggy record two of the greatest albums of his career.

THE IDIOT came first. Recorded with only Bowie and guitarist Carlos Alomar as backup, the album was released in the middle of the punk explosion of 1977. Iggy was finally in the right place at the right time. Although the connection with Bowie was obviously a factor (Bowie toured as part of Iggy's backup band as musical director and keyboardist), Iggy also benefited from a delayed appreciation of his earlier work. Since many of the young punks had already discovered and embraced the Stooges (virtually every new band from the Damned to the Sex Pistols had learned to play at least one Stooges song), they were also willing to embrace Iggy as some kind of returning messiah. Attending an Iggy Pop show in 1977 was almost akin to making a pilgrimage to some holy, ancient punk shrine. In that light, it's perhaps not surprising that THE IDIOT broke the Top 30 on the album charts in the UK and hit a very respectable No. 72 in the US. Even a reissue of RAW POWER climbed to No. 44 in Britain on the purchasing strength of Iggy's new punk constituency.

Invigorated and refreshed, Iggy made a second album with Bowie over just thirteen days that September. LUST FOR LIFE, also recorded in Berlin, was as every bit as vital and energetic as the Stooges but also enjoyed the sophistication of Bowie's guidance. The thrash-and-burn, metal-on-metal guitars of the Stooges were replaced by something more controlled, resulting in an album that will be forever remembered for two standout songs. The title track (the riff was inspired by the evening news theme of the American Forces Network, the only English language TV channel available in Berlin) captured the spirit of the newly re-energized Iggy. The second is the oft-covered *The Passenger*, Iggy's tribute to Jim Morrison. (Another Iggy legend has it that he once owned a pair of Morrison's leather pants and that Morrison's spirit had passed from the pants into Iggy's body.)

This was the new Iggy — healthy, positive, confident, and for the first time in years, (almost) drug-free. And for the first time in his career, he was selling records in significant numbers. Unfortunately, just as he hit his peak, he began another inexorably slide into mediocrity.

Iggy's ascendancy to the status of revered punk rock icon and his association with Bowie gave him a certain cachet that other big names wanted to share. But despite their best efforts, albums featuring members of the Sex Pistols, the MC5, Simple Minds, the Patti Smith group and Blondie all failed to make an impact. A promising record deal with Arista turned out to be a dead end. Even touring with the Rolling Stones didn't help; he was booed off the stage before a hometown crowd at the Silverdome in Detroit in December 1981.

This is not to say that things were all bad. In April 1983, Bowie released his LET'S DANCE album and the following month issued his recording of *China Girls* (co-written by Iggy and Bowie and originally from THE IDIOT) as a single. It was a huge success, reaching the Top 5 in the UK and the Top 15 in the US. And, thanks to the fact that LET'S DANCE sold in the millions, Iggy's net share of the profits exceeded $1 million. Another couple of Iggy songs that appeared on Bowie's critically panned but platinum selling TONIGHT and NEVER LET ME DOWN albums added a few more dollars to the bank account. After more than twenty years in the music industry, Iggy had at last achieved at least some measure of financial stability.

Iggy was to experience at least two more resurrections. In October 1986, with Bowie once again at the controls of a Swiss studio, Iggy released BLAH BLAH BLAH his ninth solo album. *Real Wild Child* (a cover of a 1957 single by an Australian rockabilly performer named Johnny O'Keefe), the album's first single, cracked the Top 10 in the UK and was a minor hit elsewhere in the world. After the metallic detour of INSTINCT in 1988, Iggy recorded the very accessible BRICK BY BRICK with producer Don Was two years later. This album featured *Candy*, a respectable stab at a Top 40 single. In 1995, a third generation of music fans were introduced to Iggy through the inclusion of *Lust for Life* in the opening sequence of *Trainspotting*. The subsequent soundtrack album became a worldwide hit.

Now on the far side of 50, Iggy's main source of income is acting in films and licensing songs for advertising purposes (*Lust for Life* has been used to sell everything from beer and Rubbermaid products to Mitsubishi automobiles and Nike footwear), although he does still commit to the occasional album and tour. He actually seems to be enjoying his role as an elder statesman of alt-rock, often appearing in documentaries on the history of rock and roll. And if there's anyone who can lecture on how this music came to be, it's Iggy. He's got the scars to prove it.

Fast Facts

o In 1970, Paulette Benson, a former lover, gave birth to Iggy's son, Eric.

o In 1984, Iggy married a woman named Suchi. They met during one of Iggy's tours of Japan. They are now divorced.

o Iggy's parent's were still living in that same trailer as of the mid-90's.

o Iggy's acting career includes film roles in *Sid and Nancy* (with Gary Oldham and a very young Courtney Love), *The Color of Money* (with Tom Cruise and Paul Newman), *Cry Baby* (with Johnny Depp) and *The Crow: City of Angels*. TV appearances include roles in *Miami Vice*, *Tales from the Crypt* and *Star Trek: Deep Space 9*.

o Iggy has become an accomplished painter and artist. An "Absolut Iggy Pop" painting is on display at the Hard Rock Café in Niagara Falls, Ontario.

o A lithograph of a portrait of Iggy painted by David Bowie can be purchase from www.bowieart.com.

o When the Stooges signed with Elektra, Humble Pie and T-Rex both turned down deals with the label. They refused to work for a company that would sign such an awful band.

o The group hired some of the toughest roadies in history including two Vietnam vets, one of whom collected machine guns for fun.

o After the group broke up, Ron Asheton formed a group called the New Order, some six years before the surviving members of Joy Division adopted that name. At last check, both he and his brother Scott were still living in Ann Arbor.

o Dave Alexander, the original bassist, died of alcohol-related illnesses in February 1975.

o Guitarist James Williamson now works for a computer company in Silicon Valley.

o Scott Thurston was recently employed as a member of Tom Petty's touring band.

Recommended Listening

o THE STOOGES (Elektra, 1968)

- FUN HOUSE (Elektra, 1970)
- RAW POWER (Columbia, 1972)
- METALLIC KO (Cleopatra, 1999)
- THE IDIOT (RCA, 1977 / Virgin, 1990)
- LUST FOR LIFE (RCA, 1977 / Virgin, 1990)
- BLAH BLAH BLAH (A&M, 1986)

Internet Resources
- www.virginrecords.com/iggy_pop/
- www.kweb.it/iggy

Recommended Reading
- Antonia, Nina. *Iggy Pop*. London: Virgin Publishing Group, 1997.
- McNeil, Legs and McCain, Gillian. *Please Kill Me: The Uncensored Oral History of Punk*. New York, New York: Grove Press, 1996.
- Pop, Iggy. *I Need More*. Los Angeles: 2.13.61, 1998.

Related Listening
The Ramones, The Sex Pistols, the Misfits, Black Flag, Metallica

The Story Thus Far . . .
The Velvet Underground inspires Iggy to head down a destructive path with the Stooges and later as a solo artist. The VU's John Cale produces some of Iggy's most essential material.

THE 1970'S

~ 3 ~
DAVID BOWIE
Shape-Shifter, Actor, Artist, Gay Icon

He's been known by many names over the years — Ziggy Stardust, Aladdin Sane, Halloween Jack, Plastic Soul Man, the Thin White Duke. In any other line of work, he might have been written off as a terminal case of Attention Deficit Disorder. But because this is the music business, David Bowie's carefully calculated makeovers became not only highly admired but widely copied. His ever-changing methods of presentation added a new and very sophisticated element of make-believe to the world of rock and roll. Under his various guises, Bowie experimented with composition, image and theater. In the process, he left an indelible mark on virtually the entire spectrum of what would eventually be called "alternative music." Few (if any!) artists have demonstrated such deftness and dexterity and fewer still can boast of influencing everyone from the early punks to the electronic and industrial acts at century's end.

It's somehow fitting that Bowie made his first appearance in this world ahead of schedule. As his father, John, was waiting for his divorce to come through, his girlfriend, Margaret Mary Burns realized she was pregnant. David Robert Jones was born shortly after midnight on January 8, 1947, some nine months before John and Peggy were able to get married. It wasn't the first time Peggy had to deal with illegitimacy; she'd already had a son named Terry with another man several years earlier.[1] Two other children completed this hodgepodge family: an adopted daughter named Myra Ann and Annette, John's daughter by a previous marriage. Home was an unremarkable red brick Victorian row house at 40 Stansfield Road in Brixton, an area populated mostly by Jamaican immigrants and a few Irish. In 1955, the family moved to Bromley, settling into another quite ordinary house at 4 Plaistow Grove.

As owner of a nearby club for wrestlers, John Jones had access to the hundreds of records destined for the club's jukebox. When he heard some Little Richard singles in 1956, an eight year old David became hooked and soon declared that one day, he would be the greatest star in England. This new infatuation with rock and roll was encouraged by Terry, who, being ten years older, was already into Bill Haley and Elvis Presley.

David found his first real musical instrument under the Christmas tree in 1959. It was a Selmer saxophone, the same kind used on some of those little Richard records. A few weeks later, Terry arranged for David to take formal lessons from a man named Ronnie Ross for £2 a session. This led to experiments on the family piano and eventually a skiffle group with George Underwood, a classmate at Bromley Technical High School. For the record, David's first public musical performance seems have been at a gathering of Cub Scouts on the Isle of Wight in 1959 when he and George entertained the troop with a couple of Lonnie Donegan songs.

Back at school, David formed his first group. With their matching suits, white shirts and striped ties, the Kon-Rads featured David on sax and vocals as they covered the popular tunes of the day. The only thing that really distinguished them from the other bands at school was David's hair — he was always changing styles and colors, even to the extent of using a few streaks of orange.

When David was fourteen, he and George got into a scrap over a girlfriend. David took several solid punches to the face. Both eyes were damaged, although the left one took the brunt of the punishment and began bleeding profusely. David ended up hospital and doctors worked for months to save his sight. An operation saved the right eye but the left pupil remained paralyzed, a condition called traumatic mydriasis. Strangely, as his eyes healed, they became different colors; to this day his right eye remains green while the left is a shade of brown.

In July 1963, David dropped out of school to take a job with J. Walter Thompson, an American advertising agency. Nights were spent prowling the jazz and R&B clubs in Soho with George, dreaming about the possibilities of forming their own group. Late that year, they took the plunge, forming a band called the Hookers who, by early 1964, had evolved into the King Bees. John Jones was so impressed by his son's attempts at a career in music that he successfully secured a sponsor for the King Bees (a washing machine company) that led to a recording session with Vocaliton, a subsidiary of Decca Records.

Picking up on the quasi-Mod sound of the day, the King Bees released their one and only single on June 5, 1964, under the name "Davie Jones [sic] with the King Bees." Since no one in the group demonstrated any song writing potential, it was decided that they would record two covers. The A-side, *Liza Jane*, was an old Negro spiritual picked out by Leslie Conn, a music publisher who was a friend of that washing machine tycoon. Side B was the King Bees' choice: a cover of a minor hit for Paul Revere and the Raiders entitled *Louie Louie Go Home*. Any illusions the group might have had of becoming as big as the Beatles were wiped out the following day when a BBC-TV program called *Juke Box Jury* declared that both sides of the single were completely devoid of any commercial potential. Interestingly enough, anyone fortunate enough to own an original copy has something worth in the neighborhood of $500 today.

Having accepted defeat, Bowie turned to the "musicians wanted" section of Melody Maker and arranged a meeting with a group from Maidstone called Band Seven. Renaming themselves the Manish Boys, they toured briefly with Gerry and the Pacemakers in November 1965 and managed to issue a single on Parlophone. Released on March 5, 1965, it featured a cover of a 1961 hit by Bobby Bland called *I Pity the Fool* on side one (the recording features a few choice guitar licks from a young session musician named Jimmy Page.) Side two was *Take My Tip*, the first-ever recording of a David Jones composition. Although the Manish Boys showed potential and had a flair for publicity (their gimmick was long hair; see the note

---

1. Terry is ten years older than David and has suffered from mental illness for most of his life. In fact, at least three of Bowie's aunts have been diagnosed with mental illness, the most common condition being schizophrenia. Is it any wonder that madness is a recurring theme in Bowie's music?

---

on the League for the Preservation of Animal Filament below), they were unable to find any chart success.

David's third stab at recording came after a merger with a group called the Lower Third (he passed the audition by ripping through the sax parts of a Little Richard song he had learned as a boy.) Raising money by writing a couple of radio commercials for an American clothing company called Youthquake, Davy Jones [sic] and the Lower Third released a single entitled *You've Got a Habit of Leaving* on August 20, 1965. Once again, the record-buying public wasn't interested.

The end of Davy Jones came as the result of an American TV show. *The Monkees* had debuted on ABC and featured a cute 20 year-old ex-jockey from Manchester named Davy Jones. Realizing that there was room for just one such creature in the music industry, several people urged David to consider a name change. The exact reasons for the choice of "Bowie" aren't clear. The most popular legend says that David was inspired by American pioneer (and Davy Crockett sidekick) Colonel James Bowie, inventor of the famous knife. Others say that he took the name from an obscure relative on this mother's side.[2]

Whatever the case, the first single to feature the name "David Bowie" on the label was released in January 1966 on Pye. *Can't Help Thinking About Me* backed with *And I Say to Myself* was credited to David Bowie and the Lower Third, even though all his live performances at the time involved a band called the Buzz. For the first time, Bowie saw a little chart success as *Can't* eventually climbed to No. 34 on Melody Maker's singles chart. It was also the Lower Third's first — and last — American release.

Less than a month after *Can't* was released, the Lower Third split up, leaving Bowie as a solo performer for the first time in his life. Using the members of the Buzz (who were paid a quick £9) he quickly recorded a single entitled *Do Anything You Say*, which was issued on Pye on April 1, 1966. Following a six week engagement at London's famed Marquee Club (a Mod-ish presentation entitled "The Bowie Showboat"), his final Pye single, *I Dig Everything*, was released on July 5, 1966. Switching to Deram Records, Bowie dashed off a couple of songs during a one day recording session on October 18 and issued *Rubber Band* in December.

Between 1967 and 1969, Bowie embarked on a number of creative experiments, originally to the detriment of his career. One of the first was a novelty single entitled *The Laughing Gnome* (released on April 14, 1967, through Deram) which was dismissed as an attempt to ape Anthony Newley, a famous song-and-dance man of the time. A follow-up (*Love You 'Til Tuesday*, released in July) was another failure. A debut album (DAVID BOWIE, June 1967) was totally ignored. A fed-up Deram gave Bowie the boot.

With no remaining alternatives as a recording artist, Bowie was forced to face the fact that he might not have a career in music. It took a stint in a Buddhist monastery in Scotland to give him the strength to continue. Back in London, he began taking mime and dance lessons from Lindsey Kemp, a former student of Marcel Marceau. Although Bowie didn't exactly consider miming to be his life's calling, these mime workshops did give him a new appreciation of theater and some new ideas about a cabaret / coffeehouse act. The work with Kemp led to an opportunity to write some music for BBC-TV in December 1967 with staff producer Tony Visconti. Over the next few months, Bowie puttered at a series of odd jobs. In addition to the BBC work, he was cast in a TV commercial for LUV ice cream and took a job at Legastat Document Copiers. Then came Feathers, a short-lived acoustic trio featuring Herimone Farthingale (Bowie's then-girlfriend) and bassist John Hutchison.

One person who had faith in Bowie was his manager, Ken Pitt. In 1968, he came up with the idea of producing a thirty-minute TV special that could then be sold to the networks. Initially, the concept was to have Feathers provide all the music but the group dissolved before anything could be completed. One song, however, soon became the centerpiece for the entire project. It was a Bowie composition entitled *Space Oddity*.

In early 1969, the entire world was caught up in America's attempts at putting a man on the moon. The summer before, movie audiences had been dazzled by Stanley Kubrick's vision in *2001: A Space Odyssey*. To Bowie, the time seemed perfect for a topical song on space, human frailty and the unknown dangers of outer space. Using *2001*'s doomed Frank Poole as a template for Major Tom, *Space Oddity* began to take shape sometime in late 1968 using a "borrowed" Dictaphone machine from Legastat (much of the

---

2. For a brief time in 1963, Bowie used the name "David Jay."

---

song was written on company time.) Encouraged by positive input from Pete Townsend and Marc Bolan, Bowie continued to refine the song until Pitt felt it was ready to be presented to Philips. In the spring, Bowie passed an audition with label executives (a recording of this audition is thoughtfully included with the SOUND+VISION boxed-set) and was signed to a deal on June 20. A chance meeting on the street with Elton John led to a meeting with producer Gus Dudgeon, who agreed to oversee the studio session. A proper single (issued in on Philips in both mono and stereo versions) was ready for release by July 11, 1969.

Bowie's timing couldn't have been better. After a slow start, *Space Oddity* finally caught on, thanks in large part to its use in TV coverage of the Apollo missions by the BBC. Musicians all across the UK began to ask about the peculiar keyboard sound on the record. Once they discovered that it was made by a pocket-sized electronic organ called a Stylophone, music shops across the country were besieged with orders (this led to a print ad featuring an endorsement by Bowie.) By December, the song had reached No. 5 on the UK charts. By the end of the year, *Space Oddity* had sold a very respectable 135,000 copies. After years of aborted attempts to break through, Bowie was finally on his way.

Bowie historians are quick to point out that the next phase of his career might not have happened had it not been for Bowie's friendship with Marc Bolan of T-Rex. Bolan was Bowie's connection to the world of the glitter and glam rock of the early 1970's. In exchange for Bowie's mime performances at several T-Rex shows, Bolan played guitar on Bowie's *The Prettiest Star*, a song dedicated to his new fiancee, Angie Barnett. (They were married on March 20, 1970 — the same month that the song was released.) By the fall, Bowie had formed a new backing band (The Hype, who debuted with Bowie on a BBC radio show on March 5, 1970) and was very interested in exploring some glam avenues.

After two unremarkable albums (MAN OF WORDS, MAN OF MUSIC and THE WORLD OF DAVID BOWIE are insignificant footnotes to Bowie's career), he and producer Tony Visconti embarked on an attempt to create a record as great as the Beatles' SGT. PEPPER. The sessions began in mid-April 1970 at Trident Studios in London and featured a new guitarist named Mick Ronson. Together with Visconti, Ronson fostered a new relationship between Bowie and the electric guitar. After some eighty-eight hours in the studio, the record was completed. Bowie called it THE MAN WHO SOLD THE WORLD.

History tells us that TMWSTW was an important record. However, in the spring of 1971, there was no indication that it was anything other than a commercial disaster. Realizing that the album would be met with indifference the UK, Tony DeFries, Bowie's new manager decided that the route to worldwide stardom lay through America. He made an unusual decision — TMWSTW had to be released in the US first and then followed up with a series of outrageous attention-grabbing promotional appearances. It sounded like a good theory, but in the end, the whole plan backfired. Blame the dresses.

Ah, yes — the dresses. Before they left England, Bowie and Angie purchased some long, flowing gowns from a Savile Row designer named "Mr. Fish." The idea appealed to Bowie, who had always enjoyed dressing to shock. Posing on the cover of his new album in his new frock sounded like a brilliant idea.

Unfortunately, this gamble was a miserable failure in America, a nation where gender-bending and cross-dressing were strictly taboo. When Bowie arrived on American soil in his gown and carrying a purse on January 27, 1971, the reaction was one of unmitigated disgust. Appearances in California and Texas (where some redneck actually pulled a gun on Bowie) were especially disastrous. As odd as it may seem today, record stores across the nation refused to display or even stock an album that featured a picture of a man wearing a dress. Those who weren't shocked by the artwork dismissed Bowie as merely another eccentric Englishman. The reaction was so negative that the original sleeve was withdrawn and replaced with something very generic and less threatening. Original versions of TMWSTW now trade for $500 and up.

However, despite selling a mere 50,000 albums in the US, Bowie's first trip to America did result in something positive. At a stop in New York, he was introduced to Andy Warhol's crowd and the underground art-and-music crowd in New York (See the previous chapter for details of Bowie's new relationship with Iggy Pop.) Inspired by his new friends (including Lou Reed, the Velvet Underground and Bob Dylan) Bowie returned to England to record HUNKY DORY (issued on RCA in December 1971), a collection of cover songs designed as a tribute to New York City.

The album was a detour of sorts. Bowie veered away from his quasi-glam image in favor of a strange neofolky, neo-hippie thing. The result was a major accomplishment, a conglomeration and synthesis of many disconnected styles and influences. Other artists had tried such a thing before but never to this extent and certainly not with this kind of critical success. In the end, HUNKY DORY made everything all right, washing away the bitterness left behind by the failure of TMWSTW. A series of well-received singles (including *Changes*, his first single for RCA) restored Bowie's confidence and laid some very important musical groundwork for the year ahead. The album also resulted in some short-term financial security. Tony DeFries was able to convince RCA that Bowie was worth at least $37,500 per album.

If wearing a dress in public was frazzling for some people, you can imagine the reaction to a simple statement that appeared in the January 22, 1972, edition of Melody Maker. In the middle of a story entitled *Oh You Pretty Thing*, writer Michael Watts got the scoop of his life. There it was — in paragraph seventeen — Bowie's answer to a question about his interest in wearing dresses. It was brief and to the point: "I'm gay and I always have been, even when I was David Jones." Today such a statement would most likely be greeted with a shrug; in the Britain of 1972, it was nothing less than an event of seismic proportions. It made him the most talked-about performer of the year.

While there was the inevitable media and public backlash (even rock critic Lester Bangs made several references to "faggot rock" in his writings), Bowie's pronouncement had an enormously positive effect on the gay population of the UK. Realizing that a respected musician was on their side, virtually every gay performer in the UK was from then on influenced by Bowie. Future stars such as Holly Johnson (Frankie Goes to Hollywood), Boy George and Tom Robinson consider hearing Bowie's admission as a turning point in both their personal professional lives.

Back in the straight world, Bowie rode the shock waves of this announcement to new levels of notoriety. Rather than hurting his image and credibility, Bowie's professed homosexuality / bisexuality added an element of danger and taboo, something that only enhanced his stature among music fans. All that was required to turn this infamy into record sales was some grand musical gesture. That gesture came in the form of an outrageous new character called Ziggy Stardust.

Inspired by the antics of Iggy Pop and the Stooges, Bowie vowed to create something even stranger. Ziggy was the answer: a doomed, space-aged alien polysexual rock star — a silvery, Erich von Däniken wet dream. He was part science fiction and part *Clockwork Orange*. He contained equal amounts of Buddhist deity, his mad half-brother and glam-era Marc Bolan. Further dissection revealed elements of underground America (Lou Reed, the Velvet Underground, Iggy Pop, the MC5, Andy Warhol and Twiggy, the famous 60's fashion model) carefully filtered through the art-school sensibilities of Britain. Hard rock and vaudeville — it was a potent combination.

Right at the core of Ziggy's persona was a huge dollop of Angie Bowie. She was the one who found a hairdresser to give Bowie a new puffball-with-a-tail haircut (copied from an ad in *Vogue* using a dye called Red Hot Red and Guard, a German anti-dandruff product. The hairdresser who executed the style was Susie Fussey, a stylist from Beckenham.) Angie also pushed Bowie to use more makeup and into wild sci-fi costumes — an important move when the standard rock start costume consisted of nothing more than long hair, jeans and maybe a few love beads.

And what about the name? That was Bowie's creation. "Ziggy" was most likely derivative of "Iggy" and "Twiggy." "Stardust" was a nod to Vince Taylor, an odd American country artist who performed under the name The Legendary Stardust Cowboy.[1] Ziggy was the world's first pre-packaged plastic rock star, a front that allowed Bowie to act out a rock and roll fantasy in full public view. It was all a facade, an excuse for strange behavior, a vehicle for taking risks — and a super-savvy marketing move. This combination of mystery and music soon mesmerized the world.

The controversy surrounding the Melody Maker interview created an instant demand for new material. *Starman*, Bowie's next single (released in April 1972) shot to No. 10 on the UK charts and whetted the public's appetite for more. It was followed by a full album on June 6, the landmark ZIGGY STARDUST AND

---

1. Vince Taylor's real name was Brian Maurice Holden. Born in Middlesex in 1939, his family emigrated to California after WWII. He adopted his stage name in 1956 and moved back to London the following year. His most lasting contribution to music was a 1959 single called *Brand New Cadillac*, a track later covered by the Clash on LONDON CALLING. Bowie became fascinated with Taylor's excesses after a chance meeting in 1966. After years of drug and alcohol abuse, Taylor became a physical and mental wreck and died in 1991. He's buried in Switzerland.

David Bowie

THE SPIDERS FROM MARS. Ziggy's public debut came at a Friends of the Earth Save the Whales benefit at London's Royal Festival Hall on July 8, 1972. With his red hair, white makeup, skin-tight space suit and red lace-up boots, Bowie approached the microphone and said "Hello, I'm Ziggy Stardust and these are the Spiders from Mars." The show and the subsequent world tour were a roaring success. A star had been born.

Ziggy provided ample fodder for the media. The world had never seen a rock star flaunt his sexuality this way — the makeup, the girly dresses, rubber space suits, the fake on stage blow jobs with guitarist Mick Ronson. Bowie used every bit of scandal to his advantage, manipulating the press in ways never before seen. Meanwhile, audiences clamored for more, pushing Bowie records further up the charts.

The Ziggy Period lasted just 360 days. After spending close to a year on the road, The Spiders from Mars appeared at the Hammersmith Odeon in London on July 3, 1973.[1] At the end of the set, Bowie declared, "This show will stay the longest in our memories, not just because it's the end of the tour but because it's the last show we'll ever do." The following day, Mainman (DeFries' management company) issued a statement confirming that Bowie was "leaving the concert stage forever." Fans reacted with shock and disappointed; what they didn't realize was that it was Ziggy who was retiring, not Bowie. A Melody Maker interview with Mick Ronson ten days later put everyone's fears at ease.

The '72-73 world tour convinced Bowie that Ziggy only had a limited life span. By the spring of 1973, he had already conceived a new persona: Aladdin Sane. Although this new character appeared to be a Ziggy clone at first glance, it soon became clear that he was a more mature creature, a creation even more theatrical than his predecessor. Bowie later claimed that part of Aladdin can be traced to Vile Bodies, a 1930 Evelyn Waugh novel about the decadent behavior of a group of young people in London in the late 1920's.

Written almost entirely on the road during the Spiders from Mars Tour, ALADDIN SANE was released on April 13, 1973. For the first time since the Beatles, an album had gathered more than 100,000 pre-orders from record stores. Initially, it received a bashing as journalists (still enamored with Ziggy) declared it to be substandard and criticizing the Aladdin Sane character as poorly defined. Fans disagreed. Singles like The Jean Genie (inspired by Iggy Pop) and Drive In Saturday were major hits in the UK while ALADDIN SANE made it into the American Top 20. Reissues of Space Oddity (the single peaked at No. 10) and SPACE ODDITY (the album peaked at No. 16) became major North American hits. Even Deram, Bowie's old label, successfully peeled off some hype for themselves as their reissue of The Laughing Gnome, a 1967 novelty single, reached No. 6 in Britain.

For the next tour, Bowie's backup band expanded to nine members. The new outfit included a saxophone player, percussionists and a second guitarist. Bowie was thus free to roam the stage, allowing the show to become more theatrical than ever. Innovative lighting effects and elaborate staging were introduced. Meanwhile, all transportation between gigs had to be by limo, train or boat since Bowie refused to fly.

By the end of 1973, Bowie was ready for another detour. His solution was PIN-UPS, a collection of his favorite songs from the 60's. Although there were several UK hits on the album, its main purpose was to buy Bowie some time so he could complete his next project, a proposed musical adaptation of George Orwell's 1984. Unfortunately, Sonia Orwell (George's widow) refused to have anything to do with Bowie and declared that she would never sell the rights to her husband's book to that freak from London. Although Bowie was disappointed, he was able to salvage three songs he had already written for the project. They became the basis for Bowie's next album DIAMOND DOGS.

The album was again very cerebral. It was a mix of rock, Kafka, William Burroughs, Aldous Huxley and Salvador Dali. Aladdin Sane was shrugged off like an old set of clothes. His replacement was the ambisexual half-canine creature that adorned the gatefold cover of the new album. (An anatomically correct half-canine, too, painted by artist Guy Peelaert. Still smarting from the TMWSTW fiasco of 1971, RCA ensured that copies of the album featuring the offending genitals were destroyed prior to release. The few albums that survived the purge now fetch upwards of $4,000 on the collector's market.) Recorded at DeFries' new £40,000 sixteen-track studio in Shepherd's Bush and released in April 1974, the album debuted at No. 1 in the UK.

---

1. This show was captured on film by D.A. Pennebaker and turned into a concert film.

Several singles quickly became hits, most notably the title track (issued in June 1974) and *Rebel Rebel*, a song that was released in three forms. The first was the North American single and featured Bowie playing all the instruments. Version two was the original album cut, while the third was a remix (the UK single released in February 1974.)

Since DIAMOND DOGS was originally envisioned as a stage musical, it was inevitable that the following tour was even more theatrical than previous road trips. Bowie lived in an old brownstone on West 17th Street in New York and had become very interested in the theater scene. Opening in Montreal on June 14, 1974, the Diamond Dogs Revue was more than a reasonable facsimile of a Broadway production — Bowie spent more than a quarter of a million dollars on elaborate staging created by New York set designer Chris Langhart, the same person who had designed a show for the Barnum and Bailey Circus. Props included two forty-foot towers and a cherry picker device that lowered Bowie out over the audience during *Space Oddity*. The show also featured dramatic state-of-the-art lighting effects (created by Jules Fisher, a noted Broadway lighting designer) and complex choreography (by Toni Basil, leader of a troop called the Lockers and hired at Angie's suggestion.) More than forty roadies and technicians were required on each of the thirty-six stops on the tour. This may have been old news to veterans of touring theater productions, but this kind of expense and preparation for a rock show was unprecedented.

Although very expensive, the tour was a giant success, culminating with a week-long run in Los Angeles in front of 35,000 people — including a large number of celebrities. A show at the Tower Theater in Philadelphia on July 12, 1974, was committed to tape and eventually released in October as a double set entitled DAVID LIVE. Reviews were good although, towards the end of the tour, Bowie was doing so many drugs that he often had trouble remembering all his cues.

During the tour, Bowie discovered the soul sounds of Philadelphia, thanks in part to Luther Vandross, one of his hired backup singers. He made a decision: his next record would be made at Sigma Sound, the same studio that was cranking out Philly soul hits by MFSB and the Gamble and Huff crew. Over a period of two weeks, Bowie and his band cranked out ten new songs. In January 1975, he set up at Electric Ladyland in New York to finish up a few ideas before handing over the master tapes to RCA. When John Lennon dropped in for a visit, he found himself playing on two songs — a rather inebriated rendition of *Across the Universe* and *Fame*, one of the singles extracted from the album. That song was destined to be Bowie's first No. 1 hit in America shortly after it was released in August 1975. Bowie called YOUNG AMERICANS his "Polaroid album" because he considered it to be a snapshot of American music at the time. This "plastic soul" approach found an eager audience immediately after the album was released in March 1975. The title track had been released as the first single a month earlier and had become a sizable hit, despite the fact two full minutes had been chopped from the 45 version.

Enamored with American culture, Bowie decided to relocate to Los Angeles. Unable to resist the temptations offered by the Beautiful People, Bowie spent much of the next two years in a cocaine-and-alcohol stupor. The problems that first surfaced during the Diamond Dogs Revue worsened as Bowie often kept large bowls of coke around the house. A drug-induced paranoia began to take hold; he was sure UFOs were monitoring him and that aliens were plotting his abduction. Between dates on the last tour, he swept the sky with a telescope from his hotel rooftop, hoping to communicated with the Masters of the Universe who had him under surveillance. He was constantly sending his personal assistant out to buy books on UFOs. Considering his fascination and fears, it only seems fitting that Bowie was soon once more cast as an alien.

Director Nicholas Roeg was planning to cast Peter O'Toole in a film about a doomed extraterrestrial entitled *The Man Who Fell to Earth*. But after seeing a BBC documentary on Bowie's drug-addled Diamond Dogs Revue, Roeg decided that Bowie would make a perfect alien. Although the role of Thomas Jerome Newton ended up being Bowie's acting breakthrough (he made an *extremely* convincing alcoholic alien), it was a fairly miserable experience. On the set, Bowie was often completely spaced out, spending hours drunk and coked up in his trailer. Speedballs would be counteracted with copious amounts of Valium and whiskey. During breaks in the filming, Bowie listened to his own records backwards on a specially-designed turntable, looking for hidden messages. Once prinicple photography was wrapped up, Bowie stole all of his alien's costumes, so he had something appropriate to wear as the Masters of the Universe watched him.

To make matters worse, Bowie's relationship with Tony DeFries and Mainman (his management company) were at an all-time low. Legal action had been launched in January 1975. An arrangment with a new manager, Micahel Lippman turned out no better. A $2 million suit was filed against him within a year. To those around him, The Man Who Fell to Earth seemed to be quickly falling apart.

In April, Bowie announced a second retirement. "I've rocked my roll," he said, "It's a boring dead end. There will be no more rock and roll records or tours from me. The last thing I want to be is some useless fucking rock and singer."

The hits, however, kept on coming. *Changes* and *Fame* had were massive success and YOUNG AMERICANS was certified gold by the late fall. As Christmas approached, a new single, *Golden Years* (a track he had written for Elvis Presley) hit the charts, offering the promise of album number ten. By time this, Bowie fans knew their hero couldn't retire — he obviously didn't know how.

By January 1976, Bowie had a new album, another tour and a new persona. STATION TO STATION went gold almost immediately upon release and continued to sell after Bowie and Raw Moon, his new band, embarked on a world tour, starting with a show in Vancouver on February 2nd. This production featured Bowie as the Thin White Duke, a character that started taking shape during DIAMOND DOGS and slowly perfected over the YOUNG AMERICANS period. The Duke made an elegant impression: blonde hair, impeccably tailored suits and a the curl of smoke from a French cigarette.

On the surface, things seem fine. Behind the scenes, Bowie was still a mess. The first indication the public had that things were going terribly wrong came on March 21 when Bowie, Iggy Pop and an assortment of hangers-on were arrested at the Flagship Americana Hotel in Rochester, New York. Caught with six ounces of marijuana, everyone faced jail terms of up to fifteen years (The case was adjourned for a year so the tour could continue. In the end, all charges were dropped.)

A second scare erupted on April 27 as Bowie tried to cross into Poland after a visit to Moscow. Border guards discovered an odd amount of Nazi literature and films amongst his belongings and detained Bowie for questioning. That incident contributed to a tabloid debacle ten days later during Bowie's carefully staged arrival at Victoria Station in London. With fans, film crews and photographers screaming from all sides, Bowie's wave to the crowd was captured in mid-gesture. When it appeared in the papers the following morning, some people interpreted this to be a Nazi salute. The fallout was fiercesome. Perhaps it was finally time to lay low for a while.

The decision to relocate to West Berlin was made that summer. By October, Bowie and Iggy were living in a quiet walk-up apartment in the Shöneberg district in a conserted attempt to wean themselves off the heroin, cocaine and alcohol that was destroying their private lives. It was to be one of the most creative periods in both their careers (see separate chapter for more on Iggy's Berlin exploits.)

Bowie spent much of his free time painting, studying art and writing music. After a few setbacks (it took a while to kick the booze and there was that time he wrote off his Mercedes in an underground parking garage), he was soon joined by Brian Eno, the electronics whiz formerly of Roxy Music. Bowie once again realized that it was time for another fresh start and, fascinated by Eno's early ventures into the area of ambient music, appealed to him for help. With his own career stalled, Eno was only too happy to help.

The compositional chemistry was powerful and immediate. Under Eno's direction, Bowie became confident enough to move in a very experimental direction, and ready to rethink his approach to music. After Eno turned Bowie on to German electronic groups like Tangerine Dream and Kraftwerk, as well as producers such as Giorgio Moroder, Bowie veered into the world of state-of-the-art electronic sounds and effects. Even more important, Eno was able to achieve a balance between challenging Bowie to write new songs and allowing him to sort out his personal demons at his own speed. It was an important theraputic experience for Bowie.

When RCA got word of what was going on at Hansa Studios, they became very concerned. The last thing they wanted was for their big star to go disco on them. But Bowie and Eno held firm. They assured label executives that they knew what they were doing.

While early media reports claimed that Bowie's next album would be another major departure in sound and style, most everyone was caught off guard when LOW was issued in January 1977. Side one consisted of seven short, mostly instrumental tracks while side two meandered through four moody pieces. The persona that went with the music was never really given it a name. Some fans assumed it to be a continuation of the Thin White Duke. Other interpreted it as an expansion of Thomas Newton, the character from The Man Who Fell to Earth. Some observers put forth the argument that Bowie had gone facist, creating some kind of undead, ultra-right-wing electronic weirdo offspring of the Master of Ceremonies in CABARET. For fans of previous incarnations like Ziggy Stardust, it was all very confusing. LOW did indeed mark a low point in many ways — sales, reviews and in terms of how his record company felt about things.

However, Bowie and Eno shrugged off all the criticisms and delivered the second Berlin album in October 1977. While the record confounded critics and confused fans in much the same way LOW did (it was once again neatly divided into vocal tracks and instrumentals), HEROES had the advantage of the brilliant title track. Bowie wrote the song after observing a young couple who met in the shadow on the Berlin Wall at the same time every day — a couple who were later killed by East German border guards. The striking vocal effects were achieved by using three microphones set up at varying distances from Bowie in the big studio at Hansa. As a demonstration of his gratitude to Kraftwerk for opening his eyes to the possibilities of electronics, the album included V-2 Schneider, a thank you to Kraftwerk's Florian Schneider.

HEROES was issued in English, French and German versions and while it lacked the commercial punch of his albums of the early and mid-70's, it sold in respectable numbers. More important, however, was that the album helped heal Bowie's psychic wounds. With his creativity re-energized, he was prepared to face the world again. He even started to travel by airplane on his 1978 world tour (a tour, by the way, that resulted in STAGE, another live set.)

The third album in the so-called Bowie-Eno "Berlin Triology" wasn't recorded entirely in Berlin, a good portion of it was recored at Mountain Studios in Montreux, Switzerland. After taking a break from rock to narrate Prokofiev's "Peter and the Wolf" for a special RCA project LODGER was released in May 1979 and had more in common with STATION TO STATION than with the previous two albums. First of all, there was no segregation of vocal and instrumental tracks. The record is also less bleak and somehow more hopeful. Hardcore Bowie fans also found that Move On sounded oddly familiar — it was a reworking of the chord sequence of All the Young Dudes (Bowie's composition for Mott the Hoople) that he put together after accidentally hearing the old song played backwards.

Having had his fill of German decadence and wanting to start the new decade fresh, Bowie moved to New York to start work on what would be his thirteenth album. With his divorce with Angie final and having won custody of their son Zowie (who was now going by the more civilized name of Joe), Bowie provided RCA with a going away present: a simultaneous No. 1 single and album in the UK. SCARY MONSTERS (AND SUPER CREEPS) debuted at the top of the charts in September 1980 at about the same time Ashes to Ashes (a semi-sequel to Space Oddity that featured the return of Major Tom) peaked at No. 1 in Britain. The song's popularity was enhanced by a visually arresting promotional video clip directed by David Mallet. Two further singles, Fashion and the title track, seemed to assure everyone that Bowie had returned to form.

With his RCA contract expired, Bowie could afford to wait until the right offer came along. Meanwhile, he was able to maintain a decent profile by recording a duet with Queen called Under Pressure. What started as a curious exercise between neighbors (Bowie and Queen singer Freddy Mercury had houses within shouting distance of each other in Switzerland) ended up becoming a worldwide smash. The following spring, Bowie teamed with Giorgio Moroder for the title theme to the film Cat People which was released as a single on MCA in April 1982.

While many labels were anxious to have Bowie's name on a contract, he was often much too busy with stage and film work to give another recording contract much thought. He won raves for his portrayal as John Merrick in a touring production of The Elephant Man, where his participation helped to attract sellout audiences in Denver, Chicago and on Broadway. Bowie played himself in Christine F, the story of a drug addicted teenage prostitute. The film eventually became the most successful release in the history of German cinema. He also played a 150 year-old vampire alongside Catherine Deneuve in The Hunger, one of the most sensual vampire movies of all time. Once photography was completed, he flew to the south Pacific to start work on Merry Christmas, Mr. Lawrence. Bowie even appeared on BBC-TV in a presentation of Bertolt Brecht's Baal.

After eighteen months away from music, a new five year, $10 million contract with Capitol / EMI required

David Bowie

a quick start on a new album. Rather than having Tony Visconti produce once again, Bowie elected to go with Nile Rodgers, one of the forces behind a disco band called Chic. Together with Rodgers and guitarist Carlos Alomar, Bowie created a sharp, tight funky album that was to be the greatest North American success of his career.

LET'S DANCE was released in April 1983 and immediately began to sell by the millions. The title track hit No. 1 on both the British and North American singles charts, a feat Bowie had been trying to achieve for years. In the process, Let's Dance became his first million-selling single since Fame in 1975. But there was still much more to come.

On May 30th, Bowie co-headlined the US Festival in San Bernardino, California and was paid $1 million for his troubles. In exchange for performing a quick fifty minute set, he earned the highest fee ever paid to a solo rock and roll performer. On June 2nd, the Serious Moonlight tour opened to sellout crowds in London, where more than 250,000 people had tried to buy tickets. The North American leg of the tour began in Montreal on July 12th and by the time everything wrapped up in Bangkok on December 12th (after lugging an eleven-piece band and 64,000 pounds of equipment through ninety-eight shows in sixty-two cities on four continents), it had become Bowie's most successful tour ever.

Perhaps then it was inevitable that Bowie treated his next album as a throwaway. Although TONIGHT rode the wave of LET'S DANCE to platinum sales numbers, it really didn't stack up. Released less than fourteen months after its predecessor, and less than ten months after the end of the Serious Moonlight tour, TONIGHT was a major letdown for fans who had been led to expect more. The good songs (Blue Jean, and Loving the Alien) were safe pop compositions, and the rest sounded too much like material that Nile Rodgers might have rejected as substandard during the LET'S DANCE sessions. A one-off Top Ten duet with Mick Jagger (a cover of Martha and the Vandellas' Dancing in the Streets) was be his last significant hit before slumping into a creative lull that lasted into the 90's.

The slide into mediocrity became more apparent when, in April 1987, Bowie released NEVER LET ME DOWN, a critical failure that had many people wondering whether he had lost all relevance in a rock and roll world that was now dominated by musicians half his age. Despite a couple of singles and the subsequent Glass Spiders tour (featuring Peter Frampton as his touring guitarist), there were legitimate concerns among both fans and critics that Bowie's best years were forever behind him. To make matters worse, Wanda Lee Nichols made a statement accusing Bowie of a "vampire-like" sexual assault in a Dallas hotel after a Glass Spiders show in the fall of 1987. (Although Bowie did admit spending the night with her, the sexual assault suit was thrown out by a judge on February 12, 1990.) Fan fears that Bowie had lost touch seemed confirmed by the end of 1988. For the first time since 1971, with no new material and without any back catalogue reissues, Bowie had gone a full year without appearing on the UK album or singles charts.

Realizing that he needed to recapture the public's interest with some new dramatic gesture, Bowie began with a long overdue economic move. He struck a deal with Rykodisc, a small Massachusetts-based label that specialized in CD releases. They were given the task of sorting through all the legal minefields of past Bowie contracts so that eighteen of Bowie's albums could finally be reissued on compact disc. This was followed up by the Sound+Vision tour, a road show that featured Bowie playing his greatest hits one more time before retiring them forever. Once the itinerary was announced — the tour began in Quebec City on March 3, 1990 — fans in each city along the route were given a chance to vote through local radio stations for what songs they would like to see in the set list. (Unfortunately, a noisy campaign led by a British music tabloid to force Bowie to perform The Laughing Gnome failed to sway Bowie.)

Threatened with never being able to see Bowie perform songs such as Ziggy Stardust or Diamond Dogs ever again, fans were coerced into making the tour a modest success with one show in Los Angeles grossing over $1.1 million. The Sound+Vision gigs also had the desired effect at the record stores — the Rykodisc reissues were soon in big demand around the world.

In an attempt to alleviate the boredom of having to rely on past glories, Bowie formed a new outfit called Tin Machine. As a stripped-down four piece featuring guitarist Reeves Gabrels and the rhythm section of Hunt and Tony Sales (sons of comedian Soupy Sales and veterans of Iggy Pop's LUST FOR LIFE sessions), Tin Machine was to be Bowie's vehicle for a return to the basics of rock and roll. Unfortunately, neither the public nor the critics fell for the band's faux-grunge approach and despite Bowie's best efforts (club shows, TV appearances, a live album), the band failed to generate any excitement and was eventually shelved.

If there was any good news, it involved Bowie's personal life. He married Iman, a 36 year-old fashion model from Somalia, a woman best known to many as the prison camp shape-shifter from *Star Trek VI: The Undiscovered Country*. There were two weddings: a perfunctory ceremony at Lausanne city hall on April 20, 1992, and a grand church affair in Florence on June 6. The couple soon settled into several homes, including a fabulous $5 million Indonesian-style retreat on the Caribbean island of Mustique.

The change obviously did him some good. In the spring of 1993, Bowie released BLACK TIE WHITE NOISE, his first solo album in five years. With Nile Rodgers producing and his old buddy Mick Ronson on guitar, the album was a comeback of sorts. Originally conceived as a wedding present for his new wife (track one on the CD is entitled *Wedding*), the album echoed back to the days of SCARY MONSTERS.

As Bowie approached his fiftieth birthday, he slowly began to receive accolades from the new generation of alt-rock performers. While many of them had not even been born when Ziggy Stardust first stepped on staged, they had nonetheless been greatly influenced by the Bowie legacy. One of Bowie's biggest fans turned out to be Trent Reznor of Nine Inch Nails. Following the release of another solid album (OUTSIDE, another collaboration with Brian Eno that was issued on Virgin on September 26, 1995), Nine Inch Nails was invited on an arena tour. The result was an inter-generational spectacle, drawing an audience comprising of teenagers and upper-end baby boomers. One of the highlights of the show was the seamless crossover between the Nine Inch Nails set and Bowie's performance. There was no intermission or set change; as Reznor wound his way through the last few songs, Bowie appeared on stage for several duets before Nine Inch Nails subtly slinked away.

Soon other artists were paying their respects, most notably Morrissey (a lifetime Bowie fan) and Nirvana (who covered Bowie material on their platinum-selling MTV UNPLUGGED disc.) On January 8, 1997 — Bowie's fiftieth birthday — a huge party and pay-per-view event were held in his honor at Madison Square Gardens in New York. A sellout crowd saw Lou Reed, Sonic Youth, Billy Corgan of the Smashing Pumpkins, Sonic Youth, Placebo, Frank Black, the Foo Fighters and Robert Smith of the Cure perform songs from Bowie's formidable repertoire.

On February 11, 1997, Bowie released the post-industrial EARTHLING, an album that showed surprising vigor for someone who was supposed to be too old to have a grasp of the music of the late 90's. A brilliant Trent Reznor remix of *I'm Afraid of Americans* (released in conjunction with an incredibly spooky video) became a highly requested track in alternative dance clubs. A return to the HUNKY DORY sound

David Bowie

was heard on … HOURS, a well-received album that was released on October 5, 1999.

By the end of the decade, Bowie seemed very comfortable yet humble in his role as an alt-rock deity. Living mainly in Bermuda (tax reasons, you understand) he continues to make music, but has also branched out into new territory that didn't even exist a few short years ago. Although Bowie's Internet ventures have been very successful (see www.davidbowie.com for a taste of what's going on), his main legacy of the 1990's may be found in the annals of Wall Street deal-making.

In February 1997, a financial player named David Pullman orchestrated a $55 million bond issue that involved nothing other than David Bowie's old music. The concept was simple: since Bowie's back catalogue generated a guaranteed cash flow (similar to what investors might expect from oil wells, fleets of trucks and real estate), it was possible to use these albums as security. These "Bowie bonds" were backed by the royalties from Bowie's first twenty-five albums over the next fifteen years. In other words, Bowie received fifteen years' worth of royalties up front in exchange for turning over his regular royalty cheques to investors. At fifty years of age, Bowie was then free to enjoy his money while investors would worry about the risks. Wall Street liked the deal (good songs don't deteriorate with age or through drug use, thus theoretically have an infinite life span) and the bonds were rated single-A-3 by Moody's, the respected investment rating service.

Since the completion of that deal, other players have begun issuing bonds secured by intellectual property — film libraries, literary estates, and syndicated TV programs. David Pullman was also the architect of a $30 million offering of bonds based on the Motown hits written by Edward Holland, Lamont Dozier and Brian Holland and $100 million package built on James Brown's back catalogue. Even Iron Maiden's music was put on the open market. The original Bowie deal also inspired the NFL to issue $600 million worth of bonds in October 1998. Agents of superstar athletes now routinely investigate the possibility of bond financing based on the potential future earnings of their clients.

David Bowie has been around for so long that it's hard to imagine life without him. His career in music has spanned an incredible forty-plus years, yet — despite his previous "retirements" — he shows no sign of wanting to give it up. Not only has his music affected at least four generations of musicians, his creative influence is being felt in the world of high finance, cyberspace, art and architecture. One thing is for sure: rock and roll will forever feel the effects of the saxophone-playing boy from Bromley.

Fast Facts

o When Bowie was producing TRANSFORMER for Lou Reed, Bowie hired his first music teacher, Ronnie Ross, to play the saxophone part in *Walk on the Wild Side.*

o In November 1964, Bowie was a founder of the International League for the Preservation of Animal Filament, a group dedicated to the protection of male pop musicians with long hair. The League's anti-persecution campaign received a surprising amount of newspaper and TV coverage.

o Fragments of a lost rock opera written sometime in 1968 turned up at an auction in the summer of 1996. It told the story of Ernie Johnson, a sad sod who planned to stage a party in honor of his suicide.

o In November 1969, *Space Oddity* was rewritten as *Ragozzo Solo, Ragozza Sola* (*Lonely Boy, Lonely Girl*) for release in Italy. Sung in Italian, this version had nothing to do with Major Tom. A French translation, *Un Homme A Disoensu Dans Le Ciel* (*The Man Who Is Lost in the Sky*) appeared in France.

o Bowie's self-titled 1969 album was reissued in November 1972 as SPACE ODDITY.

o *All the Madmen* from THE MAN WHO SOLD THE WORLD was inspired by a difficult confrontation with his half-brother, Terry, who had been sent to a Cane Hill, a mental institution, in an effort to treat his schizophrenia. Unable to cope after years of suffering, Terry committed suicide on January 16, 1985, by throwing himself in front of a train.

o Angela Bowie's maiden name is Mary Angela Barnett.

o The telephone booth featured on the back of ZIGGY STARDUST AND THE SPIDERS FROM MARS was located at the northwest end of Haddon St. near Picadilly Street. The original booth was removed in the late 70's and sold at an auction. A metal facsimile now stands in its place.

o People tend to forget that Bowie's Ziggy Stardust tour wasn't a grand commercial success everywhere. One show in St. Louis attracted just 110 people to a venue that held 11,000. Bowie played the entire show just the same.

o Bowie and Angela's son, Duncan Zowie Hayward, was born in a Bromley hospital on May 28, 1971.

o On February 14, 1973, at a show at Radio City Music Hall, Bowie collapsed from exhaustion at the end of the set. Initial rumors said that he had been shot by someone in the audience. These rumors became central to the plot of the 1998 glam fantasy film, *Velvet Goldmine*.

o Elements of LOW were incorporated into a Philip Glass symphony in 1993.

o There are perhaps fifty songs left over from the Berlin triptych, but it's doubtful they were ever all be released. They're just not that good.

o In September 1988, Bowie became one of the few humans to ever appear on the cover of *Architectural Digest* when the magazine ran a pictorial of his home in Mustique.

o Mick Ronson died of liver failure on April 30, 1993. He was 46.

o Bowie was inducted into the Rock and Roll Hall of Fame by David Byrne at a ceremony at the Waldorf Astoria in New York on January 17, 1996.

o Bowie was asked by Volkswagen to design a special limited edition millennium version of the Beetle.

o Barnes and Noble offers regular book reviews written by Bowie on their web site.

o Hardcore fans should look for a copy of the magazine design Bowie did for film director Francis Ford Coppola. Look for the summer 1999 issue (Vol. 3, No 2) of *Zoetrope: All Story*, Coppolas's literary publication. Part of the charm of this issue can be found in Bowie's take on the Zoetrope logo: the first "o" is blue while the other is brown, just like Bowie's mismatched eyes.

o Boston's Berklee College of Music granted Bowie an honorary degree on May 8, 1999.

o To date, Bowie has appeared in more than thirty films as an actor, a performer or both. Titles include *The Man Who Fell to Earth* (1976), *The Hunger* (1983), *Merry Christmas, Mr. Lawrence* (1983), *After Hours* (watch for the cameo, 1985) *Absolute Beginners* (1986), *The Last Temptation of Christ* (1988) and *Twin Peaks: Fire Walk With Me* (1992.)

o Bowie helped create a video game for Edios called *Omikron: The Nomad Soul*. The game features eight new Bowie songs plus avatars that look a lot like Bowie and his wife, Iman.

o In June 1999, the Anti-Piracy Unit named Bowie as one of the world's most bootlegged artists. Without counting the millions of illegal sound files on the Internet (only CD's, tapes and vinyl were counted), there were at least ninety-six illegal Bowie albums in circulation.

o In July 1999, Bowie finished sixth on Q magazine's list of the 100 greatest starts of the 20ᵗʰ century.

o Bowie's Internet ventures have been wildly successful, adding a new relevance to his career. His 1999 album, …HOURS (his twenty-third) was offered for sale on-line two weeks before it appeared in the stores. Expecting to sell about two hundred copies this way (a complete download with a 28.8 modem would have taken five hours), the album instead sold many times that, This prompted one HMV executive to muse aloud that perhaps artists who jump the gun and sell albums on-line before they appear in stores should perhaps be banned from retail outlets.

o Bowie's Internet company designed the official web site for the New York Yankees.

o Bowie was scheduled to greet the year 2000 with a performance in Gisborne City, New Zealand (one of the first places on the planet to enter the new year) at 12:01AM, January 1. He canceled his appearance in August 1999 when he became dissatisfied about the arrangements being made for the event.

o Wealthy Bowie fans can rent his former villa on the private island of Mustique. Rates for the Indonesian-inspired villa (with all its pools, guests houses and staff) average about $13,000 (US) a week.

Recommended Listening

o THE RISE AND FALL OF ZIGGY STARDUST (RCA, 1972 / Rykodisc, 1990 — a superior set with better sound, bonus tracks and a nice booklet.)

o ALADDIN SANE (RCA, 1973 / Rykodisc, 1990)

o YOUNG AMERICANS (RCA, 1975)

o STATION TO STATION (RCA, 1976)

o HEROES (RCA, 1977 / Rykodisc, 1991)

o Good choices for compilations include SOUND+VISION, the Rykodisc set issued in 1989 and reissued in 1994. SINGLES 1969-1993 (Rykodisc, 1993) is a solid single-disc bet along with CHANGESBOWIE (Rykodisc, 1990.) Most of Bowie's back catalogue was released in remastered (24 bit) and enhanced versions in October 1999. These CD's sound far better than the original CD issues.

o For those interested in the pre *Space Oddity* years, you might want to investigate EARLY ON 1964-1966 (Rhino, 1995) which features cleaned up recordings of tracks by the King Bees and the Manish Boys. A second option might be THE DERAM ANTHOLOGY 1966-1968 (Polygram, 1997) which features *The Laughing Gnome* in digital splendor.

Internet Resources

o www.davidbowie.com (All David, all the time)

o www.bowieart.com (Want to buy one of David's paintings or other works of art? Grab a credit card. Prices can be quoted in USD or Pound Sterling.)

o www.virginrecords.com (Bowie's current home)

o www.users.cts.com/crash/p/phil/bowielps.html (A fine resource for tracking down specific songs and albums.)

Recommended Reading

o Bowie, Angela. *Backstage Passes: Life on the Wild Side with David Bowie*. New York, New York: Putnam, 1993.

o Buckley, David. *Strange Fascination: David Bowie. The Definitive Biography*. London: Virgin, 1999.

o Gutman, David and Thomson, Elizabeth (eds.) *The Bowie Companion*. London: Macmillan London, 1993.

o Thompson, Dave. *David Bowie: Moonage Daydream*. London: Plexus, 1987.

Related Listening
Are you kidding? Anything from the Sex Pistols, the Smiths and U2 to Nine Inch Nails and Placebo.

The Story Thus Far ...
Both the Velvet Underground and Iggy Pop provide important inspiration for Bowie in the crucial months before he achieves superstardom with Ziggy Stardust. Lou Reed's post-VU attitudes are also essential components of the Ziggy persona. Bowie later becomes best friends with Iggy.

~ 4 ~
JONATHAN RICHMAN
Boston's anti-hippie punk pioneer

Punk rock didn't materialize out of thin air. Someone had to do the preliminary work, laying out the dynamite before a spark could create an explosion. A few of these pioneering demolition experts went on to sell millions of records; others, such as Jonathan Richman, did not. Richman's somewhat geeky image and quirky sense of songcraft have never materialized into chart success. It did, however, turn him into a pre-punk legend and alt-rock cult figure.

Jonathan was born at Beth Israel Hospital in Boston, Massachusetts on May 16, 1951 (some sources list May 15th.) Growing up as the son of a salesman in the western suburb of Natick, he first picked up a guitar when he was fifteen and was one of the few people who got into the Velvet Underground.

The VU was very important to Jonathan. Having discovered them during one of their many appearances at a Boston club called Tea Party. The band's noise-rock drone had such a hold on him that he began to follow them around as much as he could, becoming something of a pain in the butt. Within a year of first picking up a guitar, Jonathan's dream came true — his very first live performance was as an opener for the VU at a show in New York in 1969. Moe Tucker remembers a very shy boy who asked if it was all right if he could borrow a guitar and a couple of amps. Jonathan couldn't believe that he was actually on stage with them. He was even more excited when he was allowed to spend the next two weeks in New York at the home of the band's manager, sleeping on the couch in the living room.

Inspired by the VU's unforgiving, adrenaline-rush style, Jonathan began writing songs that were very much influenced by Lou Reed's style. He also became a big fan of Iggy Pop and the Stooges, and tried to incorporate some of their radical sensibilities into his music.[1] Unfortunately, as was the case with the VU and Iggy, most New York audiences didn't appreciate what Jonathan was trying to do. His singing voice and odd delivery were just too strange for most crowds. So, after working at a series of odd jobs, including a position at *Esquire* magazine that was even lower than the most menial mail room job, Jonathan moved back to Boston in 1970.

While working as a writer for *Vibrations* and *Fusion*, a couple of Boston-based music papers, he formed a band called Dance Band of the Highway, but that name was quickly changed to the Modern Lovers when Jonathan realized that he was on a mission to write "modern love songs." The first version of the band featured guitarist John Felice, drummer David Robinson and Rolfe Anderson on bass. Within six months, there were two important changes. Anderson was replaced by Ernie Brooks who convinced his roommate, keyboardist Jerry Harrison, to join up as well.

This edition of the Modern Lovers sounded very much like the kind of 60's-style garage band that populated every American suburb at the time — although there was obviously something more at play. The material was rough, loud and distorted. Richman liked turning up the gate on his guitar's distortion peddle while Harrison raunched up his normally sedate Fender-Rhodes piano through another fuzz pedal. This created a barrage not far removed from the Lou Reed / John Cale attack that anchored the Velvet Underground.

As raw as the music was, the songs contained equal dabs of naïveté, teenage rage and romanticism — real-world teenage things. The counterpoint was fascinating: music that rocked in a sharp, direct way but with lyrics about love, longing, sex and life in the suburbs. There were no pointless guitar or keyboard solos and certainly no flowery attempts at poetry extolling the virtues of 60's-style sex-and-drugs hedonism. Songs such as *Roadrunner* (Richman's two chord car-driving masterpiece based the VU's *Sister Ray* riff) and the offbeat *I'm Straight* (an early 70's rock song *against* drug use?) came out of this period.

Eccentric? You bet. While the long-haired hippie look and attitude was still the norm, here was a band lead by a singer with short hair and a pullover (looking very much like Dustin Hoffman crossed with Mick Jagger) who rejected everything for which the 60's stood. There are stories of Jonathan walking through the parks surrounding Cambridge University yelling "I'm not a hippie! I'm not stoned!" Jonathan and his band were certainly out of step with the times and they reveled in it.

One person who understood what the band was trying to accomplish was David Berson, assistant to Warner Brothers president Mo Ostin. Hearing about the band's impressive live shows and reading the stream of positive reviews in the New York *Daily News*, Berson was given the blessing to sign the Modern Lovers. In the spring of 1972, the group flew out to California to record some demos, with John Cale of the Velvet Underground acting as producer. Unfortunately, although nine or ten songs were put on tape (and despite A&M's underwriting the cost of more studio time), the Modern Lovers were written off as too weird to be worth any more trouble. The last straw came when Jonathan declared that he would record his old material, but would only play new material when the band played live. A second round of demos with producer Kim Fowley, and a second attempt at recording with Cale in the fall of 1973, only further underlined the fact that the band had quickly lost its way. The group was then released from their obligations with Warner Brothers insisting that the Arab oil crunch had created a shortage of vinyl for albums and, alas, spending on new acts had to be cut back. Everyone returned home to Boston angry and demoralized.

Dissension within the group grew throughout the rest of 1973, spurred in part by Jonathan's declaration that he would rather only play high schools and hospitals. The first person to quit was David Robinson after Jonathan insisted that his kit be cut down to nothing more than a snare drum with a towel laid over the skin (he soon joined a new Boston group called the Cars.) His replacement, Bob Walker, was only

---

1. In the liner notes of THE ORIGINAL MODERN LOVERS, Richman writes "If it weren't for [Iggy] and Lou Reed, this record wouldn't have existed.

around for a few shows before the band completely broke up in January 1974. Jerry Harrison spent a little more time studying at Harvard before taking a job with a computer firm. In April 1976, he was invited to join a new band from New York called the Talking Heads. Ernie Brooks ended up with a much-admired Manhattan outfit called the Necessaries.

The break-up of the Modern Lovers didn't faze Jonathan. Having temporarily lost his tolerance for loud rock, he was looking to take his music into quieter, more acoustic territory anyway. While none of the major labels would touch this stuff, a northern California indie maverick imprint called Beserkley was impressed with what Jonathan was trying to do. Jonathan quickly formed a new version of the Modern Lovers with guitarist Leroy Radcliffe, bassist Greg "Culy" Keranen (formerly of the Rubinoos) and drummer D. Sharpe.

The first thing Beserkley boss Matt "King" Kaufman did was buy up the recordings Jonathan had made for Warner Brothers. As the album was being cobbled together, Beserkley issued Roadrunner as a single in late 1974, crediting the song to Jonathan Richman and Earthquake. A full album entitled THE MODERN LOVERS, comprised mostly of recordings from the John Cale sessions, was issued in 1975. Although it wasn't exactly a sales success, the album caused a sensation in all the right places.

Why? — because in the years between the original sessions and the eventual release of THE MODERN LOVERS, an underground legend had been born. Word-of-mouth spread rumors detailing the existence of some brilliant unreleased music recorded by a group that no longer existed. The longer these tapes remained hidden, the more the legend grew. All that anyone knew was that this music was unlike anything the rock world had ever heard. When THE MODERN LOVERS hit the stores in 1975, it was immediately snapped up by people who were looking for something new, different and decidedly non-mainstream. In the same way the Velvet Underground affected a young Jonathan Richman, so did he come to affect the next generation of musicians. Songs such as Roadrunner became not only required listening but required playing (guess which was one of the first songs the Sex Pistols learned to play?) Other tracks, most notably the awesome Pablo Picasso, were performed and recorded in the manner of timeless rock and roll — even decades later, these songs still sound fresh. THE MODERN LOVERS quickly became an important template for the building punk explosion. And like THE STOOGES a few years earlier, THE MODERN LOVERS helped launch a million garage bands.

The announcement that there would be a new album in 1976 had many fans hoping for more. What they didn't know was that between the end of the first Modern Lovers and the release of that first album, Jonathan had completely retooled the band and, more importantly, his song writing style. It was inevitable that Jonathan Richman and the Modern Lovers caught most fans by surprise. Instead of getting more of the raw, garage-rock stuff that graced the first album, the new record featured quiet tales of life in New England in addition to quirky songs about Martians getting into the Kool-Aid business and meeting the Abominable Snowman at the market. In short, this record had nothing in common with the first album.

So where did the punk attitude go? The truth is that outside of this love for the Velvet Underground and his admiration for Iggy Pop and the Stooges, he never really felt any connection with the punk movement. He was on a mission to write melodic songs that could appeal to anyone, not just disaffected young people.

Still, some fans couldn't help like this goofy guy from Boston. The brooding artist was replaced by an exuberant performer who still relished in the fact that his outlook on the world was a little warped. This career makeover worked to Jonathan's advantage and throughout 1977, he was showered with critical praise in the North American music press. On the strength of a European reissue of Roadrunner, and the song's subsequent performance by bands such as the Sex Pistols, Jonathan soon attracted large cult followings in the UK, the Netherlands and Germany. A quick follow up album, ROCK AND ROLL WITH THE MODERN LOVERS, was anything but rock and roll. It not only featured lullabies and a song about waiting for the ice cream man, but also an instrumental that carried the odd title of Egyptian Reggae. Recorded in a small room at CBS studios in San Francisco, the sessions started with an attempt to lay down some tracks with the band set up in the men's room. Despite its quirks and non-punk approach, the album nevertheless proved to be quite popular in Europe.

Any other artist might have tried to milk this success for all it was worth, but not Jonathan Richman. In 1978, the Modern Lovers was once again disbanded so Jonathan could explore life as a solo act. Or so the rumor went. Instead, it was the beginning of two years of self-imposed obscurity at home in New

England and a complete turn away from rock stardom.

Richman began touring again in 1980 using a new version of the Modern Lovers that included a couple of female backup singers. However, much of his constituency had abandoned him, leaving a core of diehard loyalists. Had Richman and the Modern Lovers continued on the path they'd established in 1971 and 1972, they might have become more than footnotes (albeit important ones) in the history of new rock and alternative music.

However, these hardcore fans have been happy to indulge Jonathan over the last couple of decades. These fans understand his need to occasionally veer off in unexpected directions including pop (ROCKIN' AND ROMANCE, 1985), country (JONATHAN GOES COUNTRY, 1990) and Latin (1993's JONATHAN, TE VAS A EMOCIONAR! was sung entirely in Spanish.) He had played his cult-figure status to the hilt, which was led to frequent appearances on NBC's *Late Night with Conan O'Brien* and his weird singing cameos in the movie *There's Something About Mary* (1998.) You get the feeling that come what may, Jonathan Richman will always find ways to maintain his niche in the crowded world of music.

Fast Facts

o Jonathan has released at least seven different recordings of *Roadrunner*.
   1. A John Cale-produced version appears on THE MODERN LOVERS. This 1972 recording was briefly available as a Beserkley 7-inch in 1974 which was released under the name "Jonathan Richman and Earthquake. It later became known as *Roadrunner (Once)*.
   2. A track labeled *Roadrunner (Twice)* was issued in 1977 as an official UK single and was produced by Beserkley head Matt Kaufman. It is definitely different (less heavy and with a de-emphasized organ) than *Roadrunner (Once)*, which appears on the B-side. The A-side of this 7" release is the one that charted in Britain (peaking at No. 11) in 1977.
   3. A recording of undetermined original appears on a Beserkley compilation entitled Beserkley Chartbusters. This is the track most JoJo fans consider to be the definitive version of the song.
   4. The Original Modern Lovers contains two versions.
   5. On the B-side of *My Little Kookenhaken*, you'll find an eight minute live version.
   6. Another live performance appears on PRECISE MODERN LOVERS ORDER.
o Besides the Sex Pistols, *Roadrunner* has been recorded by the Jazz Butcher, Joan Jett and Greg Kihn.
o A brief write-up on *Roadrunner* appears in the book *Rock and Roll: The 100 Best Singles* by Paul Williams (Carroll and Graf, 1993.)
o Jonathan once played drums for Patti Smith at a gig in San Francisco in late 1974.
o John Cale thrilled Jonathan by covering *Pablo Picasso* on this 1975 album HELEN OF TROY.
o Following his two year self-imposed exile, he often played shows using nothing more than at thirty-five dollar guitar.
o Jonathan lives with his wife and two children in the Sierra Madres of California. His son played drums on one track on TE VAS A EMOCIONAR!
o His most high-profile appearance to date was his singing cameos in the film *There's Something About Mary* (1998.)

Recommended Listening

o THE MODERN LOVERS (Beserkely, 1975 / Rhino, 1986)
o BACK IN YOUR LIFE (Beserkley, 1979 / Rhino, 1986)
o A fine selection of Jonathan's legendary early work can be found on THE BESERKLEY YEARS: THE BEST OF JONATHAN RICHMOND AND MODERN LOVERS (Beserkley-Rhino, 1986)

Internet Resources

o www.base.com/jonathan/jonathan.html

Recommended Reading

o Heylin, Clinton. *From the Velvets to the Voidoids: A Pre-Punk History for a Post-Punk World*. New York, New York: Penguin Books, 1993.
o Palmer, Robert. *Rock & Roll: An Unruly History*. New York: Harmony Books, 1995.

Related Listening

Velvet Underground, Lou Reed, Iggy Pop, the Sex Pistols' demo version of *Roadrunner* from *The Great Rock and Roll Swindle*, Alex Chilton, Beck.

The Story Thus Far ...

The Velvet Underground becomes the catalyst for Jonathan's music career. John Cale produces what would become some legendary pre-punk recordings.

~ 5 ~
PATTI SMITH
The High Punk Priestess of New York

I stayed up all night with headphones on. I was 15, I think. I took it home, I put on the headphones, I sat down on the couch with a bowl of cherries — a HUGE bowl — and I listened to it and I couldn't take it off all night. I just sat there and listened to it, ate the whole bowl of cherries — I got sick to my stomach — and went to school with no sleep.

And I was a changed person. That record was such a revelation to me that it was truly one of the defining moments of my life.

— Michael Stipe of R.E.M. in an interview with the author, February 20, 1999.

Few women (or men, for that matter) can claim that their work has influenced several generations of artists. Patti Lee Smith is one of them. The effect of her Rimbaudian poet-as-tragic-figure musings can be heard in everyone from R.E.M. and U2 to the most intense riot grrl bands of the 1990's. Not only did her aggressive and emotionally raw performances (such as those captured on her first three albums) serve as a musical template for much of the burgeoning art / punk movement in New York in the middle 1970's, Smith was also elevated to the role of rock and roll suffragette. By combining the power of her poetry with three chords, she revolutionized the way women were viewed by the rock establishment. If Iggy Pop is the Godfather of Punk, then maybe Patti Smith is the Godmother.

As is the case with ultra-dramatic, ultra-legendary romantic figures, it's sometimes hard to separate fact from fiction when it comes to Patti Smith's biographical details. It seems that over the years, many people central to her story have been mythologized and / or invented along the way. This means that any fan should tread carefully when exploring Patti's past.

This much is true: she was born on December 30, 1946, on the south side of Chicago. Patti was the first of four children born to Grant (a factory worker for Honeywell) and Beverly Ann Smith (a waitress at the lunch counter of a drug store.)[1] When Patti was four, the family moved to Philadelphia where they found a house on Newhall Street on the city's north side. Although home life was fairly stable, the family was often divided along religious grounds. Beverly Ann was a devout Jehovah's witness while Grant an avowed atheist. No wonder Patti began to view God as a divisive force.

Patti was a sickly girl. Thin and scrawny, she had bouts with mumps, chicken pox, rheumatic fever, double pneumonia and — most serious of all — a case of scarlet fever at age seven. That illness gave her terrifying and recurring hallucinations, something that would plague her for years to come.

By the time she reached her senior year at Deptford High School, Patti had immersed herself in art, especially painting. Self-conscious about her thinness, she favored a tomboy look, and an outsider attitude. Her yearbook noted that some of the kids gave her the nickname Natasha because of her strange habit of lapsing into a Transylvanian accent whenever she fancied.

Patti's high school ambition to become an art teacher was bolstered by the offer of a partial scholarship

---

1. Despite Patti's later embellishments of her parents' background (they were not artists or mystics), they were simple working folk. The family also included a brother named Todd and two sisters, Linda and Kimberly.

---

by the Philadelphia Art Museum and the Philadelphia College of Art. Sadly, she had to turn it down because her parents couldn't afford to come up with the balance. Classes at the Glassboro State Teachers College would have to do. Unfortunately, she has forced to drop out shortly before graduation because she became pregnant. After giving up the baby for adoption — a decision that would haunt her for years to come — she went to live with some friends in Pine Barrens, New Jersey.[2] Still in her teens, she was forced to make ends meet by taking a menial job in a toy factory. The only escape she had from a miserable existence was her collection of Rolling Stones and Bob Dylan albums. She was eventually fired for writing poetry on the job.

After saving a few dollars from the factory gig and inspired by the biographies of Amedeo Modigliani and Arthur Rimbaud (see Fast Facts), Patti moved to New York in the spring of 1967. Determined to lead a life of art, she soon struck up a friendship with a nineteen year-old gay artist named Robert Mapplethorpe. Upon moving in together, they became muses to each other for a time. Mapplethorpe was fascinated by Patti's scarlet fever hallucinations and encouraged her to turn those experiences into something productive and perhaps even artistic. Meanwhile, Patti's neuroses and fears provided Mapplethorpe with loads of inspiration for his art.

Over the next few years, Patti worked at a series of jobs — Bretano's bookstore on Fifth Avenue, the world-famous toy retailer FAO Schwartz and, finally, Scribner's bookstore, also on Fifth Avenue. In May 1969, encouraged by Mapplethorpe to explore painting and ever more curious about Rimbaud (he's buried in Paris), Patti and her sister Linda took a two-month trip to Paris. The experience of seeing the masters in the Louvre combined with hanging out with the wannabes on the Left Bank provided Patti with a revelation — painting was not her calling. Poetry was.

Returning to New York in the fall of 1969, she and Mapplethorpe moved into the infamous Chelsea Hotel at 222 West 23rd Street and soon found themselves swept away into a new underground world filled with subversive art and music.[3] The made friends with bluesmen Johnny and Edgar Winter as well has Dylan confident Bobby Neuwirth, both of who encouraged more forays into poetry. Patti also became involved with Sam Shepard, a part-time drummer and full-time playwright. During their brief and torrid love affair, they co-wrote a play entitled *Cowboy Mouth* by sitting on opposite sides of their room at the Chelsea and sliding a typewriter back and forth across the floor.[4]

Using some of her new literary and art connections, Patti arranged an appearance at a poetry reading given by Gerard Malanga, an associate of Andy Warhol. Before Malanga took the stage, Patti was allowed to read some of her own work. The date was February 10, 1971, at St. Mark's Church in New York. About 200 people were there to witness Patti's first public performance. Accompanied by Lenny Kaye on guitar[5], she read-chanted-sung several original poems including *Oath* which began with the lines "Christ died for somebody's sins / But not mine."

The following two years saw Patti continued to perform as a poet / actress all over New York. She opened for the infamous New York Dolls at the Mercer Art Center; she helped write a few songs for a new group called Blue Oyster Cult;[6] and she found work writing record reviews for both *Creem* and *Rock Scene* magazine. In 1972, she published SEVENTH HEAVEN, her first collection of poetry featuring twenty-two original works including tributes to both doomed model Edie Sedgwick and British singer Marianne Faithful.

After experiencing some kind of vision at the Paris graveside of Jim Morrison in the summer of 1972, Patti began to think of herself as more than just a poet. When she returned to New York, she called up Lenny Kaye and explained that her new goal was a fusion of poetry and rock and roll and that she would require his accompaniment for future readings. By the spring of 1974, a piano player was added to the

2. Her only condition for putting the baby up for adoption was that it not be raised a Catholic.
3. It was at the Chelsea that Patti discovered the work of Janis Joplin and William Burroughs. She also met another young poet named Jim Carroll.
4. The character of Cavale, "a chick who looks like a crow, dressed in raggedly black," was modeled after Patti.
5. A word about Lenny Kaye: Spurred by an article on do-wop, Patti visited Village Oldies, a record store on Bleecker Street. Kaye worked at the store and occasionally wrote articles and reviews for music magazines — including that article on do-wop. He and Patti soon became friends. When the St. Mark's Church performance was booked, she asked Lenny if he wouldn't mind playing guitar in the background as she read. It was the beginning of a long association.
6. While dating BOC guitarist Allen Lanier, Patti co-wrote *Career of Evil* for the band's SECRET TREATIES album.

performance. After using a rotating cast of pianists, Richard "DNV" Sohl ended up with the full time gig. The Smith-Kaye-Sohl trio bombarded audiences with a combination of poetry, improvised wordplay, free jazz, sloppy rock, cover versions and original songs.

One of the set's strongest pieces was *Hey Joe*, the Jimi Hendrix classic combined with a poem entitled *Sixty Days* to create a tribute to kidnapped heiress Patty Hearst. With a little cash put up by Robert Mapplethorpe and Lenny Kaye, the group entered Electric Ladyland Studios on June 5, 1974. They figured they need about three hours to record the piece after which they would release it on a 7-inch single. When the session finished ahead of schedule, they decided to use up their allotted time by recording a second piece based on Patti's experience in the toy factory in Pitman, New Jersey. Patti read *Piss Factory* as Kaye and Sohl vamped in the background. The 45 was issued on a label called MER and given the number 601. Just over a thousand copies were pressed up and delivered to bookstores and record shops in Manhattan.

Much to everyone's shock, the single proved to be a big hit not only in New York but as far away as Los Angeles. When 1,600 copies quickly sold out, Patti and her group were asked to play a series of shows on both coasts. A shared residency with Television at Max's Kansas City in the summer of 1974 and at CBGB in the spring of 1975 further enhanced Patti's reputation as not only a poet but as a singer. When guitarist Ivan Kral joined the group (some accounts say he quit a band called Blondie to hook up with Patti), things really began to gel. By April 1975, hundreds of people were being turned away from most New York shows. It wasn't long before a few record companies caught a whiff of the situation.

After weighing a couple of offers, Patti chose to sign with Clive Davis and Arista Records in January 1975. Once she hired Jay Dee Daugherty and enlisted John Cale of the Velvet Underground as producer,[1] everyone returned to Electric Ladyland to start work on a full album in August and September. Referencing everything from atheism and UFOs to lesbianism and the writings of Rimbaud and Jimi Hendrix, the album was a statement of everything Patti was and wanted to be. It was art, rock and philosophy all wrapped together. Her personal description of the record was "three-chord rock merged with the power of the word." The album struck a powerful note right from the opening words of her version of Van Morrison's *Gloria* ("Jesus died for somebody's sins / But not mine") and did not let up. She called it HORSES.

By the third week of November, bits of the album had begun to leak out of the Arista offices. It wasn't long before the pre-release buzz became deafening. Publications from the New York *Times* on down heralded it as the best album of the year. New Musical Express immediately ranked it as the best debut album of all time.

Even the cover caused a sensation. Patti felt it was important that the album be adorned with an image that would capture her essence as both a seasoned poet and as serious a rock and roller. Once again, she turned to Robert Mapplethorpe. The photo was taken in natural light against a white wall in the penthouse apartment of a friend who lived near Washington Square. Striking a Frank Sinatra pose with her thrift-store jacket over her shoulder — and refusing to so much as comb her hair — Patti tried to imagine that she was Rimbaud, Baudelaire and Anna Karina all at the same time. The man's tie and butch clothing were also very calculated — Patti wanted to make a counterpoint against the accepted norm of having girl singers look sexy or, at the very least, cute. Mapplethorpe carefully placed her in front of a triangle of dim sunlight that shone through a window, giving her the effect of an angel with wings. It was a striking and powerful black-and-white photo.[2]

Predictably, Arista hated the photo. Clive Davis was appalled and wasted no time in pointing out that you could see some facial hair on Patti's upper lip. But Patti didn't care. Using the clause in her contract that gave her complete artistic control over the project, she refused all pleas by Arista to have it airbrushed out.

In the end, though, the artwork proved to be almost as important as the music. That photo established Patti Smith as a new breed of female performer; a raw, defiant outsider who was into more important things than mere appearances. In short, it was very punk.

---

1. Patti picked Cale because she was such a fan of the work he had done with her friend Jonathan Richman.
2. Untold thousands of music fans ended up buying the album on the basis of that cover artwork. When Rolling Stone published their list of the Top 100 Album Covers of All Time, HORSES finished at No. 26.

When HORSES was finally released in late November 1975, it debuted in the Top 50 of the *Billboard* album chart without the benefit of a single or significant radio airplay. This was even more remarkable in light of the fact that Patti often annoyed some journalists by refusing to answer questions that she found boring or by pretentiously name-dropping French poets in the middle of a conversation. Not only did this music and attitude win her scores of devoted fans on both sides of the Atlantic, it also somehow helped HORSES become the first of the new style of "underground" albums to break through into the mainstream.

Patti's second album came out less than a year after the first. RADIO ETHIOPIA (the title was inspired by a photographer friend's trip to Africa) was released in October 1977 under the name The Patti Smith Group. Produced by Jack Douglas and recorded over a three-week period in August, RADIO ETHIOPIA lacked the spark of *Horses* and instead plodded through Patti's deepening literary and biblical obsessions. After the commercial and critical success of her debut album, RADIO ETHIOPIA was a letdown, reaching only No. 122 on the album charts and stalling at sales of about 30,000 copies.

Some fans, however, begged to differ. They believe that as a band, the Patti Smith Group peaked with the second album. And because the album was recorded live in the studio with no overdubs, they feel that it captured the energy and aura of the band in concert. That alone made it worth looking past Patti's self-indulgence and the occasional self-righteous pronouncement.[3]

Patti's inevitable fall from grace was both metaphorical and literal. While on tour as the opener for Bob Seger and the Silver Bullet Band, there was an accident at Curtis Hixen Hall in Tampa, Florida, on January 23, 1977. Seven songs into the set and during a feverish version of *Ain't It Strange*, a dancing, spinning Patti whirled out of control and tripped over a stage monitor. She fell off the stage and crashed to the concrete fourteen feet below. After a frantic call for an ambulance, Patti was rushed to hospital. In addition to the large gash in her forehead (twenty-two stitches), x-rays revealed that she had two broken vertebrae in her neck. She was very lucky that she didn't end up a quadriplegic.

Patti returned to New York in a neck brace and was told to ride out the pain and the unexpected bout of partial paralysis. Confined to bed and often wired on painkillers, Patti wrote reams of poetry for a new collection that would be published under the name BABEL. As scary as those few months were, it provided Patti with time to gain some necessary perspective on what had happened over the previous two years.

By June 1977, the Patti Smith Group was performing short sets in New York and thinking about recording a third album. Work on EASTER (note the resurrection reference) began with producer Jimmy Iovine in early winter at the Record Plant in Manhattan. Although it was mostly unspoken, Arista was hoping for the new album to make a serious impact on the charts after the disappointment of RADIO ETHIOPIA and Patti's disappearance from public view following her accident. In short, they were quietly demanding a hit single.

As luck would have it, Jimmy Iovine's friend (and New Jersey native) Bruce Springsteen was recording

---

3. Hardcore fans should search out a sixteen minute version of *Radio Ethiopia* from a performance at CBGB in June 1977. It was issued in France on the B-side of a 12" release of *Hey Joe*. Many fans believe this to be the ultimate live recording of the Patti Smith Group.

DARKNESS AT THE EDGE OF TOWN in the studio down the hall. He gave Springsteen a rough version of a song called *Because the Night* and told him to re-write it as he saw fit. When Springsteen returned with his version, Patti and the band were not all that impressed. But after rewriting the rewrite with some new words, everyone was satisfied with the result.[1]

After more than a year of rest, recuperation and recording, EASTER was released on March 3, 1978. By the end of the month, *Because the Night* was on its way to being the hit Arista needed. The song eventually peaked at No. 13 on the American singles charts and at an impressive No. 5 in the UK. The record is also significant for Springsteen fans — it marked the first time their hero had a song reach the Top 20. The album itself reached the Top 20 on both the American and British charts. The resurrection was a success.

The following winter was spent recording album number four. Choosing her old friend Todd Rundgren to produce, WAVE was released in April 1979. The album opened with *Frederick*, another unabashed love offering to Fred Smith, Patti's lover and muse. The rest of the record wavered between acceptance, defeat, bitterness, resignation and a newfound peace in her love for Fred. Patti's powerful rendition of the Byrds' *So You Want to Be (A Rock and Roll Star)* could be interpreted as an expression of disillusionment with the music industry. Meanwhile, *Dancing Barefoot* — a song "dedicated to the rites of the heroine" — was immediately declared to be one of Patti's best-ever songs.

Despite a critical drubbing in the music press, WAVE became Patti's top-selling album to date. A five month tour followed, during which Patti was ill with bronchitis. The tour became an awful ordeal and yet another turning point in Patti's career. After the frantic pace of the last twelve years, it was time to think about retirement.

The story first broke in the New York *Daily News* on May 16, 1979. Patti told the paper that she felt that the city no longer held her in its thrall, besides, she was getting increasingly annoyed with the posturing of punk rock and the insincere romanticism of the growing New Wave scene. Perhaps it was time to move with Fred back to his hometown of Detroit where she could start fresh and maybe — gasp! — settle down. The final show for the Patti Smith Group was in front of 85,000 fans at a stadium in Florence, Italy, on September 10, 1979. The show included with an altered version of *Gloria*, which began with the words "Jesus died for somebody's sins / Why Not mine?"

Patti and Fred were married in Detroit on March 1, 1980, and for the next eight years, they lived in happy obscurity in a house in the suburb of St. Clair Shores. Their first child, Jackson, was born in 1983. Jesse came along five years later. Other than the occasional appearance for a poetry reading, Patti Smith seemed to have disappeared from the face of the earth. She had little trouble leaving her musical career behind because she knew in her heart that she had made her point and had accomplished everything she'd set out to do. She had no interest in burning out like her idol, Jim Morrison. Besides, Rimbaud had turned his back on literature after he had caused a sensation. Why couldn't Patti turn her back on music?

Patti made a brief reappearance in 1988 when she released DREAM OF LIFE, an optimistic-sounding album featuring both Richard Sohl and Jay Dee Daugherty. However, it was not the comeback for which long-time fans were hoping. DREAM OF LIFE made only a brief ripple on the commercial and critical radar.

The next several years were marred with tragedy and sadness. Patti's dear friend, Robert Mapplethorpe, died of Aids on March 9, 1989. On June 3, 1990, Richard Sohl suffered heart failure and died at his home. Most tragic of all was the death of Fred Smith. At age 45, he suffered a massive heart attack and died on November 4, 1994. Patti's grief was only underscored that November 4 is also Robert Mapplethorpe's birthday. The final blow was the death of her brother and road manager, Todd Smith. He had a stroke and died in December.

With nowhere else to go, Patti returned the world of rock and roll, starting with some low-key club shows and eventually working her way up to a surprise forty-five minute appearance with Lenny Kaye at the New York stop of the 1995 Lollapalooza tour. That fall, she was asked by Bob Dylan (one of her greatest heroes) to open ten dates on an American tour. There was also another album — GONE AGAIN, (released on July 1, 1996 and dedicated to Fred) — an album that many people consider to be as strong as EASTER. *Rolling Stone* named her as the year's *Most Welcome Comeback*.

Patti was genuinely shocked by how much people remembered her and her work. Living in pleasant

1. Patti wrote the lyrics as an ode to her new lover, Fred "Sonic" Smith of the MC5.

domestic isolation with Fred in Detroit, most of the music of the 80's and 90's had escaped her notice. And the longer she remained out of sight, the greater her mystique grew. While she was looking after Fred and the kids, the music she had made back in the 70's gradually became a powerful influence on what had become known by now as "alternative music." When someone mentioned that she was revered by riot grrls, she had to ask Thurston Moore of Sonic Youth (one of her biggest fans) to explain what a "riot grrl" was.

Patti's stature as a founding member of the alt-rock scene grew even more legendary over the last half of the 90's. Her unique combination of poetry, art, literature, sexuality, spirituality and rock has had a huge effect on several generations of musicians, both male and female. Her songs were covered by groups ranging from the Mission to U2. Michael Stipe and Peter Buck of R.E.M. constantly dropped Patti's name in interviews. Jeff Buckley, P.J. Harvey and Courtney Love have all professed to be major Patti Smith Fans. And thanks to Patti's gender-bending and gender-breaking over that short five year period in the 70's, she established a lineage that can be traced all the way through to Alanis Morissette, Tori Amos and Courtney Love — not to mention P.J. Harvey, Bikini Kill, Huggy Bear, Sleater-Kinney, Team Dresch and literally hundreds of others.

Now well past 50, Patti continues to perform and record occasionally. Much of her time is spent helping with AIDs fund-raisers and AIDs awareness campaigns. When she's at home, she continues to write poetry and bits of prose when the spirit moves her. This time, the Punk Priestess is enjoying a happy working retirement.

Fast Facts

o In order to really understand Patti Smith's work, it's necessary to know a little bit about the people who influenced her.

  Jean Genet (1910-86): A French author who spent much of his youth as a criminal and male prostitute. His 1944 novel, *Notre-Dame des Fleurs*, caused a great sensation with its tales of homosexuality and crime. His subsequent novels also explored various aspects of the underworld using a very pessimistic and mystical style.

  Jean-Luc Godard (1930-): A French film director and one of the leaders of New Wave film-making in the 1950's.

  Anna Karina (1940-): A French actress who often worked with her husband, Jean-Luc Godard.

  Amedeo Modigliani (1884-1920): An Italian painter and sculptor who often created nude images that were scandalous for his day. It was only after he died of tuberculosis that his art was recognized as revolutionary.

  Arthur Rimbaud (1854-91): A gay French poet partial to drinking and bawdy behavior, Rimbaud's work first attracted attention while he was still in his teens. In 1870, he published *Le Bateau ivre*, a collection of writings that were chock-full of evocative imagery and wild symbolism. After turning his back on literature at 19, he wandered Europe working as a soldier and gun-runner. He died of a leg infection after an amputation.

o Legend has it that Patti was the person who gave Todd Rundgren the nickname "Runt."

o Lenny Kaye released a single entitled *Crazy Like a Fox* under the name Link Cromwell in 1966. He was also very respected for his NUGGETS collections, album anthologies of singles by 60's garage bands. Lenny also wrote liner notes for a well-regarded Eddie Cochran re-release.

o There was much controversy over the cover of the EASTER album. The problem? Patti's exposed armpit hair.

o Candy Slice, one of Gilda Radner's characters on *Saturday Night Live*, was based on Patti.

o One of the last things Fred Smith did before he died was teach Patti the rudiments of guitar chords.

o *About a Boy* from GONE AGAIN was inspired by Kurt Cobain.

Recommended Listening

o HORSES (Arista, 1975)

o EASTER (Arista, 1978)

o GONE AGAIN (Arista, 1996)

o A good choice for a collection is THE PATTI SMITH MASTER: THE COLLECTIVE WORKS (Arista, 1996.) It features digitally re-mastered editions of the first five albums, each featuring bonus tracks at the end of each disc.

Internet Resources

○ www.oceanstar.com/patti/

○ www.netaxs.com/~rzepelaa/patti.html

○ Both of the above web sites will connect you to discographies, interviews and complete lists of Patti's written works.

Recommended Reading

Books featuring information about Patti Smith:

○ Heylin, Clinton. *From the Velvets to the Voidoids: A Pre-Punk History for a Post-Punk World.* New York, New York: Penguin Books, 1993.

○ Johnstone, Nick. *Patti Smith: A Biography.* London: Omnibus Press, 1997.

○ McNeil, Legs and McCain, Gillian. *Please Kill Me: The Uncensored Oral History of Punk.* New York, New York: Grove Press, 1996.

Books by Patti Smith include:

○ *Seventh Heaven.* Boston: Telegraph Books, 1972

○ *WITT.* New York: Gotham Book Mart, 1973

○ *Ha! Ha! Houdini.* New York: Gotham Book Mart, 1977.

○ *Babel.* New York: Putnam, 1974, 1978.

○ *Early Work 1970-1979.* New York: W.W. Norton, 1994

○ *The Coral Sea.* New York: W.W. Norton, 1996.

Related Listening

The Velvet Underground, Television, Iggy Pop, R.E.M., Nirvana, Hole, Tori Amos, Alanis Morissette, Liz Phair, P.J. Harvey, Soul Coughing, Sonic Youth.

The Story Thus Far ...

Not only is Patti Smith a major Velvet Underground fan, but John Cale produces her first record. Her music and attitude sets the stage for everyone from Sonic Youth to R.E.M.

~ 6 ~
THE RAMONES
Four leather jackets, two chords and an attitude

In the early 1800's, an American pioneer named John Chapman traveled west from Massachusetts, collecting seeds from Pennsylvania cider presses. For the rest of his life, he planted thousands of apple trees through what is now Ohio, Indiana and Illinois. Chapman was given the nickname "Johnny Appleseed" because wherever he went, apple trees sprouted in his wake. In the mid-1970's, four middle class kids from Forest Hills in Queens, began to have the same effect with a new style of rock and roll known as "punk." Whenever they played a town on one of their endless tours, new bands would inevitably start popping up in their wake within just a few days. Such is the legacy of the Ramones.

What began as a cartoonish attempt at making sick bubble gum music (think of the Beach Boys on a combination of crank and glue) somehow turned into something much more profound and eternal. It was all a big, happy accident. The Ramones had no illusions about changing the world with music. They were just four middle-class guys who wanted to rock in the most basic, rudimentary way. They certainly accomplished that — but they also reminded everyone that when it comes to the power and joy of rock and roll, sometimes less is more.

The roots of the Ramones go back to the day when John Cummings (a Yankees baseball fanatic, born

October 8, 1951) shared a joint with his new friend, Douglas Colvin (a collector of WW II memorabilia and a former hairdresser, born September 18, 1952.) They were both working at a construction site at 50th and Broadway in New York and often spent their lunch hours watching girls and arguing the merits of the Beatles. John had been in love with the Beatles since he first saw them on that legendary *The Ed Sullivan Show* back in 1964. Douglas (Dee Dee to his friends) didn't mind the Beatles, but he had discovered something much more interesting — Iggy Pop and the Stooges.

It was one of these discussions that led to the joint and, afterwards, a couple of beers at a local strip club. Many drinks later, a trip to Manny's Guitar Center on 48th Street was in order. Johnny and Dee Dee had decided to form a band. The date was January 23, 1974 — almost ten years to the day from that Ed Sullivan broadcast.

With about a hundred bucks between them, Johnny bought a blue Mosrite guitar ($50) while Dee Dee grabbed a DanElectro bass and a cheap amp. Four days later, they had their first rehearsal, struggling through some of the tunes found on Lenny Kaye's NUGGETS collection. In March, their friend Tommy Erdelyi (born January 29, 1952, in Budapest and a recording engineer who had worked with Jimi Hendrix) set them up with some space in his rehearsal studio and let them thrash it out using a six-foot-three drummer named Joey (born Jeff Hyman, May 19, 1951.) Joey had defected from a glitter-ish band called Sniper[1] and had grown tied of his street vendor's job of selling plastic flowers in Greenwich Village. Since he had been sharing a small living space with Dee Dee at a paint store, he was quickly drafted into service.

Anyone who had the misfortune of hearing the new trio agreed that they were simply awful. But what they lacked in ability was more than made up for with enthusiasm. Bypassing learning other peoples' songs as "too hard," the new group decided to skip ahead to writing their song material almost immediately.[2] Basic barre chords and a 4/4 beat — that would have to do. And besides, they thought, what more did you need to construct the perfect two minute pop song?

There were other rules, too. No politics. Sing about real life stuff like girls and sniffing glue. Follow the example of the Stooges. Remember your favorite pop songs, cartoons and comic books from the 60's. And don't worry about getting all the notes right.

During these rehearsals, they tried about fifty different names and had decided to go with "Spice" before someone suggested the name "Ramones." This met with everyone's approval because (a) Paul McCartney used the pseudonym "Paul Ramone" when the Beatles were still known as the Silver Beatles, (b) all the guys were big fans of Phil Ramone, the record producer who churned out some of the most memorable AM radio hits of the 60's, and (c) the name "Ramones" made them sound like a bunch of outlaw gang members. The one-for-all, all-for-one solidarity that it implied was also considered a plus. To further cement that sentiment of brotherhood, it was also decided that the members of the group would adopt "Ramone" as their last name.

The first official Ramones gig was what was kindly termed a "showcase concert" at their rehearsal space on March 30, 1974. About thirty people — mostly friends — paid two dollars apiece to see a nervous Dee Dee step on his bass and break it. It was the first and last time the group would appear as a trio.

By July, Tommy had begun to notice that this new group had some kind of potential. There was a certain appeal to the group's brash, minimalist style. What could be fresher than a group playing at the ragged edge of their ragged abilities. Tommy came to believe that the Ramones main problem wasn't their musicianship (or lack of it), it was that they lacked a frontman — and the fact that Joey wasn't a very good drummer. Everyone else seemed to agree, so on July 20, 1974, Joey was moved out front while Tommy took over on drums. The first lineup of the Ramones was now complete.

The first proper gig took place two weeks later at CBGBs on August 16, 1974 and was witnessed by five people — six if you count the bartender's dog.[3] It was the start of a long string of regular gigs at the

---

1. Joey used to dress in a stretchy black satin jumpsuit, pink-and-lavender platform boots and leather gloves that went way past the elbow. He must have been quite the sight.
2. Dee Dee didn't even know the names of the strings on his bass. He just thumped away on the open string that sounded good with the barre chord Johnny was playing.
3. A surprising amount of film footage was shot during the first six months' worth of gigs at the club. Some of it appears on the video that came with the WE'RE OUTTA HERE boxed set.

---

club. By the end of the year, the Ramones had taken the stage seventy-four times — and with each show, word on this new group spread through the underground music and art scene in New York. Soon, CBGBs was crammed with everyone from the Andy Warhol crowd and stuffy intellectual types to rich uptowners slumming it in the Bowery and kids who bored with music and needed something new and exciting.

For two bucks a head, it was interesting entertainment because at first, no one knew what to make of the Ramones. Here were four "brothers," all dressed in torn jeans and leather jackets playing what amounted to bubble gum pop songs at a million miles an hour (an early bio written by Tommy described the band's sound as "a fast drill on a rear molar".) In an era when twenty-minute guitar solos and long, complicated art-rock pieces were all the rage (think Led Zeppelin. Pink Floyd and ELP), the Ramones dispensed with everything except the basics. In a typical fifteen minute set, the group would roar through fifteen songs at jet-engine volume. There was no stage patter, no acknowledgment of the audience, no guitar solos and no letting up. The only breaks in the set came when Johnny counted in the next song: "Onetwothreefour!" After a Ramones show, everything else seemed slow.[1]

Was this a joke or were they serious? Depending on who you talked to, the Ramones were either complete idiots or minimalistic artistic geniuses. They rocked, but not like Led Zeppelin. The songs were definitely written in a 60's pop style, but were much more intense. And when the material was compared to the current state of pop (remember: Paul Anka's *You're Having My Baby* was *the* big AM radio hit in the summer of 1974), it was a big of a shock. Whatever the case, the group's raw energy and sense of fun soon had everyone's attention. Even the New York *Times* came out to see them:

> The Ramones are a highly stylized extension of the punk medium. They deliver a nonstop set of brisk, monochromatically intense songs where conventional considerations of pace and variety are thrown calculatedly into the wind.

In late 1974, the band spent about $2,000 recording fifteen demos in a cheap eight-track studio with each song running less than two minutes. Cassette copies and carefully-collated portfolios of press clippings were sent out to every record label they could find in the phone book. All they got back were rejection letters. The only label that expressed any interest was an indie called Sire. After a quick audition, they signed the Ramones on October 15, 1975, for a paltry $6,000 plus an additional $20,000 so the boys could go out and buy some new equipment. This made them the first of their CBGBs contemporaries (except for Patti Smith) to secure any kind of record deal.

Not wanting to waste any time, Sire had the band in a studio at Radio City Music Hall by February 2, 1976. By February 19, the first album was done. The whole project from start to finish cost $6,400, not counting the cost of replacing the cutter head on the mastering machine at the record pressing plant. The album had been recorded at such a high volume that the cutter head was blown clean off the machine.

Like everything else about the Ramones, it was short and to the point: fourteen songs over twenty-eight minutes. Even the cover artwork was done on the cheap. Everyone has seen it: a simple black-and-white photo of all four members standing in front of a brick wall. Behind the camera was Roberta Bayley, a woman who spent her evenings at the door of CBGBs collecting the cover charge. She had spent the last few months learning how to use her camera by shooting the Ramones whenever they played the club. Knowing that the band hated having their picture taken, Roberta knew that she had only a few minutes to get something acceptable before everyone lost interested and wandered off to do something else. After finally rounding up all four members, she marched them out to a nearby vacant lot where she snapped as many shots as she could before they got bored and wandered off. When it came time to choose something for the cover the debut album, Sire had a look through all of Roberta's contact sheets and loved what she called the "brick wall shot." It was immediately chosen for the cover.[2]

THE RAMONES was unleashed on April 23, 1976. While the world of mainstream rock and roll definitely

---

1. Okay, the group did stop occasionally — but only to fight over which song they were going to play next or when Dee Dee broke the last string on his bass. Another favorite description of Ramones material: long songs played very fast.
2. When THE RAMONES was released, Roberta's cover shot was soon hailed as a classic. Over the years, hundreds of bands would copy that look and feel. Roberta's photo was eventually selected as one of the best one hundred album covers of all time by *Rolling Stone*. What most people forget is that Roberta was paid just $125 for this classic shot.

did NOT get it — the few radio stations that gave it a spin often ended up mocking songs such as *Blitzkrieg Bop* (the first single) and *Beat on the Brat* as "noise" and "crap" — those in touch with what was happening on the street saw it as something truly special. Without the benefit of radio airplay, the album sold six thousand copies in its first week and eventually peaking at No. 181 on the *Billboard* album chart.

From that point on, the Ramones toured almost incessantly, operating under a financial plan that lasted until their last show. Things were done as quickly and as cheaply as possible. Meagre royalty payments from Sire were supplimented by healthy sales of t-shirts and other merchandise.[3]

The biggest show of the band's career — and, in fact, one of the most important concerts in the history of music — took place on July 4, 1976, at the Roundhouse in London. Playing before 2,000 people on a bill with the Stranglers and the Flaming Groovies, the Ramones nihilistic, we-can't-play-and-don't-give-a-shit set gave England a solid taste of what had been happening in New York. The following night, they gave another show at Dingwalls. The nascent punks in the crowd were awestruck. If the Ramones could build a career on this kind of attitude, what was stopping everyone else?[4] Joey Ramone remembered it well:

> It was really wild going over to England when we were selling out CBGBs. There was a wild scene going on, but when we got over to England, we were playing for three thousand kids and everybody was already tuned in to what it was that we were all about. I remember at the time the big thing going on in England was pub rock. Dr. Feelgood was the big band at the time and Brinsley Schwarz. I remember we were treated like royalty when we got there and then we did this club Dingwall's. Basically, the whole make up of Dingwall's were all these kids that would later form these kind of ground-breaking bands of their own. At a sound check, we met Johnny Rotten and Joe Strummer and all these people. They were like totally taken with the band and really after that — when we left England — they told us that we had turned them on and kind of opened them up and inspired them to form their own bands basically. When we came back in '77 the whole thing was full blown and I feel like from that point on we really kind of brought upon a radical change that would really sweep the world.

The second Ramones album, RAMONES LEAVE HOME, was released on January 10, 1977. Like the first album, it contained nothing but songs constructed with machine-gun guitars and tales of sniffing glue, weird girlfriends, dysfunctional families and poor mental health. Fourteen songs filled less than thirty minutes. It was rock and roll moronity at its finest.

The next album, ROCKET TO RUSSIA — issued on November 17, 1977 — was cut from the same now-familiar cloth and represented the peak of that special Ramones' hybrid of punk and Top 40. ROCKET contained a couple of previously-released singles (*Sheena Is a Punk Rocker* and *Rockaway Beach*) that reached the lower levels of the Top 100 chart. Another track, *Teenage Lobotomy* once again touted the benefits (?) of mental illness. And just to make sure that everyone could connect the band to their 60's bubblegum-and-surf-band roots, they included two covers — *Do You Wanna Dance* (released by Bobby Freeman in 1958 and covered by the Beach Boys in 1964) and *Surfin' Bird* (the Trashmen, 1964.)

ROCKET also marked the end of the original Ramones lineup. Because Tommy had decided to go back to being a record producer, he could no longer tour — something that the Ramones did for most of the year. His replacement was Marky Ramone (born Marc Bell, July 16, 1956), a fan and former member of Richard Hell's Voidoids. His first album with the band was ROAD TO RUIN (released on September 15, 1978), the first Ramones record to break the thirty-minute barrier and the first to feature (gasp!) an acoustic guitar.

The closest the Ramones came to a mainstream breakthrough happened in 1979 when they appeared in *Rock'n'Roll High School*, a film by schlockmeister Roger Corman. The movie told the story of Riff Randle and her encouters with the evil principal, Miss Togar, and the exploding white mice of Vince Lombardi High. (The mice exploded when exposed to *Teenage Lobotomy* at high volume.) Starring the perky P.J. Soles as Riff, the movie became something of a cult classic. The soundtrack album featured a remix of *Rock'n'Roll High School* by legendary producer Phil Spector who reportedly listened to that opening chord over and over again for ten hours before he felt it was just right.

---

3. The Ramones tended to gross anywhere from $750 to $1,000 a night — not a lot when you consider the expenses associated with touring.
4. The Clash had a jukebox in their rehearsal space that was filled with Ramones 45's.

Spector also oversaw production of the new Ramones album, END OF THE CENTURY. This pairing was something of a creative disaster, considering the Ramones' three-takes-and-out recording style and Spector's eccentricities and obsessive drive for perfection. There was a major clash of personalities, especially when the cost of recording the album ballooned to over $200,000. Even though the album was the Ramones' best-selling album to that point, they would later denounce END OF THE CENTURY as overblown, overproduced and over hyped. For years, the group felt it was their worst record.

Despite the problems with Spector, 1980 and 1981 were pretty good years for the band. Along with touring most of the worlrd, a major highlight came in September 1981 when they were invited to play in front of half a million people at the US Festival in San Bernardino, California. Then the troubles began.

By 1982, the original punk movement was dead and buried. Other groups had taken the original punk principles and advanced the evolution of music while the Ramones insisted on doing the same old thing. New Wave synthesizers became the new rage, making the minimalist guitars of the Ramones look quaint at best and at worst, irrelevant. Shortly after SUBTERRANEAN JUNGLE was released in April 1983, Marky's alcohol problems finally got the best of him. His replacement was Richie Ramone (born Richard Reinhardt. Marky would eventually return to the group in 1986.) More frightening were the events of August 14 when Joey was found by the NYPD on the street at 3:30 in the morning. He had been in a fight with Seth Macklin of a group called Sub Zero Construction after coming to the aid of a woman named Cynthia Whintney who appeared to be in trouble on East 10th Street. A kick in the head left Joey unconscious with a fractured skull. After being rushed to St. Vincent Hospital, he underwent four hours of emergency brain surgery to remove some potentially life-threatening blood clots. Fortunately, Joey was able to make a full recovery.

The Ramones spent the rest of the 80's on the road. With punk on the wane and album sales dropping off, the only way to make a living was to sell concert tickets and t-shirts. It was a grind, but they developed a rhythm — tour for the most of the year, take a break to record a new album and then tour some more. It wasn't easy, but it kept the band alive.

One person who wasn't enjoying himself was Dee Dee. The beginning of his departure from the band began in late 1987 when he strayed beyond the Ramones' punk boundaries. After being turned on to LL Cool J, Run-DMC and the Beastie Boys, he decided to release a rap record on a small label called Rock Hotel Records. It didn't attract that much attention, but he was encouraged enough to start work on a full album. In March 1989 and under the name Dee Dee King, he issued what he called a "rap and roll" record entitled STANDING IN THE SPOTLIGHT. To the shock of Ramones diehards, he began greasing back his hair and stocking up on both big gold chains and earrings.

At first, this new attitude seemed to inject some new life into the band. BRAIN DRAIN, the Ramones 1989 album, was pretty solid and received some excellent reviews from everyone from *Billboard* to *Stereo Review*. But just as the Ramones were about to celebrate the fifteenth anniversary of their first gig at CBGBs, Dee Dee quit.

Drugs and alcohol appeared to have nothing to do with his decision. Although he had been a notorious heroin user and heavy drinker earlier in his life, Dee Dee had been straight for nearly five years. The best anyone could figure was that bored with his life and with the routine of the Ramones, Dee Dee was seized by some of kind of serious midlife crisis. Within a period of just three weeks, he left his wife, left his band, left Queens and stopped going to his rehab meetings. It was the beginning of a rough ride for Dee Dee.

Naturally, this put a major strain on the Ramones. Could they survive losing a founding member? Auditions started almost immediately and one of the first people to show up was a Long Island ex-Marine named Christopher Joseph Ward (born October 8, 1965, making him exactly fourteen years younger than Joey), who, as a kid, grew up listening to Ramones albums, learning to follow what Dee Dee was playing. Enegergized by this injection of new blood, the Ramones hit the road again, stopping just long enough to record the occasional album.

As the grunge movement hit in the early 90's, the Ramones found their work being reevaluated. After years of being declared out of step with rock and roll, more and more people came to realize the enormity of what the Ramones had contributed to what was now being called "alternative music." While still failing to sell major quantities of new albums, there was a new appreciation of their old work, thanks to a series of CD compilations. Pro-Ramones articles began appearing in major music magazines as more writers began to realize the band's influence on new supserstar groups like Nirvana, Soundgarden, Pearl Jam, Green Day, the Offspring and White Zombie. By the mid-90's, the Ramones were no longer out of fashion. Quite the contrary; they were being held up as the founding fathers of the entire alternative rock sound.[1]

Joey Ramone took all this in very carefully. By the time his forty-fourth birthday rolled around, he had made a decision: after more than a dozen years in the rock wilderness, the Ramones were on top again. What better time to finally retire? Besides, animosities within the group had built to the point where no one was having much fun anymore. Playing an average of 120 shows a year had taken a psychic toll that strained relationships, both personal and professional. It was time to go.

The Ramones, circa 1983.

Rumours of the Ramones' retirement began popping up in early 1995 when word leaked that the next album would carry the ominous title of ADIOS AMIGOS. On July 11 of that year, Joey gave an interview to *USA Today* confirming that the band would soon be finished. The long farewell had begun.

After a series of shows all over the world (including a worshipful inclusion on the main stage of the 1996 Lollapalooza festival), the Ramones played their last show on August 6, 1996 at the Billboard Live club on Sunset Boulevard. The gig took place just ten days short of what would have been the twenty-second anniversary of their first show at CBGBs. More than two decades of two minute anthems had come to a close.

It's hard to overestimate the role of the Ramones in the evolution of today's rock and roll. When they first appeared in 1974, they were an refreshing slap in the face, a reminder that rock didn't have to be overblown and pretentious to be significant. They proved that all you really needed was a few chords, a little wit and a lot of energy. What started out as a joke ended up being a serious lesson for several generations of would-be musicians and fans. And for that, we should all be grateful.

Fast Facts

o The following people have appeared in the Ramones:
  Joey Ramone (Jeff Hyman), vocals
  Johnny Ramone (John Cummings), guitar
  Marky Ramone (Marc Bell), drums. After leaving in 1983, he rejoined the group in 1986.
  Dee Dee Ramone (Douglas Colvin), bass
  Tommy Ramone (Tommy Erdelyi), drums
  CJ Ramone (Christopher Joseph Ward), guitar
  Richie Ramone #1, 1974 (?), drums
  Billy Ramone, 1983 (Bill Rogers of the Heartbreakers, who played on one song on SUBTERRANEAN JUNGLE), drums
  Richie Ramone #2, 1983 (Richard Reinhardt a.k.a. Richie Beau), drums

---

1. In 1992, *Spin* magazine declared the Ramones to be one of the seven most influential acts of all time.

George Ramone (?), drums

Elvis Ramone: (Clem Burke of Blondie fame who played exactly two shows with the band before everyone agreed his style did not suit the band), drums

Charlotte Ramone (Joey's mom who sang bits of two Ramones songs on an edition of *Geraldo.*)

o The Ramones' bald eagle logo was created by Alan Vega (of the band Suicide) when he adopted the design from the belt buckle that appears on the back of the first Ramones album. The olive branch was replaced by a branch from an apple tree (symbolic of the "Ramones as-American-as-apple-pie image") and the arrows were removed in favour of a baseball bat (in deference to Johnny's baseball obsession.) The scroll in the beak originally read "Look Out Below" but was quickly changed to "Hey, Ho! Let's Go!"

o The chanting of *Blitzkrieg Bop* was modelled after a big hit of 1976: *Saturday Night* by the Bay City Rollers.

o For years, the role of Pinhead (a favourite character at Ramones shows) was played by a roadie named Bubbles. The *Gabba-gabba* chant was adopted from the *Gooble-gooble* chant heard in the 1932 film, *Freaks.*

o In addition to playing with the Voidoids, Marky Ramone was a member of a group called Dust who released a couple of records in the 60's.

o Before a show at the Capitol Theatre in Passaic, New Jersey, on November 19, 1977, Joey suffered scalding burns to his face and neck when a makeshift humidfier (basically a kettle with the lid held down with a big rubber band) blew up as he was steaming his vocal chords. Despite his injuries and a trip to the emergency ward, Joey performed as scheduled that night.

o When he was putting together *Rock and Roll High School*, Roger Corman's first choice was Cheap Trick, but they were too expensive as was his second choice, Todd Rundgren. The final script was written by Joe Dante.

o While in the Marines, CJ Ramone contracted a severe case of Rocky Mountain Spotted Fever. His fever was so high (106) that doctors were worried that he might have brain damage.

o During a police sweep of pushers and users in Washington Square on September 27, 1990, Dee Dee Ramone was arrested and charged with possession of marijuana.

o While the Ramones never sold many records, they were always a solid concert draw. A substantial portion of their income came from gate receipts and merchandise sales at live gigs.

o Joey Ramone continues to works as a solo artist. He's also interested in helping the careers of several New York-area bands including the horror ska-punk outfit, the Independents. Dee Dee and Marky appeared together in a group called the Remains (Marky also released an album with Marky Ramone and the Intruders in 1997.) Johnny Ramone is completely retired from music and spends much of his time tending to his vast collection of major league baseball memorabilia.

Recommended Listening

o The first four Ramones album are essential listening for anyone who wants to understand the true effect the band had on today's punk.

THE RAMONES (Sire, 1976)

THE RAMONES LEAVE HOME (Sire, 1977)

ROCKET TO RUSSIA (Sire, 1977)

ROAD TO RUIN (Sire, 1978)

o For a good idea of what the band was like live in their punk-rock heyday back in the late 70's, try IT'S ALIVE (Sire, 1978.) Their last show is available on a CD boxed with a video of the performance. Look for WE'RE OUTTA HERE (Radioactive, 1977.)

o There is an incredible number of Ramones compilations available. THERE'S ALL THE STUFF (AND MORE) which comes in two separate volumes (Sire / WB, 1990 and 1991) plus a "definitive" 58 song double set (containing the once-recalled *Carbona Not Glue*) called HEY! HO! LET'S GO (Rhino, 1999.) A more concise collection is the single CD RAMONES MANIA (Sire, 1988.)

Internet Resources

o www.bomis.com/rings/ramones

o www.geocities.com/SunsetStrip/Palms/6100/

○ www.cbgb.com

Recommended Reading

○ Bessman, Jim. *Ramones: An American Band.* New York, New York: St. Martin's Press, 1993.

○ Gimarc, George. *Punk Diary, 1970-79.* New York, New York: St. Martin's Press, 1994.

○ Heylin, Clinton. *From the Velvets to the Voidoids: A Pre-Punk History for a Post-Punk World.* New York, New York: Penguin Books, 1993.

○ McNeil, Legs and McCain, Gillian. *Please Kill Me: The Uncensored Oral History of Punk.* New York, New York: Grove Press, 1996.

Related Listening

Green Day, Shonen Knife and just about every other post-1978 punk band you care to name.

The Story Thus Far ...

As fans of both 60's bubble gum pop and the growing sleazy scene in the Bowery, the Ramones lay the basic foundations for the punk explosion that was to follow.

The Ramones, circa 1996.

~ 7 ~
THE SEX PISTOLS
Delivering anarchy to the UK

"Things fall apart; the center cannot hold
Mere anarchy is loosed upon the world ..."
— "The Second Coming," William Butler Yeats

Had Yeats been around in mid-70's England instead of Ireland at the turn of the century, he might have written those same words. The UK was facing a brutal recession, the continuing aftereffects of the oil crisis, high unemployment, rising crime, escalating problems with the IRA and a growing sense of social unrest. If you were young and English and unemployed, it may have seemed that things were spinning hopelessly out of control.

" ... and what rough beast, it's hour come round at last,
Slouches toward Bethlehem, waiting to be born?"

Yeats' "rough beast" was indeed waiting to be born — but instead of a manger in the Middle East, it entered the world at 430 The King's Road in London. Under the Svengali-esque guidance of the owner of this clothing shop, four petty criminals somehow held together long enough to ignite a punk explosion that continued to spread fallout long after the group had disappeared.

The Sex Pistols didn't invent punk rock and certainly weren't the first punk band. They weren't even the first punk band to release a record. At their peak, they could muddle through perhaps twenty-five songs, of which a mere fifteen were original compositions. When they broke up in January 1978, just twenty-six months after they were formed, they left behind exactly one studio album. What the Sex Pistols did manage, however, was to attract our attention. More than any other British band, the Pistols were responsible for kicking off the punk rock revolution. Without them and the media chaos they created, everything that's ever been included under the umbrella of "alternative music" would be much, much different. They were, quite simply, one of the most influential bands in the history of planet Earth.

The Pistols' legend starts with Let It Rock, Malcolm McLaren's clothing shop on King's Road in Chelsea. In 1971, McLaren (an art student) and his designer friend, Vivienne Westwood, took over the store and began selling 50's-style clothing to the neighborhood's teddy boys. It eventually became something of a hangout for a certain class of musicians and a regular stop for touring American bands like the New York Dolls. Enamored by the Dolls drunken, glamorous lifestyle, McLaren signed on as their manager and moved to New York for several months, hanging out with the underground art-and-music elite. One of the people he met was Richard Hell, a musician so poor that he had to hold his ripped and ragged clothes together with safety pins. Interpreting this as some sort of brilliant fashion statement (it wasn't; Hell really *was* that poor), McLaren took this idea back home to Let It Rock after the Dolls finally imploded.

By 1974, the Dolls finally having fallen apart and with McLaren's impresario dreams having been dashed, he had no choice but to limp home to Let It Rock to see what he could salvage. Within a few months, the shop had been renamed Sex and had moved towards specializing in fetish gear and outrageous stage clothes that were often festooned with Nazi symbols and explicit gay images. The new merchandise was an immediate hit. McLaren and Westwood were soon serving a steady clientele of clubbers, musicians and wannabes who seemed very interested in the pre-torn T-shirts, bondage clothes and rubberwear.[1]

Having been bitten by the music bug and besotted with the sort of hangers-on that his store attracted, McLaren's next idea was to form a group that would be a living, breathing advertisement for his shop and its goods. Unlike the disastrous, uncontrollable Dolls, this new band would be shaped in McLaren's own image from the ground up. Four regular loiterers were recruited — Glen Matlock (born August 27, 1956), Steve "Kutie" Jones (May 3, 1955), Paul Cook (July 20, 1956) and John Lydon (January 31, 1956), the kid with horrible green teeth nicknamed "Johnny Rotten." McLaren named his group the Sex Pistols ("Sex" after the store and "Pistols" because that sounded dangerous.)

A little extra history is in order. Jones (guitar) and Cook (drums) had been playing together in various rag-tag outfits since the winter of 1972, relying mostly on equipment stolen from a variety of rock stars.[2] By the summer of 1975, they had teamed with bassist Glen Matlock and were just a singer away from forming another band. Sometime in August, McLaren's shop assistant Bernie Rhodes (the future manager of the Clash), pointed out Lydon who had been hanging around wearing a homemade "I Hate Pink Floyd" T-shirt. After quick meeting at the Roebuck Pub to discuss his wonderfully bad attitude, John was invited over to Sex to audition as a singer. He got the job by singing along with Alice Cooper as *School's Out* blared over the store's jukebox.

The Pistols rehearsed sporadically throughout the fall, learning several songs by the Who and Small Faces as well as attempting to write a few of their own. On November 6, 1975, they played their first gig at St. Martin's Art College in front of perhaps twelve people. A screaming, squalling performance was cut after just ten minutes after the social programmer of the school found the Pistols to be so appalling that he ordered power to the stage be shut off.

Nonplused, the Pistols carried on through the winter and spring and slowly gathered an odd following of misfits and miscreants who liked loud music, weird clothes and spiky hair.[3] Gigs became more violent and more unpredictable as more young, angry and disillusioned fans began to show up to hear the Pistols spit and snarl their way through a set of loud, sloppy garage rock. To them, the Pistols were a refreshing

1. A young woman from Ohio named Chrissie Hynde worked behind the counter for a while. She and three other clerks appeared in an ad for the shop in a porn magazine called *Forum*.
2. One of their greatest heists took place on July 4, 1973 at the Hammersmith Odeon following David Bowie's final appearance as Ziggy Stardust. They managed to sneak away with some very expensive microphones as well as some PA gear. The equipment was used in a new group called The Strand (named after the Roxy Music song) that featured Jones, Cook and Glen Matlock. Bob Marley and Rolling Stone Ron Wood also had some gear nicked.
3. Fans included William Broad (soon to be known as Billy Idol), Susan Dallion (the future Siouxsie Sioux), Steve Severin (also of the future Banshees) and, of course, John's old friend, Simon Ritchie. More on him later.

blast of nihilism, an antidote to the lame rock and roll of the day. British rock of the 1970's was a stagnant wasteland dominated by over-25 millionaires like the Stones, Led Zeppelin and Wings. Meanwhile, radio was awash with sappy singer-songwriter types — James Taylor, Harry Chapin, Joni Mitchell. Lost in this mix were all the kids who couldn't identify with either scene. The Ramones (who played a triumphant show at the Roundhouse on July 4, 1976), the Sex Pistols and a few other acts offered hope that music would soon be back in the hands of the kids, even if it meant smashing the entire status quo to bits.

Suddenly, rock and roll was once again rebel music — except that this time, rock was rebelling against itself. Punk rock offered a special freedom of spirit that had gone missing from music. Unpretentious and unselfconscious, punk was quickly becoming a forum for all sorts of new ideas — and the best part was that anyone could participate. Knowing how to play an instrument wasn't important; all that mattered is that you had the guts to go for it.

This in itself was an important lesson. By the dawn of the 1970's, rock and roll had become much more sophisticated in both sound and execution. In many cases, it was a function of age. The first wave of rockers from the 50's and 60's had grown up. As better musicians, they had grown bored with simple three-chord songs. Rock had also become more complicated because it could. Guitar, amplifier and synthesizer technology had progressed to the point were the number of new sounds seemed infinite. Recording studios were refurbished, equipped with new sixteen and twenty-four track consoles and tape machines. There were racks of new boxes that added all kinds of hitherto unimaginable effects to the recording process. Starting with the Beatles and SGT. PEPPER, most of the music media had become enamoured with techincal ability and elaborate studio production.

At the other end of the pipeline, home stereo equipment had begun to improve dramatically. The old wooden "entertainment centers" with their one-pound tonearms were giving way to proper component systems featuring better speakers and especially headphones. This made it possible for the listener to pick up on subtlties that were carefully planted deep within rock recordings. Progressive FM rock stations were on also the rise. Imagine — music on the radio that was *in stereo*!

But for some, things were getting a little too sophisticated. The musicianship was a little too polished, the recording techniques a little too slick. There were those who believed that the road to technical perfection in rock was anathema to its original purpose. Deep beneath the happy blather of Top 40 radio, and beyond the slick, corporate sound of mainstream rock, pressure was building. To a growing number of people, rock had become soulless, self-indulgent and dull. There were too many millionaire rock stars. That vital connection between the fan, the performer and the music had been hijacked and corrupted. A coup d'etat was in order — a revolution that could wrest the music back from the multi-nationals and return it to the people. Young fans increasingly began to look to the underground for help — and the Sex Pistols were there for them. Technique and muscianship took a back seat to old fashioned rock and roll rage.

One of the Sex Pistols' most important shows (indeed one of the most important gigs in the history of rock) was at the Lesser Free Trade Hall in Manchester on June 4, 1976, the night that the band first performed *Anarchy in the UK*. In the awestruck audience that night was Bernard Summer and Peter Hook (back for a second look and on their way to forming Joy Division), Stephen Morrissey (who was further propelled along the road to forming the Smiths), Neil Tennant (a future Pet Shop Boy) and Howard Devoto (of the Buzzcocks.) Without even really knowing what they were doing themselves, the Pistols had begun to seed the coming punk rock explosion. Not all were impressed. The NME's review of a Pistols gig in the spring of 1976 ended with this bold prediction: "It will take a far better band to create raw music for a generation."

The Pistols repertoire slowly expanded to include not only songs from the Stooges and Jonathan Richman, but also a series of originals with lyrics penned by Rotten. Some of demo recordings were produced by soundman Dave Goodman in July and were then shopped around to various labels by McLaren. After some shrewd negotiating (and after being rejected by Island, Polydor, Rak, Warner Brothers and even Virgin), McLaren secured a deal with EMI (home of the Beatles!) worth £40,000 — the largest amount the label had ever given to a new act. Still, EMI had some serious reservations about the group. They weren't sure about their violent and insulting reputation, nor were they completely comfortable with a single that used the word "antichrist" in the lyrics.

By the time the Pistols headlined the 100 Club Punk Rock Festival in September 1976, the punk scene

The Sex Pistols

had grown to the point where the Pistols found themselves in a race to see who would become the first band to release a record. Although they were beaten by the Damned (they released *New Rose* on October 22nd), the Pistols did manage to issue *Anarchy in the UK* on EMI on November 26th.

At first, the single had little impact outside of the punk community. Even with the Pistols' enormous street credibility, *Anarchy* managed to sell just under 10,000 copies, which was a huge disappointment to everyone involved. But less than a week later, thanks to a shit storm created by a tea-time chat show host named Bill Grundy, the Pistols would be selling 10,000 copies *a day*.

Called in as a last-second substitute for the scheduled guest (Queen), the Pistols' two minute appearance transformed them from quaint curiosity to Public Enemy Number One.[1] That exchange on December 1, 1976, went like this:

Grundy:	I have been told that that group have received £40,000 from a record company. Doesn't that seem slightly opposed to their anti-materialistic view of life?
Matlock:	The more the merrier.
Grundy:	Really?
Matlock:	Oh, yeah!
Grundy:	Well, tell me more about it.
Jones:	We fucking spent it, didn't we?
Grundy:	I don't know. Have you?
Band:	Yeah.
Grundy:	Really? Good lord! Now, I want to know one thing: are you serious or are you just making this up? I mean about what you're doing?
Band:	Oh, yeah!
Grundy:	Beethoven, Mozart, Bach, Brahms have all died . . .
Rotten:	They're all heroes of ours, ain't they?
Grundy:	Really? What? What were you saying sir?
Rotten:	They're wonderful people.
Grundy:	Really?
Rotten:	Yes, they really turn us on.
Grundy:	Well, suppose they turn other people on?
Rotten:	(whispering) Well, that's just their tough shit.
Grundy:	It's what?
Rotten:	Nothing. A rude word. Next question.
Grundy:	No, no — what was the rude word?
Rotten:	Shit.
Grundy:	Was it really? Good heavens! (To the punk girls in the studio) What about you girls behind? Are you — do you love it or are you just enjoying yourselves?
Siouxsie Sioux:	Enjoying ourselves.
Grundy:	Are you?
Girls:	Yeah.
Grundy:	Ah, that's what I thought you were doing.
Siouxsie:	I've always wanted to meet you.
Grundy:	Did you really? We'll meet afterwards, shall we?
Jones:	You dirty sod! You dirty old man!
Grundy:	Well, keep going. Go on — you've got another five seconds. Say something outrageous.
Jones:	You dirty bastard. You dirty fucker. What a fucking rotter.
Grundy:	Well, that's it for tonight. I'll be seeing you soon. (To the band) I hope I'm not seeing you again. Good night.

The following day, every newspaper in the UK carried the story of how this group of snotty punk kids had used foul language on national TV. Leading the way was the *Daily Mirror* with the infamous headline "THE FILTH AND THE FURY!" Even the stodgy *Times of London* covered the incident, except that they couldn't bring themselves to print the words "Sex Pistols." All through the article, the band was referred

---

1. Legend has it that Grundy was drunk at the time of the interview.

to as "that pop group." It was a major — albeit accidental — publicity coup. Suddenly, the whole nation was talking about this new thing called "punk rock."

Embarrassed and angry by the outcry, EMI chairman Sir John Reed and the company's board members decided to cut their losses by washing their hands of the Pistols, ordering that *Anarchy* be withdrawn from sale, giving it them the dubious distinction of being the first label to delete a single while it was still going up the charts. After selling perhaps 55,000 copies of the single, the band's contract was terminated on January 22, 1977.

The label made a statement:

TV screen shot of Bill Grundy appearance

"EMI feels it is unable to promote this group's records internationally in view of the adverse publicity which has been generated over the last two months, although recent press reports of the behavior of the Sex Pistols appear to have been exaggerated."

The good news was that the band got to keep their £40,000 advance, plus they were given an additional £10,000 in publishing money.

Despite the generous payoff, the EMI debacle plunged the Pistols into a two month depression, culminating with the firing of bassist Glen Matlock. Accounts differ, but the most popular explanation is that he was forced out of the group when it was discovered that Matlock was a closet Beatles fan. His replacement was Sid Vicious (John Simon Beverly a.k.a. John Ritchie, born May 10, 1957), an ultra-violent super-fan friend of Lydon's who had been following the group from the very beginning. Although he had no clue of how to play bass, McLaren was tickled by the media angle of a fan being asked to join such a famous group.

McLaren, meanwhile, had orchestrated an even bigger coup than the contact with EMI. After holding meetings with WEA, CBS and RCA, he turned the Pistols' notoriety into a contract with A&M worth £150,000. After a cheeky 9 am signing ceremony outside of Buckingham Palace on March 10, the Pistols' entourage regrouped at A&M's London offices for a post-signing party, where they proceeded to tear the place apart.

Within hours, news of the signing and the sacking of the offices was sending shivers throughout the company. Complaints from board members, managers and artists (including Peter Frampton and Karen Carpenter) quickly convinced A&M brass that having the Pistols on the roster was a bad idea. Nerves were rattled when it was revealed that the first single on the label would be a song called *God Save the Queen*, a track that allegedly called the Queen a "moron." Issuing something so offensive in the year of Queen Elizabeth's Silver Jubilee would have been corporate suicide. Faced with an internal revolt and with the possibility of a public embarrassment, A&M decided that drastic measures were required to correct what was obviously a horrible lapse in judgment. On March 16 — just six days after the Buckingham Palace photo op — A&M issued a statement saying that they were severing all ties with the group. The £150,000 contract was canceled and the band was paid £75,000 to go away.[1]

McLaren was delighted. In the space of less than six months, he had swindled £125,000 pounds from two record companies. Meanwhile, word on the Sex Pistols' reputation had begun to push their market value down. Although many different labels considered signing the band after the A&M disaster, all of them — including Polydor — decided to take a pass. With his choices exhausted and with no new offers on the

---

1. A&M had pressed up 25,000 copies of *God Save the Queen* during those six days. When the contract was canceled, all those 45's were ordered destroyed. The few surviving copies of *God Save the Queen* that were rescued from the A&M warehouse are now worth thousands of dollars each.

---

table, McLaren's asking price began to drop. By the time Virgin offered Pistols a £15,000 deal on May 12th, McLaren was only too happy to have his boys sign so he could cash the cheque.

After some initial problems at the pressing plant (workers refused to manufacture a single so insulting to their queen), *God Save the Queen* was unleashed on May 27, 1977. Not only did the song refer to the monarch as a "moron," but the picture sleeve featured a drawing of Queen Elizabeth with a safety pin stuck through her mouth. No one — let alone a rock group — had ever expressed such blatant anti-monarchist sentiments in centuries. The press went crazy. Radio stations and the big chain stores banned the record. Local authorities banned the group from playing shows. Clergy screamed that punk rockers were the devil's children and bound for hell. Politicians stood up in Parliament and condemned the Pistols and other punk groups. Newspapers ran editorials demanding that something be done about punk rock bands. Half the country wanted the Pistols executed for treason. Both Johnny Rotten and Paul Cook were beaten up by monarchists. And *God Save the Queen* sold 150,000 copies in five days.[1]

Two more singles followed over the next few months: *Pretty Vacant* (released July 1, 1977 and backed with a version of the Stooges' *No Fun*) and *Holiday in the Sun* (released October 15, 1977.) Between covert UK shows (the infamous S.P.O.T.S. tour — Sex Pistols On Tour Secretly), the band worked on what would become their one and only studio album. It was finally ready on October 28, 1977.

Despite the fact that stores began banning NEVER MIND THE BOLLOCKS literally within an hour of its release, the album entered the UK charts at No. 1. Most radio stations even refused to run commercials for the album, despite the fact that Virgin was willing to spend £40,000 on advertising. Ten days later, in a farcical example of prudeness, the manager of the Virgin Records shop on King's Road in Nottingham was arrested for displaying a poster of the album in the window. According to the arresting officer, the display of the word "bollocks" in a public place contravened the 1889 Indecent Advertisements Act (the case was eventually thrown out.)

By the end of November, discouraged by the difficulties his group was encountering in Britain, Malcolm McLaren began to think that the Pistols had tapped out all their opportunities in Britain and Europe. Perhaps it was time to take his act to America.

The first attempt was a messed up by a series of bureaucratic errors — and by the fact that everyone in the band had lengthy criminal records (assault, drug possession, and theft.) Unable to get their visas on time, the Pistols had to forgo an appearance on *Saturday Night Live* on December 17.[2] After some last-second scrambling and a final UK show on December 25 (a benefit for widows and orphans of firefighters), the Pistols left for the US and one of the greatest touring disasters in rock history began to unfold.

McLaren had decided to avoid the major centers of the US in favor of taking the Pistols the American

1. Johnny Rotten was stabbed in the leg when he was attacked by monarchists in a car park outside the Pegasus Hotel. Had he not been wearing thick leather pants, he might have been crippled. As it stands, the razor cut he received on his hand in the attack has made it impossible for him to play a guitar properly.
2. Their replacement was Elvis Costello who turned in his infamous *Radio Radio* performance. In a gesture of thanks for the opportunity, Elvis' drummer wore a T-shirt that read "Thanks Malc."

hinterland. Cities like New York, Philadelphia and Washington were bypassed in favor of a dubious route through the South. Perhaps he was hoping to incite some kind of spontaneous punk insurrection among the musically-oppressed people of the hinterland. He couldn't have been more wrong.

Before he went to sleep on the night of January 3, 1978, Andy Warhol wrote the following in his diary:

> The Sex Pistols arrived in the US today. Punk is going to be so big. They're so smart, whoever's running the tour, because they're starting where the kids have nothing to do, so they'll go really, really crazy.

At the exact moment Warhol was writing those words, Johnny Rotten and Sid Vicious were in the parking lot of the Squire Motor Inn in Atlanta, trying to explain to a redneck Georgia state trooper what they were doing with that bottle of vodka. Shortly after the encounter with the cop, Sid managed to get himself beaten up by his own bodyguard. It wasn't long before he began missing rides to the next gig because he was out trolling for drugs. When he was around, he was either drunk or high or both and since he never thought to wash, he quickly became quite rank. Unable to stand the smell anymore, McLaren ordered the road crew to bathe dear Sid whenever he passed out.

The crowds were both weird and surly. At the first show in Atlanta, the group was bombarded with pig

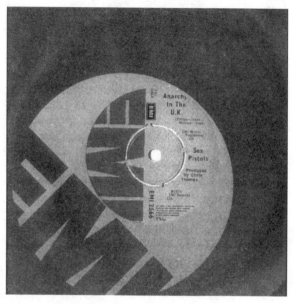

The withdrawn EMI single

snouts.[3] They threw seafood in San Antonio. Baton Rouge tossed tomatoes. And no matter where they went, they were showered with beer cans. A few were even empty.

Sid didn't help matters much, spitting into the audience and picking fights with anyone who looked at him funny (he discovered that if you swing a bass guitar like a cricket bat, you can do some satisfying damage.) In his more loving moments, groupies were invited to give him blow jobs on stage — and on least one occasion, a woman was happy to oblige. And all the while, Sid never played a note. Knowing that he was too stoned and too stupid to be trusted with playing his parts, his amp was never hooked up. A roadie played all of his parts from backstage. Poor Sid didn't have a clue.[4]

On January 14th, the wretched tour limped into San Francisco for one final show. Everyone was tired, frustrated, stoned, drunk and extremely surly. Rotten was perhaps the angriest. He was tired of being pelted with garbage, fed up with his friend Sid, bored with the antics of Steve and Paul, and was especially pissed at McLaren and his scheming ways. The last straw came backstage after that last show at the Winterland Theatre (featuring Johnny's famous remark "Ever had the feeling you've been cheated?") Although more than 5,000 people had paid to see the Pistols that night, their total profit after expenses added up to $66. When McLaren insisted that everyone get on a plane in order to play some dates in Brazil instead of going back home, Rotten quit. The Sex Pistols were finished.

Everyone began to scatter immediately. Jones and Cook stuck together and ended up in Rio after all as guests of Ronnie Biggs, England's notorious "Great Train Robber." Upon returning to England and before

---

3. The date was January 5, 1978. In the audience that night was a young punk fan from Emory College named Peter Buck. He would later form R.E.M.

4. For a fabulous account of this awful tour, see *12 Days on the Road: The Sex Pistols and America* by Noel Monk and Jimmy Guterman (Quill, 1990.)

The Sex Pistols

The ultra rare A&M edition of *God Save The Queen*.

splitting up, they tried to form several other groups, most notably the Professionals. Matlock later formed Rich Kids with future Ultravox singer, Midge Ure. Sid flew tried to fly back the UK, but ended up stopping in a New York hospital after an in-flight overdose. He ultimately died of a heroin overdose on February 2, 1979, while awaiting trial in the death of his girlfriend, Nancy Spungen. Malcolm McLaren went on to a reasonably successful career as a band manager (Adam and the Ants, Bow Wow Wow) and as a performer, releasing several decent albums and singles. He even got to direct TV commercials for Coca-Cola and several chocolate bars. Rotten cooled off with a trip to Jamaica before reverting to his real name and forming the rather excellent Public Image Ltd. PiL became a tremendously influential band in their early years, making some important contributions to the evolving industrial music scene.

Meanwhile, the Sex Pistols business legacy was in shambles thanks to Glitterbest, McLaren's management company. Where did all that record company money go? Where were all the royalty cheques? Who owned the rights to the Sex Pistols' name, logo and merchandise agreements? Who owned the rights to Sex Pistols songs? Who gave Malcolm the authority (and the money) to produce the Pistols' film, *The Great Rock & Roll Swindle*? At first it was Lydon against Glitterbest, Jones and Cook. After a series of hasty alliances of convenience between 1979 and 1986, Lydon, Jones, Cook and Sid's mom finally filed a strong suit against Glitterbest, asking for £1 million. After years of trying, they finally found a judge who agreed with them.

By 1992, with most of the legal hurdles (and McLaren) out of the way, the four original Pistols had begun to discuss the possibility of somehow recouping years of lost royalties and opportunities by releasing some kind of definitive collection of Sex Pistols material. Four years later, the group held a press conference in London on March 18, 1996, to announce that they were re-forming for what they called the Filthy Lucre Tour. This time, the swindle would be on their terms.

To many, the Sex Pistols are to punk what Elvis and the Beatles were to rock and roll. They were the musical and media focus of their era, attracting attention and fans to a new form of music, a new type of youth culture, a new style of expression and a new political and social movement. Although NEVER MIND THE BOLLOCKS still smokes as a rock and roll album, perhaps the Pistols' most important contribution was their attitude: the DIY punk ethic that stated that anyone could make music and that anyone could screw the system. All that was required was the will and the energy. By tearing apart the traditional trappings of the Rock Star, the Pistols made sure that at least a portion of the rock and roll spectrum was delivered back to the youth of the UK.

Although their role as the "voice of a generation" is still debated, there's no arguing that the Pistols were the grand symbol of British punk. In their original incarnation, they were young and loud and they didn't give a damn about what anyone thought. They were crude, full of fire and only too happy to offend. More than any other group, they were responsible for spreading the spirit of punk. By spreading this new gospel, they became the catalyst for a chain reaction of fresh, new ideas that has continued for decades, cleansing the world of rock and roll of the stale and the boring.[1] The status quo of the music industry

---

1. Just think of all the artists that say they got into the music as the direct result of seeing the Sex Pistols perform or after

The Sex Pistols

had been challenged and ultimately broken and changed. After the Pistols, there was no going back.

Fast Facts

o Despite the fact that the Pistols released exactly one proper studio album, there are more than seventy Pistols releases available (most are bootlegs, many of dubious quality.)

o Part of the reason for Johnny's intimidating stare and bad eyesight caused by a childhood bout with spinal meningitis. He was hospitalized for about a year starting at age seven and floated in and out of a coma for six months.

o It was Johnny Rotten who gave his friend the nickname "Sid Vicious." The "Sid" part came from Johnny's pet hamster and the "Vicious" had to do with his friend's habit of entering fights using a bicycle chain.

o One version of *Anarchy in the UK* features more than twenty layers of guitar.

o *God Save the Queen* was written on Johnny's mother's kitchen table as he was cooking some baked beans.

o *Pretty Vacant* was thematic riff from Richard Hell's *Blank Generation*. The opening guitar sequence was inspired by the beginning of *SOS* by Abba.

o The original title for NEVER MIND THE BOLLOCKS was GOD SAVE THE QUEEN.

o Before he joined the band, Sid Vicious was involved in a series of violent altercations. He was accused of throwing a glass that shattered and blinded a girl at a show at the 100 Club in London.

o Because they were banned from playing most everywhere in the UK after the release of *God Save the Queen*, the Pistols were forced to play a large number of gigs in Europe. This is why so many live bootlegs originate from Swedish performances.

o In July 1977, Malcolm McLaren approached soft-core porn director Russ Meyer about developing a film project centering on the Pistols. *Who Killed Bambi?* was scheduled to be written by future film critic Roger Ebert.

o When Sid Vicious finally got home after that final show in San Francisco, he and his girlfriend, Nancy Spungen, moved to New York. In July 1978, Sid sang for the Vicious White Kids, a one-off group featuring Rate Scabies of the Damned and a resurrected Glen Matlock. On October 11ᵗʰ, police were called to room 100 of the Chelsea Hotel where they found Spungen's body. Sid was arrested and charged with her murder. He never made it to trial. Sid died after OD'ing on the heroin his mother had thoughtfully purchased for him as a getting-out-of-jail present. He was 21.

o There are many questions regarding the murder of Nancy Spungen. Although she was stabbed with Sid's knife, some evidence suggests that she was killed by a drug dealer who also stole $3,000 from the room. Another report suggest that Spungen had stabbed herself while in the depths of a heroin stupor. Sid's alibi was that he was unconscious at the time, so he had no idea what happened. When he died, his ashes were spread over Nancy's grave in at King David Cemetery in Philadelphia.

o Room 100 at the Chelsea no longer exists. After years of attracting both fans and curiosity seekers, management became fed up and had the walls knocked down.

o Steve Jones has carved out a reputation as an LA session guitarist, working with everyone from Iggy Pop to Guns 'N Roses.

o After playing with Steve Jones in several post-Pistols groups, Paul Cook ended up as the producer, manager and, occasionally, the drummer for Bananarama.

o The relationship of Sid Vicious and Nancy Spungen was turned into a movie in 1986 by director Alex Cox. *Sid and Nancy* starred Gary Oldham and Chloe Webb.

o Despite being such a genre-defining album, NEVER MIND THE BOLLOCKS didn't sell as well as most people think. It wasn't certified platinum (sales of 1 million) in the US until March 26, 1992 — nearly fourteen years after it was first released.

o The Filthy Lucre Tour began outside of Helsinki, Finland, on June 21, 1996.

---

hearing NEVER MIND THE BOLLOCKS: Joy Division (and ultimately, New Order), Elvis Costello, Billy Idol, Siouxsie and the Banshees, the Pet Shop Boys, Morrissey, and Sonic Youth are just a few. Now think of the influence these performers had on others!

---

o In August 1996, Anne Beverly (Sid's 53 year-old mom) announced that she was forming at band called Road Rage. On September 6, 1996, she followed her son. Depressed at the notion that the Sex Pistols would dare reunite without her Sid and discouraged at the lack of success with her new band (who, by the way, often performed Sex Pistols covers), she carefully packed her bags and wrote out a suicide note before deliberately overdosing on a mixture of drugs and alcohol.

o *The Filth and the Fury*, a Pistols documentary directed by Julien Temple, received its world premiere at the Toronto Film Festival in September 1999. The film contains footage shot during that horrible 1978 American tour.

Recommended Listening

o NEVER MIND THE BOLLOCKS (Warner Brothers, 1977.) Everyone should have a copy of this album in their library. For an added thrill, search out a couple of the special double CD edition released through Virgin that features a legitimate edition of the SPUNK bootleg. If features all the original demos produced by Chris Spedding.

o THE GREAT ROCK & ROLL SWINDLE (Warner Brothers, 1979.) Buy it if only for Sid's snarling version of *My Way*.

o Virgin also released a collection of interviews and oddities entitled *SOME PRODUCT / CARRI ON SEX PISTOLS* [sic]. This combines a couple of former famous bootlegs onto one CD.

o The Pistols performance at the 100 Club Punk Rock Festival was captured on a bootleg entitled INDECENT EXPOSURE. Copies are still floating around. Beware of the sound quality of other bootlegs.

o The Pistols were a tight rock band during The Filthy Lucre tour. They have been older and slightly fatter, but their playing was better than ever. For proof, check out FILTHY LUCRE LIVE (Virgin, 1996.)

Internet Resources

o www.virginrecords.com/sex_pistols/

o www.users.wineasy.se/ludde/

o http://perso.club-internet.fr/fakirpro/music/pistols.htm

Recommended Reading

o Dalton, David. *El Sid: Saint Vicious*. New York, New York: St. Martin's Press, 1997.

o Gimarc, George. *Punk Diary, 1970-79*. New York, New York: St. Martin's Press, 1994

o Heylin, Clinton. *Classic Rock Albums: Never Mind the Bollocks*. New York, New York: Schirmer Books, 1998.

o Lydon, John. *Rotten: No Irish, No Blacks, No Dogs*. New York, New York: St. Martin's Press, 1994.

o Matlock, Glen. *I Was a Teenage Sex Pistol*. London: Omnibus, 1990.

o Monk, Noel and Guterman, Jimmy. *12 Days on the Road: The Sex Pistols in America*. New York, New York: Quill, 1990.

o Savage, Jon. *England's Dreaming: Sex Pistols and Punk Rock*. London: Faber and Faber, 1991.

o Scrivener, Tony. *Agents of Anarchy*. London: Kingsfleet Publications, 1992.

Related Listening

The Ramones, Nirvana, Black Flag, the Minutemen, Green Day, the Offspring and many others. Some of Malcolm McLaren's solo work, while not at all punk, also makes for good listening.

The Story Thus Far . . .

Inspired by the basic rock and roll of both Jonathan Richman and the Stooges, enchanted by Bowie's sense of style (not to mention the equipment they stole), and encouraged by the machine-gun guitar antics of the Ramones, the Pistols spark the UK punk scene.

~ 8 ~
THE CLASH
The Only Band that Matters

In its infancy, punk was limited to two re-occurring basic themes. The first was the *nihilism* preached by the Velvet Underground, the Ramones and, in their dumber moments, the Stooges. The second was various shades of spiritual and political *anarchy*. This was the gospel according to the Sex Pistols, Patti Smith and, when they were feeling surly, the Stooges. But then, in June 1976, the Clash appeared. More political than the Pistols and less goofy than the Ramones, it wasn't long before their fans anointed them as "the only band that matters."

At first, the Clash followed the standard bees-and-buzzsaw power chord / fuck-off-and-die approach of their contemporaries. However, by the time punk moved into its second summer, the Clash had made it clear that they were a band to be taken seriously. Not only had their music developed beyond the basics, incorporating elements of reggae, dub and rockabilly into their sound, but the Clash also managed to combine punk sensibilities with political awareness, social observation and personal integrity. Instead of just trying to destroy the system indiscriminately (and instead of being indifferent to it), the Clash were protesters, revolutionaries on a mission to fight injustice and racism while preaching the Truth. Abrasive, ambitious and politically correct (or incorrect — the Clash often displayed some glaring inconsistencies as they conducted their affairs), the Clash managed to broaden the base of the punk movement. In doing so, they formed the important third leg of the holy Punk Trinity with the Ramones and the Sex Pistols.

The Clash evolved out of punk's most famous stillborn band. The London SS was formed by Mick Jones (born June 26, 1955) in 1975 while Britain's punk scene was still in its primordial development. Consisting mainly of Jones, guitarist Keith Levene (later of Johnny Lydon's Public Image Ltd.) and manager Bernie Rhodes,[1] the extent of the London SS "scene" was a café in the Paddington part of London. Try as they might to find the right combination of musicians,[2] the group was never able to get it together long enough to play a proper gig.

One of the last people to join the group was Paul Simonon (born December 15, 1955), an art school student who had never played an instrument before. He, however, didn't consider that to be much of a handicap because he thought he was applying for the position of lead singer. Forced to fake his way through a version of Jonathan Richman's *Roadrunner*, he somehow demonstrated the right stuff (his good looks didn't hurt — he would eventually be voted one of the world's hunkiest men in *Playgirl*) and was allowed to join. Still short a singer, they approached Joe Strummer (born John Graham Mellor, August 21, 1952) just after he finished a gig with his band, the 101ers at the Red Cow pub. The offer came at just the right time. Strummer had grown disenchanted with the direction of the 101ers and was looking for a new band. On June 6, 1976, less than 24 hours after Jones made the offer, Strummer agreed to join this new group — whatever it was going to be called.

Soon, Jones, Strummer, Simonon and Levene were all living in a hideously run-down squat at 22 Davis Road in the Shepard's Bush area. It was an old warehouse set near a British Rail yard that had little going for it other than the fact that the accommodations were free. After a little cleaning up and a little paint, the squat was renamed Rehearsal Rehearsals and became the center of Clash operations for the next two years.[3]

After the warehouse was made somewhat presentable, the still-unnamed band auditioned a parade of drummers. The position was somewhat reluctantly given to Terry Chimes (born January 25, 1955), someone who had once failed to make the cut for the London SS several months earlier.

It was Paul Simonon who came up with the name. The group had already been experimenting with

---

1. Rhodes was a clerk at Sex, the clothing and fetish gear shop owned by Malcolm McLaren.
2. Other people known to have rotated through the London SS include Chrissie Hynde (who later formed the Pretenders), Tony James (soon of Generation X) and Brian James (who left to form the Damned.)
3. A frequent overnight guest was an otherwise homeless Sid Vicious.

dozens of names — the Weak Heart Drops, the Outsiders, the Psycho Negatives, the Phones, and the Mirrors. The debate was settled as Simonon stumbled on a headline in the *Evening Standard*; something about a "clash with police." When he suggested that they should call themselves the Clash, the others immediately agreed.

On July 4, 1976, at the exact same moment the Ramones were playing their historic gig at the Roundhouse in London, the Clash made their first official appearance, an unannounced opening slot for the Sex Pistols at the Black Swan in Sheffield. The second show was just as low-key. On August 13th, some friends and three music writers were invited around to Rehearsal Rehearsals see the group run through a couple of dodgy originals. Most witnesses left impressed by the Clash's sense of honesty and raw energy.

Encouraged by growing fan support, the Clash forged ahead, agreeing to several dates with the Sex Pistols including a set during the 100 Club Punk Rock Festival in September. These were the last shows with guitarist Keith Levene. He was more-or-less booted from the band for not exhibiting the proper discipline expected from a member of the Clash. (Levene also had problems with drugs.)

Now a four-piece, the Clash played wherever and whenever they could throughout the rest of 1976 — which is to say they didn't get much work. Touring on a bill with the Sex Pistols (a group that got themselves banned from playing virtually anywhere), Clash performances were few and far between. When they did get to play, Terry Chimes found the violence to be too much. After a thrown wine bottle narrowly missed his head during a show, Chimes decided that enough was enough. He had had enough of the violence and the political posturing. He just wanted out. His temporary replacement was a drummer named Rob Harper (born c. 1955.) Meanwhile, the other three members found themselves to be so short of cash that they often had to eat the flour-and-water paste they used for gluing up their posters.

The good news was that Bernie Rhodes was determined to out-do his old boss, Malcolm McLaren. When the Sex Pistols signed the first of their aborted record contracts, Rhodes was driven to find a better deal for this band. On January 25, 1977, he was successful, arranging for the Clash to sign a worldwide deal with CBS for £100,000 that trumped Polydor's offer of £25,000. Vowing to corrupt the record industry from within, the band nevertheless faced fierce criticism from the hardcore punk compatriots who accused them of selling out.

Now that the Clash had a record contract, they needed to make an album. They were more than ready to go into the studio — an album's worth of material had been written in the quiet confines of the council flat occupied by Jones' grandmother on the eighteenth floor of a building on Harrow Road. But before they could go anywhere, they had to solve their drummer dilemma. Rob Harper wasn't working out and their next choice, Jon Moss (a future drummer of the Culture Club!), wasn't available, so they called up Terry Chimes. Once he agreed to help out, the Clash booked three four-day sessions over the next month in Studio 3 of CBS Studios in London using soundman Mickey Foote as producer.[1]

The first official Clash single, *White Riot*, was in the stores by March 18th. Inspired by a riot in Notting Hill on September 1, 1976, the recorded version ran at about half of the speed that it was played live. Their debut album — a fourteen track effort entitled THE CLASH — followed on April 8th and received generally positive reviews across the UK, reaching No. 12 on the charts.[2]

His obligation to help the Clash through their debut album completed, Chimes once again took his leave, forcing the band into another long round of auditions. Legend has it that they went through 206 hopefuls, finally settling on Applicant #207: Nicky "Topper" Headon (born May 30, 1955), another one-time London SS reject and a recent hire of rock guitarist Pat Travers. The four-piece lineup once again restored, the Clash stormed Britain as a headliner on the White Riot Tour, a road trip that ended with a

---

1. This is the same studio in which the Stooges recorded RAW POWER.
2. A couple of notes about THE CLASH: Only three members are featured on the cover because at the time of its release, the group still did not have an official full-time drummer. And although the band had a planet-wide deal with CBS, the label declined to release it in the US, saying that punk was too raw and abrasive for American tastes. After all, they said, America is in the thrall of disco. Why would anyone care about the Clash? As it turned out, Americans bought more than 100,000 copies of this album, making it the biggest-selling import record of all time. When CBS finally relented, the American version of THE CLASH featured an altered (and inferior) track listing.

London audience literally tearing the seats from the floor of the Rainbow Theater and tossing them on stage.

By the summer of 1977, the Clash's fanbase was exponentially larger than it had been just a few months earlier. The blistering live shows and the powerful lyrical messages had been amplified by the band's carefully managed image as honest truth-seekers. The faithful saw the Clash as a group that not only sang about the injustices of this world, but one that was also price sensitive. The Clash were very serious about remaining affordable, insisting that the price of their records and concert tickets be kept lower than the going market rate. To the kids caught in the crossfire of Margaret Thatcher's right wing policies and the awful economy of late 70's Britain, the Clash seemed to articulate their frustrations.

It also didn't hurt that the Clash had their own well publicized (albeit minor) scrapes with the law. On June 10, 1977, both Strummer and Headon were arrested for spray-painting the group's name on a wall. When they were booked, it was discovered that they had both failed to appear before a magistrate on a charge of stealing a pillowcase from a hotel. That resulted in a night in jail and a £100 fine. The following October, the entire band spent an afternoon in a German jail over an unpaid hotel bill. Then in February 1978, police vehicles and helicopters responded to a call in Camden where Simonon and Headon were arrested for shooting down racing pigeons with pellet guns from the room of their warehouse. That cost them £800.

The second Clash album, GIVE 'EM ENOUGH ROPE, was recorded in San Francisco over three weeks in July 1978 with Sandy Pearlman, a producer best known for his work with Blue Oyster Cult. The months leading up to the release of the album were, to say the least, chaotic. After a series of confrontations with CBS regarding American releases, the Clash finally delivered an ultimatum: no new album until we're assured that this record comes out in America. Soon after CBS agree to those conditions, the band fired Bernie Rhodes over a series of financial disagreements and over some of his future plans for the group.[3] On October 21, 1978, lawyers for the Clash informed Rhodes that his services would no longer be required. Rhodes responded with a lawsuit, claiming that he had a management contract with the group guaranteeing him twenty per cent of the group's earnings. Just days before GIVE 'EM ENOUGH ROPE was scheduled to hit the stores (November 10, 1978), Rhodes persuaded a judge to order all the Clash's money routed directly into his account. It was the beginning of a legal battle that dragged on for a couple of years. Meanwhile, Rhodes' management duties were assumed by Caroline Coon, a writer for *Melody Maker* and a longtime fan of the group — not to mention Paul Simonon's live-in girlfriend.

Following a brief UK road trip (sarcastically dubbed the "Sort It Out" tour), the Clash made plans for their first tour of North America. Beginning with a show in Vancouver (with Bo Diddley as their opening act!), the Pearl Harbor '79 Tour swung through San Francisco, Los Angeles, Texas, Washington DC, New York and Toronto, collecting converts along the way. By the time the Clash headed back to England, GIVE 'EM ENOUGH ROPE had been voted Album of the Year by *Time*. Epic (their American label) was dumbfounded by the group's popularity.

Several projects awaited the Clash back in London. The first was a four-track EP entitled COST OF LIVING (released May 11, 1979) featuring the live favorite *I Fought the Law* and a newly recorded version of *Capitol Radio*. The second was to find at least a partial solution for the management problem. Coon was relieved of her duties on June 23rd. Finally, Epic had finally recovered from the shock that their punk group had sales potential in the US and were agitating for a third album.

New material certainly wasn't a problem. Not only had their first North American tour provided them with a ton of new ideas, but the group, sensing that punk was over, made a conscious decision to grow out of the standard three-chord anger-and-rage format. Using the music of their new neighborhood as inspiration (the Clash had relocated to a new rehearsal space in Pimlico), they began to slow things down, incorporating elements of dub and reggae into their sound. Lyrically, the album was fueled by the bad feelings from the split with Bernie Rhodes, the continuing poor economic state of the UK and the group's growing debt. No wonder they came across angrier and more apocalyptic than ever.

Choosing Guy Stevens as a producer (he oversaw the Polydor demo sessions at the end of 1976), the Clash blasted through twelve songs in just three days in August. In fact, they recorded so much material

---

3. One plan was to allegedly replace Mick Jones with Steve Jones, now ex of the Sex Pistols.

so quickly that it was obvious that the third album could end up as a double.[1] This was fine, except that both the band and the label had to keep in mind that the average Clash fan didn't have that much money; a double album might be too expensive. After some protracted negotiations, a compromise was reached — the Clash could release a double album providing that both records were included in a single sleeve, thereby saving on costs. It was also agreed that the set would sell for a reduced price with the Clash taking less in the way of royalties to make up for the label's lost revenue. And just to prove that they were more concerned about their art than they were about money, the Clash agreed to continue to each draw a salary of just $200 per week.

LONDON CALLING was finally released on December 14, 1979.[2] Critics and fans were stunned by not only by the band's undiminished ferocity but also by the breadth of the Clash's new musical landscape. Beginning with the opening anti-nuke diatribe of the title track and ending with the pop-ish *Train in Vain*, LONDON CALLING traveled through punk, reggae, rockabilly, R&B, jazz and dub. The Clash let it be known that they would not be limited by the expectations and norms of the punk world — punk was just one of the worlds they were out to change. Less intense and thus more accessible than the first two Clash albums, yet still brimming with fire, LONDON CALLING was nothing short of a masterpiece. *Rolling Stone* would later name it the No. 1 album of the 1980's.[3]

The Clash began the new decade with a hit album, several big singles on both sides of the Atlantic, a new management team, and a film. Although the Clash had originally sought to prevent the release of *Rude Boy* (a fictionalized documentary of a Clash roadie featuring footage of the band shot over the previous eighteen months), they eventually relented in time for the movie to debut at the Prince Charles Cinema in London on March 15. The band embarked on several tours, at least one of which (in Hamburg on May 21) deteriorated into a riot.[4]

Still on a high from the critical success of LONDON CALLING, (the New York *Times* called it "an album prized for its seriousness even as it reaches out to the millions"), the Clash began work on what they thought was going to be a single self-titled album. Despite growing tensions between Jones and Strummer (creative and political disagreements), the sessions proved to be productive — in fact, they were a little *too* productive. Within a few weeks, it became obvious that the next Clash album was going to be even more sprawling and more expansive than LONDON CALLING. With no outside producer to tell the band when to stop or where to cut — and with apparently no desire to impose any self-restraint — the length of the new album (and the band's debts) kept growing.

When SANDINISTA! (a *triple* album — thirty-six tracks in a single sleeve) was finally released on December 13, 1980, it was immediately savaged by both fans and critics. Although the six sides did contain flashes of brilliance (most notably *The Magnificent Seven*, *Police on My Back* and *The Call Up*), the album would have benefited by some serious pruning. Unable to distinguish true songs from self-indulgent crap, the Clash elected to release virtually everything they had recorded. Had it been cut down to a single record, SANDINISTA! might have been able to rival LONDON CALLING for power and bombast. Still, momentum was on the band's side, and the album reached a respectable No. 19 in the UK and No. 24 in the U.S.[5]

The SANDINISTA! ordeal (and the band's continued financial vulnerability) convinced Joe Strummer that the group was in dire need of stable management. In January 1981, he called up Bernie Rhodes after a chance meeting in London to discuss the possibilities of him returning as the Clash's full-time manager. Within two months, all the old legal problems had been solved and Rhodes was once again directing the band's career.

---

1. The band loved working with Guy Stevens because he was concerned more with feel than technical perfection. For example, notice how *Brand New Cadillac* speeds up along the way. When the Clash pointed out this error in tempo, Stevens dismissed their concern, saying that "all rock and roll speeds up." The version that appears on LONDON CALLING was actually a run-through of the song that Stevens taped without the band's knowledge.
2. LONDON CALLING was supposed to be called THE NEW TESTAMENT.
3. The Top 5 on that list included Prince's PURPLE RAIN at No. 2, U2's THE JOSHUA TREE at 3, REMAIN IN LIGHT from the Talking Heads at 4 and Paul Simon's GRACELAND at 5.
4. Strummer was arrested for braining a violent member of the audience with his guitar. After spending a few hours in jail, he was released.
5. Faced with another album with expensive retail price, the Clash fought with CBS to have this triple album released at the price of a double. To further sweeten the deal, the Clash reportedly agreed to forgo royalties on the first 200,000 copies. This was especially risky considering that LONDON CALLING had only sold 180,000 to that point.

One of the first things he arranged was a sixteen-night residency at Bonds International Casino in New York. Tickets that sold at the box office for ten dollars were sold for five times their face value. The crowds were so big and boisterous that there were concerns of overcrowding, the fire marshal and a series of building inspectors were brought into the club. In the end (apparently, the City Building Commissioner was pressured to let the gigs go ahead by two hardcore Clash fans — his children), the residency was a great success. The Clash was once the toast of New York.

That was the good news. The bad news is that internal dissension had once again taken hold, threatening to tear the band apart. There were serious concerns about Topper Headon's drug and alcohol use and it wasn't uncommon for squabbles to break out between Strummer and Jones. There were fights over music, politics, outside projects, girlfriends — you name it. There were stories about fights with producer Glyn Johns, who was working with them on a new studio album. No wonder the UK music papers carried a constant stream of rumors that the Clash was about to break up. Then Joe Strummer disappeared.

Having wrapped up the sessions for COMBAT ROCK (working title: RAT PATROL FROM FORT BRAGG) in March 1982, the Clash were rehearsing for what was to be called their Know Your Rights tour. After conducting a phone interview with a Scottish newspaper at the Clash offices, Strummer walked out the door and vanished. Although he was apparently spotted boarding a train and then a ferry for France, no one had any idea where he might have gone or what his motivations were. With Strummer still AWOL by the middle of May (despite Rhodes' public plea on April 21 for any information regarding his whereabouts), the Clash had no choice but to cancel almost the entire tour. The only good news was that Joe had contacted some relatives and was thus able to tell everyone he was fine without revealing his location.[6]

COMBAT ROCK was issued during Joe's disappearance — May 14, 1982 — to generally positive reviews (it debuted at No. 2 in the UK.) With no choice but to go ahead with several scheduled gigs, the Clash were forced to play several shows without him. Then, as suddenly as he vanished, Joe reappeared in the third week of May. No formal explanations were ever given.

Meanwhile, troubles with drummer Topper Headon had reached a peak. The morning after Strummer returned the fold, Headon either quit or was fired. One account said that he announced his intentions to leave after a final show in Holland, complaining that the Clash was too politicized for his liking. Another suggested that drugs had gotten the best of him (he was arrested for heroin possession in December 1981.) In any event, he was soon in front of a judge, charged with stealing a stop sign and with possession of some stolen stereo equipment.

With a North American tour set to start in five days, the Clash were once again forced to go to the bench for the reliable Terry Chimes. Taking time out from his work with a project called Cowboys International, Chimes joined up with the band in time for a quick spin through the US in the summer of 1982. This road trip was their most successful to date, pushing COMBAT ROCK into the Top 10 on the album charts. Even more surprising was that Rock the Casbah (first released June 11, 1982) reached No. 8 on the Top 40 chart.[7] A second single, Should I Stay or Should I Go (released September 24, 1982, and often incorrectly assumed by fans as a real-life question posed by Mick Jones regarding his status with the Clash — it was actually inspired by Ellen Foley, Strummer's then-girlfriend) also received significant radio airplay, reaching No. 45 on the US singles chart.[8]

In September, the Clash made what to many fans consider to be a fatal tactical blunder — they accepted the opening slot for the Who's farewell tour of America. Although they played before the largest crowds of their career (eight dates including two sellouts at Shea Stadium in New York), longtime Clash fans began to fear the worst, that their anti-establishment heroes had finally been co-opted into the mainstream. Britain's NME openly wonder about the band's "No Elvis, no Beatles, no Stones" policy. Was this the same band that built a career on raging against capitalism, commercialism and American cultural imperialism?

6. One suggestion is that the whole thing was a publicity stunt orchestrated by Bernie Rhodes. Strummer confidants say Joe went to Paris because his girlfriend's mother was in jail there.
7. Ironically, this was Topper's song. He had been messing with the central piano riff for years. During the sessions for the album at Electric Ladyland, he recorded the piano, bass and drums by himself. The rest of the band added their parts later.
8. Should I Stay or Should I Go was re-released in the UK in 1991 and went to Number One.

Feeling the heat, the Clash laid low until the spring of 1983 when they once again launched a series of American dates. On drums was twenty-three year-old Pete Howard (ex of a group called Cold Fish and allegedly the successful candidate of out 300 Clash hopefuls.) The tour took the band through the American Southwest, culminating with a first day main stage appearance at the US Festival in San Bernardino, California, on May 28.

Not much was heard from the Clash that summer, although there were more than enough rumors to go around. One of the most popular was that Strummer believed that the Clash had been carried away by success and that Jones had become what he detested; a rich pop star, a fake punk. When there finally was some news, it was a bombshell. According to a "Clash Communiqué" issued in September "Joe Strummer and Paul Simonon have decided that Mick Jones should leave the group. It is felt that Jones has drifted apart from the original idea of the Clash." It was nothing short of a coup — Strummer kicked Jones of the band that he had founded back in 1976.

> "Mick was my best friend at one time," Strummer told the Los Angeles Times in 1984. "We were
> partners and I don't dispense my partners easily ... but he became indifferent. He didn't want to
> go into the studio or go on tour. He just wanted to go on holiday. He wasn't with us anymore.
> I did him wrong. I stabbed him in the back."

Nevertheless, Joe Strummer set about rebuilding the Clash in his own image immediately. After auditioning close to 350 guitarists, he settled what he called "two desperate men." The first was Vince White, a student from Southampton. He was joined by Nick Sheppard, formerly of a British punk band called the Cortinas. The new lineup (the Clash MK II, "a whole new Clash era," according to Strummer) began with the a show in Santa Barbara, California, on January 19, 1984.

The new — and inferior — version of the Clash spent most of the year playing gigs on both sides of the Atlantic, stopping only long enough to record an album entitled CUT THE CRAP. Released in the fall of 1985, this is an album so unworthy of the Clash name that many official discographies don't even list it. Although the album peaked briefly at No. 16 in the UK, it was quickly written off as a disappointment and a sham. Two years later, Strummer himself admitted that the album had been a mistake. By the end of 1985, the Clash had disbanded. There was no formal announcement. The last documented Clash gig was in Athens, Greece, on August 27, 1985.

The spirit of the Clash, however, lived on in several different forms. Within weeks of his ousting, Mick Jones created Big Audio Dynamite, a band that had several strong-selling albums. After a stint as an actor (see in him Alex Cox's Straight to Hell, a movie that also featured a pre-nose job Courtney Love) Joe Strummer still works as a solo artist. His latest band, The Mescalaros, released a 1999 album entitled ROCK, ART AND THE X-RAY STYLE. Paul Simonon resumed painting, creating some artwork for Big Audio Dynamite. He also fronted Havana 3AM, a decent enough sounding band who released a self-titled album in 1990.

Other members of the Clash cast have moved on to other things. After working with Billy Idol, Hanoi Rocks, Black Sabbath and Samantha Fox, Terry Chimes retired from music and now works as a chiropractor and acupuncturist. Topper Headon released a solo album called WAKING UP in 1986 while continuing his battle with heroin addiction before dropping out of music altogether. In 1987, he was sentenced to fifteen months in jail after supplying junk to a friend who then died of an overdose. At one point, he was said to have been driving a cab somewhere in London, living off the handsome royalties generated by Should I Stay Or Should I Go. Now it's believed that he's living somewhere in Dover. Drummer Roy Harper played with Adam and the Ants for a while. And what of Pete Howard, Vince White and Nick Sheppard? They have faded into obscurity.

Looking back, it's remarkable that the Clash stayed together as long as they did. Rejecting conformity, driven by integrity and dogged by adversity (much of it self-induced), they lifted the entire punk scene beyond the simple search-and-destroy approach. By showing how punk could be melded with ska, reggae and rockabilly (not to mention political and social commentary), the Clash confused, angered and confounded some followers while challenging, inspiring and teaching others. U2, Fatboy Slim and John Squire were just a few of the band's young students.

As 1999 drew to a close, the world saw something of a Clash renaissance, complete with a TV documentary, a photo exhibition, a tribute album and a long overdue live record entitled FROM HERE TO

ETERNITY (first released in the UK on October 4, 1999.)

"Punk was about change," Simonon told *Rolling Stone* in 1981, "and rule number one was: there are no rules." No wonder that out of all the bands that emerged from the punk stew of the 1970's, few mattered more than the Clash.

Fast Facts

o Joe Strummer, the son of a British Foreign Services worker (not a diplomat as Joe once suggested in an early interview), was born in Ankara, Turkey, and grew up in Cyprus, Egypt, Mexico City and West Germany. He also attended a series of upper-crust boarding schools (he dropped out in his teens to form the 101ers.) He was nicknamed "Strummer" after the unique way he strummed *Johnny B. Goode* on his ukulele while busking in the streets of London. He eventually fashioned something called a "strum guard," a bandanna taped around his right wrist to prevent it from being shredded by the stings.

o Strummer had a younger brother named David who, for reasons known only to himself, became immersed in racist activities as a teenager. After dabbling in the National Front and Ian Smith's Rhodesian UDI movement, David was found dead in London's Regent Park on July 19, 1970. It was apparently a suicide. David's politics forced his brother into becoming more politically aware and pushed him in the activist direction he would achieve with the Clash.

o There is much dispute over how Keith Levene spelled his last name. Some sources spell it "Levine."

o Terry Chimes is listed as "Tory Crimes" on the first Clash album. This was a shot at his right-wing political views, something that didn't sit well with the rest of the band.

o Joe Strummer says he was once so desperate for money that he agreed to marry a woman for £150 so he could buy a guitar and she could get her British citizenship. After the ceremony, he lost track of her. He didn't even get her name. It took years for him to straighten out this fiasco.

o Manager Bernie Rhodes' car once bore the license plate CLA 5H.

o The 101ers were named after the house where Joe lived and the band rehearsed.

o Joe Strummer was hospitalized in February 1978 with hepatitis. He had the misfortune of having his mouth open when some ill individual in the audience managed to hit him with a large gob of spit.

o The cover of LONDON CALLING is a photo of Paul Simonon smashing his bass at the Palladium in New York during the Clash Take the Fifth tour. We know that this picture was taken at exactly 10:50 PM, September 21, 1979, because along with his bass, Simonon also busted up his watch in the process. He handed the debris to a journalist offstage who noted that it had stopped at 10:50.

o During the period from 1979 to 1981, the Clash went through three different sets of management. At one point, the band owed close to a quarter of a million dollars to various creditors, despite having had a hit with LONDON CALLING.

o *Train in Vain* was the mysterious final track on LONDON CALLING. Originally slated to be released as a flexi-disc through the *NME*, the group decided to include it on the album after all — but not until after all the sleeves had been printed. Since LONDON CALLING was being produced on a tight budget, the decision was made not to reprint the sleeves. Since then, *Train in Vain* has never been listed in the liner notes of any version of the album, thereby becoming one of the first hidden bonus tracks in rock and roll history.

o In July 1982, Flushco Inc., the manufacturer of a toilet bowl cleaner, sued the Clash for using a portion of their 2000 Flushes TV commercial in *Inoculated City* on COMBAT ROCK. They maintained that the inclusion of their jingle in a punk rock song hurt the company's image.

o Strummer's one-time girlfriend, Ellen Foley, is the voice who sings with Meatloaf on *Paradise by the Dashboard Life* on BAT OUT OF HELL.

o Why did a re-released *Should I Stay Or Should I Go* become a No. 1 hit in 1991? Because it was used in a TV commercial for Levi's 501 jeans. British Telecom applied to use *London Calling* in a long-distance telephone service TV campaign. Their request was refused.

o Joe Strummer temporarily filled in as singer for the Pogues in 1987, replacing Phil Chevron, who was sidelined with a stomach ulcer. Some audiences were treated to performances of *I Fought the Law* and *London Calling*. And while we're on the subject of the Pogues, Shane McGowan had his ear nearly bitten off by his girlfriend at an early Clash gig.

The Clash

o While it's true that the Clash were offered bags of money to reform for a Lollapalooza tour, the exact amount of the offer depends on who's telling the story. It can range anywhere from $1 million to £10 million. Meanwhile, the closest we've come to a Clash reunion was when Strummer helped out with the production on the second Big Audio Dynamite album.

o Strummer is an avid runner and still competes in the occasional marathon.

Recommended Listening

o THE CLASH (CBS, 1977) Make sure you look for the British version. Don't fall for the inferior American reissue.

o LONDON CALLING (Epic, 1979)

o COMBAT ROCK (Epic, 1982)

o There are several compilations from which to choose. For a single set, try THE CLASH: THE SINGLES (Sony International, 1999) If you want to step up to a double CD, go for THE STORY OF THE CLASH, VOLUME I (Epic, 1988.) Finally, there's THE CLASH ON BROADWAY (Epic / Legacy, 1991), a three CD boxed set that comes with an informative booklet.

Internet Resources

o www.geocities.com/SunsetStrip/Palladium/1028/

o www.bradstanley.com/clashalternative/

o members.tripod.com/~casbahclub/

o www.well.com/user/jeffdove/clash.html

Recommended Reading

o Du Moyer, Paul. *Modern Icons: The Clash*. London: Virgin Publishing, 1997.

o Gimarc, George. *Punk Diary, 1970-79*. New York, New York: St. Martin's Press, 1994.

o Gimarc, George. *Punk Diary, 1980-1982*. New York, New York: St. Martin's Griffin, 1997

o Gray, Marcus. *The Last Gang in Town: The Story and Myth of the Clash*. London: 4th Estate, 1995.

o Green, Johnny and Barker, Garry. *A Riot of Our Own: Night and Day with the Clash*. London: Faber and Faber, 1998.

o Peachy, Tobler and Miles. *The Clash: The New Visual Documentary*. London: Omibus Press, 1992.

Related Listening

Any solo Joe Strummer, Big Audio Dynamite, Operation Ivy, Rancid, Green Day.

The Story Thus Far ...

Using the basic approach of the Ramones and Jonathan Richman as a musical template, the Clash added angry and political comment to become one of the most relevant and dangerous bands of the original punk era.

~ 9 ~
KRAFTWERK
The Man Machines

At 24 Hochstrasse, on a nondescript street near the train station in the center of Düsseldorf, there's a yellow building across the street from a Turkish grocery store. There's no sign on the door, nor will you find any formal reception area once you step inside. At first glance, the austere, low-key surroundings might make you think you've stumbled upon a high-security computer complex or perhaps a Level Four biological containment laboratory. Actually, it's just a recording studio. Although it been there since 1971, it remains an extraordinarily mysterious place. Unlike other famous recording studios, like Abbey Road in London or Electric Ladyland in New York, Kling Klang is not for available to anyone, no matter who they might be. In fact, only one group has every used the place: the owners. Kraftwerk.

Welcome to the world of music's most famous *klangchemikers* — sound chemists — men dedicated to the pursuit of a visual and aural art form known as *gersamkunchverk*. Although Kraftwerk can't claim to have sold that many records over their thirty year existence (they haven't), they could, if they chose to do so, boast of influencing the development of modern music on a dozen different levels. Their innovative use of electronics, computers and on-stage imagery ultimately affected the course of everything from disco, house and hip-hop to pop, dance and industrial music. Had it not been for Kraftwerk's relentless electronic pursuits, today's music would be much, much different.

Florian Schneider-Esleben was born on April 7, 1947, in a small town in the Bordensee area of what was then the southern part of West Germany. In 1950, the family moved to Düsseldorf were his father, Paul, became a well-known architect, designing and rebuilding the airports and train stations that were destroyed during the war. Ralf Hütter was born on August 20, 1946, in Krefeld, a town northwest of Düsseldorf. As the son of a doctor, he studied classical piano for a number of years before moving on to the electric organ at the Kunstakademie (Academy of Arts) in Remschied, a city east of Düsseldorf. This is where he met Schneider, who was studying the flute. The two became friends and began exploring a common interest in avant-garde music.

One concern for many young German artists in the 50's and 60's was a loss of cultural identity. Caught between West and East in the cold war, German pop culture was becoming increasingly Americanized. There was no real German scene or sound. Local bands were content to perform covers of American or British artists, while the visual arts (film, theater, etc.) were dominated by foreign content. This gave birth to a loosely knit movement of post-war artists who were determined to recapture, rebuild and advance a new cultural identity for their country.

One of the first areas to be revitalized was music. In 1953, a German composer named Karlheinz Stockhausen started working on electronically generated music in an experimental studio built by West German radio. It wasn't long before he attracted a group of disciples who were all eager to push the edge of the musical envelope. Two of Stockhausen's students, Holger Czukay and Irmin Schmidt, eventually formed Can, a Cologne-based classical-cum-rock outfit that specialized in adding layers of sound over a steady beat. Others followed, most notably Neu! and Tangerine Dream. Although this music demonstrated little in the way of traditional song structure, it proved popular enough to set the foundations for a sound eventually dubbed "Krautrock" by the British music press.[1]

As fans of Can, and as students of free-form improvisational jazz, Schneider and Hütter were soon caught up in the possibilities of mating the avant-garde with rock and roll. In 1969, Schneider and Hütter attended a show at a Munich gallery that feature music created by several sine wave oscillators. These were primitive and temperamental electronic devices that generated tones. By careful manipulation of voltage, it was possible to get something resembling a musical composition. At the very least, it was an interesting art statement.

Like many German musicians of the era, Schneider and Hütter believed this new, modern, electronic approach could be the route to creating a distinctly German sound — what they began to call "European industrial folk music." Their first attempt at forming a band came in the late 60's with Organisation. As a five-piece, dedicated to improvisational performance art using feedback, repetitive rhythms and traditional instruments such as guitar, violin and flute, Organisation performed at universities and art galleries. One album exists although TONE FLOAT (RCA, 1970) gives little indication of where Schneider and Florian were headed.[2]

Organisation was disbanded in early 1970. Schneider and Florian then formed Kraftwerk, using the German word for "power plant." In the summer of that year, they recorded a debut album with Klaus Dinger and Andreas Hohman on drums and percussion. More structured, more melodic and more electronic than their first attempt, KRAFTWERK (Philips, 1970) offered a blend of sounds that could be both soothing and disturbing depending on the time of day, the volume at which it was played and the mood of the listener. *Ruckzuck* (the opening track — German for "do it quickly") would eventually

---

1. UK singer Julian Cope is an authority on this genre. For more, try his book *Krautrocksampler*.
2. Legend has it that TONE FLOAT was recorded in a studio situated inside an oil refinery. That's because their label was owned by Siemens, a large German industrial conglomerate.

---

became a favorite of the band when they played live.

Realizing that their strengths may lie in experiments conducted in a recording studio, Kraftwerk created Kling Klang in late 1970. Using a rented sixty square meter space on Hochstrasse, they fitted the room with sound insulation, tape machines and exotic pieces of electronic equipment. The first album to be created in the new studio was entitled KRAFTWERK 2 (Philips, 1971), a project that was recorded in the space of seven days at the end of September 1970. One of the most interesting things about the album was the piece *Kling Klang*, which may be the first pop recording to ever feature a drum machine.[1] KRAFTWERK 2 album sold a respectable 60,000 copies in Germany, although it might have sold more had the cover artwork (depicting an orange traffic cone) not been so similar to that of the first album. It was enough, however, to help keep Kling Klang operational.

After some personnel shifts, Kraftwerk was temporarily put on hold. Reduced to a duo for the time being, Hütter and Schneider (with important help and inspiration from artist-musician Emil Schult), issued RALF AND FLORIAN (Philips) in November 1973. Although it was filled with austere synthesizer sounds, the fact that the album also featured woodwinds and strings disqualifies it from being a pure electronic record. Those who bought the record also received a bonus comic book.

Resurrecting the Kraftwerk name, Hütter and Schneider decided to abandon the free-form, hit-and-miss approach of their first three albums. From now on, they decided, they would endeavor to make precise, exacting music. Discipline and structure replaced improvisation. Unlike, however, contemporaries such as Tangerine Dream, the music was to employ a pop song approach rather than a neo-classical or avant-garde jazz one. And to make sure that everything remained regimented and well-ordered, they would rely on machines. Investing in several Moog synthesizers and a sequencer (a device that could be programmed to play long, repetitive sequences of notes endlessly and perfectly), they set about recording what would become a landmark album in the history of music. Hired to help with the album were Wolfgang Flur (born July 17, 1947) and Klaus Roeder (birth date unknown.)

The third Kraftwerk album was recorded at a time when the West German government was spending huge sums of money on a national highway building program. Not only did these wide, speed limitless freeways open the countryside to German city-dwellers, they made German drivers the envy of Europe. Seizing on this metaphor of the *autobahn* as *freedom*, everyone went for a ride in Hütter's Volkswagen. Few drivers and passers-by noticed the microphone handing out the window. Returning to the studio, that drive down the autobahn became the basis of an all-electronic pop album.

Alternating between mesmerizing minimalistic pop and cold, robotic, electronic sounds, AUTOBAHN became a major hit on both sides of the Atlantic. The album contained an astonishing sonic landscape, featuring sounds and textures never before heard on a pop record. In the UK, the album peaked at No. 4 and remained on the charts for eighteen weeks. In America, the album hit No. 5 on Billboard. A four minute edit of the title track (a necessity for a single release — the album version is close to twenty-three minutes long) climbed to No. 6 in Britain and a respectable No. 25 in the US.

AUTOBAHN was a major musical milestone, not only for Kraftwerk, but for music in general. In the early 70's, synthesizers were at best nothing more than expensive electric curiosities. At worst, they were viewed as evil — machines used by lazy and / or untalented people who couldn't be bothered to learn how to play a *real* instrument like a guitar or piano. Others went so far as to suggest that electronic music was a plot designed to prevent real musicians from making a living. Furthermore, there were those who insisted that the rise of the machine meant the death of music as we knew it.

To others, however, Kraftwerk's mechanical, high-tech, disembodied approach to pop music was nothing less than a window on the future. To them, synthesizers, sequencers and drum machines represented a whole new universe of creative possibilities — the infinite tonal range of a synth pulse and the guiding program of a sequencer (which removed the potential for human error) had unlimited potential. This technological and creative breakthrough immediately began to affect all music, from classical to dance to rock. In a few short years, an entire genre of music (dubbed techno-pop, electro-pop and electro-beat) was born, rooted firmly in the premise of AUTOBAHN.

---

1. A drum machine was also used for a show in Paris in February 1973. This may have been the first-ever appearance of a drum machine in a concert situation.

Kraftwerk built on these new electronic foundations for their next album. Using Wolfgang Flur again and replacing Klaus Roeder with an electronic percussion specialist named Karl Bartos (born May 31, 1952), the new four-piece decided to build the album around the central theme of radio, especially the type of radio broadcasts used to spread propaganda. They also settled on a change in the way they presented themselves. Gone were the beards and the long hair. Instead of looking like a bunch of aging European hippies, each band member adopted a generic look that was a cross somewhere between a German rocket scientist and a storm trooper. This was the beginning of the group's image as serious sonic engineers. With Kling Klang as their laboratory, Kraftwerk viewed themselves as sound chemists: *klangchemikers.*

Since AUTOBAHN had cost next to nothing to record, its enormous success resulted in loads of new investment for Kling Klang. New equipment was purchased and installed. What they couldn't buy (Kraftwerk often found that the marketplace hadn't kept up with their technological needs), they constructed themselves.[2] Within a few months, Kling Klang was transformed from a crude rehearsal space into a fully-functioning, state-of-the-art recording facility.

The next album was the first under a new deal with EMI. First released in Germany in November 1975, RADIO-ACTIVITY (entitled RADIO-AKTIVITÄT and sung in German; RADIO-ACTIVITY was released in an English form in January 1976) was both a success and a failure. First of all, since it lacked the catchy novelty value of a single like *Autobahn,* the album didn't sell well. Inside Germany, the band were dogged by the fact that they were perceived as supporters of nuclear power. That hurt sales at home. Meanwhile, hardcore avant-garde fans were worried that the album mirrored the structure of a regular rock album — twelve tracks with six per side. About the only territory where the album could be considered a success was France.

On the other hand, the album provided further inspiration for musicians who had become hooked on this new minimalist, electronic, non-organic approach to rock. One person who was very intrigued was David Bowie, one of the biggest stars in the world. Not only did he often use Kraftwerk as entrance music for some of his shows on the Station to Station tour, they were a big part of his decision to quit Los Angeles in favor of Berlin as he searched for new musical inspiration. Kraftwerk is the reason behind the sounds of Bowies so-called "Berlin trilogy" of Brian Eno-produced albums in the late 1970's — LOW, HEROES and LODGER — not to mention two Bowie-produced albums from Iggy Pop.[3]

By 1977, Kling Klang was equipped with the most esoteric electronic equipment of the day. Still financially independent thanks to AUTOBAHN, Kraftwerk was free to spend as much time as they wished experimenting with (and occasionally, building) new gear. Two years of this messing about (not to mention travels by train to the south of France) produced another landmark album: TRANS-EUROPE EXPRESS.

The album was released through EMI in May 1977. Although the music may sound a little dated by today's standards, it featured sounds never heard by the human ear before 1977. The title track was especially engaging in its subtleties and versatility. Played soft, it provided futuristic background music for, say, a planetarium show or an art installation; turn up the volume and it became radical disco music. Other tracks on the album (most notably *Showroom Dummies*) were just great pop songs.

Here's where the Kraftwerk effect begins to multiply. What the Sex Pistols and the Ramones were to punk and guitars so Kraftwerk was to the world of electronic music. Disco performers began adopting Kraftwerk's synthesizer-and-sequencer approach for their records. Starting with Donna Summer and the Giorgio Moroder-produced *I Feel Love,* some elements of disco began moving away from their funk roots towards something more pulsating, throbbing and robotic. Rap, break dancing and hip-hop can also trace roots back to TRANS-EUROPE EXPRESS, thanks to Afrika Bambaataa, whose ultra-influential *Planet Rock* was built around a sample of the title song. The dehumanized electronics and sequenced sounds provided an early template for what was quickly become known as "industrial music." Nitzer Ebb, Nine Inch Nails, Front 242, Laibach, Ministry — they all owe Kraftwerk a debt of gratitude. Kraftwerk was also being studied by a series of post-punk groups who were toying with the idea of dumping the guitar-bass-drums idea completely. Like Kraftwerk, they were interested in using synthesizer pulses to create cold, robotic pop songs. Followers included future members of Depeche Mode, the Human League, Soft Cell,

---

2. Kraftwerk were always building drum machines. One of the first was made from a beat-box in an electronic organ.
3. LOW contains a tribute to Florian Schneider called *V2 Schneider.*

Orchestral Maneuvers in the Dark and, in fact, the entire techno-pop movement.[1] Follow this line of thinking to its present-day conclusion and you arrive at the many flavors of techno and ambient music.

And it didn't stop at just music. Dance — from modern to ballet — was being affected by the Kraftwerk method. Their influence had begun to spread to film as arty expressionist movies embraced the cold, dehumanized atmosphere conjured up by some of the group's more detached pieces. In short, TRANS-EUROPE EXPRESS should be viewed as one of he most influential albums of the 70's.

Exactly one year after the release of TRANS-EUROPE EXPRESS — May 1978 — came THE MAN MACHINE (DIE MENSCH MASCHINE, EMI.) By this time, Kraftwerk had become much more than just a musical group, they were a living, breathing artistic statement and nothing typified that attitude more than the cover of this album. Dressed in suspiciously fascist-looking paramilitary gear (red and black were the Nazi colors) but looking east (towards their communist foes? Brethren?), the artwork was carefully modeled after the work of Russian artist Eli Lissitzsky.[2]

Kraftwerk became more immersed in their emotionless Teutonic-science-fiction-automation imagery. Just prior to the release of THE MAN MACHINE (and inspired by *The Robots*, one of the tracks from the album), they commissioned the construction of a four of mannequins in the image of the band. So began the robots' duties as stand-ins for the group at press conferences, record releases and even concerts. Kraftwerk loved to play up this special relationship with their dummies and their incomprehensibly complicated musical gear. "We play the machines but the machines also play us," said Ralf Hütter in an interview. "We try to treat them as colleagues so they exchange energies with us."

THE MAN MACHINE sold very well, spawning a UK hit single in *The Model*, and selling over 300,000 copies in Europe. Their reputation as artists and futurists secured, Kraftwerk retreated to Kling Klang and remained sequestered there for three years. What were they doing in there?

All four members were fascinated with the possibilities of the new personal computers that were starting to be sold. They experimented heavily with the new machines, incorporating them into new custom-designed equipment. The band was so entranced by computers that they became the central theme of the next album, appropriately entitled COMPUTER WORLD (EMI.)

By the time the record was released in May 1981, the techno-pop revolution was in full force, vindicating Kraftwerk's *Blade Runner* vision of the future from back in 1974. The feel of many of the seven tracks on COMPUTER WORLD is livelier and occasionally playful (good examples are *Pocket Calculator* and the UK hit *Computer Love*.) Still, with so many new electronic-based groups now making music, Kraftwerk was starting to sound a little old.

The band, however, seemed unconcerned. They just kept working at Kling Klang, day after day, month after month, year after year. The silence was broken, briefly, in 1983 when they released *Tour de France*, a 12-inch single based on their passion for cycling.[3] The single was a double-A side, one side featured the song in German, the other in French.

Five years passed before Kraftwerk got around to releasing a new album.[4] While most fans were glad to hear anything new, ELECTRIC CAFÉ (released in November 1986 and the first Kraftwerk album to be totally digital) was viewed as a bit of a disappointment. Although it does contain some wonderful minimalist moments (the first side with *Boing Boom Tschak*, *Techno Pop* and *Musique Non Stop* is worth the time), it's generally agreed that the band didn't break any new ground. Another complaint was that at thirty-five minutes, it was too short for an album that supposedly took five years to make.

After just a handful of live dates, Kraftwerk once again disappeared into the confines of Kling Klang. Their next appearance was in May 1991 when they released THE MIX, a collection of old Kraftwerk material

---

1. One of the world's biggest Kraftwerk fans was Daniel Miller. He was so moved by this all-electronic approach to pop that he eventually created Mute Records, home to Depeche Mode, Erasure and many of the world's best-known techno-pop bands.
2. A note acknowledging his influence is included in the artwork. The band was concerned about possible charges of plagiarism.
3. This piece was commissioned by the organizers of the famous bicycle race.
4. It wasn't supposed to be this way. In 1983, ads started to appear in German magazines regarding the imminent release of an album called TECHNO POP. The album was even given a release number (EMC 3407) and some artwork had been prepared, but after two postponements, the album disappeared from all release schedules. Rumors abound about this lost album. One of the most popular is that it was to have contained *Tour de France* and a twenty minute-plus title track.

that had been re-jigged and remixed using Kling Klang's new digital gear. This album, however, came at price. Upset and frustrated at the lack of activity, both Wolfgang Flur and Klaus Bartos left the group, leaving Schneider and Hütter to fend for themselves.

According to the current legend, the two men still keep regular hours at Kling Klang, working from 8am to 4pm, Monday to Friday. Despite Schneider's distaste for touring, Kraftwerk continues to play the occasional live show to appease both hardcore fans and as a way of supporting various charities and activist groups such as Greenpeace. In the late 90's, the band's status as electronic pioneers had reached mythical godlike status amongst fans of the newly born electronica scene.[5] When Kraftwerk shows were scheduled (there was a brief American tour in 1997), they were instant sellouts.

Kraftwerk is responsible for injecting more technology into modern music than any other single group. Once again, current legend suggests that they are working on new machines and electronics, such as a way of playing simultaneous concerts in different cities using robots and holograms. A common rumor circulating amongst fans is that Kraftwerk will not release any new material until they perfect their latest invention — a musical interface that's played using brain waves. No keyboards and no external input devices whatsoever are needed — the musician *wills* the music to come forth.

Whatever they may (or may not) do in the future, Kraftwerk have already brought incredible innovation to music through their use of technology and through their artistic vision. While the machines may have been complex, the arrangements of the songs were quite simple. The careful display of that juxtaposition of complexity and simplicity was almost as important as the music itself.

Kraftwerk's whole approach changed the way people listened to music, made music and reacted to music. Call it what you want — de-personification of music, Bauhaus-era modernism, retro-futurism, neo-classical modernism — their influence will be felt for years to come.

Fast Facts

o While Kraftwerk was responsible for introducing the synthesizer to millions of people, they were hardly the first rock / pop outfit to use one in a recording. That honor apparently belongs to the Monkees who included a brief synth solo in a 1967 song called *Star Collector*.

o *Autobahn* wasn't the first all-electronic song to become a pop hit. Most historians will point to *Popcorn*, a 1972 Top 10 hit by a group called Hot Butter (featuring Stan Free on synthesizer.)

o The Morse code at the beginning of *Radio-Activity* spells out R-A-D-I-O-A-C-T-I-V-I-T-Y. This single was also the first song to be recorded in English.

o The working title of THE MAN MACHINE was DYNAMO.

o By the late 70's, Kling Klang had been redesigned in such a way that it would be broken down, packed up and sent on tour with the group.

o During a promotional tour of the UK for ELECTRIC CAFÉ, Ralf Hütter appeared to have a heart attack. After a week in hospital, doctors determined that his heart had raced into overdrive as the result of way too much coffee.

o The voice of the woman on *The Telephone Call* belongs to Samdhya Whaley, Florian Schneider's girlfriend.

o Ralf Hütter runs marathons and cycles. It's not uncommon for him to cycle 200 km a day.

o The fabulous 12-inch mixes of *Tour de France* are still unavailable on CD.

o The group remains swathed in mystery. All communication with the outside world (including their record company) is been done through faxes and e-mail. Interview requests are either turned down or ignored. Visitors are discouraged at Kling Klang.

o In 1998, a poll was conducted among musicians and music industry professionals. The question was simple: "Who is the top music star of the last thirty years?" When all the votes were counted, Kraftwerk finished eighth, ahead of even Bob Dylan.

Recommended Listening

o AUTOBAHN (Warner Brothers, 1974)

---

5. Kraftwerk's legendary anonymity fits in perfectly with the techno concept of dance music made by anonymous, faceless DJs.

- RADIO-ACTIVITY (Capitol, 1975)
- TRANS-EUROPE EXPRESS (Capitol, 1977)
- THE MAN MACHINE (Capitol, 1978)
- COMPUTER WORLD (Warner Brothers, 1981)
- ELECTRIC CAFÉ (Warner Brothers, 1986)

Internet Resources
- www.kraftwerk.com
- www.bham.ac.uk/busbykg/kraftwerk/FAQ
- www.geocities.com/SunsetStrip/8880/
- www.swcp.com/lazlo-bin/discogs?kraftwerk

Recommended Reading
- Bussy, Pascal. *Kraftwerk: Man Machine and Music.* London: SAF Publishing, 1993.

Related Listening
Early Depeche Mode and OMD, Tangerine Dream, the Orb, Orbital, Bowie's "Berlin Trilogy), Neu!, Air, Chemical Brothers, Crystal Method, Spaceman 3, Afrika Bambaataa.

The Story Thus Far . . .
By dragging the synthesizer into the rock and roll arena, Kraftwerk changes the way the world regards electronic music. David Bowie becomes a firm believer, as do future members of Depeche Mode.

~ 10 ~
JOY DIVISION
Here Come the Young Men

It's a rare accomplishment for a band to continue after losing their lead singer. It's even more unusual for a group to carry on after any member — let alone their lead singer — dies tragically. The odds against three friends forming two successful bands are astronomical. And the chances of *both* these groups being good enough to actually change the courses of musical history are so remote that it defies calculation. Yet it has been done. It's the story of Joy Division and New Order.

Each band created its own distinct sphere of influence. While they existed, Joy Division created an essential link between the original punk movement and many of the styles and sounds that came later. When the group died with singer Ian Curtis in 1980, their influence was perpetuated for years, swaddled in myth and mystery. Meanwhile, the survivors regrouped as New Order and went on to build musical bridges that created a rock-solid alliance between techno-pop, dance, New Wave and the new indie alt-rock scene. Taken together, the combined effect of Joy Division and New Order is nothing less than staggering.

Ian Curtis was born in Manchester, England, on July 15, 1956. The son of a police detective, Ian loved to read, preferring to skip school in favor of staying in his room with his books and his Velvet Underground, David Bowie and Iggy Pop albums. Part of his reticence regarding school was that he and his classmates were obligated to spend time at the local retirement homes, keeping company with the aged residents. The only thing that made these visits bearable was that Ian and his friends often found time to rifle through the old folks' medicine cabinets, helping themselves to interesting pharmaceuticals. These excursions into medication resulted in at least one stomach pumping and one expulsion after Ian returned to school high on cough medicine.

On August 23, 1974, Ian married his girlfriend, Deborah Woodruff. Even though they were just nineteen, they managed to buy themselves a house at 77 Barton Street in Macclesfield, south of Manchester. One room was eventually given over to Ian so he could write poetry and music in solitude.

Perhaps the most important event of his life was seeing the Sex Pistols in their first appearance at the Lesser Free Trade Hall in Manchester on June 4, 1976. He was dumbstruck by the power and the fury of the new punk movement. From that show on, Ian was more determined than ever to be involved in the new movement as a performer.

In the audience with him that night were two friends, Peter Hook (born February 13, 1956) and Bernard "Barney" Dicken (born January 4, 1956 — See Fast Facts for more on Barney's many surnames.) Inspired by the Pistols, they went home to form their own band the following day, despite the fact that they had no idea how to play any instruments. Still, they were resourceful enough to rig up a crude amplifier by running a signal from an old guitar through the pickup in the tone arm of an old console stereo. Bernard had his old guitar, while Hooky spent £35 on a cheap bass.

Because Ian, Peter and Bernard kept bumping into each other at punk shows, it was perhaps inevitable that the three of them decided to form a band together. Their first attempt was called Stiff Kittens (Pete Shelley of the Buzzcocks is the one who came up with the name), but that name was soon discarded because it made them sound too much like just another punk group. Their second choice was Warsaw, inspired by an instrumental piece entitled *Warsawa* on David Bowie's LOW album. After pulling together a few songs and hiring drummer Tony Tabac,[1] the group made their debut at the Electric Circus in Manchester on May 29, 1977. Reviews were decidedly mix, but the group did get a couple of nice lines in the NME — "There's an illusive spark of dissimilarity," the reviewer said. "I liked them and will like them even more in six months time."

Warsaw was adept enough to earn several more gigs, most of which received good reviews, which, of course, resulted in more bookings. They were even invited to contribute a song called *At a Later Date* to a long-deleted 10-inch compilation entitled SHORT CIRCUIT: LIVE AT THE ELECTRIC CIRCUS. It was also around this time that Bernard Dicken changed his name to Bernard Albrecht.

After about a half-dozen performances, everyone pooled their money and rented ten hours of studio time at Pennine Studios in Manchester in July 10. Although the demos went unreleased (at least officially), the tapes were used successfully to pique the interest of various club owners and promoters in and around Manchester.

There were two more important changes in the summer of 1977. On August 24, the group finally settled on a permanent drummer. Even though Stephen Morris (born October 28, 1957) was the only person to apply for the job, as a longtime school friend of Ian's, he seemed to fit in well and was made a full-time member. This change in personnel was soon followed by another name change. Our Warsaw — the band from Manchester — kept getting confused with Warsaw Pakt, a heavy metal group from London. Rather than fight, Warsaw decided that it would simply be easier to change their name. But to what?

By this time, the group had become very serious about making a proper record. The recording sessions at Pennine were financed by a £400 loan Ian had wrangled from his bank with a little while lie (he told them he need to buy some dining room furniture) and resulted in four finished songs: *No Love Lost*, *Failures*, *Warsaw* and *Leaders of Men*. Some of the bank loan was also invested in creating artwork and packaging. It was here that Warsaw found their new name.

While researching for the Nazi themes that adorned the cover of the IDEAL FOR LIVING EP (originally released as a 7-inch on Enigma on June 4, 1978, and then re-released as a 12-inch on Anonymous Records on October 10th), Ian discovered a book by Karol Cetinsky entitled *House of Dolls*. In the book, he describes a "joy division" as an area of a Nazi concentration camp where women are forced into service as prostitutes for officers and soldiers. The darkness and the irony of the term "joy division" somehow appealed to the band and, after one last gig as Warsaw on New Year's Eve, 1977, the group officially became Joy Division in time for a show on January 25, 1978.[2]

---

1. Tabac wouldn't last long. Hired less than forty-eight hours before that first show, he remained with Warsaw for about a month before leaving for "health reasons." His replacement was Steve Brotherdale. He joined the band in time for a gig on June 30, 1977.
2. Barney insists that the group was never known as Warsaw. He maintains that they changed their name to Joy Division in time for their first gig.

Once IDEAL FOR LIVING was ready to hit the stores (only 1200 copies were pressed up and sold out quickly), the group attempted to record an album for RCA in May 1978. Unfortunately, the chemistry was all wrong and after just four days, the project was abandoned.[1]

Joy Division's spirits were lifted by a strange break. After entering a local Battle of the Bands contest scheduled for April 14, 1978 at a Manchester club called Rafters, Ian discovered that among the dozens of producers and label representatives attending that night would be Tony Wilson, host of a TV show called So It Goes. Determined to make an impression, Ian assaulted Tony with a torrent of abuse, complete with a very angry, profanity-riddled note, badgering him about booking Joy Division on his program. This odd bit of reverse psychology worked — instead of blowing off this drunken yob, Wilson was impressed by Ian's gall and immediately agreed to have Joy Division appear at his club, the Russell. Stunned by this wonderful turn of events, Joy Division turned in a furious set that night, impressing more people, including Rob Gretton (a former insurance clerk, Wilson's friend and part-time DJ at Rafters) who agreed to become the band's manager.

This was followed by another chance occurrence. Shortly after that night, one of Wilson's relatives died, leaving him (much to his surprise) a small inheritance. This became the seed money for Wilson's next project; his own record label featuring bands that regularly performed at his club, now renamed The Factory.[2] In December, Joy Division, Durutti Column, John Dowie and Cabaret Voltaire all appeared on A FACTORY SAMPLE (FAC 2, released December 24, 1978) which consisted of two 7-inch records (Joy Division's contributions were Digital and Glass.) Word of mouth on the release — especially Joy Division — was very good. It seemed that the band was finally on their way. Then came December 27, 1978.

Ian Curtis was not really what you would call a sickly child, but he did have some health problems. For one thing, he was allergic to sunlight — if he stayed outside for too long, his hands would swell up like big, red balloons. While waiting for the antihistamines to work, Ian would have to have his hands bandaged for several days. Beyond that, he seemed fine — except for that incident with a strobe light at a concert in his mid-teens. After staring at it for several minutes, he collapsed to the floor. The security guards thought it was just another dumb kid on drugs and were rather rough when they tossed him out on the street. As Ian was growing up, people around him learned to deal with his increasingly large mood swings and violent temper. When he developed a strange phobia for foam rubber, friends and family just dismissed it as another one of Ian's eccentricities.

In 1977, Ian found a civil service job that required he learn something about epilepsy. Part of his job was to make sure people received the health benefits they were due — and it just so happened that a great number of his clients were epileptics. His boss enrolled him in a course to learn more about the condition and by the fall of 1977, he was somewhat of a lay expert on epilepsy.

On December 27, 1978, Hooky, Barney, Stephen and Ian were in the car, returning from their first-ever gig in London. It was a difficult ride on a cold night. The gig had gone poorly (some reports say the band's net profit was 60 pence after expenses) plus Barney had a bad case of the flu. About halfway back to Manchester, Ian started grabbing at Barney's sleeping bag. He then began to lash out, punching at the windows of the car. Stephen pulled over and there, on the side of the road, the band helped Ian ride out his first confirmed epileptic seizure.

When he was released from the hospital, Ian went to see his doctor who simply shrugged and placed him on a waiting list to see a specialist. Meanwhile, the seizures continued, coming more frequently, sometimes up to four times a week. When he finally saw his specialist, Ian began to try a series of prescriptions for anti-convulsive drugs. But while some of the drugs helped control his seizures, he was unable to eliminate them entirely; in fact, some made his mood swings even more pronounced. Those

---

1. Most of the problems seemed to have resulted from a poorly-worded contract with the label. Apparently, some of the conditions of the agreement — which was modeled on a typical American recording contract — would not have stood up under UK law. This was further complicated by RCA's unwillingness to give the band any advance nor would they budge on their meagre royalty offer. Unable to reach a compromise on money and the wording of the contract, the deal was formally scrapped and the album was killed. The eleven tracks from that short series of sessions soon turned up on a bootleg called Warsaw.

2. Wilson's Russell Club was renamed The Factory for Friday nights. The first "Factory night" was May 27, 1978. The poster proclaiming the night (designed but never distributed because of printing problems) was named FAC 1, thereby beginning the tradition of cataloguing every single Factory project — no matter how big or small — as if it were a record. For example, when New Order opened the Hacienda nightclub, it was officially known as FAC 51.

around him began to wonder what was making him more unhappy, the epilepsy or the anti-epileptic medication.

Then there was the matter of Ian's dancing. When Joy Division played live, Ian would often disappear into a trance of herky-jerky, arrhythmic moves. To the uninitiated, he looked like a marionette being electrocuted. After a while, it was literally impossible to tell if he was dancing or enduring another seizure.

As his conditioned worsened, Ian's lyrics and poetry had grown darker, more gloomy and more depressing.[3] When these lyrics were mated to music, it was inevitable that Joy Division's sound became more somber and minor key. There was, however, a sizable audience for this approach. Joy Division gigs were getting quite crowded as more people began to hear about this somber, aloof band that often performed in the shadows of a deliberately poorly lit stage. Unlike their punk contemporaries, the members of Joy Division favored short, simple haircuts and dressed in black, gray, brown and dark green. After Ian appeared on the cover of the NME wearing a dark raincoat in January 1979, die-hard fans began turning up to shows dress in the same kind of coat, proudly displaying a series of metal Joy Division badges on the lapels. After a powerful appearance on John Peel's BBC radio show on Valentine's Day 1979, word was that this depressing band from Manchester was on its way to doing something significant.

In April 1979, the band booked three weeks at Strawberry Studios with producer Martin Hannett. He had been watching the band from a distance for quite some time and was actually quite eager to work with them. The sessions were stormy affairs with Hannett forcing the group to bend to his vision of Joy Division. On the third day of recording, upset with Stephen's inability to come up with a distinctive drum sound, Hannett ordered him to strip his kit down to the last lug nut and rebuild it from scratch. Once he had the drum sound he wanted (a hollow, ghostly beat treated with delay and echo), he cut away the band's rock leanings, leaving behind stark, minimalist, naked arrangements. Using all his psychological studio tricks, Hannett had the band record standing close together with the lights down low in order to enhance the somber mood of the lyrics and music.

The recordings that resulted were, frankly, substantially different from how the band had envisioned them. To those on the outside, the finished product was a lo-fi masterpiece.[4] It wasn't punk, nor could it be slotted with the growing power pop / New Wave scene. Loaded with atmosphere, urgency and a sense of desperation, UNKNOWN PLEASURES was very, very different from any other album from 1979.

Tony Wilson was thrilled with the results — so much so that he put up everything Factory Records had (£8,500) to press 10,000 copies. When it was released in the second week of June 1979, the music press fell over themselves trying to come up with adjectives for the sound of the album: brooding, mournful, eerie, dark, depressing, frightening, intense, painful. Drums and keyboards seem to have been treated as lead instruments, guitars and keyboards were used mainly as accents. The album reeked with genuine grief and gloom.

Even the cover art was singled out as something special. Designed by Peter Saville, the sleeve was all black with a tiny amount of text on the back in small white letters — the name of the band, the title of the album and the Factory Records name. On the front was what looked like a sketch of a mountain range. It was, in fact, the scream of a dying star — a graphical representation of one hundred consecutive pulses from Pulsar CP 1919, the object found in the center of the Dumb Bell Nebula in the constellation Vulpecula. Inside, there were hardly any liner notes nor were the songs listed anywhere on the label. And if you looked closely, you might be able to discern some strange messages scratched into the run-off grooves. (For example, the message scratched into the grooves of the 12-inch for She's Lost Control reads "Here are the young men / But where have they been?") No punk record had ever looked like this.

UNKNOWN PLEASURES (FACT 10, released in June 1979) became a huge underground hit in the summer of 1979, with that initial pressing of 10,000 copies selling out almost immediately. The record was especially popular at home in Manchester during that awful summer. The economy was bad, unemployment was high and, to make matters worse, the city's sewer system collapsed, spreading a

---

3. Ian carried a plastic bag full of notebooks wherever he went. When the mood struck him, he'd set down and write. As both the epilepsy and the medication took hold, Ian's minor key scribblings increased.
4. Very low-fi. If you listen carefully, you can hear the strainer on Morris' snare buzz whenever Hooky hits his bass. This sort of noise is almost never tolerated on a recording, even today.

stench throughout the streets. Joy Division had managed to articulate the mood of their city and their fans.

Despite this commercial and critical success, Ian was descending deeper into his private hell. When his daughter, Natalie, was born on April 16, 1979, Ian was as proud and thrilled as any new father could be. But as his epilepsy became more severe, he became more afraid of picking her up or even touching her for fear that she might be hurt during one of his unpredictable seizures. His depression deepened.

As Joy Division's popularity increased, the more gigs they played. The harder they worked, the worse and more frequent the attacks became. After a particularly arduous stretch of shows in May 1979, Ian suffered four *grand mal* seizures in one night. When his mood swings became even more erratic, he and Deborah went back to the doctor. He wasn't much help at all. After leaving his office, they had a feeling that the doctor was himself a little disturbed. That bit of intuition turned out to be correct. He shot himself several weeks later.

Exhausted and depressed by his condition, Ian became more withdrawn and difficult over the ensuing months. Although it was indisputable that the seizures were coming more frequently, Ian was now known to fake a convulsion or two as a way of manipulating those around him. He was also mixing his prescriptions with a lot of illegal drugs and alcohol. Deborah was justifiably concerned with her husband's behavior. She was also a little suspicious of the relatively new and unwritten Joy Division rule that wives and girlfriends were no longer welcome at gigs.

Ian was, in fact, playing around. At a show in Brussels, Belgium, at a club called Plan K on October 16, 1979, Ian met Annik Honoré. Before long, they were engaged in a full-blown affair. Telling Deborah he was off to a soccer match or down to the pub for a pint, he would instead rendezvous with Annik. Meanwhile, money was getting tighter and tighter around the house. Finances deteriorated to the point where the family could no longer afford to keep their dog. As 1980 rolled around, it was obvious that the marriage was on the rocks.

In March 1980, Joy Division began sessions for a new album called CLOSER with producer Martin Hannett. Once they were finished, the group embarked on a grueling series of gigs, sometimes playing two shows in two cities on the same day. And the more the band played, the more ill Ian became. The pressures and obligations were mounting — the album, a couple of singles, the UK tour, a planned North American tour, his failing marriage, his continuing relationship with Annik Honoré, his drug use, the late nights, the epilepsy. Something was bound to give.

During a show in London on April 4, 1980, Ian suffered three attacks during the first five songs of the set before collapsing entirely. The band might have stopped playing sooner, but it had become impossible to tell whether Ian was having a seizure or just dancing in his trademark jerky manner. While opening for the Stranglers on April 6, the erratic electricity of Ian's brain once again sent his body into convulsions. Depressed and angry, Ian overdosed on his medication (phenobarbitone) on purpose, but had his stomach pumped before any damage was done. Although this was clearly a suicide attempt — Ian had reportedly left a note — the psychiatrist at the hospital concluded that Ian wasn't suicidal and, incredibly, after being admitted overnight, he was driven directly to the next gig at Derby Hall in Bury, Lancashire.

That was a mistake. The Bury crowd was loaded with Joy Division faithful, many of who had come a long way to see their heroes. After an obviously exhausted Ian appeared to sing just two songs, the audience became surly and a riot broke out. Five people (including one of the band's roadies) had to be taken to the emergency ward. The incident only fed Ian's depression. Desperately trying to help, Barney tried to hypnotize Ian (Barney is apparently a pretty fair hypnotist) and after a little probing evidently discovered that in a previous life, Ian had once been a very old man who had spent a long time on his deathbed.

The final Joy Division concert was on May 2, 1980, at Birmingham University. During the last song in the set (a new track called Decades), Ian suffered another major seizure and collapsed. Although he was helped from the stage, he was able to return for an encore.[1]

At this point, the best thing for Ian would have been a three month stay in the hospital, but instead Factory pushed ahead with plans for a North American tour. To make sure Ian remained as healthy as

---

1. This event is captured on Still (FACT 40, released in October 1981.)

possible, Tony Wilson hired a minder for Ian, someone to make sure that he took his medication and stayed away from all the temptations of the road. Everyone was given two weeks off and told that they were to be on a plane on May 19ᵗʰ. This, Factory believed, was the tour that was going to make Joy Division one of the biggest bands in the world.

During those two weeks, things went from bad to worse for Ian and Deborah. He moved out, eventually ending up at his parents' place while she moved towards filing for divorce. Annik Honoré was still on the scene and although she wanted to spend more time with Ian, she had a hard time coping with his illness. All this battered Ian's psyche even further, driving him deeper into depression.

On Thursday, May 15, Ian hung out with Peter Hook, playing pool in a local pub. The following day, Peter dropped Ian off at his parents' house

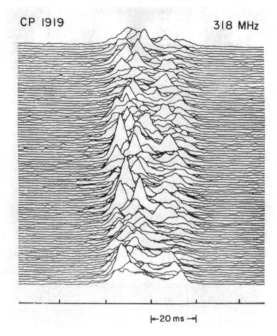

CP 1919   318 MHz

|←20 ms →|

The basis of the artwork for Unknown Pleasure

with instructions to start packing for the tour that was scheduled to leave on Monday. On Saturday the 17ᵗʰ, Ian called Barney saying that he wasn't going to come over that night because there was a movie on TV that he wanted to see. That was one of the last times anyone heard from Ian Curtis.

That Saturday night, Ian went back to his house at 77 Barton Street. Deborah was on her way out to work as a bartender at a wedding reception, but before she left, Ian told her that he needed some time alone and made her promise not to come home until after 10 the following morning. Exasperated and not wanting to fight anymore, she agreed to spend the night at her parents' house.

Once she was gone, Ian sat down to watch his movie, a 1977 film entitled *Stroszek* about a musician and former mental patient who travels to the US and is unable to decide between the two women in his life. During the movie, he drank several cups of very strong coffee, chasing it all down with a shot of whiskey. Then, with pictures of his wife and daughter sitting on the table in front of him, Ian began to write a very long note to Deborah. He wrote until sunrise, finishing with "At this moment, I just wish I were dead. I just can't cope anymore." It was the morning of Sunday, May 18ᵗʰ.

Ian put down his pen, went over to the stereo and put on his favorite album, THE IDIOT by Iggy Pop. He then retrieved a big clothesline from the garden. As the sun came up and Iggy Pop sang, Ian hanged himself. Deborah found him a few hours later, the needle still scratching on the turntable.

An inquest was held and the official verdict was asphyxia with ligature around the neck. His body was cremated on May 23ʳᵈ, and it was Deborah who selected the inscription for Ian's headstone. It reads "Ian Curtis 18-5-80 Love Will Tear Us Apart."[2]

The transformation into legend began immediately. To many, Ian Curtis' suicide was seen in a tragic, romantic light — the last, desperate gesture of a tortured artist. Comparisons abounded with the deaths of poet John Keats and painter Jackson Pollock. With 20/20 hindsight, lyrics of older songs were scoured for meaning and much was made of the eerie prescience of the new single *Love Will Tear Us Apart* (FAC 23, released on June 28, 1980.) When CLOSER was finally released in June (FACT 25), fans and critics examined songs like *Isolation* and then wondered why no one had seen it coming. The mystique had

---

2. The Macclesfield Crematorium on Prestbury Road sees many Joy Divison fans every year who come to pay their respects.

become myth.

To be continued . . .

Ian Curtis' tombstone:
"LOVE WILL TEAR US APART"

Fast Facts

o As a child, Peter Hook lived in Jamaica where his stepfather held a job with a glass company.

o Barney grew up never knowing his real father. Living with his mother and grandparents in Salford, he originally used the surname Sumner, which was his mother's maiden name. When she remarried, he adopted Dicken, his stepfather's name. For a period of time, he wished to be known as Bernard Albrecht, although the reasons for that remain private and thus unknown. When New Order was formed, Barney once again went back to being a Sumner.

o There's a long-lost, unfinished Joy Division cover of a Northern Soul track. In 1978, they attempted to record N.F. Porter's *Keep On Keepin' On*, but gave up after three days in the studio.

o *She's Lost Control* was apparently inspired by the time Ian Curtis witnessed a woman suffer an epileptic seizure.

o Strawberry Studios no longer exits. Owner Nick Turnbull closed the place in 1991 to concentrate on making music videos.

Recommended Listening

o UNKNOWN PLEASURES (Factory, 1979)

o CLOSER (Factory, 1980)

o STILL (Factory, 1981)

o There are several collections that offer an overview of the band's short career. A good first choice is SUBSTANCE (Qwest, 1988.) You may wish to follow that up with PERMANENT: JOY DIVISION 1995 (Qwest 1995), although there will be some inevitable overlap. A more complete collection is the four-CD HEART AND SOUL box. It still leaves some gaps and the liner notes are mostly incoherent drivel, but the sound quality is excellent. Beware the mistakes in the annotations and song sequences.

o For a genuine live experience, the only full-length legal release is FRACTURED MUSIC ARCHIVE PRESTON (Factory Too, 1999.) Recorded at The Warehouse in Preston on February 28, 1980, this is the full gig, complete with technical breakdowns and noise from a surly crowd. A fine Joy Division artifact.

Internet Resources

o www.worldinmotion.net/joydivision.htm

o www.angelfire.com/vt/jejune/joy.html

o www.magnix.demon.nl/jd.htm

o www.warren.org.uk/music/joyd_frames.html

o www.geocities.com/SoHo/Bistro/3907/joyd_english.html

Manchester Music Links

o http://webgate.poptel.org.uk/mar.tin/music.htm

Recommended Reading

o Curtis, Deborah. *Touching from a Distance: Ian Curtis and Joy Division*. London: Faber and Faber, 1995.
o Edge, Brian. *New Order + Joy Division: Pleasures and Wayward Distractions*. London: Omnibus Press, 1988.
o Middles, Mick. *From Joy Division to New Order: The Factory Story*. London: Virgin Books, 1996.
o Suatoni, Alfredo. *Joy Division: From the Centre of the City*. Rome (?): Stampa, date unknown.

Related Listening
    The Cure, Bauhaus, Sister of Mercy, Birthday Party, Nick Cave, The Mission UK, Nine Inch Nails, Marilyn Manson.
The Story Thus Far ...
    A Sex Pistols concert springs the earlier incarnation of Joy Division together. Together with Martin Hannett, they creates a unique post-punk sound that provides inspiration for everything from goth and industrial music to lo-fi indie rock.

THE 1980's

~ 11 ~
NEW ORDER
Band of Substance

Long before Ian Curtis' death, the members of Joy Division had formed an odd suicide pact — should any member leave for any reason, Joy Division would be broken up. Once Ian died, Hooky, Barney and Stephen kept their word.

Conventional wisdom said that they were faced with three choices: (1) They could retire from music, dedicating their time to preserving the myth, in the same way that the Doors have done since the death of Jim Morrison; (2) They could try to find a new singer and launch a new band under a different name; or (3) they could do what Led Zeppelin did after John Bonham died and break up for good. In the end, the surviving members of Joy Division chose none of those options. Instead, they decided to regroup and start from scratch.

A month after Ian died, there were short, tentative rehearsals. With no singer, no name and no real direction, they weren't really sure where things were headed. Using the moniker the No Names, the trio made a surprise appearance at the Beach Club in Manchester on July 29. Running through a series of instrumental pieces, the gig went well enough. In September, they played four shows in the US at venues that were supposed to have hosted Joy Division that spring. Again, things went well.

Meanwhile, they had come up with a name. While manager Rob Gretton was watching a TV documentary on Cambodia (then called Kampuchea) and Khmer Rouge leader Pol Pot, he remembered an article from the Manchester *Guardian* on Prince Sihanouk's new anti-Pot military unit called The New Order. The named admittedly sounded a little too Nazi-esque, a little too fascist — but it undoubtedly conveyed the message that this new group was a reorganization of the old. It truly was a "new order."[1] And there was one more thing — in this spirit of rebirth, Barney changed his last name yet again, going from Barney

---

1. As pointed out earlier in this book, the name New Order had already been used by Ron Asheton upon the breakup of the Stooges. Chances are that the Manchester band had never heard of his group. Other names thrown about for this post-Joy Division project included The Eternal, Stevie [Morris] and the JDs, and the Sunshine Valley Dance Band (the name of one of Morris' pre-Joy Division outfits.)

Albrecht to Barney Sumner.

The next job was to find a singer. Barney, Hooky and Stephen each took turns at the microphone, singing and playing at the same time seemed to be a bit much. Out of the three, though, Barney seemed to be the best, so he'd would just have to learn how to play and sing at the same time.[1]

To make things a little easier, and to fill in a few gaps in the new band's sound, Rob Gretton suggested that the group hire keyboardist Gillian Gilbert (born January 27, 1961), a friend and fan from Peel Green near Macclesfield. The group had known Gillian since 1978 and her days with an all-girl punk band called the Inadequates (they used to rehearse next door to Joy Division.) Somehow knowing that Gillian's style could be molded into whatever shape New Order required, she was offered the job — but only after she proved that she was up for the part by successfully playing Jingle Bells at the piano. Evidently passing the audition with flying colors, she left the graphic design course she had been talking at Stockport Technical College and joined the group. After rehearsing in a drafty rented farmhouse on the outskirts of town, Gillian's first gig with the band was on October 25, 1980, at the Squat Club in Manchester.

Ceremony, the first New Order single (FAC 33), was released was a 7-inch in January 1981. The song had been around for quite some time and even existed in demo form before it was re-recorded after Gillian joined the band. This first foray back onto the charts was reasonably successful — the song peaked at No. 34 in the UK.

Everyone trooped back to Strawberry Studios in April to begin two weeks of work on what would become the first New Order album. Martin Hannett was once again at the helm and as the sessions progressed, it became very apparent that even after discounting the effect of a new leader singer, New Order was going to sound very different from Joy Division. It was a learning ordeal for everyone, including Hannett who soon decided that it would perhaps be best if the group produced themselves. With that, he excused himself from the proceedings.

Following those recording sessions, the band embarked on a series of small tours and TV appearances throughout the summer before releasing Procession backed with Everything's Gone Green (FAC 53) in September 1981. That was followed by MOVEMENT (FACT 50), New Order's debut album, which was released in November. Although most reviews were tepid, the album did manage to climb into the Top 30 on the UK charts.

Most of 1982 was spent working out the bugs in the band's sound. As they messed about with new keyboards and sequencers, New Order found that this new technology was leading them in a more danceable direction. The band was delighted to learn that by pressing a few buttons they could create all kinds of new and interesting sounds, all without having to be brilliant musicians. A single, Temptation (FAC 63, April 1982) was reasonably well received, as was an EP of UK and Belgian singles entitled NEW ORDER 1981-1982 (FACTUS 8, November 1982.) Still, people weren't exactly stampeding to the record stores, demanding the next New Order release. And here's where we run into one of those strange quirks of fate, an innocent act that somehow ends up changing the course of music history — the real story behind Blue Monday.

In 1981, after building a few drum machines from do-it-yourself kits, Stephen began messing around with a series of rhythms that eventually became known as Prime Time 586. Over the next few months, its title was shortened to 586 and was used to set the atmosphere for the gala grand opening of the Hacienda on May 21, 1982, Factory's foray into the world of nightclubs.[2] Stephen continued to experiment with the track and eventually came up with an idea of how the band could avoid doing encores.

New Order hated doing encores. Using Stephen's pre-programmed drum machine rhythms as a base, the band began to layer sequence after sequence on top: keyboards, a bass line, a little guitar. The goal was to simply be able to switch on all the machines and let them run, allowing the band to get backstage before the audience realized they were gone. But before they realized it, they had the foundations for a brand new song that sounded far removed from anything Joy Division had ever written. Legend has it that before New Order took this idea into the studio in October 1982, every member dropped a tab

1. This is key to understanding New Order's musical future arrangements. Because he found it difficult to sing and play at the same time, Barney would stop playing his guitar when a vocal part came up, leaving it to Hooky and Stephen (and later, Gillian) to carry the song forward. Songs were often written with that in mind, resulting in a more propulsive, rhythm-heavy sound.
2. 586 was also featured on John Peel's show in June 1982. It ended up being included on POWER, CORRUPTION AND LIES.

of LSD. They somehow managed to get all the basic tracks down, but they were so wasted that once they were done, the studio engineers sent them to a café across the street so they could finish mixing the song in peace.

When the song was released on March 9, 1983, as FAC 73 (backed with The Beach), Blue Monday had an immediate and startling effect. Released only as an eight minute 12-inch (there were never any plans to release an edited 7-inch version — a move that some predicted would be commercial suicide), the song took off, selling 250,000 copies immediately. Although the record received some radio airplay, its real impact was felt in the dance clubs. At the time, people were dancing to songs like Physical by Olivia Newton-John and I Love Rock and Roll by Joan Jett. To club patrons, the sudden appearance of a powerful dance track like Blue Monday must have been overwhelming. This 12-inch single forged all sorts of new links between the indie scene, the lightweight techno-pop sound, mainstream rock and dance music. For many people, Blue Monday was the song that made dancing cool again. The single went on to sell over three million copies and will probably be forever known as the best-selling 12-inch single of all time.[3]

The release of Blue Monday set the stage for a profitable couple of years. The group's second full album, the synth-heavy POWER, CORRUPTION AND LIES (FACT 75, May 1983) reached No. 4 in the UK. Thieves Like Us (FAC 103, March 1984) was another Top 20 UK hit. Meanwhile, American super-producer (and Michael Jackson's best friend) Quincy Jones was so impressed with what the band was doing that he signed New Order to his personal record label in February 1985. It wasn't long before America was finally getting domestic versions of New Order releases. LOW-LIFE (FACT 100) was issued in May 1985, the same day as The Perfect Kiss, the album's first single. Both did extremely well on the UK charts and in dance clubs around the world.

People were also noticing the improvement in Barney's singing voice, although it was generally acknowledged that he would never become a great vocalist. But that somehow was part of New Order's charm. Even though he could only manage the simplest of melody lines, his singing floated atop an incredibly complex computerized wall of sound. It was important combination — it had a good beat, and just about anyone could sing along while dancing.

More releases followed. BROTHERHOOD (FACT 150) was issued in September 1986 and featured Bizarre Love Triangle (originally released as FAC 163 in the UK, there were a myriad of others around the world), the band's most enduring hit since Blue Monday. Even more important was the two-disc SUBSTANCE 1987 (FACT 200, August 1987), a collection of New Order's greatest 12-inch releases, a re-recording of Ceremony and True Faith, another huge worldwide dance club hit.[4] The collection sold close to 400,000 copies in Britain alone and was one of the few albums to ever be released to the public on prerecorded DAT tape. (The collection wasn't certified platinum in the US until January 18, 1991.)

After a two year break, New Order came back with TECHNIQUE (FACT 275, January 1989), an album that debuted at No. 1 in Britain. The previous month, the group had a hit with Fine Time, (FAC 223, December 1988) which reached No. 11 in the UK.[5] After a long bout of touring, New Order won the right to record the official theme song for the 1990 English World Cup team.[6] Despite the fact that the single didn't say much about soccer, the song went to No. 1 in the UK and became an especially popular track in gay dance clubs.

Meanwhile, things were not going so well at Factory headquarters. Debts were piling up — bad real estate investments, problems with the Hacienda and large recording studio bills were threatening to sink the entire organization. The situation was made worse by the late delivery of New Order's next album

---

3. Incredibly, New Order and Factory lost money on Blue Monday. Because the production and distribution costs of the single were so high (a serious Factory business faux pas), New Order actually lost about £30,000 by issuing the world's favorite dance record.

4. True Faith was produced by Stephen Hague and was accompanied by a surrealistic video directed by John Baptiste Mondino.

5. Fine Time was not a band favorite. All four members considered it to be akin to a novelty song. Manager Rob Gretton disagreed and bet the band £250 that it would make the Top Ten. He lost. When the follow-up, Round and Round (FAC 263) was issued, Tony Wilson put his position with Factory on the line with Gretton, saying that it was a definite Top 5 hit. He lost and temporarily resigned.

6. World in Motion (FAC 293, May 1990) was issued under the name England New Order. Written by the band and comedian / actor Keith Allen, the song featured a rap by soccer star John Barnes. The rhythm track was taken from a Morris / Gilbert composition originally destined to be a TV theme for a show called Reportage. The BBC didn't think much of the song and ended up substituting a Luciano Pavarotti aria for their World Cup coverage.

(which cost a reported £430,000 to record) and by the huge bills resulting from the Happy Mondays' recording stint in Barbados (£380,000.) On November 24, 1992, it all finally fell apart. With more than £2 million in outstanding bills, Factory declared bankruptcy. Bits of the Factory empire were picked off by other labels and New Order ended up with London in the UK. They issued REPUBLIC in May 1993.

Once REPUBLIC and its subsequent tour ran their course, New Order dropped from sight. Barney drifted away to devote more time on Electronic, a side project he had developed with ex-Smiths guitarist Johnny Marr. Peter Hook formed Revenge (the band bombed) and then Monaco (they were a hit.) Meanwhile, he went through an extremely messy and expensive divorce with his wife, Caroline. Gillian and Stephen remain together (they're now married) and released material under the name The Other Two. By late 1996, the assumption was that New Order was finished.

But not so fast. On February 16, 1998, the BBC reported that New Order was reforming to headline a UK summer festival. Sure enough, the group made their first live appearance in five years at the Manchester Apollo on July 16th. Five days later, they played Reading Festival. That was followed up with a show at Manchester G-Mex on December 29th. As of mid-1999, reports indicated that New Order was back together working on a new album for release in 2000. Two planned boxed sets entitled RECYCLE (each featuring eleven CD's for a mind-boggling total of twenty-two!) have apparently been indefinitely postponed for financial reasons.

Whatever the future may hold, Joy Division and New Order both left an indelible stamp on the psyche of alt-rock. Joy Division's dark, brooding cry of desperation was an essential element for variety of post-punk genres, ranging from goth and grunge to industrial and techno. Casting aside the darkness, New Order's highly mechanized post-modernist, post-disco approach became the blueprint for a whole new style of danceable rock (ranging from U2 and Primal Scream to the Pet Shop Boys and the Prodigy), making them one of the most important synth-based pop bands of all time. The fact that three musicians could make that much difference in two completely separate areas of the musical spectrum may never be duplicated. Think of it this way: how many times can one person win the lottery and then be struck by lightning on the way home with the cheque?

Fast Facts

o There are many theories on the inspiration for *Blue Monday*. One is that the Monday in question was May 19, 1980, the day after Ian Curtis committed suicide. Another suggestion (often trotted out by Rob Gretton) was that the song is about a series of student suicides that occurred in Sweden in the 1950's. According to this story, six very depressed students took their own lives after listening to *Blue Monday* by Fats Domino. Others suggest the song is somehow related to the work and subsequent suicide of Hungarian author Arthur Koestler. That, however, is unlikely — his death was reported on March 3, 1983, just six days before *Blue Monday* was released. The song had already been recorded.

- Legend has it that due to some superstition, *Blue Monday* has never been played at the Hacienda.

- Fellow Mancunians the Happy Mondays chose their name as a counterpoint to *Blue Monday*.

- During the *Blue Monday* era, each member of New Order agreed to a financial plan whereby everyone was paid a salary of £70 a week. Any profits were reinvested in new equipment. At one point, money was so tight that Hooky was restricted to spending £2 a week on gas for his car.

New Order (left to right): Peter Hook, Stephen Morris, Bernard Sumner, Gillian Gilbert.

- The Hacienda (FAC 51, 11-13 Whitworth Street) was a former yacht showroom. It was joined by a more upscale bar called Dry 201 (FAC 201, 28 Oldham Street) designed for the day crowd. Liam Gallagher has been tossed out many times.

- Although they were involved in the ownership structure of the Hacienda (they liked the idea of a nightclub where local bands could perform), New Order soon ran into disagreements with Factory on how the place should be run. When there was a dispute over whether to invest in an expensive studio keyboard (a Fairlight) or the club, a long-running — and ultimately fatal — schism developed over finances.

- Despite the disagreements, the Hacienda transformed night life in Manchester. It became the physical and spiritual birthplace for many different sounds and groups, including the rave scene (think Happy Mondays and Primal Scream) and "Madchester" (Stone Roses, Charlatans, et al.) The club has also hosted shows by Grandmaster Flash, the Smiths and Madonna.

- There was much controversy when the Hacienda was temporarily forced to close in 1991 after a 16 year-old died after taking Ecstasy. More problems erupted when an alleged drug dealer pulled a machine gun when told to take his business elsewhere. The Hacienda has remained vacant since mid-1997 because of a crushing debt load of more than £500,000. On June 5, 1999, more than a thousand people clashed with police after squatters took over the abandoned building and started a party. At last word, the building's owners are considering an offer to transform the site into luxury condominiums.

- SUBSTANCE 1987 is New Order's largest-selling album. The rarest must be the flexi-disc given out at the Hacienda on Christmas Eve 1982. Side one features *Rocking Carol*, while the B-side is New Order's version of *Ode to Joy*.

- Both Joy Division and New Order were known for their innovative sleeve designs, thanks to artist Peter Saville. *Blue Monday* was originally released in an expensive sleeve shaped to look like a floppy disc. A more mysterious design appeared in 1983. Using the color wheel that appears with POWER, CORRUPTION AND LIES, it's possible to decode a number of secret messages. For instructions on the use of the color wheel, see www.niagara.edu/~rpk/Factory/faq96.html

- Sunkist wanted to pay New Order £100,000 to turn *Blue Monday* into an orange juice commercial. Barney went as far as recording some new lyrics for the ad ("How does it feel / When you're drinking in the sun / All you've got to believe / Sunkist is the one".) Manager Rob Gretton vetoed the idea and the spot never aired. However, some of the new lyrics turned up in a Steve "Silk" Hurley remix of the song.

- Tony Wilson has made a second foray into the record business after the financial debacle of Factory. In 1994, he started Factory Too.

- Producer Martin Hannett died of apparent heart failure on April 18, 1991. Manager Rob Gretton died of a heart attack at his home on May 15, 1999.

Recommended Listening

o POWER, CORRUPTION AND LIES (Factory, 1983)

o BROTHERHOOD (Factor, 1986)

o TECHNIQUE (Factory / Qwest, 1989)

o BBC RADIO 1 LIVE IN CONCERT (Windsong, 1992)

o *Touched by the Hand of God* (Single release, FAC 193, December 1987. Stick with the 12-inch mix; the 7-inch edit is vastly inferior.)

o *World in Motion* (Single release, FAC 293, May 1990.)

o The best collection (as of the end of 1999 and pending the release of any long-promised box sets) remains the double CD set, SUBSTANCE 1987 (Factory, 1987.) Beware some of the strange twists included on (THE BEST OF) NEW ORDER (Qwest, 1995.) Side projects include ELECTRONIC (Sumner), REVENGE, MONACO (Hook), THE OTHER TWO (Morris and Gilbert.)

Internet Resources

o http://slashmc.rice.edu/ceremony/neworder/no_disc/nodisc.html

o http://welcome.to/neworder

o www.waterrat.com/neworder.htm

Manchester Music Links

o http://webgate.poptel.org.uk/mar.tin/music.htm

Recommended Reading

o Edge, Brian. *New Order + Joy Division: Pleasures and Wayward Distractions.* London: Omnibus Press, 1988.

o Middles, Mick. *From Joy Division to New Order: The Factory Story.* London: Virgin Books, 1996.

Related Listening

The Stone Roses, Happy Mondays, Underworld, the Prodigy, Moby

The Story Thus Far ...

While maintaining some of Joy Division's bleak visions, New Order adds some Kraftwerk-ish electronics to bridge the gap between post-punk music and dance.

~ 12 ~
U2
Four Hearts Beat as One

There's a well-defined pecking order among performers. First, there's your basic unsigned indie band. They play a lot of clubs and parties and may even have scraped together enough money to put out one or two records. Next are the groups who have a major label contract. Although most of the members have probably quit their day jobs, the truth is that they sell just enough records to stay afloat. The third level consists of genuinely successful groups, bands with gold and platinum albums. Their music careers have turned into well-paying jobs, with all the rights, privileges and perks pertaining there. In the press and among fans, they are often referred to as "stars" and even "superstars." In other words, these bands have *made* it.

There is, however, another level beyond "superstar." In the upper reaches of celebritydom, there are performers whose albums sell in the tens of millions. Not only are they rich beyond their wildest dreams, but everything they touch creates an enormous trickle-down effect. While many profit from the albums and concert tickets they sell, thousands (perhaps even tens of thousands) of ordinary people benefit from the fallout of their investments in real estate and the stock market. They're so huge that national governments begin to depend on the tax revenue these groups generate for the economy. In fact, their gigantic profits may even have an impact on the country's GDP. These bands are far beyond being mere superstars — they're industries.

U2 is such an industry. Record sales are approaching 100 million units. Gross revenues have been tallied at $1.5 billion. Estimates of the group's net worth range from $250 to $500 million. U2's actions have even been known to affect the stock price of their record label. Through their entertainment and real estate ventures, their organization provides employment for hundreds of people.

But, unlike your normal run-of-the-mill faceless multinational, U2 has a conscience. They're fiercely loyal to their hometown, reinvesting some of their enormous profits into various Dublin ventures, including the local arts scene. They contribute incredible amounts of time and money to charities, both big and small. They're politically active, railing against the injustices of governments and corporations. In fact, U2 has probably encouraged more people to think about political, social and human rights issues than any other rock group on the planet.

Underlying all this is the fact that U2 has accomplished everything with music. They've been very good at walking a series of fine lines: the line between good Christian values and bombastic preachiness; the line between constructive political dialogue and propaganda; the line between rock, punk and Irish folk; the line between genuine passion and cartoonish buffoonery; and the line between being ultra-superstars and four regular guys from Dublin. Commercially successful, critically acclaimed and highly influential, U2 remains one of the most important groups in the history of all of rock and roll.

It all began with a note on the bulletin board at Mount Temple Comprehensive School in Dublin in the fall of 1976. It was placed there by fifteen year old Larry Mullen (born October 31, 1961.) Having played the drums since he was nine in such prestigious outfits as the Post Office Worker's Band, Larry was finally going to form his own rock group. He'd already approached a student named Adam Clayton (born March 13, 1960) because Larry thought he was "cool looking." It also help that Adam already owned a bass guitar.

Several people responded to the notice. Dik Evans came by with his little brother, Dave, who brought a guitar that he had bought in a garage sale for £1. Peter Martin, one of Larry's friends, supplied a guitar and an amp. He was accompanied by guitarist Neil McCormick and an older, swaggering student named Paul Hewson.[1] Although he owned a guitar and boasted he could play like a pro, he was actually quite inept. Everyone eventually told him to put the thing down.

This, however, was when things started going right. Paul instinctively assumed command of the rehearsals, directing everyone else and somehow inspiring everyone to play better. He also started to sing along as the band struggled through their favorite Stones and Bowie tunes, bumping and grinding like some young Elvis. The others were impressed. Even without any formal vocal training, Paul's voice wasn't bad and he had a commanding presence. When it was all over, a vote was taken: Paul could stay providing he took the job as singer — and if he promised to leave his guitar at home. Out of the cacophony that reigned throughout those first rehearsals, the band found themselves a name, Feedback.

Operating as a quartet (Paul, Larry, Adam and Dave; Dik was unavailable at the time), Feedback made their first public appearance several weeks later, performing Peter Frampton's *Show Me the Way* as part of a ten minute set during a talent contest at school. By the time the group played their second show (this time as a quintet) at St. Fintan's School some time later, they had changed their name to the Hype.[2]

There were also two more name changes. As members of a new quasi-gang known as the Village (perhaps best described as a street gang crossed with *The Dead Poet's Society* and an escapist Gaelic study group), Paul and Dave had acquired new nicknames. Derek Rowen — Guggi to the guys in the Village — was the person who christened Paul. While walking together down O'Connell Street in Dublin, they came across a hearing aid shop across from the old Gresham Hotel. The store, at 13 North Earl Street, was called "Bonavox [sic] Hearing Aids." From that moment on, Guggi declared, Paul would forever been known as Bonovox (or, alternatively, Bono Vox) — Bono for short. Meanwhile, because of the apparent angular

---

1. For the uninitiated, Dave Evans (born August 8, 1961) soon became the Edge. Paul Hewson (born May 10, 1960) is now known as Bono. More on those names later. Peter Martin and Neil McCormick lasted just that one rehearsal. Although Martin's whereabouts are unknown, McCormick is now a music journalist.
2. There were two reasons for this. First of all, "hype" is what they wanted to stir up. Second, as huge Bowie fans, they thought it would be cool to name themselves after the backing band that came before the famed Spiders from Mars.

The Bonavox Hearing Aid Store, source of Paul Hewson's nickname.

shape of his skull, Dave Evans was renamed the Edge.

The Hype rehearsed as often as they could over the next year, usually in the Mullens' front room. When Adam was expelled from school, he threw all his energies into the band. He tried to learn all he could about equipment, sought advice on getting gigs and generally tried to spread the word on his new group. Adam's work slowly began to pay off as word of Hype began to spread. As far as anyone can remember, the Hype's first professional gig was played at a Dublin club called McGonagle's in early 1978. Opening for a band called Revolver, they spun through a short set that mainly featured Stranglers and Sex Pistols tunes.

On March 17, 1978, the Hype performed in a talent contest in Limerick that was sponsored by a beer company. After making it through the early rounds, the group's final three-song set won them the £500 first prize and an opportunity to record a demo for CBS Records. Although the session turned out poorly (CBS told them to come back and try again later in the year), the group was energized by the experience. Adam was especially jazzed and redoubled his efforts at making things happen.

Adam certain wasn't shy. He was fearless on the phone, once ringing up Thin Lizzy's Phil Lynott for advice on how to choose a manager. On another occasion, he called Steve Averill, singer of an Irish band called the Radiators, who just happened to work at an ad agency by day. Talking about the importance of finding the right name for the band, Averill suggested that the Hype may wish to consider going with "U2." It was short, snappy and had a vaguely political ring to it. Shortly after the group returned from Limerick (March 1978), the Hype played a show at the Howth Community Center. Midway through the show, Dik Evans bid everyone farewell, walked off the stage and out of the band forever. At that moment, the Hype became U2.

The next important step was to find a manager so that Adam could concentrate on making music with the rest of the group. His first attempt consisted of putting a fake ad in the classifieds of the NME. It read "Manager seeks the whereabouts of the Hype after an amazing gig. Please ring Brian. It was great, lads." Of course, there was no Brian, the phone number belonged to Adam. No one called.

The second attempt was much more successful. After badgering Hot Sounds writer Bill Graham, Adam was connected with his friend, Paul McGuinness, a person with some experience in band management.[1] Although he wasn't much into punk or New Wave, Adam convinced McGuinness to check out U2 when they played the Project Arts Center on May 25, 1978. After some reticence, McGuinness made the effort and was immediately impressed by what he saw — a young band of true friends, bound together by spirit, energy and honesty. The singer, he thought, was especially charismatic. Musically, they still needed work. Nevertheless, McGuinness felt that with time and effort, their ambitiousness would overcome their technical deficiencies. As the group continued to play in front of ever larger crowds at schools, youth centers and pubs like the Baggot Inn and the Moran Hotel, he was proven correct.

U2's first official release was U2:3, a three-track record that was issued as both a 7-inch and a 12-inch by the Irish division of CBS in September 1979. Production was limited to about a thousand individually numbered copies. Reaction was generally positive, especially to Out of Control, a song that Bono had written in honor of his eighteenth birthday. CBS also released a second Ireland-only single, Another Day, in February, 1980. However, when it came to commit to underwriting a full album, CBS decided to pass.

---

1. McGuinness' real experience lay in film and the production of TV commercials. His only previous foray into band management was with a folk outfit called Spud, a spin-off from Horslips. His agreement with U2 (which still stands today) allows him a 20% share in the group's net profits. All U2's money has always been evenly divided five ways.

So did EMI. It wasn't until U2 played an electric show at Dublin National Stadium in February 16, 1980, that Island Records agreed to take a chance on the band. One of the key parts of the contract (a world-wide, four year, four album deal) stated that U2 was to retain complete creative control over whatever they produced, right down to the finished artwork.

Over the next six months, Island issued three U2 singles: *11 O'Clock Tick Tock* (actually a re-working of an older song called *Silver Lining*, May 1980), *A Day Without Me* (August) and — on October 20, the same day as the group's debut album — *I Will Follow*.[2]

U2, circa 1984

BOY did nothing for about three weeks. Doubts began to set it as U2 began to wonder if they had miscalculated their popularity. Paul McGuinness, however, was not to be denied. He booked the band on a quick tour of the UK, Europe and North America, forcing U2 to take their music to the fans. Spurred by this tour, *I Will Follow* started appearing on the radio in Europe in November and December and in North America in March 1981. Once it began to get airplay, reaction was swift. Although the song contained just two chords, the sharpness of the guitar and bashing of the drums made it stand out from the lightweight post-punk / New Wave / insipid pop that was being heard at the turn of the decade.[3] Those who heard it immediately realized that U2 was somehow different, a fresh approach to the standard guitar-bass-drums lineup. Some suggested that they sounded like a more optimistic version of the Clash.

The group spent 1981 playing in front of larger and larger crowds as casual listeners were turned into fans by the group's seemingly inexhaustible passion and idealism. Plans were made to start work on a second album as soon as possible in order to capitalize on this wave of popularity.

Then disaster struck after a gig at the Fog Horn in Portland, Oregon on March 22, 1981. After the show, three young girls made it backstage to talk to the band. They hung out for about an hour and then left. They also stole Bono's briefcase. Inside was $300 cash — and all of Bono's lyrics for the next album. Twelve months of inspiration and work walked out the door in that briefcase.

This was a serious crisis. U2 was committed to going into the studio to record the next album in just twelve weeks. Bono was frantic. It had taken him three years to write all the lyrics for BOY and he a solid years' work had just disappeared. When they got back to Dublin, producer Steve Lillywhite was sympathetic but firm. "You can write a song in five minutes," he said, "Do your job."

---

2. Some of these singles were released in Ireland on CBS. The group then became the exclusive property of Island.

3. *I Will Follow* is another example of how technical naiveté can lead to wonderfully inventive playing. At the band's inception, the Edge was never very good at playing chords. His tendency towards piercing lead lines and arpeggio figures stems from this long, productive battle between imagination and technical limitations.

So it came to pass that a confused, angry and desperate Bono was forced to improvise many of the words to the new songs on the spot. One track was inspired by an album of Gregorian chants that Paul McGuinness always seemed to have on. With the help of his friend Jeremy and one of his old high school teachers, Bono worked out a few Latin phrases and hurriedly came up with the words to *Gloria*, the first big single from OCTOBER. (*Gloria* was released in September 1981. OCTOBER followed on, appropriately, the 21st of October.)

Once the album was out, U2 hit the road again for an extended tour. Audiences continued to get bigger and Bono became more impassioned with each passing performance. Words spread of this young Irish singer who would seemingly do anything to get the crowd going: stage diving, climbing the PA stacks and the lighting grid, running all over the stage and through the audience. His enthusiasm seemed boundless. The resulting feedback was good for the band, too.

A third album was written during that ten-month road trip in 1982. WAR was issued on February 25, 1983. It was a mature and confident record, full of political and social comment. One of the big songs from the album was *New Year's Day*, the sixth or seventh song written for the project (released in January 1983, prior to the album.) Adam Clayton came up with the bass line during a sound check. It was then mated to a simple piano line that the Edge had invented in the studio. Once they had the basic structure of the song, it became Bono's job to come up with some appropriate lyrics. Try as he might, he had real problems crystallizing what he wanted to say — he had all these images in his head, but he couldn't find the words to describe them. After dozens of attempts at improvising the lyrics in the studio, U2 actually considered leaving the song off the album. In the end, Bono decided to wing it one more time, treating it — believe it or not — as a love song to his wife.

Another strong track dealt with the events of Sunday, January 30, 1972. During a civil rights march in Londonderry, Northern Ireland, members of a British army unit opened fire and killed fourteen unarmed people. One of the enduring TV images of that day was a Catholic bishop waving a white handkerchief as a flag of surrender as he crawled towards the dead and injured. When Bono wrote the words for *Sunday Bloody Sunday*, he made sure that it was clear he wasn't offering support for either side. He wanted to capture the feelings of young people in Ireland, how tired they were of the fighting and the dying. This began the tradition of Bono's waving of a big white flag during live performances of the song. It was not a flag of surrender, however; it was meant to symbolize a clean slate — a flag free of the red, white and blue of the Union Jack and the green, white and orange of the Republic of Ireland.

Thanks to songs like these, U2 finally had an album on the North American charts (neither BOY nor OCTOBER had cracked the Top 40 on the *Billboard* album charts.) WAR was the critical and commercial breakthrough that they needed. With the group's idealistic Christian values plainly in view, and with each concert a raw and exhilarating experience, U2 quickly became known as "the band with a conscience." By the end of the year, *Rolling Stone* had started calling them one of the best bands on the planet.

As U2 began to think about their fourth album, a realization set in: they knew that they'd taken their original vision about as far as they could. If they were going to remain relevant in a changing world, they would have to change themselves. One of their main concerns was that they were beginning to sound shrill and preachy as the "Bono is God" perception began to spiral out of control. Something had to be done if U2 expected to survive past the mid-80's.

After taking a little time off — Bono maintains that the group broke up and then formed another band using the same members and the same name — U2 decided to go with a new producer. After three albums with Steve Lillywhite, the band believed that it would be best if they found someone with a different perspective on things. They chose Brian Eno, who then brought in Canadian Daniel Lanois for backup. Most of the early sessions were loose, casual affairs that took place in an old Irish castle (Slane Castle) using a mobile recording unit. Lanois was especially good with rhythms, encouraging Larry and Adam to get a little funky from time to time. One day, as a joke, everyone decided to record some tracks in the nude. The only person who seemed to be struggling was Bono. As the basic tracks were coming together, he still didn't have all his lyrics written. To make matters worse, he had less than ten days to write and record his parts because the band was scheduled to go on the road again. But, like always, he managed to pull through.

Eno brought an innovative structure to the recording process, encouraging the band to feel out ideas and then piece the better bits together later. After rolling miles of tape as the band jammed and improvised, everyone reviewed the results. A prime example of this approach is Pride *(In the Name of Love)*. It was based on a jam recovered from an old tape made at a sound check in Hawaii on November 16, 1983. Once the guitar lick and the rhythm were reintroduced in the studio under Eno's tutelage, the song fell together in about fifteen minutes. It also became the band's first American Top 30 hit, reaching No. 33 in the winter of 1984.

Within a few months, THE UNFORGETTABLE FIRE (released in September 1984) was their best-selling album ever.[1] Critics and fans pointed out how the album marked a creative rebirth for U2. Not only had their lyrical focus changed slightly (becoming less preachy and more spiritual), but working with Eno and Lanois had made them better musicians. It was a refined studio album, sonically honed in a way many thought was beyond the group's abilities. But even as powerful as FIRE appeared, it turned out to be something akin to a dress rehearsal for the group's next studio effort.

U2, circa 1987

Following the release of FIRE, U2 spent much of the next eighteen months doing what might be best described as "community service." On May 17, 1986, U2 took part in the Self Aid concert in Dublin. Impressed by the accomplishments of Live Aid in July 1985, the group accepted an offer on the Conspiracy of Hope tour for Amnesty International before Bono left on a tour of the civil war zones in Nicaragua and El Salvador. Meanwhile, the Edge scored a film entitled *Captive* which featured the first recorded vocal performance of an Irish teenager named Sinead O'Connor.

Work on U2's fifth album began about six months after the final show on the Unforgettable Fire tour. At first, the group did nothing more than jam at Larry's house in Danesmoate and the Edge's home in Dublin. When Eno and Lanois were recalled for their production and engineering expertise in August 1986, they brought along Flood (a young and promising English producer) to help with the recording process. Settling in at Windmill Lane Studios in Dublin, work began on approximately thirty new songs, many of which had been inspired by Bono's new appreciate of folk, American R&B and roots music.

With the Edge often working late into the night on his own, and with Eno forcing the band to extend themselves even further, the album began to coalesce in unexpected ways. One of the greatest stories from the sessions involves the time when Eno, frustrated by the group's inability to make a particular song work (and angry that they were wasting so much time on it), he tried to erase the master tape, effectively killing the track. It was only after an assistant engineer at the studio blocked Eno from the tape machine with his body did he relent to take another stab at it. The song? *Where the Streets Have No Name.*

THE JOSHUA TREE was released worldwide on March 9, 1987, and was immediately heralded as one of the best albums of the decade. Prior to its release, there was little argument that U2 was one of the

---

1. Although it equaled WAR's climb to No. 12 on the album charts, it sold twice as many copies.

---

biggest bands in the world; THE JOSHUA TREE confirmed that there was, indeed, none bigger.

o Entering the US charts at No. 7, THE JOSHUA TREE climbed to No. 1 by the end of April, staying there for nine weeks. It was the first album by any Irish band to reached No. 1 in America.

o More than 300,000 copies were sold in Britain during the first week of its release, making it the fastest-selling album in history. It would remain on the British charts for 129 weeks.

o THE JOSHUA TREE sold more than ten million in America and close to twenty million worldwide.

o The album spawned several hit singles including *With or Without You* and *I Still Haven't Found What I'm Looking For*, both No. 1 hits around the globe.

o Not only did the album top the year-end critic and reader polls, U2 won Grammy Awards for Album of the Year and Best Rock Performance by a group for *With or Without You*.

o The first spin through North America in support of the album is a virtual sellout with 99.77% of all tickets sold through twenty-nine dates. In Europe, thirty shows attracted 1.2 million people (this includes the 92,000 tickets that were sold in one hour for a show in Holland.) On the American leg of the tour, the group is seen by more than 1.5 million people over fifty (average gig attendance: 31,350.) The total box office gross exceeded $27 million.

o After editing more than 160 miles of film that were shot during the tour by director Phil Joanou, *Rattle and Hum* (complete with a soundtrack filled with new material) was released on October 27, 1988.

o The tour that started on April 2, 1987, in Arizona didn't really come to an end until January 10, 1990, in Rotterdam.

U2's POPMART stage, 1997

In November 1990, more than four full years after they first started work on THE JOSHUA TREE, U2 began working on their next studio album in Berlin. They'd picked a perfect time to be in the city — the Wall was coming down and the air was filled with hope and optimism.[1]

What began with high expectations nearly ended in disaster. The sessions were torn by creative divisions and personal tensions which sometimes descended into ugly shouting matches between Bono and Lanois. No one could agree on what to do next. Nothing constructive was being written or recorded. After three months' work, only two songs emerged, and everything else seemed to be nothing more than directionless crap.

Brian Eno, who was eventually called in to clean house, was ruthless in his assessment of the group's work, throwing out any material be thought was substandard. He laid down some firm ground rules to bring some much-needed order to the session and basically whipped everyone back into shape. Moving everyone back to Ireland in March 1991, things finally began to come together in some kind of calm and logical manner.

On November 18, 1991, U2 issued ACHTUNG BABY, their first proper studio album since THE JOSHUA TREE in 1987. For a project that initially deteriorated into chaos, ACHTUNG BABY not only turned out to be a coherent album, but one that also demonstrated a sense of fun. What's more is that the album provided a series of sonic shocks: the industrial-ish clank of *Zoo Station*; the funky club beats of *Mysterious Ways*; and the almost unbearable intimacy of *One*. It was another critical and commercial success, spawning four Top 40 singles and selling close to ten million copies worldwide.

---

1. A point of trivia: U2 arrived in Berlin on the last commercial airline flight before the Wall came down.

When U2 announced that they were about to head out on tour again, the demand for tickets outstripped the supply on a ratio of ten to one. By any measure, the Zoo TV tour was massive — 157 shows between February 29, 1992 in Lakeland, Florida and Tokyo, Japan, just before Christmas 1993. With its elaborate stage set up and complex production requirements, it reigned as the most expensive concert tour spectacle in history — so expensive, in fact, that despite selling hundreds of thousands of tickets, it nearly bankrupted the band.

During a six month break in the middle of the world tour, U2 used their pent-up energy to record another album. It really began when the Edge needed something to keep himself occupied following the breakup of his marriage. While the other three members were out having fun and relaxing, the Edge was content to fiddle about in the studio, recording demos as a way of working out his frustrations. One of the things he discovered was an old experimental jam from some long-forgotten ACHTUNG BABY session. Fiddling with it for a while, he began to think that perhaps Bono could rap

The Clarence, U2's luxury hotel in Dublin.

some kind of vocal over the loop he had created. However, Bono was nowhere to be seen, so the Edge decided to do the rap himself. When the rest of the band heard his deadpan delivery of the song he called *Numb*, things really started to roll. Before anyone realized what was going on, another complete album was in the can. ZOOROPA (issued on July 5, 1993) was a quirky, techno-tinged album that once again showed the world that U2 was still unafraid to take risks in order to remain relevant.

The tours that encompassed the ACHTUNG BABY and ZOOROPA periods were so long and expensive that U2 needed another extended break in order to recharge themselves — and their bank accounts. When everyone finally made it home in early 1994, it wasn't long before the group began to think about how they could reinvent themselves yet again. In 1995, they began work on what they thought was going to be another U2 album; instead it turned out to be far too experimental for anyone's tastes (including Larry Mullen — he HATED the album) and was issued instead under the name the Passengers (See Fast Facts.)

The next official U2 project was born out of the band's growing interest in techno, jungle and various flavors of electronica.[2] During their extended break, each member had independently discovered the sounds coming out of the UK club scene. Groups like Leftfield, the Prodigy and Underworld became big favorites. This fascination with dance beats grew deeper after the group purchased a dance club in Dublin.

---

2. Rumours were that this was going to be a down and dirty rock and roll record that they planned to bang off in about six months. They should have known better; it's been decades since U2 made a record that quickly. Once they start working on a project, things have a way of mutating, sometimes to the point where the finished product sounds absolutely nothing like what they started with. In the case of POP, one of the mitigating factors was Larry Mullen's back. Early on in the sessions, it became so painful that he was out of action for weeks. This is when Flood and Howie B had the rest of the band work with pre-programmed techno and trip-hop beats. We soon learned the effect that this would have on the rest of the album.

DJs spinning the latest dance tracks exposed U2 to new sounds and new attitudes. Although everyone was on side with this new direction, it became a battle to organize all the new ideas. For the first time in more than a decade, Brian Eno wasn't involved, declining all invitations to participate. His place was taken by two dance specialists, Howie B and Nellee Hooper. Under pressure by their fans and their record label to release something, U2 had to rush a little more than they would have liked. While they wouldn't admit it at the time, POP was still a little less than what they'd wanted it to be when it was released on March 4, 1997.[1] Despite lackluster sales, the subsequent PopMart Tour — an even more expensive and elaborate outing than Zoo TV — was a major success, thanks in part to an innovative agreement with promoter Michael Cole. In exchange booking the entire tour (and for assuming the financial risks involved), U2 was guaranteed a set fee, thereby avoiding the money pitfalls which had threatened the band throughout Zoo TV.[2]

What does the future hold for U2? As of the summer of 1999, they were back in the studio working with Brian Eno and Daniel Lanois on an album due sometime in 2000. Having been rushed with POP, the group has vowed not to release anything until they're absolutely sure it's perfect. In an on-line chat in June 1999, Bono hinted that this is the album where U2 will return to its rock and roll roots. We'll see.

Fast Facts

o Fans still make pilgrimages to Bono's boyhood home at 10 Cedarwood Avenue in the Ballymun area of Dublin. The first rehearsal of the band that was to become U2 took place at Larry Mullen's home at 60 Rosemount Avenue in Artane.

o As a teenager, Bono pumped gas and once took a job at the post office arranged by his father.

o On December 4, 1979, U2 were mistakenly billed as "The V2s" at the Hope & Anchor in London. A grand total of nine paying customers showed up. A week later, *Melody Maker* slipped up, listing them as "UR" at another club.

o Close examination of the lyrics to *I Will Follow* may offer some insight into Bono's relationship with his mother. Iris Hewson died of a brain hemorrhage on September 10, 1974 — the same day has his grandfather's funeral. Bono was devastated by the loss and, according to friends, was never the same thereafter.

o On March 16, 1981, U2 played a show in Anaheim, California, at a club called Woodstock. Although they'd played to a sellout crowd of 600 the night before in Reseda, someone forgot to advertise this next show. Total paid attendance: 12.

o Two weeks later (March 30, 1981), a club owner in Lubbock, Texas, insisted that U2 take a cheque as payment for their appearance. To make sure manager Paul McGuinness didn't object, the owner pulled a gun.

o The young child on BOY, WAR and on the 1998 greatest hits collection is Peter Rowen, brother of Guggi (the friend who first called Paul Hewson "Bono".) Guggi got him to pose in exchange for a box of chocolates. Peter now lives in Dublin as a photographer's assistant. He claims to have never owned a copy of BOY or WAR. Rumor has it that Michael Jackson tried to buy the billboard for WAR that appeared on Sunset Boulevard. In May 1999, an Italian neo-fascist group co-opted Peter's picture on the greatest hits album for one of their posters (much to U2's horror.)

o **Breakup Crisis Number One:** One part of U2's past that a lot of people have forgotten was a period in the early 80's when three-quarters of the band was involved in an evangelical non-denominational Christian group. Founded by Bono, the Edge and Larry Mullen when they were still in their teens, Shalom was eventually dominated by zealots who began asking hard questions like "How can you be in a rock band and be a Christian at the same time?" Such debates created a philosophical crisis and, for a while, the future of U2 was in real jeopardy. After some serious soul-searching, U2 decided that they, in fact, could be both religious and in a rock band. Any moral conflicts would be dealt with as they came up.

o **Breakup Crisis Number Two:** When U2 was invited to appear during the Wembley Stadium segment of Live Aid on July 15, 1985, they intended to play three songs: *Sunday Bloody Sunday, Bad*

---

1. Believe it or not, in the last twelve hours before their deadline, U2 mixed four songs, recorded vocals for three and were even writing new lyrics up until the last possible second.
2. ZOO TV was rumored to cost $125,000 a day. Figures for Popmart indicate expenses of $200,000 per day.

and *Pride (In the Name of Love)*. However, during *Bad*, Bono decided he needed a dance partner and spent long minutes trying to pull someone out of the audience. By the time he was finished, the song had gone on for fifteen minutes. U2 had used up their alloted time without being able to play what was, at the time, their biggest song. Backstage, there was a big fight over what the other three members saw as unnecessary theatrics. Emotions got out of control — and Bono allegedly said he was quitting the group. Flying back to Dublin alone, he eventually found himself driving through the Irish countryside in order to clear his head. That's when he chanced upon a hitchhiker. Stopping to pick her up (this is where the story starts to take on the trappings of an urban legend), she recognized Bono right away and immediately began to tell him how moved she had been by the band's Live Aid performance. The conversation made Bono think that perhaps his resignation had been too hasty. When he returned to Dublin, he apologized to the rest of the band for his behavior. Who knows what might have happened had it not been for that anonymous hitchhiker?

o Bono is allergic to both aspirin and whiskey.

o In Spain, U2 is known as U-Dos.

o The cover photo of THE JOSHUA TREE was taken in the Joshua Tree National park in California, home to a species of strange, gnarled trees. Daniel Lanois maintains a recording studio in the nearby town of Twentynine Palms.

o In 1992, Bono, the Edge and Harry Crosby (a Dublin businessman) bought the Clarence Hotel (6-8 Weillington Quay in Dublin.) After investing close to IR£5 million in renovations, the hotel opened as a five-star property in 1996. For reservations (and beware, it's not cheap!), call (800) 447-7462.

o U2 maintains ownership of a nightclub called The Kitchen in the basement of the Clarence. Legend has it that this is the site of the same pub where an underage U2 used to slip in for the occasional pint. The grand opening was February 12, 1994.

o The artwork of ACHTUNG BABY turned out to be surprisingly controversial, thanks to a small full-frontal nude shot of Adam Clayton tucked within the photo collage.

o U2 agonized over the title of ACHTUNG BABY. They considered CRUISE DOWN MAIN STREET (too much like a Stones album), FEAR OF WOMEN (too pretentious) and MAN (as a logical extension of BOY.) ACHTUNG BABY comes from the fictional musical called *Springtime for Hitler* in the Mel Brooks movie, *The Producers*.

o *Hold Me, Thrill Me, Kiss Me, Kill Me* from the *Batman Forever* soundtrack actually dates back to the earliest ACHTUNG BABY sessions. At the time, Brian Eno considered it substandard and ordered it shelved.

o Like many stars, Bono often receives death threats. At one point in 1980's, U2 was targeted by white supremacists in the Southern US. The FBI received a tip indicating that Bono would be assassinated should he try to sing *Pride (In the Name of Love)*. Defiant, the performance went ahead as scheduled and no shots were fired.

o Bono has been married to Ali (a film producer) for years and they have two daughters. The first, Jordan, was born on Daddy's birthday in 1989. The Edge's current companion is Morleigh Steinberg, the *Mysterious Ways* belly dancer on the second half of the Zoo TV tour.

o **Breakup Crisis Number Three:** A soured relationship with supermodel Naomi Campbell created some terribly awkward moments towards the end of the Zoo TV tour. Devastated by being dumped (apparently in favor of Robert Di Niro), Adam Clayton went on a big bender just hours before the band was supposed to perform in Sydney, Australia, on November 26, 1993. Too drunk and disorientated to take the stage (officially, Adam was laid up with a virus), bass roadie Stuart Morgan had to fill in for the gig. That marked the first time in U2's history that they played a show as less than a full unit. Fans learn later (thanks chiefly to Bill Flanagan's wonderful book, *U2 at the End of the World*) that Adam came very close to leaving the group.

o The Passengers project caught most fans completely off guard. ORIGINAL SOUNDTRACKS I supposedly contains music from fourteen art films (only four of which were real.) The only track that received any widespread airplay was *Miss Sarajevo*, featuring a lead vocal by Luciano Pavarotti. Here's a tip: read the liner notes carefully for all kinds of clues that this is actually a U2 album. An example would be track 4 which describes a villain named "Pi Hoo Sun" (Paul Hewson.) If you unscramble the name of actress "Venda Davis," you will get "Dave Evans." Also look for anagrams for Brian Eno and pay particular attention to the lengths given for several of these "movies."

○ The business wing of the U2 empire is called Principle, a company headquartered in Dublin and with a branch office in New York. Although overseen by manager Paul McGuinness, Principle is staffed and run almost entirely by women. People who have worked for and with the company say it's one of the most efficient and professional organizations to be found anywhere in the music industry.

○ When it was announced that POP wouldn't be in the stores in time for the 1996 Christmas shopping season, the stock price of U2's parent company dropped on exchanges around the world.

○ The equipment manifest for the PopMart tour included:

1. The world's largest television. Measuring 150-by-56 feet, the video screen used twenty-two miles of cable, 21,000 circuit boards, 120,000 connectors and 150,000 pixels made up of one million LED's. Covering 833 square yards and weighing 65,000 pounds, it was manufactured specifically for U2 by a company in Montreal.

2. A main stage of 181-by-71 feet plus a 100-ft. runway to a secondary stage. Each stage set up took three days and three thousand man-hours to complete. This meant that two separate stages were needed for the tour.

3. Thirty tons of PA equipment (all in mono) that generated over one million watts of power. The system included 149 speaker enclosures of various designs and incorporated 298 eighteen inch woofers, 428 10" midrange drivers and 604 high frequency tweeters.

4. One 100-ft golden arch inspired by the arch in St. Louis (not, despite appearances, McDonalds) garnished with a twelve foot illuminated stuffed olive one a 100-ft. toothpick and one thirty-five foot, lemon-shaped mirror ball.

5. One thousand lighting fixtures including 5,000 feet of disco lighting, a Plexiglas dance floor, six lightning machines, twenty Xenon search lights, 100 strobe lights, six TV cameras and one headset camera.

6. The three power generators supplied four million watts of electricity (enough to supply 1,500 homes) through thirteen miles of cable.

7. More than 1,200 tons of equipment and 250 tour personnel were moved in seventy-five semi-trailers, fifteen buses and one customized fifty-seat Boeing 727. An additional 200 people were hired at each stop on the tour.

○ U2 also had some very specific requirements when it came to backstage snacks on PopMart. Bono needed raw broccoli and cauliflower, celery, olives and a small loaf of white bread. Larry Mullen wanted soy-veggie burgers, jack cheese, some salsa, some guacamole and some potato chips. The Edge required mushrooms stuffed with feta cheese. Adam Clayton preferred tofu spinach salad with croutons and a Dijon dressing. Everyone also demanded different brands of bottled water along with a case of raspberry Snapple for the Edge and peach Snapple for Larry.

○ *The Sweetest Thing*, which originally appeared as a bonus track to *Where the Streets Have No Name*, was written by Bono as an apology to his wife for missing her birthday. She owns all the rights to the song (and its 1998 re-recording) and donates the royalties to charity.

○ One of the most interesting U2 collectibles is a collection of remixes entitled MELON (Island, 1995) which was released only to members of the band's fan club.

Recommended Listening

○ BOY (Island, 1980)

○ WAR (Island, 1983)

○ THE UNFORGETTABLE FIRE (Island, 1984)

○ THE JOSHUA TREE (Island, 1987)

○ RATTLE AND HUM (Island, 1987)

○ ACHTUNG BABY (Island, 1991)

○ At the close of the century, there is only one official greatest hits collection: THE BEST OF: 1980-90 (Island, 1998.) If you can, source out the limited edition original version which came with a bonus disc of B-sides.

Internet Resources

○ http://zoonation.com/indexB.html

- www.u2dublin.com/
- www.u2station.com/u2ography.html
- www.uslink.net/~candym/highres.htm
- www.geocities.com/SunsetStrip/Towers/9218/

Recommended Reading

- Alan, Carter. *Outside is America: U2 in the U.S.* Boston: Faber and Faber, 1992.
- Dunphy, Eamon. *Unforgettable Fire: The Definitive Biography of U2.* London: Viking Penguin, 1987.
- Flanagan, Bill. *U2 at the End of the World.* New York, New York: Delacorte Press, 1995.
- Jal del la Parra, Pimm. *U2 Live: A Concert Documentary.* London: Omnibus Press, 1994.
- Stokes, Niall. *Into the Heart: The Stories Behind Every U2 Song.* Dubai: Carlton Books, 1996.

Related Listening
The Alarm, Simple Minds, Radiohead.

The Story Thus Far ...
Born from equal parts punk, Patti Smith and David Bowie. U2 eventually finds their own niche to become one of the first ultra-superstars of the alt-rock kingdom.

~ 13 ~
THE CURE
Faith, Pornography and Sometimes, Love

The first thing newcomers notice is The Hair. It is, after all, one of the most famous haircuts in all of music. Even so, Robert Smith may appear a most unlikely candidates for superstardom. In fact, a 1993 cover story on the Cure in *Q* magazine ran with the headline "How Did *This* Get to be Superstar?"

Outward appearances aside, this much is undisputed: Robert Smith has steered the career of the Cure for better than two decades, creating one of the world's most successful doom-and-gloom outfits. As a result of Smith's unrelenting, eclectic and highly romanticized vision of what the Cure should be, the band has sold more than 25 million albums. And despite the occasional protestation from Smith ("We're *not* goths!"), the band has had a lasting effect on alt-rock, especially with the black-clad eyeliner and lipstick crowd — including a significant portion of the goth community. With songs that often obsessed on mournful things, the Cure found an audience desperate for a way to express their feelings of futility, purposelessness and alienation. In the Cure, they found someone who could express those feelings, validating the way they looked at the world and thereby offering some measure of comfort. As they say, misery loves company.

While it's true that the Cure is known mostly for gloomy and sometimes morbid songs that focus on the absurdities of the universe (they've been called "the messiahs of melancholy," among other things), Smith has been known to write some dandy pop songs, all featuring thin, tinny guitars, synth-pop embellishments and, of course, his trademark quirky vocal style. This combination of light and dark has made the Cure one of the most influential bands in the post-punk world.

The Cure begins — and will ultimately end — with Robert Smith (born April 21, 1959.)[1] The earliest roots of the band can be traced back to Christmas Day 1972 when Robert found his first guitar under the tree. Within a couple of years — and having learned a few basic chords from his older brother, Richard — he was writing songs with Laurence "Lol" Tolhurst (born February 3, 1959), a friend he had met on a

---

1. Over the years, about twenty people have rotated in and out of the band. The list of alumni includes a mailman, a hairdresser, one of the band's guitar roadies and the proprietor of a clothing shop. At various times, the Cure has existed as a trio, a quartet and a quintet. Robert Smith — an admitted control freak — has been the only constant.

---

school bus back in 1964. As a particularly precocious child, Robert did not respond well to authority nor did he have any intentions of fitting in with the other kids. A prime example might be the time Robert wore a black velvet dress to school on a dare. He was then promptly beaten up by four classmates.

Music soon became a way to avoid school. When he was fourteen, Robert formed his first band — dubbed the Crawley Goat band — with brother Richard, his sister Janet and a few friends from the neighborhood. This was followed by an outfit simply known as The Group — since they were the only rock band at the school, a name wasn't necessary. Starting in January 1976, a series of groups came and went: The Obelisks ("Horrible," says Robert); Malice (mid-to-late 1976, they even had a gig at a local church posing as a folk group); and finally, the Easy Cure (January 1977), an incarnation that took their name from a song Lol had written. Meanwhile, Robert found himself expelled from school for being a rather malignant influence on the other children. Much of his newfound free time was spent brewing his own beer at home.

During this year-long metamorphosis, a parade of would-be pop stars came and went including Richard and Janet Smith, Alan Hill, the Ceccagno brothers, and a drummer named Graham. But by January 1977, things had settled down somewhat. The new lineup featured Robert, Lol, a former waiter at Gatwick Airport named Porl Thompson and a singer named Peter O'Toole. Inspired by the growing punk movement, the Easy Cure entered — and won — a song writing contest sponsored by Ariola-Hansa in the summer of 1977. Things became complicated when singer Peter O'Toole quit to work in a kibbutz in Israel.

With more gigs and some demo sessions coming up, decisive action was needed. From the beginning, Robert had been the undisputed leader of the group, directing rehearsals, defining musical direction and writing the majority of original material. Once O'Toole left, Robert decided that if things were going to proceed the way he intended, then he would have to assume the role as lead vocalist. It was a simple case of "if you want something done right, then do it yourself."

Another crisis soon appeared. Following months of work with Hansa, the Easy Cure discovered that the label had plans to manipulate their image into something less threatening and more radio-friendly.[1] Smith was appalled. Refusing to be remade into something they weren't, the group and Hansa parted company. There were two more changes in the spring of 1978. The first came when guitarist Porl Thompson decided to quit, the second was when the band's name was simplified to just "The Cure" in early May.

Now working as a trio — Smith, Tolhurst and Michael Dempsey (born November 29, 1958) — the Cure recorded a four song demo on May 27, 1978, and circulated the results among a number of different record companies. After some discussion, the group becomes the first signing of Fiction, a new label set up by Polydor A&R man Chris Parry. Within six months, yet another new recording of *Killing an Arab* (the band's first single, officially released on December 22, 1978) was being played on the John Peel Show.

Killing an Arab certainly stood out as a single in the winter of 1978-79. Not only did it have a decidedly quirky feel, but the subject matter proved to be a little more touchy than the Cure had anticipated. Smith had written the song after reading *L'Etranger* by Nobel prize-winning author Albert Camus — but many people saw it as a simple case of Arab-bashing.[2] Still gripped by the impact of the oil embargo of the early 70's, and alarmed by sheiks buying up swaths of British real estate with their buckets of petro-dollars, Arab xenophobia was still running high. No wonder *Killing an Arab* was misconstrued as racist hate propaganda. Various Arab groups claimed to have been defamed. Meanwhile, scuffles began to break out whenever the Cure played the song live, thanks mainly to intrusions by members of the ultra-right National Front. Naturally, the track was banned by the BBC. The outcry was so fierce that Fiction deleted the single just ten weeks after it was released.

Undeterred, the band began work on their debut album and released THREE IMAGINARY BOYS on May 5, 1979. Despite the fact that the group was initially disappointed with the production, most critics seemed to appreciate the Cure's thin, minimalist sound, which stood in sharp contrast to the noise of

---

1. Hansa paid for the recording of two five song demo tapes in October and November 1977. When the label rejected all ten songs — including *Killing an Arab*, the band's choice for their first single — the agreement fell apart. The prize ultimately went to a new band called Japan.
2. Written in 1946, *L'Etranger* (*The Stranger*) tells the story of a man who is pulled into a senseless murder on a beach in Algeria. If anything, the book is an *anti*-racist rant.

punk and the pop of New Wave. The first single, *Boys Don't Cry*, featuring what would soon become known as Robert's trademark economical guitar stylings, also received good reviews, but surprisingly didn't even crack the Top 100 on the British charts.

By the summer of 1979, Robert Smith was beginning to demonstrate a strong penchant for make-up and outrageously teased jet-black hair. This, perhaps more than anything, attracted the attention of Steve Severin of Siouxsie and the Banshees who offered Robert a part-time job as the Banshees' guitarist (two Banshees had suddenly quit, leaving the band in the lurch.) He accepted, playing in both bands for the duration of a British tour.

Once things wrapped up in November, Robert had to face another lineup change, this time in his own band. Michael Dempsey had quit, saying that he felt uncomfortable in the background and wasn't allowed as much input into the Cure as he would have liked. Once he left to join the Associates, he was replaced by Simon Gallup (born June 1, 1960), an old friend from a Surrey band called Lockjaw. In addition to Gallup, Smith hired Mathieu Hartley (born February 4, 1960), an ex-hairdresser and keyboard player from a group called the Magpies. This new lineup made its debut at Eric's in Liverpool on November 16, 1979.

Much of the winter of 1979-80 was spent on the road as the Cure's cult following continued to build. After spending a few weeks in the studio in the spring, the group's second album, 17 SECONDS, was released on April 26, 1980, and eventually peaked at No. 20 on the UK charts. The extracted single *A Forest* (released in late March) crept up to No. 31. More touring followed (Europe, North America, New Zealand, and Australia) after which Hartley quit, reducing the group to a trio once again (Smith, Tolhurst and Gallup.)

The Cure's grueling pace continued through the fall and winter of 1980. In the space of just a couple of months, there were rehearsals for the third album, a round of recording demos (which were ultimately scrapped), a virtually sold out trip through Scandinavia, followed by another spin through the UK. By February 1981, the Cure was back in the studio, working on what would become known as FAITH.

Released on April 11, 1981 (and preceded by a single called *Primary*), FAITH was, by the band's own admission, a rather morbid-sounding album. Described by critics as "grammar school angst" (*NME*), the doom-laden, self-loathing, semi-religious themes of FAITH were the group's first real foray into a sound that made them a favorite of alienated teens everywhere. Robert Smith was cast as a somber soul, someone who ranked up with Ian Curtis as one of the most depressed musicians on the planet.[3] There was, however, a market for this kind of material; *Faith* debuted at No. 14 in the UK.

The descent into bleak darkness continued on PORNOGRAPHY, the Cure's fourth album (released April 18, 1982.) Although the album received mixed reviews from the critics, it did finally give the group their Top Ten breakthrough, debuting at No. 8. To their growing mob of black-clad, made-up, angst-ridden fans, the album clearly and effectively articulated their feelings of isolation and alienation. The situation within the band, however, was as bleak as the music. In mid-1981, Smith had hinted that the Cure was on the verge of splitting up, having failed to attract the same kind of respect and following as Joy Division. The gloom extended into the next tour where the everyone came to blows after a show in Strasbourg, France, in May (Smith and Gallup both quit the band for a week), which resulted in Gallup's total departure in June.

On the insistence of producer Chris Parry, Smith and Tolhurst (now playing keyboards) with the help of session drummer Steve Goulding returned to the studio to record a single to demonstrate to fans that the group was still together. Smith, however, was disappointed with the result ("Too contrived," he said) and at first wanted *Let's Go to Bed* released under the name Recur. Once he was convinced that it was indeed worthy of the Cure name, the single eventually peaked at No. 44.[4] Still confused and angered about his musical future, Smith went off to rejoin Siouxsie and the Banshees for a short tour. For the time being, the Cure ceased to exist.

It's quite possible that the band's story might have ended there had it not been for a last-minute invitation by the BBC to perform on program called *The Oxford Roadshow*. Having undergone a sudden change of

---

3. There were valid reasons for the band's dark mood, not least of which was the terminal illness of Lol's mother and the death of Robert's grandmother. These personal tragedies led to a lengthy period of doubt, anger and re-evaluation.
4. Despite hating the song and what Smith saw as "disco clichés," *Let's Go to Bed* eventually became a fan favorite. The subsequent video also marked the beginning of a long and profitable relationship with director Tim Pope.

heart, Smith quickly enlisted Tolhurst and hired drummer Andy Anderson (born January 30, 1951 and formerly of the band Brilliant) and bassist Derek Thompson (from SPK.) The performance went so well that Smith decided to give the Cure another shot. After hiring Anderson and bassist, engineer and producer Phil Thornalley (born January 5, 1960), a new single called The Walk (chart peak at No. 12) was in stores by the summer. By January, the Cure had released The Love Cats (UK No. 7), a compilation of early material called BOYS DON'T CRY, and a mini-album entitled JAPANESE WHISPERS (released in December 1983.)

Following the release of a dour and inconsistent album called THE TOP (in May 1984), the balance of the year was spent on the road, culminating with a bizarre incident in the Far East in September when an Andy Anderson drinking binge led to a physical attack on the rest of the band.[1] After using Vince Ely (the original drummer from the Psychedelic Furs) as an emergency replacement for eleven dates, the band hired Boris Williams (born April 24, 1957) in order to complete the tour. And if all that weren't enough, bassist Phil Thornalley quit in December, leading to a forced reconciliation with Simon Gallup in January 1985.

After the darkness and uncertainty of 1983 and 1984, the next three years were a welcome relief. Not only did the Cure release three of their best singles and videos in 1985, (In Between Days, Close to Me and an updated version of Boys Don't Cry), they also had a decent hit with THE HEAD ON THE DOOR (released in August 1985.) But the best was yet to come.

In 1986, the Cure struck pay dirt with a greatest hits collection entitled STANDING ON A BEACH (released in May of that year.)[2] The album reached No. 4 in the UK and a then-impressive No. 48 in America, selling several million albums in the process. A 1987 double set entitled KISS ME KISS ME KISS ME (released in May 1987) featured a series of impressive singles (including an American Top 40 hit with Feels Like Heaven) which led to the band playing for some of their largest concert crowds ever. The Cure had reached a new commercial peak — STANDING ON A BEACH and KISS ME sold a combined six million copies worldwide. Even the group's lineup enjoyed a period of unprecedented stability (Smith, Tolhurst, Gallup, Williams and Porl Thompson with touring help coming from Furs keyboardist Roger O'Donnell, born October 19, 1955.) Robert even found time to settle into domestic bliss with his longtime sweetheart, Mary Poole (see Fast Facts.)

Naturally, it couldn't last. In December 1988, Smith reassembled the Cure in a form that did not include Lol Tolhurst (Smith, Gallup, Williams, Thompson and O'Donnell.) By February 1989, Tolhurst had been officially fired under the auspices that he was no longer making any significant contributions to the group.[3]

The first album of the post-Tolhurst area (much to Lol's chagrin) was DISINTEGRATION. Released on April 28, 1989 — less than a week after Robert's much-anticipated, much-dreaded thirtieth birthday — the album was a solid collection of songs that finally displayed the Cure's long-held potential for creating mope-rock for arenas and stadiums. Often foreboding and occasionally downright icy, the album contained no fewer that four essential songs from the Cure catalogue (Lullaby, Pictures of You, Lovesong and Fascination Street), propelling it into becoming the best-selling release of the band's career.[4] DISINTEGRATION was the Cure's long-awaited commercial breakthrough, peaking at No. 3 in the UK and at a strong No. 12 on Billboard. The following Prayer Tour played to large crowds all over the world. Some audiences were so appreciative that the band often played beyond the curfews imposed by the venues.

---

1. The Cure was a quintet at this time: Smith, Tolhurst, Anderson, bassist Phil Thornalley and Porl Thompson, who rejoined the band earlier in the year.
2. This can be confusing. The vinyl edition of this release was entitled STANDING ON A BEACH. The CD and cassette versions (featuring many B-sides not included on the vinyl release) were issued under the title STARING AT THE SEA.
3. Tolhurst later sued the Cure (specifically Robert Smith and Fiction head Chris Parry) for a greater share of the band's royalties. The case finally went to trial in February 1994 and on September 16, Justice Chadwick threw out all charges, leaving Tolhurst with a legal bill of more than £1,000,000. In court, Smith described his former best friend as a "tired, shambling shadow of his former self." He also made no efforts to defend Lol's often-ridiculed simplistic keyboard style. In fact, Smith described Tolhurst's non-contributions to the band by saying his role was "almost that of a court jester."
4. Many of the songs on the album were no doubt inspired by Robert's marriage to his longtime sweetheart, Mary Poole, in August 1988 (See Fast Facts.) Lovesong reached an unbelievable No. 2 on the US singles charts in October 1989. And while we're on the subject of inspiration, rumor has it that the title track was written on the day of that much-feared thirtieth birthday.

Even though this meant that the Cure had to pay thousands of dollars in fines for going overtime, Smith was only too happy to keep playing in order to keep the fans happy. However, as good as fortunes were, the Cure's lineup was still in a state of continuous flux. After appearing at the 1990 Glastonbury Festival on June 24, Roger O'Donnell quit and was replaced by one-time Cure roadie, Perry Bamonte (born September 6, 1960.)

Following a much-needed six month break, the Cure returned with MIXED UP (released in November 1990), a greatest hits sort of album featuring remixes of ten favorites from the group's career.[5] Designed mainly as a present for hardcore Cure fans (many of the new mixes were far too radical for general consumption), the album was launched in a unique way. For as long as he can remember, Robert Smith has held a certain fascination with radio and broadcasting. When MIXED UP was about to be released, Smith paid to set up a pirate radio station at a secret location in downtown London. For four hours on the night of September 1, 1990, Smith went on the air, playing tracks from the new CD as well as interview clips, live recordings, bootlegs, commercials and weather and traffic reports. Although the album initially received a critical hammering — a remix album was considered very pretentious in 1990 — it started a trend and soon other artists were issuing remix albums of their own.

When the Cure got around to issuing WISH (released April 21, 1992), it had been three years since the band had released a proper studio album. On the surface, the record was positively *jolly* in places (check out the bouncy fun of *Friday I'm in Love*), but below the surface, the much-loved Cure angst (*Open, High*) was very much intact. Fans responded in droves. WISH debuted in America at No. 2. The group's thirty-nine date North American tour sold out in virtually every city, while trips through Australia and Europe often saw box offices grosses approach $1 million USD.

Once things wound down, it was time for another long break. Smith spent much of the latter half of 1993 and most of 1994 fighting a court case against Lol Tolhurst (see previous footnote) while supervising the release of two distinctly different live albums. SHOW (released on September 21, 1993) featured newer, pop-oriented material while PARIS (released on October 26, 1993) concentrated on the songs that made the Cure cult favorites. Naturally, there was the almost predictable — and by now, inevitable — shift in the band's lineup. As a huge Led Zeppelin fan, no one was surprised when Porl Thompson accepted a chance to play in the backup band supporting Jimmy Page and Robert Plant on their reunion tour. Roger O'Donnell returned on keyboards, prompting Perry Bamonte to switch to guitars. Then just as the band was about to record a follow-up to WISH, drummer Boris Williams quit. After placing ads in the British music papers,[6] Jason Cooper (born January 31, 1967) won the job.

Finally, after a wait lasting four years, the Cure released their tenth proper studio album. WILD MOOD SWINGS (released May 7, 1996) was a departure from the pop stylings of WISH, returning the band to somewhat darker and occasionally edgier territory. The title was most apt considering how the sound and feel of the album veered between light pop to heavy dirges — not to mention strange detours, such as the mariachi horns (!) that graced *The 13ᵗʰ*.[7]

The Cure is still very much a going concern, with an album planned for late 1999. When he's not writing, recording or touring, Robert Smith leads what amounts to a fairly quiet — some would say boring — life. Together with wife Mary, he lives in a large house on the southern coast of England where his favorite pastimes remain soccer and nipping down to the local pub for a few pints.[8] As the century drew to a close, word slipped out of a new Cure album — possibly the group's last — entitled BLOODFLOWERS, due for release on February 15, 2000.

---

5. The original idea was to collect together all the Cure's previous remixes a la New Order's SUBSTANCE collection, but that was abandoned in favor or creating all-new remixes of past hits. One new song, *Never Enough*, was also included.

6. The ad read "Very famous band needs drummer. No metalheads." Applicants were filmed as they played two new demos. No one knew the name of the band for which they were auditioning until they made the first cut. Jason Cooper was the successful candidate from a final field of twelve.

7. Perhaps the location of the studio had something to do with Smith's sensibilities. WILD MOOD SWINGS was recorded in the library and ballroom of an English mansion in Bath, England, owned by actress Jane Seymour. St. Catherine's Court is a real 14ᵗʰ century castle, once owned by Henry VIII. It has eight bedrooms, six-and-a-half bathrooms, stables, a tennis court, a full church and is surrounded by fourteen acres of gardens that are literally fit for a king. By the way, anyone can rent St. Catherine's Court — for $13,000 a week. Radiohead also recorded portions of OK COMPUTER in the castle.

8. Smith is a fanatical football supporter. Cure recording sessions and tours are scheduled around major tournaments — and don't ever dare come calling during the World Cup.

Although he generally enjoys his position as a senior member of alt-rock's aristocracy, Robert Smith says he still has moments of melancholy and can slip quite unexpectedly into doleful moods. He insists that ninety per cent of the time, he's completely normal and emotionally well balanced. But when that final ten per cent takes hold, the only way he can shake it is to express it through music. That's good — because as long as he's able to dwell on the purposeless and futility of humankind's existence, there will be material for Cure albums.

Fast Facts

o Robert Smith grew up in Crawley, a suburb of London that's quite noisy due to its location beneath the flight path of aircraft going in and out of Gatwick Airport.

o Robert and Mary Poole have been inseparable since they first met in drama class at age fourteen. They were married August 13, 1988, at a Benedictine Monastery in Sussex. *Lovesong* (from DISINTEGRATION) was written as a wedding present to his new wife. Mary can be seen in the video for *Just Like Heaven*.

o In September 1979, the Cure was dropped from a tour with Generation X after Lol Tolhurst accidentally discovered Billy Idol having sex with a groupie.

o Bizarre things tend to happen at Cure shows. At a gig in Bournemouth on February 28, 1979, an angry woman pulled off her boyfriend's ear. On July 27, a fan named Jon Moreland, distraught after being dumped by his girlfriend, jumped on stage during a show in Los Angeles and proceeded to stab himself repeatedly. He survived.

o In December 1979, Robert Smith, Lol Tolhurst and an ex-postman named Frank Bell released a one-off single called *I'm a Cult Hero* under the name The Cult Heroes. They played just one gig: March 23, 1980, at the Marquee in London.

o The Cure is quite good at releasing compilations of previously issued material. The first was BOYS DON'T CRY, a collection that was first released in North America in February 1980, but not in the UK until three years later. JAPANESE WHISPERS was a collection of singles released between November 1982 and November 1983. In 1986, the Cure issued STARING AT THE SEA / STANDING ON A BEACH (see footnote above.) A twelve-CD boxed set was issued on the Alex label in 1991. Finally, GALORE (October 1997) featured all the singles from KISS ME KISS ME KISS ME to WILD MOOD SWINGS, i.e. 1987-1997.

o In January 1981, the Cure provided the music for a short film called *Carnage Visors* which was then used as entrance music for Cure concerts. The first appearance of that track appeared on the cassette version of FAITH.

o Smith plays guitar on the HYENA album by Siouxsie and the Banshees. That's him on guitar on *Dear Prudence*. Smith and Steve Severin of Siouxsie and the Banshees collaborated on a project called THE GLOVE in 1983.

o *The Love Cats* was originally based on a fantasy involving the deliberate drowning of some kittens.

o The Hair first appeared sometime in 1982 around the release of PORNOGRAPHY. After a couple of years becoming of long and swoopy (peaking with an incredible spider-web do in about 1984 that was imitated by fans around the world), Smith shocked fans by getting a military-style haircut in late 1986. Reaction among fans was intense, recalling the day when Elvis' locks were shorn upon his induction in the army. The Hair reappeared within a year before Smith went short again in 1992.

o Smith has long been afraid of flying. When the band embarked on their 1989 tour of North America, he insisted on crossing the Atlantic on the QE2.

o Since Smith was terribly disappointed in the state of English radio (too much pop, not enough good indie music), he invested substantial amounts of money in setting up a London station called XFM. After finally receiving a full-time license, the station under-performed in terms of ratings (and thus revenues) and was eventually sold to arch-rival Capitol Radio in 1998.

o According to friends and bandmates, Robert Smith almost never practices playing the guitar — or any other instrument, for that matter.

o Smith is a secret fan of 1940's jazz and big band music. In 1985, he threatened to record an EP of Frank Sinatra songs.

o Barry Gibb of the Bee Gees is a huge fan of the Cure. No one knows what to make of this.

○ Robert once invented a cocktail that he calls the Oracle. It contains orange juices, rum, apple slices, calvados and lemon juice.

○ Robert has refused to dance in any Cure videos every since he saw himself in the clip for *Why Can't I Be You?*

○ A group called Cogasm appeared on FOR THE MASSES, a 1998 Depeche Mode tribute album. The group, consisting of Jason Cooper, Reeves Gabrels and Robert Smith, contributed a version of *World in My Eyes*.

○ In 1998, Robert Smith provided the voice for an animated version of himself on the TV series *South Park*. He helps Stan, Kyle, Kenny and Cartman defeat the evil Mecha-Streisand.

Recommended Listening

○ FAITH (Elektra, 1981)

○ *KISS ME KISS ME KISS ME* (Elektra, 1987)

○ *DISINTEGRATION* (Elektra, 1989)

○ As for the rest of the band's catalogue, the best way to sample the most important tracks are with the following compilations:
  STARING AT THE SEA (Elektra, 1986)
  GALORE (Elektra, 1997)

Internet Resources

○ www.thecure.com

○ www.prayersforrain.com

○ http://ourworld.compuserve.com/homepages/ChainofFlowers/

Recommended Reading

○ Bowler, Dave and Dray, Bryan. *The Cure: Faith*. London: Sidgewick and Jackson, 1995.

○ Butler, Darren. *The Cure On Record*. London: Omnibus Press, 1995.

○ Thompson, Dave and Green, Jo-Anne. *The Cure: A Visual Documentary*. London: Omnibus Press, 1988.

○ Thompson, Dave. *The Making of the Cure's Disintegration*. Burlington, Ontario: Collector's Guide Publishing, 1996.

Related Listening

Bauhaus, Siouxsie and the Banshees, Joy Division, Love and Rockets, the Mission UK, Sisters of Mercy, the Smiths, Swans, Depeche Mode, and Nick Cave.

The Story Thus Far . . .

The Cure provides music and comfort for the disenchanted and the depressed in the post-punk world.

~ 14 ~
DEPECHE MODE
Music for the Masses — and Then Some

For the first twenty years of the rock and roll era, the electric guitar reigned supreme. As rock charged across the globe, the electric six-string was held aloft by conquering hordes of young people, who revered it as if it were some holy relic. As a scepter, a weapon and as a powerful sexual talisman, the electric guitar came to symbolize everything that was rock and roll to the point where if the music didn't contain a fuzzed out ax, then it just didn't rock. No exceptions.

Then, quite unexpectedly, the synthesizer appeared in the early 1970's. At first, these electronic keyboards were considered to be nothing more than expensive curiosities, unwieldy tools best left in recording studios where they could be programmed and played by classical musicians. But as the technology improved and prices dropped to within the reach of young musicians, rock and roll underwent a fundamental re-examination. Perhaps the guitar wasn't so essential after all.

Kraftwerk became the first band to show how electronics and computers could be incorporated into the rock and roll landscape. They were soon followed by scores of imitators, bands who based their entire identities and presentation around the fact that they did not play guitars. Nor, for that matter, did they seem to need a drum kit or any of the other traditional rock instruments. It was out of this stew of transistors and printed circuits that Depeche Mode arose.

Originally just another bouncy techno-pop band of the short-lived New Romantic movement, Depeche Mode grew into something more. As their music darkened and their presentation became more dramatic, the Basildon boys began to have a serious effect on the direction of alt-rock. Their use of keyboards, computers and studio technology set new worldwide standards for creativity, their obsession with remixes became legendary, and the attention to detail lavished on both their videos and stage production helped position them as true alt-rock superstars. And if that weren't enough, behind all the glitter was enough gossip and intrigue to sink a dozen supermarket tabloids.

As a kid, Andrew John Fletcher (born July 8, 1960) was always getting involved in activities at the local church. Along with his friend Vince Clarke (born July 3, 1961), he joined the Boy Scouts and sometimes volunteered at the local chapter of the Salvation Army. Once he left school, he settled into a steady and predictable position as an insurance clerk. The only real corrupting force in their lives was a love of pop music — not the snarling and spitting of punk rock, mind you, but the milder sounds of the Beatles and the Eagles. By late 1977, both Fletch and Vince had ditched the serious instruments and musical pursuits of their youth and began to noodle with a guitar and bass in a band they called No Romance in China.[1]

Martin Lee Gore (born July 23, 1961) started out as something of a school bully, someone who once beat another kid over the head with a brick. Much to the relief of his parents, he eventually straightened out, participating in a variety of student exchange trips before taking a safe position as a bank teller. Like Andy and Vince, he began hanging around a local club called the Van Gogh. When another local group of wannabes called Norman and the Worms brought a Moog Prodigy synthesizer into the club one night, he became hooked on the weird, otherworldly sounds it produced. Saving whatever he could from his job at the bank, Martin soon had a Prodigy of his own which he used in a band called French Look.

With the lineup of No Romance in China constantly rotating, it was only a matter of time before Martin came into contact with Fletch and Vince and soon, they had a new group called Composition of Sound. Powered by a finicky drum machine, Vince (guitar), Fletch (bass) and Martin (synth) played a series of forgettable gigs in and around Basildon in late 1979. Things went so poorly that Vince decided to give up the guitar — it was too hard to play and sing at the same time — in favor of the infinite possibilities of the synthesizer. How could anyone not like a machine that made a novice sound like a virtuoso with a few twists of a knob? The synthesizer was truly a wonderful equalizer among the musically-inclined, not to mention the musically-challenged.

To complete the lineup, they started looking for a singer. They found Dave Gahan (born May 9, 1962), a skinny ex-punk who was also one of the worst juvenile offenders in town. Dave had a habit of stealing cars. The ones he couldn't steal, he set on fire. Graffiti, theft, vandalism — Dave was into all of it along with pills, pot and hash. By the time he left school, not only had he been sent to juvenile court three times, but Dave had gone through close to twenty different jobs ranging from a selling soft drinks to a position at a perfume bottling factory. One of his most identifying characteristics was a broken-line tattoo around his neck that was captioned "Cut Here." As he approached his late teens, most people had already written off Dave as a lost cause until he seemed to settle down, taking a college course in window design.

Given his attitude, it's not surprising to learn that when punk hit, Dave glommed onto the new scene, gravitating towards the angst and aggression of the Clash, the Sex Pistols and older performers like David Bowie and the Iggy and the Stooges. When Vince heard that he was a fellow Bowie fan looking for a gig as a singer in a group, he invited Dave to the church where Composition of Sound rehearsed.[2] After

---

1. Fletch took oboe lessons while Vince sang in a gospel duo. Both were big fans of a new post-Punk band called the Cure.
2. Vince was especially enamored with Bowie during the period he was making electronic-tinged records with Brian Eno in Berlin.

running through a rough version of *Heroes*, Dave was given the job.

All that was necessary to re-launch the group was a new name. Many different combinations were considered: Peter Bonetti's Boots, the Lemon Peels, the Runny Smiles and the Glow Worms. Dave came up with the winner: Depeche Mode, which just happened to be the name of a popular French fashion magazine. In fact, the literal translation of the phrase is "fast (or rapid) fashion."

As the new decade began, Depeche Mode made a crucial decision — all guitars would be jettisoned in favor of keyboards. Caught up in the modernism of post-punk music, and fascinated by the all-electronic approach of groups such as OMD and the Human League, Depeche Mode believed that synthesizers were the wave of the future. Besides, they were easier to carry from gig to gig than bulky guitars and amplifiers.

In October 1980, the new group recorded a three-song demo that was sent to all of the clubs and record labels that their meager postage funds would permit. Although most labels were somewhat underwhelmed by what they heard, Depeche Mode did manage to get some gigs at a club called the Bridgehouse during their occasional Futurist nights. Several weeks into this engagement, they were approached by Daniel Miller, leader of another synth-happy group and Futurist regular called the Fad Gadget. Miller had a new synth-only label called Mute and was looking for acts to add to the roster. When he offered to finance the recording of a single, Depeche Mode jumped at the chance.[3]

The first Depeche Mode single (and the thirteenth release in the short history of Mute) was issued on February 20, 1981. *Dreaming of Me* started slow, but eventually managed to peak at No. 57 in April. This was encouragement enough to release a second single, *New Life*, in June (No. 11) and a third, *Just Can't Get Enough* on September 7 (No. 8.) By time SPEAK AND SPELL, their debut album was released on October 5ᵗʰ, Depeche Mode was considered to be one of the leading acts of the short-lived sub-genre of techno-pop known as New Romantics.[4] The album reached a solid No. 10 in the UK. Even more impressive, however, was that this unknown British act managed to place their debut album in the Top 200 in America. Airplay of import copies of SPEAK AND SPELL (the album wasn't released domestically in the US until March 1982) pushed the record to No. 192. Of course, things just had to come to a crashing halt.

The sudden success of Depeche Mode had left Vince Clarke mysteriously gloomy. He grew to prefer the friendly and manageable silent confines of the recording studio to clubs, concert halls and TV studios. As the momentum of SPEAK AND SPELL threatened to force the band on a long serious of performances, Vince decided that he needed out. While his decision to leave had been made back in the fall, it wasn't until after a tour wrapped up that he made it official. On December 1, 1981, Clarke announced that he, the chief songwriter of one of the hottest acts of the year, was leaving. His last appearance with Depeche Mode was at the London Lyceum on December 3.

Some radical surgery was necessary in order to save the patient. As Martin Gore prepared to grab the song writing reins, a small ad appeared in *Melody Maker*: "Name band. Synthesizer. Must be under 21." The successful applicant was Alan Charles Wilder (born June 1, 1959), a programming whiz and singer who was more than capable of filling the technological void left by Vince Clarke.[5] After a six month probation period that lasted through the band's first North American tour, Wilder was hired full-time.

The transition from Clarke to Gore was virtually seamless as a succession of Gore-penned songs (*See You*, *The Meaning of Love*, and *Leave in Silence*) turned into hit singles throughout 1982. The first post-Clarke album, A BROKEN FRAME (released on September 27), peaked at a comforting No. 8 in the UK despite the fact that most of the material had been lying around Martin's house for years. Some of the songs on the album were written when he was just sixteen.

---

3. DM and Mute had an understanding whereby all proceeds would be split 50-50 in the UK and 70-30 internationally. So great was the trust between the two parties that no one got around to writing this down in a formal contract until 1986!

4. New Romantic bands specialized in superficial techno-pop that was antipodal to punk. Instead of heavy themes that dwelt on politics and anarchy, New Romantics chose to be lighter and more dance-oriented. Gone where the safety pins, Nazi symbols and torn clothes. They were replaced by designer clothes, vaudevillian sensibilities, high-tech musical keyboards, a sly sense of humor, fancy hairdos and — gasp! — the occasional dalliance with effeminate makeup. The flamboyant New Romantics were direct descendants of David Bowie's Thin White Duke era and Roxy Music's mid-70's look.

5. Yes, Wilder lied about his age in order to get the job.

The next album, CONSTRUCTION TIME AGAIN (released on August 22, 1983), was a major step forward in the evolution of Depeche Mode. The music and the arrangements were more sophisticated, while the lyrics were more heartfelt and meaningful. Technical innovations were also apparent in the form of something called "samples." With contributions by engineer Gareth Jones, a freelance sample pioneer, Gore construction clanking, metallic-sounding rhythm tracks — a far cry from the cheesy beats that could be coaxed from the drum machines of the era. Recorded at the headquarters of Hansa in Berlin (home of the world's only fifty-six track recording console), CONSTRUCTION was easily the most complicated project Depeche Mode had ever attempted. On the whole — and despite their new leanings toward darker themes and heavier sounds — the band seemed more assured than ever before.[1]

Following a major world tour that saw hysterical fans beaten back with truncheons by Hong Kong riot police, Depeche Mode returned to the studio to begin working on their fourth album. One of the first songs to emerge from the sessions was *People Are People*, a clanking, mid-tempo number that, on the surface, was a somewhat effeminate-sounding plea for equality, peace and harmony. However, closer inspection revealed that the band was once again using new and radical recording techniques. For example, the uniquely powerful bass drum sound was achieved by hitting the skin with a chunk of metal. Instead of a plastic pick, the guitar was strummed using a coin. The effect was cold, mechanical and above, all, very serious. While many of the group's techno-pop and New Romantic contemporaries (Heaven 17, Flock of Seagulls, Soft Cell, Spandau Ballet, Human League, etc.) were either running out techno-pop ideas or turning away from a pure synthesizer approach, Depeche continued to evolve. This evolution also had some unexpected consequences, the harsh percussive approach of CONSTRUCTION were soon adopted by the still-developing industrial music scene.

SOME GREAT REWARD was released on September 29, 1984, almost exactly one year after CONSTRUCTION TIME AGAIN. With this album, Martin Gore found his niche — bleak, minor key synthesizer songs that focused on sex, religion and despair. *Master and Servant* (released in August 1984), a psycho-sexual S&M tribute, was considered a risky follow-up to *People Are People*, especially since the band's main constituency was obsessive teenage girls. The third single, *Blasphemous Rumors* (September 1984) was particularly fatalistic when it came to the question of God and spiritual doubt. Two true stories sparked this particular crisis in faith. One told of a sixteen year old who attempted suicide but survived, while the other involved an eighteen year-old who was killed in a car crash a few days after embracing religion. When the song became the controversial choice for a single in September 1984, conservatives bristled at its anti-religion sentiments. After the Church of England spoke out, the song was relegated to the status of a B-side and was hurriedly paired with the future wedding reception favorite *Somebody*. Needless to say, the blustering and pontificating at the BBC over the appropriateness of these songs made sure that the album was a success.

Depeche Mode's 1986 album BLACK CELEBRATION (released on March 17 1986) continued to expound on themes of sex and corruption — and fans couldn't seem to get enough of Gore's grim hooks and melancholy lyrics. As the singles piled up — *Stripped* (one of the first DM songs to prominently feature a guitar), *A Question of Lust*, and *A Question of Time* — the band played to ever larger crowds on both sides of the Atlantic.[2] While the screams got louder, and as the pay cheques got bigger, Depeche Mode found themselves in the middle of a pack of "underground" bands (R.E.M., New Order, the Cure, the Smiths) that were somehow managing to sell millions of albums and concert tickets in North America with only a smattering of radio airplay. The scent of change was in the air.

Switching producers in an attempt to re-energize and re-channel the recording process, Depeche Mode started work on what would become MUSIC FOR THE MASSES in Paris in February 1987. Peter Bascombe (a favorite of Tears for Fears and Peter Gabriel) encouraged the band to experiment with "found sounds," noise made by everyday objects that could be manipulated and incorporated into the music. Tape machines rolled as toys were bashed, kitchen implements were hit, rubber bands were plucked and bottles were tapped with the results run through a variety of processing devices until the sounds were

---

1. The atmosphere of working in Cold War Berlin had the same effect on Depeche Mode as it had on David Bowie five years earlier. There's something about working in a city surrounded by soldiers with AK-47s that can darken the mood of any songwriter.
2. Almost supernaturally photogenic, Depeche Mode were, by now, MTV favorites. In fact, a good deal of MTV's early success — and the success of other video channels such as Much Music — was rooted in their use of clips by good looking, theatrical and non-threatening UK pop groups like Depeche Mode, Human League and especially Duran Duran.

unrecognizable. Loops were made and sometimes played backwards for added effect. Meanwhile, the group's arsenal of electronics continued to grow. Not only could Depeche Mode afford access to the latest and greatest keyboard devices, they also found new ways to use the now-vintage synths of their early days.

Fan reaction to this new approach was immediate. When, on April 13, 1987, Depeche Mode released *Strangelove* as a single in advance of the new album, demand for new material proved so insatiable that the group authorized no fewer than *fourteen* different remixes of the song.[3] This orgy of mixing continued with *Never Let Me Down* (more than a dozen versions) and reached a peak with *Behind the Wheel / Route 66* (even Martin Gore doesn't know how many versions there are.) In the end, MUSIC FOR THE MASSES (released on September 28, 1987) sold over two million copies worldwide and culminated with a show before a sellout crowd of 75,000 at the Rose Bowl in Pasadena, California, on June 18, 1988.[4]

In the summer of 1989, a strange ad started showing up in the personal section of newspapers and magazines in Britain. All it said was "Your own personal Jesus" followed by phone number. Most people dismissed this as some low-budget attempt at evangelism. Those who dared call heard a snippet of the first new single from Depeche Mode in two long years.

Reaction was, by this time, predictable. When *Personal Jesus* first appeared on August 28, 1989, it was the start of a frenzy that eventually built into a full-scale riot. Soon after VIOLATOR was released on March 19, 1990, all four members of the group agreed to appear at The Wherehouse, an LA record store on La Cienega Boulevard the following day. Forty-eight hours before the autograph session, crowds started gathering in the parking lot. By the time the appointed time arrived — 9 PM — traffic in the area was in gridlock. The thirty security guards hired to keep the peace soon realized that they were no match for the 25,000 screaming DM fans waiting outside.

As the band took their place at a table, the mob surged dangerously against the plate glass windows along the front of the store. As pressure on the windows built up, and as more people poured into the parking lot, it was decided that, for safety's sake, the event would be aborted. That's when all hell broke loose.

Bricks and rocks started flying and two large neon signs were destroyed. Bits of trim and plaster were literally kicked off the building. Close to 150 members of the LAPD responded, most wearing full riot gear. In the end, seven people were sent to hospital — and The Wherehouse was given bills totaling $25,000 for police and fire department services, as well as being hit with a huge clean-up charge from the city.

After teetering on the verge of superstardom for years, VIOLATOR was the album that finally pushed Depeche Mode over the top. Debuting at No. 2 in the UK and peaking at No. 7 in the US, the album quickly became the band's best-selling album ever.[5] Concert attendance had never been higher, either. A triumphant return to Los Angeles resulted in a gross of more then $2.4 million over two nights at Dodger Stadium in August 1990. The rise of alt-rock in the 90's had begun.

By the time the tour for VIOLATOR ended, it was obvious to everyone close to the band that Dave Gahan was finally ready to crack. He was often angry and irritable, distraught about turning thirty and no doubt upset at the breakup of his marriage.[6] To make matters worse, he couldn't even find sanctuary at home. He'd already moved twice, after waking up to find Depeche Mode fans singing on his front lawn. One obsessive fan even went so far as to hire a private detective to find Gahan's address by tracking him from the recording studio to his house.

While the rest of the band scattered to spend some time with their families, Dave was cast adrift. With too much free time and temporarily without the support system of the Depeche Mode organization, Gahan's personal crisis led back to Los Angeles. Depressed and confused, he let loose, getting involved

---

3. Here's where the DM discography starts to really go nuts. Previous to 1987, the band was usually content to issue three or four different mixes of a song. With MUSIC FOR THE MASSES, it became common for there to be ten, fifteen or even twenty-five different remixes of each single. To those of you attempting to amass a complete collection, best of luck.
4. The event was captured by renowned filmmaker D.A. Pennebaker in the DM concert film *101*.
5. VIOLATOR was DM's first ever million-seller in America.
6. Dave married Joanne, the secretary of DM's fan club, on August 4, 1985, in a quiet civil ceremony. They had a son, Jack, on October 14, 1987.

---

with Teresa Conway, the group's former press officer.[1] The "Rock God" thing got worse as Gahan's intake of drugs and alcohol reached gargantuan proportions. Insiders hint that the only thing that kept him from flying off into oblivion was his new wife and daughter.

When Depeche Mode reappeared with SONGS OF FAITH AND DEVOTION on March 22, 1993, it was with a very different Dave Gahan. The hair, the clothes, the tattoo — it was hardly the effeminate-looking singer of the *Just Can't Get Enough* video. In interviews, he adamantly insisted that he had cleaned up and straightened out, thanks to the support of his new family. At the same time, Depeche Mode had evolved yet again, incorporating everything from the newest keyboards and computers to real drums and a twenty-eight piece orchestra. And although Martin Gore maintained that none of the songs were written with Gahan's tribulations in mind (*Condemnation, Walking in My Shoes*), fans were left to speculate on about Gore's real inspirations. Regardless of his motivations, fans responded like never before, and the album debuted at No. 1 in both the UK and the US.

People associated with the tour following the release of SONGS will go on at length about the non-stop party that surrounded every show. Depeche Mode's reputation for backstage decadence was already legendary — but past antics paled in comparison to what happened on the road in 1993 and 1994.[2] Vast quantities of alcohol and drugs were consumed as parties continued well into the night. Two arrests were documented. On November 4, 1993, Martin Gore was picked up at the Westin Hotel in Denver for refusing to turn down his stereo at four in the morning. A second arrest occurred in Quebec City when Gahan and the band's road manager scuffled with security at their hotel.

Back in the indulgent, anything-goes environment of a world tour, Gahan was once again seized by his Rock God tendencies. Fans saw the hair get longer and the tattoos get bigger.[3] What they didn't see was the return to booze and drugs. Gahan had started using heroin in 1991 after being introduced by Teresa to some of the hangers-on in Jane's Addiction circles.[4] During the SONGS tour (which employed at least a hundred people, including a psychiatrist and a drug-buyer), Gahan would often spend days in his hotel room in an opium haze. There was even an occasion in New Orleans on October 8, 1993, where the band had to abort an encore because Gahan had OD'd after the band had left the stage following the final song of the main set. At a July 8, 1994, show in Indianapolis, he leapt into the crowd, breaking two ribs and causing internal hemorrhaging. By the time the long tour finally ended, Gahan had partied and drugged himself down to a body weight of just over one hundred pounds.

The other guys in the band weren't in great shape, either. When it was announced that Andrew Fletcher was staying behind in England to sort out some business affairs for the band rather than appear on the second leg of the tour, most fans accepted this explanation. In truth, Fletch had suffered a nervous breakdown, depressed over his sister's death of stomach cancer, and exacerbated by the craziness of life on the road. His anxiety reached a point where he required treatment for a severe case of depression. Unable to meet his touring commitments with Depeche Mode — he was that ill — his spot on the remainder of the tour was taken by keyboard roadie and age-old friend of the band, Daryl Balmonte.

Martin Gore was also feeling the effects of years of overindulgence. In addition to the panic attacks that were coming more frequently, he had a grand mal seizure in the middle of business meeting in Los Angeles. Doctors diagnosed the attack as the result of stress, drugs and unbelievable amounts of alcohol. Even Alan Wilder had to be hospitalized in South Africa after an attack of kidney stones.

Far more troubling was Wilder's deteriorating relationship with the rest of the group. Along with being fed up with the sex-and-drugs-and-rock and roll antics of his bandmates, and with Martin Gore's authoritarian hold on the song writing duties, he also had a painful case of gallstones. On June 1, 1995, he made it official. After thirteen years as a member of Depeche Mode, he quit.

"Due to increasing dissatisfaction with the internal relations and the working practices of the

---

1. That relationship resulted in a baby daughter. After Dave divorced Joanne, he married Teresa at the Graceland chapel in Memphis in April 1990. The music for the service was provided by an Elvis impersonator.
2. Even the mighty Metallica is in awe of DM's capacity for partying after seeing them in action first-hand. Few (if any) associates of DM are willing to go on the record regarding some of the rumors and stories. They're that foul.
3. One shoulder tattoo took ten painful hours to apply. Another tattoo, this one beneath a picture of a heart in a cage, read "TCTTM-FG." That stood for Teresa Conway To The Mother-Fucker Gahan.
4. Living in Los Angeles and plugged into the inner circles of the city's rock and roll crowd, drugs were cheap and plentiful. One of his favorite wedding presents was a big lump of black heroin.

group, it is with some sadness that I have decided to part company from Depeche Mode. My decision to leave the group was not an easy one, particularly as our last few albums were an indication of the full potential that Depeche Mode was realizing.

Since joining in 1982, I have continually striven to give total energy, enthusiasm and commitment to the furthering of the group's success, and in spite of a consistent imbalance in the distribution of the workload, willingly offered this. Unfortunately, within the group, this level of input never received the respect and the acknowledgment that it warrants.

Whilst I believe that the caliber of our musical input has improved, the quality of our association has deteriorated to the point where I no longer feel the end justifies the means. I have no wish to cast aspersions on any individual. Suffice to say that relations have become seriously strained, increasingly frustrating and ultimately, in certain situations, intolerable.

Given these circumstances, I have no option but to leave the group. It seems preferable therefore, to leave on a relative high, and as I still retain a great enthusiasm and passion for music, I am excited by the prospect of pursuing new projects.

The remaining band members have my support and best wishes for anything they may pursue in the future, be it collectively or individually."

In Los Angeles, Dave Gahan's situation was also deteriorating rapidly. With a constant supply of heroin available, it had become as essential to his life as drinking water. He grew paranoid and began carrying a gun even if he just meant a quick a walk to the mailbox. Locked in his house and spaced out, he often watched the weather channel for twenty-four hours at a stretch and talked to his collection of stuffed animals. When his friends and family convinced him to take a stab a rehab, the results were disastrous. After checking out of an expensive clinic in the Arizona desert on August 17, 1995, he returned to L.A. to find that his house had been completely looted. He moved into the Sunset Marquis and there were rumors of least two a suicide attempts and one stint in a psychiatric ward over the next few weeks.[5]

Despite the turmoil, Martin Gore had not given up on his band. In late 1995, he sent Gahan a tape of demos for the next Depeche Mode album. He flew to New York to put some vocals to the new songs, but he was often too strung out to get much done.[6]

Dave Gahan's drug crisis reached a crescendo on May 27, 1996. After flying back to L.A. after some discouraging recording sessions on the east coast, he checked into the Sunset Marquis and immediately secured a supply of drugs. After injecting a mixture of heroin and cocaine, he suffered a massive overdose. At 1:15 AM on the morning of the 28th, someone — a woman who refused to give her name — called 911. When the paramedics arrived, they found Gahan unconscious and turning blue because he had gone into full cardiac arrest. He was clinically dead for two minutes before he was revived.

When Gahan was released from hospital — and from jail on drug charges — he went right back to his stash of smack. Only this time, there was no buzz, no familiar feeling of euphoria. His body had become so accustomed to the drug that it no longer had any kind of effect. That's when he decided to check into the Exodus Recovery Center in Marina Del Ray, California. As far as anyone knows, this trip to detox was successful and Gahan remains clean to this day.

The first post-Wilder Depeche Mode album was released on April 15, 1997. Although as gloomy and minor key as ever, with its industrial-ish percussion and loops, ULTRA backed away from the arena-rock anthems of the previous two albums. Instead, it featured a series of songs that were loaded with subtle references to Gahan's drug problems, Fletch's nervous breakdown and Wilder's departure. While the album didn't sell as well as expected (given that electronica was supposed to explode into popular consciousness in 97-98), its very existence provided fans with a much-needed sense of relief that their band was going to survive after all. That relief proved justified in 1998 when Depeche Mode embarked on a world tour in support of a greatest hits collection entitled THE SINGLES, 86-98 (released October 6, 1998.) Opening on September 2, 1998, in Tartu, Estonia, the four month road trip covered sixty-five

---

5. The most persistent rumor was that Gahan was admitted to Cedars-Sinai Medical Center on August 17, 1995 for treatment of "lacerations." The cause of those lacerations was never officially reported. Meanwhile, Steve Malins' 1999 bio on DM includes quotes from Gahan himself saying that yes, it was definitely a suicide bid.
6. The vocals for *Sister of Night* on the *Ultra* album were recorded while Dave was on a heroin high.

shows without incident. Anyone who drifted throughout the backstage area or the band's hotel rooms would have been hard-pressed to find any sign of alcohol or drugs among the band or crew. It was the driest, straightest tour in Depeche Mode history.

Depeche Mode certainly wasn't the first group to drop their guitars for synthesizers and computers. Nor can they even lay claim to being the first techno-pop band or even a founding member of the New Romantic movement. History, however, does recognize the group as being electronic pioneers who have left their fingerprints on much of the electronica that arose in the late 80's and throughout the 90's. The effect of Martin Gore's introspective lyrics shouldn't be discounted either. Back in the early and mid-80's, when macho spandex-and-hair metal bands ruled the day, Depeche Mode offered a sanctuary to sensitive souls who needed someone to articulate their deepest, darkest feelings. Once Gore demonstrated that he could express this world-weariness succinctly and consistently, he earned their undying loyalty and respect. In fact, you will be hard pressed to find someone more willing to go to war for their favorite band than a Depeche Mode fan. They will be defenders of the faith to the very end.

No, Depeche Mode wasn't the first all-synth band — but they were the quintessential synth band of the 80's. With great hooks, heartfelt lyrics and a video image to die for, they did more to bring artsy electronic music into the mainstream than any other band since Kraftwerk. And when you reach heights like those, you're bound to steer at least a segment of rock and roll in a whole new direction.

Fast Facts

o   The version of *Photographic* that appeared on SOME BIZARRE ALBUM (Mute, March 1981) was lifted directly from the band's first three-song demo tape.

o   After leaving Depeche Mode, Vince Clarke formed Yazoo with Alison Moyet and then Erasure with Andy Bell.

o   Depeche Mode was one of the pioneers of the 12-inch remix. Their first was an altered version of *New Life* in February 1981 followed by the formerly long-lost "schitzomix" of *Just Can't Get Enough* in September.

o   Before Alan Wilder joined the group, he played in a series of groups. As Alan Normal, he appeared with Daphne and the Tenderspots when they released a 1978 single entitled *Disco Hell*. The following year, he appeared on Real to Real's debut album TIGHTROPE WALKERS. His final pre-DM gig was with the Hitman, who issued a single called *Bates Motel* in 1980. The Korgis single *If I Had You* features Wilder on keyboards.

o   If you look closely at the artwork for BLACK CELEBRATION, you'll see a notation that reads "Life in the so-called space age." This is actually the title of the only Depeche Mode song ever written by Andy Fletcher. Somewhere along the line, the track was deemed too awful to include on the album — but since they liked the title so much, Depeche Mode decided to at least print it in the artwork.

o   The title of *Pimpf* was taken from the name of the Nazi youth organization for pre-teens.

o   The original 12-inch mix of *Personal Jesus* became the biggest-selling remix in the history of Warner Brothers, vastly outperforming remixes by Madonna and Prince.

o   The working titles of 101 were A BRIEF PERIOD OF REJOICING and MASS. A French reissue was entitled TOTAL LIVE.

o   The first album to feature pictures of the band members on the cover was SONGS OF FAITH AND DEVOTION.

o   On September 1, 1994, Alan Wilder was driving through the Scottish countryside when a jet fighter

— an out of control RAF trainer — almost crashed right on top of his car. It hit the ground less than 200 yards away, showering him with metal and debris. Two airmen were killed in the incident.

o If you're ever in London, you might want to drop into Fletch's restaurant. Gascognes is at 12 Blenheim Terrance.

o Along with being a successful song writer, Martin Gore is also a shrewd real estate investor. One of his properties in the Docklands area of London takes in close to £200,000 a year in rent. In one of the most delicious rock and roll ironies, one of the tenants of the building is a branch of the same bank he worked for as a teller back in the late 1970's.

o Following the depths of his drug addiction in 1995-96, Dave Gahan has made a serious — and successful — attempt at staying straight. Along with attending Narcotics Anonymous meetings, he sticks to an exercise routine that includes yoga. His first wife, Joanne, now lets him visit their son, Jack. Meanwhile, Teresa, his second wife, has filed for divorce.

o In 1998, Depeche Mode became one of the first bands to sell advance tickets to concerts through their official web site. The practice is now standard throughout the industry.

Recommended Listening

Depeche Mode has gone through a serious of phases in their career. The best way to get an overview of how they've evolved (and of how their influence has spread) is with their greatest hits collections.

o CATCHING UP WITH DEPECHE MODE (Mute / Sire, 1985)

o THE SINGLES 81-85 (Mute, 1985)
CATCHING was released in North America while 81-85 was the UK release. Although their contents are similar, there are marked differences. CATCHING excludes any tracks that appear on PEOPLE ARE PEOPLE (a collection not released in the UK) but includes *Fly on the Windscreen* and *Flexible*.) The original UK collection features thirteen European singles on vinyl, while two more were added for the cassette and the CD.

o THE SINGLES 86-98 (Mute / Reprise, 1998)
The North American and UK editions of this double set are identical. Other collections (including the outrageous expensive X series of Japanese releases, plus the 1998 SINGLES BOXES) are also available.

o The rest of the DM discography is made complicated by an almost uncountable plethora of remixes, alternate versions and bootlegs available on singles and EP's. If you want to investigate this labyrinth of CD's, vinyl and cassettes, try ftp://www.CommLine.com/pub/bong/Discog/

Internet Resources

o www.depechemode.com

o www.bongbishop.com/

o www.tcn.net/~pcyopick/alamode/

o http://members.tripod.com/dv_101/dm_main.htm

Recommended Reading

o Clarke, Martin. *Depeche Mode*. London: Omnibus Press, 1999.

o Malins, Steve. *Depeche Mode: A Biography*. London: Andre Deutsch Ltd., 1999.

o Thompson, Dave. *Some Great Reward*. New York, New York: St. Martin's Press, 1994.

o The book on DM by Dave Thomas and the photography collection published by Anton Corbijn are out of print.

Related Listening

The Cure, Joy Division, New Order, Soft Cell, Tears for Fears, Erasure, Recoil (Alan Wilder's group), and early Cabaret Voltaire, Kraftwerk.

The Story Thus Far . . .

Along with the Cure, the Smiths, Joy Division and New Order, Depeche Mode was able to speak to the hearts of a distinct group of alt-rock fans. Although these music fans often found their tastes gravitating towards the gloomy and depressing, they also liked to dance. Meanwhile, Depeche Mode's innovative use of keyboards, computers and clanking percussion stirred up something in the industrial community, directing it away from the factory floor sounds of Einsturzende Neubauten and Throbbing Gristle and more along a direction that would result in Nine Inch Nails, Stabbing Westward and the Prodigy. And don't forget DM's use of remixes. Once they got into the act of releasing multiple mixes of the same song, the whole world followed suit.

~ 15 ~
R.E.M.
Radio Free Athens

The city of Athens, Georgia, lies about an hour east of Atlanta. If you exit off Highway 29, you can get onto Broad Street, which is the main drag through town. A few blocks past the entrance to the University of Georgia, a street called Ocanee veers off to the right. Ahead on the left, just past the railway tracks, at what used to be 394 Ocanee, are the remains of an old church, with the steeple of St. Mary's Episcopal teetering precariously next to the Steeplechase condominium development.

It was hard enough saving that steeple. When the condo developer started work in the late 80's, he wanted to remove all of that church, but some of the townsfolk would have none of that. The church was a *shrine*. How *dare* someone destroy it? But don't get the wrong idea. These weren't old parishioners or members of some religious sect. They were simply music fans who wanted to preserve at least part of Athens' most precious musical artifact — the location of the first-ever R.E.M. concert. That first gig — a birthday party for their friend Kathleen O'Brien on April 5, 1980 — was the first step that ultimately led towards hit singles, platinum albums, world tours and Grammy awards, not to mention hundreds of millions of dollars.

Like U2, R.E.M. carved out their niche as household names by charting their own course through the music industry. Stylistically, they weren't all that much different from the dozens of jangly post-punk college rock combos that started popping up in the wake of New Wave. And unlike the Ramones, the Sex Pistols or Kraftwerk, R.E.M.'s sound didn't define a genre or a specific musical movement. They did, however, have a chemistry, a charisma, a cloak of mystery, that set them apart from the pack, and by the time the 80's ended, they'd proven that brainy post-modern indie rock had a place in the marketplace.

When he reported for work at Wuxtry Records in Athens (197 E. Clayton Street), Peter Lawrence Buck (born December 6, 1956), a punk fan from way back, would keep a guitar behind the counter that we could strum when business was slow. Set up with a place to sleep in the old church on Ocanee by the owner of the store, Buck had entertained ideas of forming a band, but couldn't quite make the commitment. Then John Michael Stipe (born January 4, 1960) started hanging out in the store.

Although he was born in the Atlanta suburb of Decatur, Georgia, Stipe — an Air Force brat — had spent much of his life growing up on bases around the country and even in Germany. After the Vietnam war, the family settled in East St. Louis, Missouri, where he discovered the music of Patti Smith, the Velvet Underground, Television and Wire. By the time he was eighteen, Michael was singing with a punk group called Bad Habits. When they fell apart, Michael moved back to Georgia (his parents had relocated to Watkinsville, which is just outside of Athens, in 1978) and enrolled in art and photography at the University of Georgia at Athens. He soon became a frequent customer at Wuxtry, and he and Peter had long discussions on the merits of Patti Smith versus the Stooges.

William Thomas Berry born in Duluth, Minnesota, on July 31, 1958, moved with his family to Macon, Georgia in 1972. His first instrument was the ukulele, but when he reached grade four, he began playing drums in the school band. One of his bandmates was Michael Edward Mills (born December 17, 1958), a sousaphone player originally from Orange County who took to beating up Bill after rehearsal. The pot-smoking, shit-disturbing, class-cutting Mike despised Bill for his goody-goody attitude towards teachers and school. When Mike switched to bass and found himself at the same jam session as Bill (a short-lived high school thing called Shadofax), they decided to make the best of the situation. By the time the group broke up, Bill and Mike had become a fairly formidable rhythm section.

The person responsible for bringing R.E.M. together was the aforementioned Kathleen O'Brien, a mutual friend who worked at WUOG, the campus radio station. She lived with Peter and a bunch of other people in the broken down church, paying about $75 a month along with Peter, his brother Kenny and a variety of other bohemian types.[1] In about March 1980, she introduced Bill and Mike to Peter and Michael. Talk inevitably turned to music and, with Kathleen's twentieth birthday party only a couple of weeks away, it was decided that the four guys would throw together a group in time for the big blow-out on April 5th.[2] Rehearsals were organized and the unnamed group learned about eighteen songs, mostly covers by the Sex Pistols, the Stones and Jonathan Richman. It was agreed that they would play with two other local groups, Side Effects and Turtle Bay.

That Saturday night was cold and rainy — so cold that Peter remembers having to wear gloves for most of the night. Something like 125 had been invited, but by midnight between three and four hundred people had pushed their way into the church and, by most accounts, a good time was had by all. And that might have been that for Michael, Peter, Bill and Mike had it not been for the problem with the beer kegs.

Kathleen had rented a couple of taps for the kegs, but at some point in the evening, someone had stolen them, leaving her on the hook for about two hundred dollars. Some birthday present. That's when someone suggested that they hold a second party in order to raise money to pay for the taps. One of the guests at the original party was Mike Hobbs, a talent booker for Tyrone's, one of Athens' music clubs. He offered Peter's band the opening slot, suggesting that they could donate their $100 in earnings to the tap cause. Somewhat dazed at being offered a professional engagement, the new group accepted, mostly as a favor to Kathleen. With the show set for May 6th, the band knew they had to come up with a name. After much debate over much beer, they finally settled on R.E.M. just hours before the show at Tyrone's.[3]

When that gig turned out better than expected, the members of the newly christened group began to believe that there was something to their new hobby and began to actively pursue new bookings. The rest of 1980 was spent playing shows in and around Athens, although they did make it into Atlanta from time to time. In fact, R.E.M. opened for the Police when they played the Fox Theater on December 6th. Most of the time, however, R.E.M. stayed close to Tyrone's. The first known R.E.M. recording was made during a Tyrone's gig on October 6, 1980, and by the end of the year, the group had close to thirty original songs. Some were pretty thrashy and punky, but others — such as *Gardening at Night* — gave hints that the band had the potential of rising above mere frat-boy party band stuff.

There was a major development in the spring of 1981. Bill Berry had grown tired of being the band's *de facto* manager, accountant and van driver. These jobs were assumed by Jefferson Holt, a big fan of the group and the former owner of a failed record store. Once he had familiarized himself with R.E.M.'s situation, he arranged for the group to make some proper demos, booking time at a studio in Winston-Salem, North Carolina called The Drive-In. After making the trip up I-85 the night before, R.E.M. made their first real studio recordings on April 15, 1981. One of the three songs committed to tape that day was *Radio Free Europe*, a song inspired by the years Stipe spent listening to European radio while living on that Air Force base in Germany. Four hundred cassettes were run off and tarted up with photocopy artwork before being sent off to anyone they could think of — including, believe it or not, such long shots as *Women's Wear Daily*. There were few responses.

Several months later, Jonny Hibbert, an Athens law student who wanted to start an indie label, persuaded the band to let him remix and release *Radio Free Europe* backed with *Sitting Still*. Despite a bad pressing (the new Hib-Tone single sounded vastly inferior to the original demo),[4] the song created a much bigger

---

1. The church, by all descriptions, was a dump — a concrete box divided into ugly rooms. There was no heat and no running water.
2. Legend has it that Bill pushed for the gig because he was besotted with Kathleen and thought that this might win her favor.
3. Some blanks need to be filled in at this point. The unnamed group played their second gig on April 19th at the Koffee Klub in Athens, but didn't get to finish the gig once the cops moved in to shut the place down because of overcrowding. As for the name — R.E.M., in the context of the group, doesn't stand for anything. Although dream researchers use R.E.M. as short for "rapid eye movement," this abbreviation does not apply to the band. The group pulled it out of a dictionary as an alternative to some of their other choices: Negro Eyes, Twisted Kites and Cans of Piss. And yes, the periods between the letters ARE necessary. An early rider drawn up by then-manager Jefferson Holt for a promoter read as follows: "Please note that R.E.M. is three letters with periods. It does not serve as an abbreviation and is not pronounced as a word. Please bear this in mind in all promotional activities."
4. Hear this version on R.E.M.'s EPONYMOUS (IRS, 1988.)

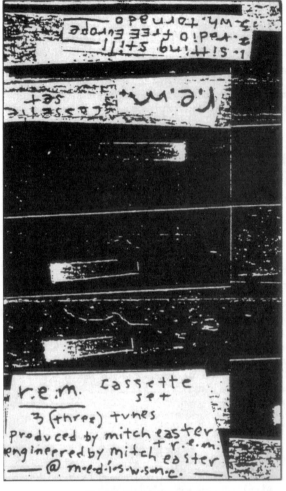

The *Radio Free Europe* cassette

buzz than anyone had anticipated. First of all, it was a little weird for its day. While the world remained awash in synthesizers and metal bands, here was a rock song that wasn't played through Marshall amplifiers and didn't feature any guitar solos. Second, what was the singer singing about? He was obviously singing with great passion — but what was he saying?[1] And third, although the song rocked, there was a weird country and folk tinge to everything as well. Whatever the case, many critics and college radio programmers recognized this as fresh and exciting stuff for 1981. At the end of the year, *Radio Free Europe* was named as independent single of the year by *The Village Voice* (way up there in New York City!) A cult following was starting to build.

R.E.M. was quickly leaving their punk-ish leanings behind. Although the change in sound and attitude had been dramatic over the first twelve months of their existence, there was one particular incident that changed things even more. It was what has become known in R.E.M. lore as the "Nashville Incident."

In late 1981, R.E.M. was booked to play a show in Nashville. The venue was a tent with a very low ceiling and the stage was nothing more than a few tables lashed together with duct tape. When R.E.M. went on, Peter Buck's attention was immediately transfixed on a gorgeous woman down front who was wearing a plastic shirt that was virtually transparent. And wonder of wonders, she appeared to be flirting with him. Loaded on beer and adrenaline, Peter began to show off, leaping into the air and executing fancy split-leg maneuvers. Unfortunately, one jump was a little too high and he smashed his head — and the neck of his guitar — on one of the steel supports holding up the tent. His head — and pride — would eventually heal, the Fender Telecaster would not. His one and only guitar was ruined beyond repair.

This was a disaster. A series of gigs was now in jeopardy because their lead guitarist had gone and destroyed his guitar. With no choice, Peter scraped up $175 and headed over to Chick Pianos in Athens in hopes of finding a decent used guitar — hopefully, another Telecaster. As it turned out, the only guitar in stock in his price range was a Rickenbacker, an instrument with a different feel and sound than a Telecaster. It was a little weird; after all, this is what the Beatles and the Byrds used — a Rickenbacker was not very punk rock. But with no choice, and with shows lined up, Peter took it.

Fortune smiled on R.E.M. that day. It just so happens that at the time of the Nashville Incident, Peter had been content to play straight chords, although there were times that he liked to pick at the strings for effect. The technique sounded okay on the Telecaster, but what he tried the same thing on the

---

1. During the sessions, Stipe actually sang most of the song with his hands almost over his mouth.

Rickenbacker, he was amazed at how much better it sounded. As he began to apply this technique to R.E.M. originals, they suddenly sounded newer, fresher and more exciting. This discovery encouraged Peter to experiment further with this new style, leading him off in a completely different, completely unexpected direction. In the years ahead, R.E.M.'s music — and bank accounts — would benefit immeasurably, thanks largely to a flirtatious girl in a see-through plastic shirt.

In October 1981, R.E.M. recorded twelve more originals, hoping to issue a debut album. But upon hearing the playback, they realized that much of what they had recorded was substandard and threw six of them out. Rather than go back and hurriedly write enough new material to fill out an album, they decided to stick with those six solid songs and issue an EP instead. In March 1982, CHRONIC TOWN appeared on an American indie label called IRS. After it was released, the band spend the rest of the year on the road. R.E.M. played everywhere, from college campuses to fried chicken restaurants in the middle of Nebraska. When they weren't on tour, they were working on material for what would become their debut album.

Studio sessions started in January 1983 and when the album hit the stores on April 12th, it immediately created a sensation among fans of underground rock and roll. With music still dominated by New Wavers like Duran Duran and with safe, corporate rock monsters like Styx and Journey playing to stadiums, R.E.M.'s new made-in-America sound might as well have been beamed from space. There were no guitar solos, no synthesizers, no drum solos, no ultra-slick, multi-track production techniques. The guitars jangled while the bass often seemed to carry the melody as much as the singer — but then again, what exactly was the singer saying? It was simple, striped-down, melodic rock that created an oddly haunting atmosphere, reminiscent of the promise once offered by Jonathan Richman and Television. Although it was ignored by much of mainstream radio — even after *Rolling Stone* declared it to be a better album than both Michael Jackson's THRILLER and SYNCHRONICITY from the Police — MURMUR connected where it counted. R.E.M. found themselves the darlings of a surprisingly large and loyal underground rock audience. It peaked at No. 36 on the album charts and stayed on the charts for thirty weeks. All in all, it was a very respectable performance for a first effort. In retrospect, MURMUR was one of the most important and influential debut albums of the 80's.[2]

The effect of the Nashville Incident was even more pronounced by April 14, 1984, the day R.E.M. released RECKONING. With breezy singles like *So. Central Rain*, *Pretty Persuasion* and *(Don't Go Back To) Rockville*, R.E.M.'s status as college radio heroes began to build even more. The understated production, the mysterious, mumbled lyrics and the cryptic artwork of their albums all endeared them to a growing fanbase composed of college kids and music fans who hated the mainstream rock of the day. They bought enough copies of RECKONING to push the album into the Top 30 on the *Billboard* album charts.[3]

After a seemingly endless tour, R.E.M. moved to London in January 1985 to start work on their third album. In retrospect, this was a mistake. The last tour had been too long and everyone really should have taken a break from music. London was also snowy and cold that winter, and the trip to the studio required a long walk outside each day — not exactly ideal conditions for a bunch of guys from Georgia. The weather was especially tough for Stipe who, prone to chills, took to wrapping himself in layer after layer of clothing. To make matters even worse, R.E.M. found themselves in the midst of a song writing slump. Even though they were determined to advance their sound, they were stymied as to how to do it. Tensions increased to the point where Michael Stipe had a mini mental and physical breakdown.

When the album was finally released on June 10, 1985, fans were confused. Something wasn't right. The songs were darker, folkier and somehow obsessed with rural life in the South. And what was the title of this record, anyway? Was it FABLES OF THE RECONSTRUCTION or was it RECONSTRUCTION OF THE FABLES? The artwork made it hard to be sure. In the end, all attempts to find a hit single from the album failed, and although it eventually went gold, initial sales were disappointing — at a minimum, they had expected to sell 600,000 copies right away. Instead, they sold only half that, and after the promise of the last two albums, FABLES was looked upon as a step back. For the time being, R.E.M. was a band in trouble.

---

2. MURMUR had the good fortune to be released just as more music fans turned to college radio stations for their fix of new music. Disappointed and angry with the pap being played on commercial stations, campus radio offered listeners music that couldn't be heard anywhere else. R.E.M. became a favorite of campus stations across the US as college radio began to exert a greater and greater influence when it came to breaking new bands and, ultimately, record sales. The rise of R.E.M. went hand in hand with the rise of college radio.

3. MURMUR had also done surprisingly well, peaking at No. 36 on *Billboard* the previous year.

When everyone reconvened to record album number four in April 1986, R.E.M. set about to change things. The dark, folky experiment of FABLES was abandoned and a concerted effort was made to return R.E.M. to their original ways. And no more recording in London in the dead of winter. Spring in Indiana was a much better idea. Using producer Don Gehman, the album once again featured R.E.M. as a stripped-down, understated, jangly pop band who sounded like they were having fun.

One of the best songs from the record wasn't an R.E.M. original. Back in his days as a record clerk at Wuxtry in Athens, Peter loved to rummaged through stacks of old 45's. One of his favorite discoveries was a Texas band called the Clique who, in 1969, issued a minor hit (No. 22) called *Sugar on Sunday*. On the B-side of that single was a pop gem called *(I Am) Superman*. After Peter played the song for the rest of the band, everyone decided to take a shot at recording it, thinking that if things turned out well, it might end up as a B-side to some future R.E.M. single. In the end, the recording turned out so well that they decided to stick the song onto the album at the last minute, not only making it the first cover to show up on an R.E.M. album, but also the first song featuring Mike Mills on lead vocals.[1] You can probably imagine the surprise of the composer of *Superman* — Gary Zekley, now an operator of a computer supply house in California — when he suddenly started receiving huge royalty cheques in the mail.

Although LIFES was a strong return to form for R.E.M., it still wasn't the commercial breakthrough that most people had expected. Even though it was another gold record for the band, there were those who had expected more. But then again, even though the last six years had been spent carefully laying all the groundwork, R.E.M. had never really aggressively courted mainstream success. Invitations to support bigger acts on the road were rejected in favor of smaller headlining tours of their own. There was a continuing aversion towards doing videos. And there was the matter of R.E.M.'s low-key production sound, which, for many music fans in the mid-80's, was still somewhat of an acquired taste. Besides, they were making a nice living at being a cult band, and enjoyed the level of credibility and integrity generally accorded to cult groups.

At the same time, R.E.M. knew that they'd hit the Cult Band Wall. At first, obscurity was a virtue, a badge of honor to be worn proudly. But after a while, many cult bands realize that if they are to survive creatively, they have to grow. They come to the realization that music is their life's work. What's the point of pouring your heart and soul into music if only a few people will ever get to hear it? And if you honestly believe that this music could change rock and roll for the better, shouldn't you do everything in your power to make sure that it got to as many people as possible?

The transition from college rock faves to mainstream force came in 1987. R.E.M.'s cult following had grown so large over the previous couple of years that it was perhaps inevitable that their sheer numbers would force R.E.M. onto the mainstream stage. That big shove came in August 1987 when the group issued DOCUMENT, an album that came to be recognized as a commercial and creative breakthrough. Demand for new product was so great that the album went gold almost immediately while *The One I Love* rocketed up the singles charts before settling in at No. 9 on *Billboard* and well into the Top 40 in the UK. Meanwhile, critics took note of the muscular production of Scott Litt, who managed to give the band a bright, clean sound without sacrificing R.E.M.'s trademark lo-fi energy. Much was also made of Stipe's lyrics which alternately exploded with righteous anger and dripped with irony. Suddenly, the whole world was paying attention to this band of college geeks from Georgia.

DOCUMENT also marked a turning point in the general public's perception of what it took to be a successful rock band. Firstly, R.E.M. proved that it was possible to be in a big group without having to sound like Van Halen, Boston or Def Leppard. Marshall amplifiers, layers of screaming guitars and outrageous stage productions were not always necessary to attract attention. Second, DOCUMENT also showed what could happen if a record label was patient enough to let an artist develop, not over weeks or months, but over *years*. Third, with DOCUMENT, R.E.M. demonstrated that it was possible to grow into something huge without having to resort to artistic compromises — it apparently *was* possible to go from cult band to major mainstream stars without selling out and alienating all your longtime fans. And finally,

---

1. And that noise at the beginning of the song? That's a talking Godzilla doll that the band picked up during a tour of Japan. The reason you can't understand what's being said is because he's speaking Japanese. Here's the translation: "This is a special news report! Godzilla has been sighted in Tokyo Bay! The attack on it by the Self-Defense Force has been useless! He is heading towards the city! Aaarrrghhhhh!"

R.E.M. proved that you didn't necessarily have to be on a major label to succeed — the right indie label would do just fine. Or would it?

R.E.M.'s association with IRS through the 80's had, for the most part, been both cordial and profitable. The label was both patient and indulgent toward R.E.M., assuring them of complete creative control over all aspects of their music. R.E.M. appreciated this arrangement, but they couldn't help being concerned over the problems IRS had with the biggest bugaboo faced by any indie label — distribution. The group was faced with a common problem — what's the point of having all this control if the label can't guarantee that they'll get the records into the stores? IRS had a solid distribution arrangement for North America, but

Hib-Tone single

in other parts of the world, they were, well, *lacking*. R.E.M. knew that if they were going to be a truly global band, they had to make a decision involving not only their fundamental business principles, but their basic artistic philosophies.

The end of their affiliation came with IRS came shortly after Mo Ostin of Warner Brothers offered the group $6 million (US) for five albums. Even more important than the money were the promises of solid, worldwide distribution, and that R.E.M. would be allowed to retain complete creative control over everything; music, artwork, merchandising — the works. It was an offer R.E.M. couldn't refuse, and in June 1988, R.E.M. finally became a major label act.[2]

The band entered this new phase of their career completely re-energized and, largely because of the Reagan presidency, much more politicized than ever before. Now that they were guaranteed to have all their records shipped all over the world, they set about on a new mission to conquer the planet, without falling prey to artistic compromises, and without having to dilute their musical vision. Their first album for Warner Brothers, GREEN, was released on November 8, 1988. In the beginning, the album suffered from the predictable backlash from hardcore fans who believed that R.E.M. had sold out the moment they left IRS. Some even misinterpreted the environmental sentiments of the word "green," thinking that this was an allusion to the group's new found wealth. Nevertheless, GREEN sold faster than DOCUMENT as Warner's strong distribution helped open new markets for the group. The subsequent tour took the band through 130 shows in seventeen countries. No more clubs and small theaters either, most of these gigs were in arenas and stadiums. The star of these shows was Michael Stipe. His outrageous costumes, his make-up, his anti-macho rock god poses and oddball stage patter caused everyone to take notice of the kid from Georgia. The shy, obtuse art student had completed his slow transition to major rock icon.

When R.E.M. finally returned to Athens, the original plan was for everyone to take six full months to recover. But as sometimes happens, the energy felt at the end of a successful tour turned into another round of writing and recording. Within a month of returning home, everyone but Michael Stipe was back rehearsing new material. He soon followed with a batch of new lyrics.

Peter Buck had begun his recovery from the Green tour by doing little more than drinking beer and watching football through December 1988 and January 1989. During the games, he kept fiddling with his new mandolin. After a few quarters, he recorded some parts on a boom box and then gave the tape to Mike Mills who then added a bass line. The tape then made its way to Michael Stipe who added some

---

2. Even the head of IRS said that the offer was too good to turn down.

words based around an old Southern saying that described someone who was losing all hope and faith. As the song evolved and was given a title — *Losing My Religion* — the decision was made that it would be the first single from the next album.

When it came time to issue OUT OF TIME (released March 12, 1991), Warner Brothers balked at their choice of a first single, saying that it was inappropriate for a rock band of R.E.M.'s stature to risk releasing a song featuring a mandolin. R.E.M., pointing out that "complete creative control" clause in their contract, insisted that they get their way. Wisely, the company backed down. Once it was released, the brilliantly confessional and highly intimate nature of *Losing My Religion* was an immediate hit with fans. Not only did it become a No. 4 hit on the singles chart in America, it also propelled OUT OF TIME to the No. 1 slot on the album charts. Critics and fans went crazy, awed by the accomplished musicianship of R.E.M. and entranced by the group's new experiments with song textures. Thanks to several other major singles (*Radio Song, Shiny Happy People*), R.E.M. had done what many thought impossible — they had bested both DOCUMENT and GREEN. The flood of accolades was not far behind: Grammy Awards, MTV Video awards and uncountable "best of the year" votes from fans and critics

Most people would have assumed that R.E.M. was happy with things following the release of OUT OF TIME. The truth was that these people were not so shiny or happy. Peter Buck was especially miserable, and, having seen his marriage fall apart, began drinking more than he should. Mike Mills was also battling personal demons, while a rapidly balding Michael Stipe looked thin and ill. Everyone was also feeling out of sorts from a creative perspective. Even as OUT OF TIME lingered on the charts, the grunge movement, with its streetwise indie bands playing loud guitars through big amplifiers, began to boom. R.E.M. began to fear that perhaps their approach to music — the old American indie rock vision of the 80's that allowed for quieter, more subtle-sounding groups — was no longer relevant. The band was in such a deep funk that for the first time ever, they declined to tour in support of an album.

Considering the weirdness and the personal crises each of the members endured through 1991 and 1992, it was only natural for their somber moods to manifest themselves on the next R.E.M. album. The group turned inward, becoming even more emotional and introspective, creating what Michael Stipe defiantly described as a "punk rock record — just a very quiet one."

Issued on October 6, 1992, AUTOMATIC FOR THE PEOPLE[1] featured many songs about death, longing and sadness. The prime example was *Everybody Hurts*, a song inspired by a true story told to Michael by his schoolteacher sister, Lynda. One of her students had attempted suicide after a prolonged bout of depression. Michael — well aware of the effect depression can have on a person's will to live — decided to write a song that might offer people hope, thereby giving them the strength to continue fighting. The powerful video clip (shot on I-10 just outside of San Antonio, Texas, and directed by Jake Scott, son of Ridley) was one of the finest examples of the medium and won several major awards. While grunge was making ears bleed and opening new markets for flannel shirts, AUTOMATIC FOR THE PEOPLE was quiet and melancholy. It was also R.E.M.'s most successful album ever, selling more than 15 million copies worldwide.

While AUTOMATIC was mostly soft and acoustic, the next album was not. MONSTER (released on September 27, 1994) was one of the hardest R.E.M. records ever. Rather than sit around in a circle writing songs on acoustic instruments — a method that had become standard practice over the years — the band set up as if they were playing a concert. Sometimes they went as far as rehearsing in a parking lot in order to recreate a live atmosphere. Themes of life and death were once again in evidence, spurred along by real-life events that created an explosive emotional atmosphere.[2] Unbeknownst to fans, the making of MONSTER took a serious emotional toll on the group. Tensions rose to such a level that R.E.M. actually called it quits shortly after the album was finished. It was only after a brief cooling down period that everyone began talking again, and the temporary breakup was hushed up.

---

1. A word about the title of this album: "Automatic for the People" is the motto of Weaver D's restaurant on East Broad Street in Athens. Not only is the food good (Lynda Stipe had the place cater her wedding), but the service is excellent. Instead of responding with a "thank you" after they take your order, many of the serving staff acknowledge things with a swift "Automatic!" In Weaver D's world, that means ready, quick and efficient preparation and service of your food. It's another little piece of Athens that's been immortalized on an R.E.M. album.

2. Life: Peter Buck became a father of twin girls, while Michael Stipe became an uncle for the first time. Death: River Phoenix — a close friend of Michael's — died of a drug overdose on October 31, 1993. Then Kurt Cobain was found dead on April 8, 1994.

MONSTER was another major success for R.E.M. When it was issued in the fall of 1994, it became the first R.E.M. album to enter the *Billboard* charts at No. 1. Upbeat and recovered from their short-lived split, the group decided to embark on a world tour for the first time in five years. It was to be a long, strange trip.

Things started well enough on January 13, 1995, in Perth, Australia, and continued more-or-less on course until March 1st in Lausanne, Switzerland. About ninety minutes into the set, and just as the band was getting into the falsetto part of a song called *Tongue*, Bill Berry recalls a pain so intense that it felt like someone had dropped a bowling ball on his head. The agony was white-hot, and he had to be carried from the stage. At first, doctors thought it might just be a bad migraine exacerbated by the altitude, but after a CAT scan, they realized that they were dealing with two potentially fatal brain aneurysms. Berry underwent emergency brain surgery at Lausanne's University Hospital Center and spent eight long weeks recovering. It wasn't until May 15th that he was well enough for the tour to resume in San Francisco.[3]

However, R.E.M.'s problems weren't over yet. In July, Mike Mills discovered that he needed surgery to correct a lesion on his intestine and more shows had to be canceled. No sooner were the sutures out when R.E.M. played an outdoor show in Ireland where two fans drowned while swimming in the river that flowed through the concert site. A few weeks later, Michael Stipe had to fly back to Georgia to have an iguinal hernia repaired. By the time the tour ended at the Omni in Atlanta on November 21, 1995, R.E.M. was happy just to make it home in one piece.

One of the positive things that arose from that horrible world tour was that the band now had a backlog of new ideas for songs. As the new tracks took shape over the course of the tour, some of them were introduced as part of the set. Over 110 concerts were taped and more than a hundred hours worth of sound checks were also recorded. Once everyone got home, they were faced with the task of analyzing all those recordings in order to isolate the best bits.

For example, a Peter Buck riff from the sound check before the comeback show in San Francisco led to the rough outline of a chorus two days later. When the tour checked into Memphis, a piano was added. That tape was then taken to a studio in Seattle where Mike Mills added some organ and a few more keyboard parts. The tape then transferred back to Peter who inserted a few additional layers of guitar (okay, so he added *forty* layers) before it was given to Michael who then contributed his vocals. Finally, the song was given a title — *Bittersweet Me* — and was included on the next R.E.M. album, NEW ADVENTURES IN HI-FI.

NEW ADVENTURES (released on September 10, 1996) was the first album under a brand new deal with Warner Brothers. The previous month, they'd signed a new contract that called for an additional five albums. But because OUT OF TIME and MONSTER had been the answers to many an executive's multi-platinum dreams, the dollar value of R.E.M.'s new contract increased substantially. The payout went from $6 million to $80 million, making it one of the richest deals in the history of rock and roll. On the negative side, NEW ADVENTURES did not offer much of a return on this new investment. After starting strong, the album fell out of the Top 20 only a month later.[4]

Meanwhile, R.E.M. had unexpected problems of their own. Jefferson Holt, their longtime manager, had been suddenly terminated on May 22, 1996. Although both parties refused to talk about what led to Holt's dismissal, gossip of allegations of sexual harassment involving a member of R.E.M.'s staff at the home office in Athens periodically bubbled up throughout the industry. Most serious of all was the surprise announcement that R.E.M. was about to undergo its first lineup change in seventeen years.

---

3. This was not the first time Bill Berry almost died while on tour. In April 1989, he collapsed on stage in Germany, suffering from a bout of Rocky Mountain Spotted Fever that he'd picked up from a tick in his garden before the band hit the road. Doctors in Germany had never seen a case of Spotted Fever because, after all, Munich is a few miles away from the Rockies. Despite his delirium and bright red skin blotches, Berry was diagnosed with a bronchial infection. By sheer coincidence, the drug they prescribed to treat this particular type of infection is identical to what a Georgia doctor would give a person with Rocky Mountain Spotted Fever. Had this not been the case, Berry might have very well died.

4. Some believe that R.E.M.'s choice of *E-Bow the Letter* as a first single did the album in. When UP was released, the label picked *Daysleeper* as the first single, determined that the new album would not be introduced to the world through a gloom-and-doom song.

On what was supposed to be the first day of rehearsals for the next album, Bill Berry told the rest of the band that he was quitting. A near-fatal brain aneurysm will do wonders when it comes to changing your perspective on life. The news was made public on October 30, 1997, when Bill read a statement to an unbelieving audience:

> I've been playing drums since age nine. I'm at a point in my life where some of my priorities have shifted. I loved my seventeen years with R.E.M., but I'm ready to reflect, assess and move on to a different phase of my life. The four of us will continue our close friendship and I look forward to hearing their future efforts as the world's biggest R.E.M. fan.

Michael Stipe responded stoically:

> It's the end of an era for us and that's sad. I'm happy for Bill. It's what he really wants and I think it's a courageous decision. For me, Mike and Peter, are we still R.E.M.? I guess a three-legged dog is still a dog. It just has to learn how to run differently.

Had Berry left the group after they had just released an album or finished a tour, R.E.M. would probably have broken up. But because they were just about to begin making a new record, Michael, Peter and Mike realized that they could turn this turmoil into a golden opportunity. Now that they were, in effect, a new band, the old rules and assumptions that governed the former incarnation of R.E.M. need not apply. The forty-five new songs that had been prepared for the sessions could be approached from completely different angles, free from old biases and habits. The creative challenge of not only refurbishing but *reinventing* R.E.M. was a creative challenge that was too enticing to ignore.

Sessions for the new album began in earnest on January 31, 1998, two months after Berry handed in his resignation. The result, UP, was released on October 27, 1998. Loops and drum machines (originally introduced by Berry as far back as AUTOMATIC FOR THE PEOPLE in 1992) were used with greater frequency, allowing the band to create sonic landscapes which were far removed from the original R.E.M. blueprint of the 1980's. They concentrated more on mood and texture, deliberately dispensing with the jangly guitars of the old days and, for the first time, electing to print Stipe's lyrics in the liner notes. While UP didn't feature much in the way of singles that jumped out at listeners — the album takes a while to "get", and requires repeated listening before the songs begin to sink in — it was a well crafted album that hinted at what R.E.M. might accomplish as a trio in the future. The group believed in the album enough to embark on another world tour (a risky venture, considering what happened last time) beginning in Lisbon on June 17, 1999.

Like U2, R.E.M. has become legendary for their ability to sell tens of millions of albums while being able to maintain an unwavering artistic vision. Unaffected by musical trends or the machinations of the music industry, R.E.M. has remained true to their original indie ideals. They've also been quite successful in serving two generations of fans: their original followers from the IRS years (many of whom are now in their 40's and 50's) and those that they picked up after OUT OF TIME or even AUTOMATIC FOR THE PEOPLE. It takes a special type of band to bridge that kind of gap.

Although their musical influence has been far-reaching — think of all the jangle-pop bands that followed in their wake — R.E.M. will forever be remembered for how they paved the way for indie / college rock culture in America. R.E.M. proved conclusively that, with a little determination and patience, it was possible to rise to superstardom without having to succumb to the compromises often demanded by record labels. After R.E.M. made it, more labels were suddenly willing to take a chance on some of the weird bands heard only on campus radio stations. This, in turn, encouraged more bands to continue to fight for their artistic principles, setting in motion the dynamic that resulted in the explosion of alt-rock in the early 90's. The R.E.M. model is now followed by hundreds of alt-rock bands as they fight their way from obscurity to mainstream acceptance. Had it not been for the R.E.M., we might still be living in the era of Styx and Journey.

Fast Facts

- Michael contracted a serious case of scarlet fever when he was two years old. He was also a very popular kid with his teachers in kindergarten. They called him "Mike the Shining Light."
- There's a big scar on Stipe's forehead from an auto accident when he was nineteen. His car hit a deer. He has tattoos of a couple of 1920's-era cartoon characters on his right arm (Krazy Kat and Ignatz Mouse.)

o At the time R.E.M. chose that name, there were at least six other band using the name R.E.M., but since no one challenged them, the boys from Athens were the ones who got to keep it.

o *Radio Free Europe* (the re-recorded IRS version) peaked at No. 78 on the American singles charts in August 1983.

o *(Don't Go Back To) Rockville* was a plea to Ingrid Schorr, a short-lived member of Oh-Ok, a group headed up by Michael Stipe's sister, Lynda. Mike Mills was besotted with her and didn't want her to move back to Rockville, Maryland.

o R.E.M. has always been known for their quirky artwork, especially when it comes to labeling the sides of their albums. The tradition extends all the way back to CHRONIC TOWN and, with the brief exception of MURMUR, all R.E.M. albums have stayed away from the obvious "Side 1 - Side 2" style of labeling. For example, the original vinyl version of RECKONING wasn't labeled in the traditional side one / side two manner. Instead, we were given the L(eft) side and the R(ight) side. FABLES features an A Side and Another Side. AUTOMATIC FOR THE PEOPLE was *Drive and Ride*, while MONSTER was labeled C and D.

o The photos that adorn MURMUR were shot by Michael Stipe. The front cover features the kudzu vine in a field near the Normaltown area of Athens. The kudzu is an incredibly fast-growing Japanese weed that infests much of the Deep South. The train bridge on the back was originally envisioned as the front cover.

o The liner notes and track listings of LIFES RICH PAGEANT are all mixed up and a few songs are missing along with the apostrophe in LIFES.

o During the dark period surrounding the FABLES album, Peter Buck, feeling the need to clear his head, when back to work at Wuxtry Records for a while. As a "guest clerk," he bagged records at the cash in late 1985 and 1986 before the crowds of fans made work impossible.

o The title LIFES RICH PAGEANT was taken from a line in a Pink Panther sequel entitled *A Shot in the Dark*.

o The video for *Fall on Me* (the first single from LIFES, released on August 18, 1986) was shot for $650.

o Hardcore followers of Michael Stipe are often called "Distiples."

o Michael Stipe realized a life-long dream when Patti Smith agree to duet with him on *E-Bow the Letter* from NEW ADVENTURES IN HI-FI.

o After Bill Berry returned to duty after his emergency surgery, the remainder of the road trip was dubbed the Aneurysm Tour. Some programs sold at the shows featured a nice picture of the emergency room CAT scan of Bill's brain.

o There's an odd story behind *What's the Frequency, Kenneth?* In October 1993, CBS news anchor Dan Rather was walking down Park Avenue in New York when he was attacked by a man who kept yelling "Kenneth! What's the frequency?" One theory was that Rather had been mistaken for Kenneth Schaffer, an electronics expert who had built a system for intercepting secret Soviet satellite transmissions. Later, it was discovered that the assailant was William Tager, a mentally ill man who believed that the media was beaming hostile messages into his brain. He wanted Rather to give him the frequency of the transmissions so he could shut off the voices. Later, after R.E.M. had written the song, Rather turned up with R.E.M. to lip-sync the song on *Late Night with David Letterman*.

o R.E.M. has performed under a variety of pseudonyms over the years. They include Pink Pajamas; the Neon Mud Men; It Crawled from the South; Fat, Drunk and Stupid; Hornets Attack Victor Mature and Bingo Handjob.

o The group is one of the most politically active bands in the world. As "unabashed liberals" (their term) R.E.M. has supported causes ranging from Greenpeace and Amnesty International to various animal rights organizations and pro-choice groups.

o R.E.M.'s activism is also apparent right at home in Athens. Since Michael Stipe and Mike Mills still live in Athens (Stipe owns three blocks' worth of real estate that has been assessed at close to $1 million), they often get involved in a variety of civic issues ranging from historic preservation to the environment. They've also been known to make substantial campaign donations to their favorite civic government candidates.

o Along with his interest in photography, Michael Stipe owns two movie production companies. Single

Cell is based in Hollywood and concentrates on Hollywood-style releases. C100 is based in New York and focuses on a style called "guerrilla-style indie films."

o Bertis Down has acted as the band's legal advisor from the very beginning.

o The rumor about R.E.M. playing one last show on December 31, 1999, before breaking up for good started with a joke Peter Buck made during an interview.

o World headquarters for R.E.M. is on Clayton above a cookie shop. Joining the official fan club costs $10 US for American fans, $12 US for people in other countries. Your membership needs to be renewed every year. The address is

R.E.M.
P.O. BOX 8032
ATHENS, GA.
30603

Recommended Listening

o MURMUR (IRS, 1983)

o LIFES RICH PAGEANT (IRS, 1986)

o DOCUMENT (IRS, 1987)

o OUT OF TIME (Warner Brothers 1991)

o AUTOMATIC FOR THE PEOPLE (Warner Brothers, 1993)

o MONSTER (Warner Brothers, 1994)

o DEAD LETTER OFFICE, a collection of interesting and amusing B-sides and rarities also comes with all six tracks from the CHRONIC TOWN EP (IRS, 1982.) The import version features two bonus tracks. EPONYMOUS (IRS, 1988) is a good overview of the IRS years. As a bonus, it features the original Hib-Tone version of *Radio Free Europe*. One other collection that might appeal to serious R.E.M. fans is IN THE ATTIC: ALTERNATIVE RECORDINGS 1985-1989 (EMI, 1997.) The CD features fifteen tracks from the obscure corners of the R.E.M. catalogue that were acquired by EMI when IRS folded.

Internet Resources

o www.remhq.com

o www.murmurs.com

o www.retroweb.com/rem.html

o http://come.to/r-e-m/

Recommended Reading

o Bowler, Dave and Dray, Bryan. *R.E.M.: Documental.* London: Boxtree, 1995.

o Editors of Rolling Stone. *R.E.M.: The Ultimate Compendium of Interviews, Articles, Facts and Opinions.* New York, New York: Hyperion, 1995.

o Fletcher, Tony. *R.E.M.arks: The Story of R.E.M.* London: Omnibus Press, 1989.

o Gray, Marcus. *It Crawled from the South: An R.E.M. Companion.* New York, New York: Da Cao Press, 1993.

o Greer, Jim. *R.E.M.: Behind the Mask.* Boston, Massachusetts: Little, Brown, 1992.

o Rosen, Craig. *R.E.M.: Inside Out; The Stories Behind Every Song.* Dubai: Carlton Books, 1997.

o Sullivan, Denise. *R.E.M.: An Oral History; Talk About the Passion.* Lancaster, Pennsylvania: Charles F. Miller Books, 1994.

Related Listening

Patti Smith, Jonathan Richman, Television, the Feelies, Gin Blossoms, Toad the Wet Sprocket, Live, Dream Syndicate, the dBs, and Let's Active.

The Story Thus Far ...

Prompted towards a certain musical sensibility by Patti Smith (and encouraged in that direction by the Velvet Underground, Television, Wire and the Sex Pistols), R.E.M. added 60's-style jangly guitars (the Byrds) to create a brand new made-in-American indie rock sound.

~ 16 ~
SONIC YOUTH
Beautiful Indie Noise

The problem with revolutionaries is that they tend to burn out very quickly. They have one, maybe two, wild and crazy ideas that bore deep holes into the status quo — and then, spent, exhausted and irrelevant, they disappear forever.

It's especially tough to be a musical revolutionary. Changing the world's perception of how music should be made and enjoyed borders on the impossible. Even the most rabid of musical rebels will eventually get tired of banging their heads against the wall, at which point they'll either compromise their original vision in order to get some kind of attention from the mainstream, or quit music entirely.

This is why Sonic Youth has been so special to the evolution of alt-rock. They've been unwavering in their methods since the early 80's — no compromises, no shortcuts, no attempts to water things down for the masses. By challenging the conventions and traditions of rock and roll — everything from the controlled chaos of their song structure to the odd ways they tuned their guitars — Sonic Youth has had a massive effect on everything from hardcore punk to grunge to lo-fi indie music.

By the late 1970's, the core of the original punk scene with Patti Smith, the Voidoids and Heartbreakers had faded away. Angered by how quickly some of these once cutting-edge bands had been co-opted by the mainstream (and, as a general rebellion, at how quickly the New York underground had been institutionalized, commercialized and rendered brainless), a small group of self-styled avant-garde *artistes* slowly came together in a new scene. Bound by a determination to put the "anti" back into rock (they were basically anti-*everything*), they called this new scene "No Wave" (after a 1978 Brian Eno sponsored collection entitled *No New York*.)

Musicianship was the last thing on the minds of these art-punks. Many had no idea of how to hold a guitar, let alone play one. All that was required was an intense hatred of mainstream rock, and a determination to make music so extreme and so negative that no one would like it — except, of course, other No Wavers.[1] Often the result was nothing more than deliberate excruciating noise. Even some of the earliest Velvet Underground jams seemed like pop songs in comparison. Even so, the No Wave scene grew to include a surprising number of groups — Teenage Jesus and the Jerks, DNA, Mars, the Contortions, Tone Deaf, Red Transistor, the Gynecologists and Glenn Branca's Theoretical Girls.

The problem with being this *avant-garde* is obvious. Because these bands set out to be unpopular and unlistenable, they were. After an initial flurry of interest in this new brand of (supposedly) intelligent art-rock, it became tougher for these groups to find gigs. And because there were far more musicians than places to play, No Wave faded faster than it was born. But while it lasted, the scene served as an odd musical laboratory, a place where many different and often unrelated musical concepts could freely mix. It was out of this stew that Sonic Youth emerged.

Thurston Moore (born July 25, 1958) was a six-foot-six kid from Bethel, Connecticut who worshipped all the right idols; the Velvet Underground, the Stooges, Television, the Ramones, and Suicide. Having moved to New York in the fall of 1977, he eventually hooked up with several like-minded individuals in at least three different bands — Even Worse, the Coachmen and, finally, in a Glenn Branca project. It was while floating around with Branca that Moore met Long Island native Lee Ranaldo (born February 3, 1958.) Ranaldo also had some previous experience in bands with names like the Fluks (also known as the Flucts) and Plus Instruments. The two vowed to stay in touch.

Moore's next band was called Male Bonding and featured Dave Keay (the last known drummer of the Coachmen), Ann DeMarinis (an art-school punk with some keyboard ability) and guitarist Kim Gordon (born April 23, 1958, not, as some sources list, 1953.) Kim had come to New York via Los Angeles and

---

1. In Robert Palmer's *Rock & Roll: An Unruly History*, Lydia Lunch (of Teenage Jesus and the Jerks) is quoted as saying "We can't stand to hear *ourselves* play for more than fifteen minutes."

Toronto, and had already been in a noisy band called CKM. After some quick rehearsals, Male Bonding (now known as Red Milk) made their debut on December 17, 1980. Within a month, the group (now known as the Acadians) was skirting the edges of what remained of the No Wave scene.

The following summer, Moore organized a nine day noisefest at a New York venue called White Columns. On the third day of a festival — June 18, 1981 — a new band called Sonic Youth[1] took the stage. Consisting of Moore, Gordon, DeMarinis and drummer (actually, he was a trumpet player and actor) Richard Edson, this first version of the band specialized in nothing more than a wall of white noise. Lee Ranaldo, another participant in the festival, apparently liked what he saw because, within weeks, DeMarinis was out and he was in as the group's second guitarist.

The first Sonic Youth recording session was held over two days in December 1981 at Radio City Studios in Manhattan. Spending $2,000 for the two days, the group recorded five original songs and released them on a self-titled 12-inch EP through Neutral (a tiny label set up by Glenn Branca) early in 1982. This was the only recording made with original drummer Richard Edson, who soon left to pursue a career in acting. By the end of the year, Edson had been replaced with Bob Bert, a big No Wave fan from New Jersey, who found himself hired, fired and rehired in the space of a year.[2]

Sonic Youth issued three releases in 1983 — CONFUSION IS SEX, KILL YR IDOLS and a the live set (initially on cassette only and through Moore's own Ecstatic Peace label), SONIC DEATH.[3] Along with a handful of post-punk underground freakmeisters (most notably the Butthole Surfers, the Minutemen and the Meat Puppets, and reminiscent of both the Stooges and the MC5), Sonic Youth alternately confused, amused and angered audiences with a violent wall of sound. The music became more challenging, more confrontational and sometimes just plain weird as Moore came up with radical guitar ideas. Not only did he and Ranaldo experiment with strange tunings (F# F# G G A A is a fairly typical example), they came up with odd ways of playing the instrument. Sometimes — just for the hell of it — they'd prop up a dozen guitars on stage with each one tuned a different way, going for a new one with each song. Anyone who looked closely might have even noticed the screwdrivers and drumsticks jammed between the fretboards and the strings as some kind of weird capo. As far as Moore and Ranaldo were concerned, anything was fair game in the search for different sounds.[4]

Out of necessity (remember, there wasn't much of an American indie scene back in the early 1980's), Sonic Youth did things incredibly cheap. During the CONFUSION IS SEX sessions, one of the studio's big reel-to-reel machines ate a section of the master tape. Since it was too late to go back and re-record those sections — it would have been prohibitively expensive, anyway — the group just smoothed out the tape as best they could by hand and repaired any tears with a little cellophane tape. Then someone knocked over a can of Coke while everyone had their backs turned, soaking the master tape in a sugary mess. Once again, after a bit of desperate cleaning, the group simply soldiered on. In the end, CONFUSION IS SEX became one of those rare albums that had a serious impact on almost everyone who bought it. Building new musical bridges between the extremes of No Wave, hardcore punk and more traditional types of music, the album did come across as weird and different — but it still rocked.

After a series of false starts in late 1983 and early 1984 (and unable to find an American label interested in the band's developing pop-noise approach), Sonic Youth was signed to Blast First Records, an indie label based in Britain and distributed by Rough Trade. For the first time in its career, Sonic Youth was with a label that could guarantee that their records would make it to a large number of stores around the world. The first album under the deal was BAD MOON RISING (1985), a deliberately discordant, intentionally dissonant recording drenched in feedback, but with a definite nod to traditional song structure. The underground music press loved the album, with good reviews leading to a deal with SST,

---

1. The name was Thurston's idea. It's a cross between two of his favorite bands: Big Youth (a late 70's reggae outfit) and Sonic's Rendezvous Band (Fred "Sonic" Smith's first gig after leaving the MC5.)
2. There were other drummers during this era, including Jim Sclavunos, who was briefly with the band in 1983.
3. One of the most confusing things you will ever see is an official Sonic Youth discography. Using fly-by-night indie labels that were often based in Europe, it's a real challenge to keep track of everything the band issued in their early years. The best I've found is on-line at http://pent21.infosys.tuwien.ac.at/Staff/lux/sonic-youth/ascii.html.
4. Okay, this behavior had just as much to do with laziness as it did with art. Back then, neither Moore or Ranaldo had the patience to learn the proper finger techniques for chords. Odd open tunings allowed for cheating. It made it easy to play all these cool sounding chords without really having to work the fretboard.

the hardcore label formed by Black Flag and home to Hüsker Du and the Minutemen. Following the release of the EP DEATH VALLEY 69 (on yet another label — Homestead — in 1985), Bob Bert departed the band for good and was replaced by ex-Crucifucks drummer Steve Shelley (born June 3, 1962.) He was on board by the time the band recorded, their second album, BAD MOON RISING (1985.)

By the end of 1985, Sonic Youth had become indie darlings, especially in the UK where Blast First gave them better distribution. A series of British tours, which also featured the Butthole Surfers and Big Black, created a strong awareness and appreciation of what was happening below the surface in America. Meanwhile, back home in the States, many of these Blast First releases were selling surprisingly well as imports. Although a few major labels took noticed and began making polite inquiries about their availability, Sonic Youth refused every temptation sent their way.

In 1986, they severed ties with Blast First in favor of a new exclusive deal with SST. The first album under that deal was EVOL ("love" spelled backwards, 1986), a release that showcased Sonic Youth's growing ability to tame noise with melody and a new found sense of discipline. The music was still raw and different, but it was played and recorded with a greater understanding of the need for some kind of basic structure. Gone were the long free-form jams, replaced instead with songs constructed of simple phrases that were repeated throughout the piece. Beyond the curtain of fuzz and noise were wisps of melody. It didn't always work, but when it did, the effect was hypnotizing. A further advance in this direction came with SISTER in 1987, an album so powerful and different for its day that even *Rolling Stone* had to admit that it was a pretty good record.

Now that the group had evolved beyond an oddball performance-art outfit, Sonic Youth became favorites with US college radio, which spread the music to an even wider audience. Thanks to these campus DJs, Sonic Youth (and underground bands like them) started gaining acceptance in college towns around the country: Seattle; Olympia, Washington; Chicago; Boston; Athens, Georgia; Los Angeles and Orange County. As new, young bands in these cities bought Sonic Youth albums, they were inspired by what they heard — the infinite sonic potential of the guitar.

The biggest lesson was tabled in 1988 when Sonic Youth released DAYDREAM NATION (on still another label — Enigma — after SST failed to pay them all the money they were owed) to widespread critical acclaim. A long, sprawling double set, the album was a near perfect synthesis of hardcore punk, No Wave noise and conventional rock — a freshly defined sonic landscape for a new generation. It took the band to a top of a lot of national critics and readers polls, and sold about 100,000 copies (a *huge* number for an indie record in those days), as well as influencing the next wave of young musicians who were bored with the status quo. But just as Sonic Youth had became the undisputed leaders on the American indie stage, they came to the end of an era.

As successful as DAYDREAM NATION was, it couldn't prevent Enigma from sliding into bankruptcy. With no money to pay distributors, the supply of Enigma releases began to dry up. Soon it was impossible to find any of their product — including Sonic Youth — in any record store. Tired and frustrated of having spent the better part of a decade dealing with cash-poor indie labels who offered big promises and poor distribution, Sonic Youth made the biggest decision of their career — they signed to a major label.

In the late 80's, many of the large labels in the United States had begun to realize that there was more to rock than lightweight, spandex-clad metal bands and clunky classic rockers. As they investigated the indie / college rock scene, they realized that they'd better grab a piece of this action lest they miss out on an opportunity to inject new blood into an increasingly moribund rock scene. Hüsker Du was one of the first, jumping from SST to Warner Brothers. Warner had also cherry-picked R.E.M. out of the ashes of IRS. Soundgarden (formerly with SST and Sub Pop) was being wooed by several labels and appeared ready to jump ship. And now that Enigma was finished, the members of Sonic Youth found themselves in the enviable position of being free agents who were in big demand.

After weighing a variety of different options, Sonic Youth did what would have been unthinkable just a few years earlier. With their indie options exhausted, they struck a deal with struck with DGC, the wing of Geffen Records formed to specifically exploit the coming wave of "alternative" music. Sonic Youth's terms were clear; they would be allowed to operate in their normal fashion with complete creative control. No interference from the label would be tolerated. What's more, the group demanded that they be free to act as informal A&R reps for the label. DCG was only too happy to agree. After all, their label had just achieved what they believed was instant credibility. They'd just signed the biggest, most revered indie band of them all. A major precedent had been set.[1]

The first Sonic Youth album for DCG was GOO. Because indie bands all over America (and indeed, all over the world) were watching to see what would happen, it was crucial for this album to succeed on both an artistic and commercial level. While it was true that GOO was more focused than past albums, the trademark Sonic Youth noise was still there. Sales-wise, it became the biggest selling record of the band's career, becoming the first Sonic Youth record to crack the Top 100 on the *Billboard* album charts. The result was one of the greatest domino-effect situations in the history of music. Once indie groups realized that they could maintain their creative autonomy while enjoying the financial benefits of a major label, many of them abandoned their anti-corporate stance and signed contracts. The indie scene assault on the mainstream had begun.

By the time Butch Vig produced DIRTY (1992) for Sonic Youth (an even more structured, listener-friendly album that sold more than 300,000 copies), the group was being acknowledged as the godparents of modern alternative music. As groups such as Nirvana and Soundgarden received more attention, more respect was directed towards Sonic Youth. The effect was measurable on DCG's spreadsheets. When EXPERIMENTAL JET SET, TRASH AND NO STAR was released in 1994, it entered the Billboard charts at No. 34 and at No. 10 in the UK. This, in turn, led to a headlining slot on the 1995 Lollapalooza tour in time to promote WASHING MACHINE (1995.) Taking the proceeds from that tour, Sonic Youth was finally able to build their own recording studio. This remains the band's headquarters and the source of the experimental EP's (released on their own SYR label) as well as the band's 1998 album, A THOUSAND LEAVES.

Despite never being able to sell large numbers of records, Sonic Youth's musical influence is nothing short of gigantic. Their dissonant harmonic adventures laid the groundwork for the countless noisy, raw, lo-fi bands that followed. And not only did they establish a new vocabulary for the guitar, they showed how it was possible to maintain artistic credibility while finding a home on a major record label. This legacy is arguably even more important than their music. Consider how many wannabe musical rebels learned from this example — i.e. Nirvana. Had Sonic Youth not signed to DGC, would we have seen the explosion of alternative rock in the early and mid-90's? Would there have been that trickle-up effect that now allows us to trace a line from Sonic Youth through Nirvana, the Breeders, the Smashing Pumpkins, Hole, Offspring and Green Day? The thought is almost too scary to contemplate.

Fast Facts

o In addition to a general laziness (see footnote above), a lot of Sonic Youth's tendencies towards radical guitar tunings had to do with the fact that the group could only afford ultra-cheap instruments in the early days. Because these guitars kept going out of tune, Moore and Ranaldo decided that they might as well exploit the situation rather than fight it. This lead to experiments with different tunings. For example, *I Love Her All the Time* from BAD MOON RISING requires that the guitar be tuned to D# D# C# C# G G. (Standard guitar tuning is E B G D A E.)

o What about all those old drummers? Richard Edson returned to acting and won small-ish parts in more than forty movies, including *Do the Right Thing, Ferris Bueller's Day Off* and *Platoon*. After Bob Bert left the band for good in 1985, he appeared with Pussy Galore, Action Swingers and Chrome Cranks. Jim Sclavunos' post-Sonic Youth activities included stints with Nick Cave and the Bad Seeds and the Cramps.

o Because she helped narrow the gender gap — not only did she sing, but she played bass, a formerly decidedly unladylike instrument — Kim Gordon is revered as one of the inspirations of the riot grrl movement. This is one reason why Courtney Love insisted that Kim co-produce the first Hole album, PRETTY ON THE INSIDE.

o DGC encountered some problems with the artwork of GOO. Some record stores refused to carry and album that featured the phrase "We killed my parents" on the cover. Sonic Youth refused to change the artwork.

---

1. At first, the deal with DGC raised some eyebrows; after all, the label's parent company was home to Guns N'Roses, Whitesnake and Cher. But because of the unique "complete creative control" clause in Sonic Youth's contract, some of the edge was taken off many criticisms. DGC had no idea how much signing Sonic Youth would mean until a few years later when they bagged a trio from Aberdeen, Washington. This group stated that the only reason they signed with DGC was because if the label was all right for Sonic Youth, it was all right for them. The group? Nirvana.

---

o After GOO was released, Sonic Youth accepted an invitation to open for Neil Young on his Ragged Glory tour. Although the road trip was difficult (winning over old-time hippies with the feedback blasts of *Starpower* was a non-starter), the tour did help Young gain some cred with the alt-rock crowd, leading to his elevation to "grandfather of grunge" status.

o Sonic Youth has at least two celebrity fixations. The first is with Madonna (most notably, the Ciccone Youth side project in 1988 and *Sean, Madonna and Me* on EVOL.) Before she got big, Madonna used to hang around a lot of the same New York clubs as Sonic Youth. At first, the band thought she was kind of cool. That soon changed. The second fixation is with doomed Carpenters' singer Karen Carpenter. Kim Gordon, fascinated by Karen's fears of inadequacy, has written several songs about her, including *Tunic* on GOO. It's also why Sonic Youth performed *Superstar* for a 1994 Carpenters tribute album.

o Thurston Moore and Kim Gordon were married in 1983. They have a daughter named Coco Haley (born 1994.) Kim also runs a line of clothing called X-Girl.

o In May 1996, Sonic Youth recorded a version of the theme from an episode of *The Simpsons* that closed an episode entitled "Homerpalooza." All four members were animated for the show.

o On July 4, 1999, the band's Ryder truck was stolen from the parking lot outside of a Ramada Inn in Orange County, California. They lost many one-of-a-kind, specially-modified guitars, amplifiers and effects pedals, prompting the group to consider taking their sound in a new direction.

Recommended Listening

o EVOL (SST, 1986)
o SISTER (SST, 1987)
o DAYDREAM NATION (Blast First / Enigma, 1988. Reissued by DGC)
o GOO (DGC, 1990)
o DIRTY (DGC, 1992)
o WASHING MACHINE (DGC, 1995)
o A THOUSAND LEAVES (DGC, 1998)
o A quick way to sample SY's career is with SCREAMING FIELDS OF SONIC LOVE a broad (yet incomplete) survey of the band's indie years. And finally, a word of caution: SONIC YOUTH LIVE (SST, 1982) is as close as you may ever come to a unlistenable album. If you're into video, a good buy is 1991: THE YEAR PUNK BROKE.

Internet Resources

o www.geffen.com/sonic-youth/
o www.geocities.com/Eureka/Enterprises/1594/tbd.html#sy
o www.lasource.net/soniclife/
o http://home.nordnet.fr/~sjeziorny/indexson.htm
o http://members.tripod.com/syproject/

Recommended Reading

o Foege, Alec. *Confusion is Next: The Sonic Youth Story.* New York, New York: St. Martin's Press, 1994.

Related Listening

Velvet Underground, the Stooges, Dinosaur Jr, Husker Du, Minutemen, My Bloody Valentine, Nirvana, early Hole, Pavement, Pixies and many others.

The Story Thus Far ...

Taking the Velvet Underground's sonic attack to the next level (thanks to a liberal dose of post-punk performance-art attitude), Sonic Youth blazes a trail as American's premiere indie band.

~ 17 ~
SKINNY PUPPY
Digging It, Industrially

Music doesn't always have to be pretty. Sometimes it needs to be harsh, ugly and evil if the mission is to capture the harsh, ugly and evil aspects of everyday life. This music can make us uncomfortable and agitated at first — but if we can hold on long enough, the message might get through to us. Aural ugliness can be a powerful art statement.

Skinny Puppy specialized in these kinds of statements. Their unique brand of musical brutality alternately shocked, disgusted, amused and inspired a legion of followers, some of whom used Puppy's methods to advance not only the evolution of industrial music, but also the art of sampling and esoteric studio production techniques. They didn't just record music and sound, they manipulated and mutilated it, sculpting audio into something new. And although they didn't sell many albums (perhaps a million in total), their work through the 80's made it possible for other extreme bands like Nine Inch Nails and Marilyn Manson to exist. Since the band's tragic demise in the mid-90's, their legend has grown ever stronger.

The Puppy story started in 1982 when cEvin Key (born Kevin Crompton, February 13, 1961), a former lead singer for a Depeche Mode-like Vancouver band called Images in Vogue, teamed up with Nivek Ogre (born Kevin Ogilvie, December 5, 1962.)[1] Having discovered the industrial-grade thumping and noise terrorism of UK bands such as Throbbing Gristle and Cabaret Voltaire and the moodiness of Bauhaus, Joy Division, early New Order and Depeche Mode, cEvin and Nivek set about creating their own brand of electronic attack. All pop and rock conventions — such as melody — were immediately discarded in favor of distortion, thunderous rhythms, more distortion, aggressive electronic sounds and still more distortion.

Together with an acquaintance named Wilhelm Schroeder,[2] Key and Ogre scraped together enough money to issue BACK AND FORTH, a seven song cassette with an original run of just fifty copies, of which only thirty-five were actually released.[3] In early 1983, one of these tapes landed on a desk at Nettwerk Records, a new Vancouver indie label. Nettwerk was looking to sign new bands in order to live up to a reciprocal distribution agreement they had with a variety of foreign labels who specialized in aggressive electronic dance music. Having already signed Moev (featuring one of the label's founders) and the Grapes of Wrath, Nettwerk decided to give Skinny Puppy a shot. Although the group had never played a live gig to that point, their sound fit in well with the Cabaret Voltaire and Front 242 records Nettwerk had agreed to distribute. They agreed to a two-album deal.

The first official Puppy release was REMISSION, a 1984 record that, while containing eleven tracks, was nevertheless classified as an EP. REMISSION was also the beginning of a decade-long relationship with producer Dave "Rave" Ogilvie. In October 1985, Puppy issued the Ogilvie-produced BITES. Although neither record was even remotely radio-friendly, the band's punishing dance beats and goth / industrial / electronic fusion found an enthusiastic audience in dark clubs on both sides of the Atlantic. Songs like Assimilate and The Choke became turntable standards whenever the industrial set turned out to dance.

In the summer of 1986, Schroeder was replaced by Dwayne Rudolph Goettel (born February 1, 1964), a former member of a band called Psyche and an Edmonton outfit called Water. His first release with the band was MIND: THE PERPETUAL INTERCOURSE, an album that's now considered to be a classic of the

---

1. Yes, you spell his name "cEvin." Note that "Nivek" is "Kevin" spelled backwards. He is NOT related to producer Dave Ogilvie, nor is he related to Rosie Ogilvie. Although she did contribute some backing vocals to Puppy tunes, it should be made clear that she's Dave Ogilvie's wife.
2. This is the pseudonym of Bill Leeb, the future founder of Front Line Assembly. He based Wilhem on his first name and picked Schroeder because he thought it sounded cool. He left Skinny Puppy when he felt his musical contributions weren't being appreciated.
3. These tracks were later officially reissued as BACK AND FORTH SERIES 2 (Nettwerk, 1993).

industrial genre. With its heavy use of samples — dialogue from obscure movies, sound bites from newscasts and documentaries, half-whispered *somethings* drifting in and out in the background — the album captured a special sort of postmodern angst. While anyone who claimed to be able to make out the lyrics to a song like *Dig It* was surely lying, the inherent violence and menace in the beat, and the electronically-altered guitars, had a certain appeal to music fans tired of the lightweight techno-pop of the mid-80's.[4] Campus radio grabbed the album, turning MIND into a late-night favorite across North America.

Skinny Puppy

After completing their first-ever tour, Skinny Puppy issued CLEANSE, FOLD AND MANIPULATE on Nettwerk in October 1987. Intense and sometimes frightening, the album was more finely-honed than anything Puppy had done to date. With Key credited as playing "radio" along with his usual array of synthesizers and sequencers, and with Ogre in charge of "audio sculpture," "punishments" and "objects," the group continued lyrical attack on what they saw as a sick world. While Adrian Sherwood remixes of both *Addiction* and *Deep Down Trauma Hounds* became hits with the industrial crowd, the group's reputation began to spread far beyond the black-clothes-and-mascara set. Raves came from *Melody Maker* and the *NME*, who likened CF&M to the best horror books and films. Even *People* magazine ran a review, calling the group's music "insanity" and comparing the album to "stepping into a nightmare being experienced by the Phantom of the Opera." Puppy had become masters of setting mood and atmosphere.

When VIVISECTVI (pronounced "Vivisect Six" — notice the "666" imagery inherent in the spelling) was released in October 1988, fans noticed a new acknowledgment of melody. The rhythms were still brutal and robotic, and the samples were still harsh, but songs like *Testure* were, for Puppy, oddly accessible. Lyrically, the album was still as in-your-face as ever, espousing sociopolitical concerns ranging from chemical warfare (*VX Gas Attack*) to medical experiments on animals. Two singles were issued: the aforementioned *Testure* (a surprise Top 20 hit on the Billboard dance charts) and *Censor* (the alternate title of a song actually called *Dogshit*.) In concert, the band had become even more theatrical with pyrotechnics, fake blood, simulated torture and often projecting disturbing film footage. To attend a Skinny Puppy show was to witness an exercise in extreme industrial performance art.

The beats got harder and the guitars got louder for RABIES (released in November 1989), thanks in part to the contributions of Ministry's Al Jourgensen, a Puppy fan from way back. His quasi-metal guitars and signature production sound added something of a new twist to the group which was perhaps best exemplified in the choices of *Tin Omen* and *Worlock* as singles.[5] A little concert controversy also helped Puppy's notoriety when the band was arrested in Cincinnati while making an anti-vivisectionist statement using a stuffed dog.[6]

As solid as the band's reputation was among fans, both Key and Ogre were getting a little board with the Skinny Puppy approach and began to drift off into various side projects. Key was the first to work outside the group with Edward Ka-Spell of the Legendary Pink Dots. Calling their outfit Tear Garden, they issued TIRED EYES SLOWLY BURNING in 1987. In 1990, he and friend Alan Nelson formed Hilt who subsequently

---

4. One such person was a kid from Pennsylvania named Trent Reznor. Having spent the last few years playing Thompson Twins covers in bands like Option 30, Skinny Puppy opened his eyes to a new type of bottom-heavy electronic music. He would later confess that *Down In It* from PRETTY HATE MACHINE was his attempt at aping *Dig It*.

5. The video for *Worlock* was often banned for its violent imagery.

6. Puppy's stuffed mascot was named CHUD. He was once stolen by a fan after a show in Detroit, but was eventually safely recovered

Ogre of Skinny Puppy

released two decidedly non-Puppy sounding albums.[1]

As TOO DARK PARK hit the stores in October 1990, a rift had begun to develop within the group. Key and Goettel were often annoyed with Ogre's growing interest in pursuing projects outside the band. Complicating matters was Goettel's escalating drug use. Most fans didn't notice because they were only too happy to buy another album of death, doom and despair. TOO DARK PARK also had its quirks. An initial vinyl pressing was defective (there was forty seconds of unintended silence before each song) and an eleventh song (*Left Hand Shake*) had to be dropped at the last minute when the sample of a rant by drug guru Timothy Leary couldn't be cleared (oddly, those same samples turn up in *Fistfuck* on the Nine Inch Nails EP, FIXED.)

After another intense tour of shock-theater and the release of the predictably intense LAST RITES (issued on March 24, 1992), Nettwerk Records shocked the band by declining to extend their contract. Without a deal, and with no label interested in releasing new material, Puppy took a long break leaving fans to speculate on the literal meaning of the title of their last Nettwerk album. Although there were few takers (despite the fact that industrial music was now very big business, thanks to Puppy disciples like Ministry and Nine Inch Nails), the band did managed to snag a deal with American Recordings. But almost as soon as the ink on the contract was dry, the group's implosion began in earnest.

Even before American approached them with a deal, personal tensions within the band had made any sort of harmonious working relationship impossible. With each member determined to follow his own musical agendas — and with each agenda clashing with the other — Skinny Puppy was as good as done by the end of 1992.[2] Longtime producer Dave Ogilvie was no longer in the picture. The band had frozen him out, completely underestimating this importance in the Puppy scheme of things. Complicating matters was the clause in the new contract that clearly stated that the band was not going to have complete creative control over their material. They agreed to that initially — they were that desperate to get a deal — but soon, that clause was going to be the source of more trouble.

The sessions for the next album, which started in October 1993, were doomed from the start, especially after Dwayne Goettel started coming apart. Key and Ogre thought about firing him, but decided against any drastic moves until after the album was completed. Thousands of dollars were spent renting a beach house studio (ironically named Shangri-La) in Malibu that was located just up the hill from where *Baywatch* was being filmed. The distractions of the beach (not to mention periodic evacuations caused by

---

1. CALL THE AMBULANCE BEFORE I HURT MYSELF (Nettwerk, 1989) and JOURNEY TO THE CENTRE OF THE BOWL (Nettwerk, 1991.) Tear Garden also released THE LAST MAN TO FLY (Nettwerk, 1992) and SHEILA LIKED THE RODEO (Nettwerk, 1993.)
2. One major source of contention was whether or not to continue using distortion treatments on vocal tracks.

that year's wildfires and the occasional California earthquake) proved to be too much. After four months of writing and recording in that house had resulted in very little — and after Key was injured during a film shoot — Puppy knew it that their inspiration had dried up. The demos were so substandard that they were even ashamed to show them to the producers assigned to the project.[3] When American Recordings finally heard a sample of the new work, they accused the band making an album that was totally unlistenable. Several successive attempts were also rejected by the label before Ogilvie was called in to salvage what he could.[4]

By March 1995, with production costs exceeding $750,000 and the album at least a year behind schedule, American demanded that the band's contract be re-examined. Puppy's deal was cut from three albums to one. When the band insisted that they be paid American's original promise of $1.3 million regardless, there were more delays. The fatal moment came on June 2, 1995. Just as the rent on the house in Malibu ran out and everyone was preparing to move back to Vancouver, Nivek Ogre quit. He told everyone that he was going to remain in California and that the rest of the band could do as they liked. That move that automatically rendered the contract with American null and void. Puppy was dropped from the American Recordings roster.

Out of everyone in the band, Dwayne Goettel took the news the hardest. As perhaps the hardest-working member of the group (he would often spend long hours on the tiniest details of a song) and the member most passionate about music, the collapse of Skinny Puppy was the worst thing that could happen to him. Already in an ultra-fragile emotional state over the disastrous failure of the Malibu sessions, he fell into a destructive depression. Even though he and Key continued to work on the album in Vancouver, there was a sense that Goettel was loosing his grip. When he decided that he needed to get out of town for a while, everyone agreed that a break from music would be a good idea.

Goettel flew back to his parents' home in Edmonton where he soon received a package mailed by a friend from Vancouver. Inside was a quantity of heroin. On August 23, 1995, Dwayne Goettel was found dead in his old bedroom, the victim of a massive accidental overdose.

After Goettel's death, Key and Ogre finished up the album, after they were assured that American had decided to release THE PROCESS despite any previous disagreements. After three years in the making, the album finally hit the stores in February 1996. It is now deleted.

When Skinny Puppy first came together in 1982, industrial music as we know it today did not exist. In their thirteen years together, Puppy pioneered this new sound, reinventing and shaping it along the way. Like some of alt-rock's other great ground breakers — the Velvet Underground, Jonathan Richman, Sonic Youth — Puppy never sold great quantities of albums. But like some of those great performers, their records managed to get into the hands of some important people — people that would eventually add their own lasting impressions on hard and heavy music: Al Jourgensen of Ministry, Trent Reznor of Nine Inch Nails and Brian Warner, later to be known as Marilyn Manson.

Skinny Puppy provided that vital bridge between the European industrial approach and the scene in North America. Electronics and guitars mated over a stew of samples and computers, allowing for a new branch to grow from the industrial family tree. Those who believe in the creed "better dead than mellow," are eternally grateful.

Fast Facts

o cEvin came up with the name "Skinny Puppy" before he met Ogre. The name can be interpreted many ways with the most popular being that the band's view of the world is similar to that of an a hungry, abused and neglected dog.

o A major influence on Nivek Ogre's way of thinking were the works of a 19th century writer named Comte de Lautremont, a contemporary of Rimbaud, who died in obscurity in 1873 at age 24. Laurement's views — especially those depicted in his book, *Maldoror* — had an influence on the surrealist movement of the 1930's. Ogre also credits the Cure's *Pornography* album as opening his eyes to a new world of music.

---

3. Contributing producers included Roli Mosimann of Swan and industrial expert Martin Aitkins.
4. There's some dispute as to why Ogilvie wasn't the main producer from the beginning. Some suggest that American Recordings insisted on using someone else in a hope that they might steer Puppy in a more commercial direction.

---

o Dave Ogilvie first worked with cEvin as an engineer when he was still playing drums for Images in Vogue. Key quit IIV on the date BITES was released in 1985.

o One of cEvin Key's pre-Puppy, pre-IIV bands was called the Fuck Brothers

o Along with stints in Psyche and Water, Dwayne Goettel was also a member of Voice and Office. He wrote his first song with Skinny Puppy within twenty-four hours of joining the band. *Antagonism* appears on MIND: THE PERPETUAL INTERCOURSE.

o During the months that the band worked on THE PROCESS at the house in Malibu, Goettel became more and more unstable. At one point, he tried to break down Ogre's bedroom door after wrapping himself in barbed wire.

o Original reports regarding a death in Skinny Puppy got it wrong. They listed the victim as Nivek Ogre.

o Since the demise of Skinny Puppy, both cEvin Key and Nivek Ogre have been involved in numerous other projects including Download (Key), along with Rx and W.E.L.T. (Ogre.)

o Nivek, cEvin and Dwayne all appeared in the movie *The Doom Generation*. Watch for them in a fight scene with actor Jonathan Schaech. It was during the shooting of this scene that Key fell off a car and broke his arm.

o Ogre lost most of his record collection when he was addicted to drugs. He sold off most of his records in order to buy more dope.

Recommended Listening

o MIND: THE PERPETUAL INTERCOURSE (Nettwerk, 1986)

o CLEANSE, FOLD AND MANIPULATE (Nettwerk, 1987)

o VIVISECTVI (Nettwerk, 1988)

o RABIES (Nettwerk, 1989)

o Industrial fans will appreciate the remixes on TWELVE INCH ANTHOLOGY (Nettwerk 1989) and the live set recording at the Concert Hall in Toronto (June 1, 1987) called AIN'T IT DEAD YET? (Nettwerk / Capitol, 1989.) For a historical document, BRAP (Nettwerk, 1996) is pretty good. It features the four tracks from that first Skinny Puppy tape plus outtakes from both the TOO DARK PARK and LAST RIGHTS sessions.

Internet Resources

o http://skinnypuppy.homepage.nu

o http://userpages.aug.com/sgraham/

o www.evansville.net/~tgodsend/brap.html

o www.geocities.com/SunsetStrip/Underground/4140/puppy.html

o www.geocities.com/SunsetStrip/Alley/5317/skinnypuppy.html

o www.monmouth.com/~sgoldberg/faqraw.txt

Recommended Reading

o Thompson, Dave. *Better to Burn Out: The Cult of Death in Rock and Roll.* New York, New York: Thunder's Mouth Press, 1999.

Related Listening

Nine Inch Nails, Ministry, Front 242, Marilyn Manson, Pigface, Lard, and Revolting Cocks.

The Story Thus Far . . .

Influenced by the darkness of bands ranging from Joy Division and Echo and the Bunnymen to Throbbing Gristle, Skinny Puppy adds computers and samples to an ultra-heavy drumbeat leading to the establishment of a beyond-heavy-metal brand of industrial music. It's the foundation for groups like Nine Inch Nails and beyond.

~ 18 ~
THE SMITHS
Those Charming Men

Once upon a time, just about every rock and roll band on the planet seemed to be suffering from an overdose of testosterone. The macho swagger of the Guitar God, the Robert Plant wannabes, the power-chord arena-rock anthems, the sex-drugs-and-rock-and-roll mentality — these were the things that were standard issue to thousands of performers throughout the late 60's to the early 80's. The only real competition came from the all-synthesizer techno-pop outfits that began swarming in the late 70's. With their sense of theatrics, their makeup and often effeminate / androgynous / bisexual personas, it appeared that some of these groups might have traded their guitars for a few injections of estrogen.

This is the world that the Smiths entered. Caught between the unbridled machismo of the Rock Gods and the otherworldly wash of synthesizers, the Smiths' approach was unique. Morrissey, the Smiths' ultra-charismatic, sexually ambiguous frontman, pursued a lyrical path of self-absorption, self-loathing, selfishness and general anguish that somehow made him one of the most-adored figures of the 80's. Behind him was a basic but solid band, led by guitarist Johnny Marr. With an exquisitely tasteful playing style that was new and fresh, Marr ensured that the Smiths didn't fit into any existing place in the rock and roll order. Worshipped and scorned in equal amounts, the Smiths, during their short four-year life span, helped lay some of the essential groundwork for much of the alternative rock that was to come.

Although much of the Smiths' story is now surrounded by myth and legend, it's still possible to come up with an accurate historical account of who they were and what they accomplished. Everything starts on May 22, 1959 when Steven Patrick Morrissey was born at Park Hospital in Manchester. Growing up at 384 King's Road in Stretford (still a shrine for Smiths fans), Steven began to buy records in 1965 at age six, his first purchase being *Come Stay with Me* by Marianne Faithful. Through the early 70's, he became a big fan of England's glam-rockers, especially Marc Bolan of T-Rex and David Bowie, two performers he came to idolize for their sense of style and fashion as well as their music. In late 1973, he discovered punk via the New York Dolls and began writing a series of letters on the subject, some of which were printed in *Sounds* as well as *Melody Maker* and the *NME*.[1]

Seeing the Sex Pistols at the Lesser Free Trade Hall in Manchester on July 20, 1976 only reinforced Steven's growing musical ambitions. As he grew tired of the drudgery of a regular job (he worked for both the British civil service and Inland Revenue, as well as in a hospital morgue, thanks to his father), he began to think seriously of pursuing music as a full-time vocation. His first audition was for the position of bassist for the CJs, an amateur Manchester group, in early 1977. That summer, through some mutual New York Dolls fans, he met guitarist Billy Duffy, and worked with him in a group called Sulky Young (later called the Tee-Shirts) and later in the Nosebleeds.[2] With Morrissey assuming the role of lyricist, he bombarded Duffy with a series of compositions with titles like *(I Think) I'm Ready for the Electric Chair* until he agreed to give Morrissey at shot as the band's singer. The Nosebleeds played exactly two gigs before breaking up in June 1978. For the next few years, Steven did little except to collect unemployment, attend concerts and write letters to the music papers.

Morrissey first encountered John Martin Maher (later Johnny Marr, born October 21, 1963) in May 1982.[3] Growing up, Marr showed promise as a potential soccer star, but once he discovered music — especially the guitar playing of Rory Gallagher, Neil Young and Nils Lofgren — it became his obsession. After playing in a series of bands (Sister Ray, Paris Valentinos, White Dice and the funky Freaky Party), Marr was introduced to Morrissey by Billy Duffy, thinking that the two of them might make a nice song

---

1. If you care to look through some back issues, the letter in *Sounds* (about the New York Dolls) appeared on December 29, 1975. His comparison of the Dolls and the Sex Pistols was in both *Melody Maker* and the *NME* on June 18, 1976. A critique of the Pistols was published in the November 11, 1976 edition of *Melody Maker*. There were also several other missives on topics such as Warsaw (later known as Joy Division), the Ramones and his new goddess, Patti Smith.

2. Yes, this is the same Billy Duffy that would later form the Cult with Ian Astbury.

3. A note about the spelling Johnny's last name. He changed it to "Marr" so that he wouldn't be confused with John Maher, drummer of another Manchester band, the Buzzcocks.

---

writing team. After a now-legendary meeting in Morrissey's bedroom — Morrissey immediately fell in love with his guitar style — Marr set about writing music to Morrissey's lyrics. Within a month, they were rehearsing together and that summer several eight-track demos were made at Decibel Studios in Manchester.

Even though the new group's lineup did not expand beyond Morrissey and Marr through the summer of 1982, they had at least found a name. As a direct affront to the long, pretentious names of the day (think Orchestral Manoeuvres in the Dark), Morrissey deliberately chose a name that was short, simple, basic and, most importantly, quintessentially English. He was determined that this be a straightforward pop band that sang about real people in real situations. With no possible connotations, a name The Smiths was perfect for discouraging preconceptions of what the group might be about. Besides, such a name gave Morrissey a chance to honor his hero, Patti Smith.[1]

With new drummer Mike Joyce (born June 1, 1963 and ex of a band called Victim) and a bassist named Dale (an engineer from the those first demo sessions), the Smiths made their first live appearance on October 4, 1982 at the Ritz in Manchester. By December, Dale was out and replaced by Andrew Rourke (born January 17, 1964), a former bandmate of Marr's in the Paris Valentinos. With a few weeks' rehearsal time, the Smiths headlined their first gig on January 6, 1983, performing at Manhattan Sound in Manchester and accompanied by a gay go-go dancer hired by new manager Joe Moss.

After the Smiths played their first London gig on March 23rd, a very persuasive and insistent Johnny Marr convinced Geoff Travis of Rough Trade Records to listen to a demo of *Hand In Glove*. After being cornered in the kitchen at the label's offices, Travis was forced to agree that the song had its good points and agreed to it as a one-off single. *Hand In Glove* (backed with a live version of *Handsome Devil* recorded live at the Hacienda) appeared in the stores in May 1983.

Although the single failed to make much of a dent on the mainstream pop charts (it did, however, top the indie chart), the Smiths were nevertheless starting to generate a buzz, thanks in large part to the singer's powerful stage presence. Openly displaying his influences and obsessions (Patti Smith, the New York Dolls, 50's singer Johnny Ray, and writer Oscar Wilde) and often presented with enough gladioli to smother a florist, Morrissey made sure that Smiths' gigs were intimate communions with fans. Word spread on this simple pop band who looked and sounded nothing like the keyboard-driven and foppish Depeche Mode or the computer-powered and mechanical Human League. Late that spring, Geoff Travis decided that he'd better grab the band while he could. Offering them the biggest advance in the label's history — an offer that swayed the band from signing with their hometown Factory Records — the Smiths agreed to a long-term contract with Rough Trade. It was a decision they'd later regret.

After much gigging and an aborted attempt to record a debut album that summer, the second Smiths' single, *This Charming Man*, was finally released on October 28, 1983. Along with the customary 7-inch single, Travis had also taken it upon himself to release four extended remixes. Morrissey was apoplectic at Travis' gall; how *dare* he bastardize his beautifully simple pop songs by adding meaningless filler? How dare he mess with the Smiths' image? And how dare he do it without permission? All remixes were recalled and turned into instant collector's items for the next decade.[2] Despite the confusion and controversy among fans (or perhaps because of it), Smiths shows became more and more crowded.

Following a third single (*What Difference Does It Make*, released on January 20, 1984), the Smiths released a self-titled debut album on February 20, 1984. Recorded over a period of just two weeks with producer John Porter, the Smiths were rather unhappy with the results, believing that if they had had just a little more time and money, they could have created something better. Many of the tracks were hurriedly re-recorded in frantic all-night sessions towards the end of the second week.

Fans and critics didn't seem to notice any of the shortcomings with which the band was obsessed. On the contrary — the rough, stark minimalism of the arrangements combined with Morrissey's wavering, almost crooning vocals resulted in a record that sounded like no other. Morrissey's ability to capture the

---

1. There's yet another interpretation to the name. It evoked memories of "Mr. Smith's," a Manchester club that was very popular back in the 60's. Other rejected names included Smith Family and Smithdom.
2. A seven-track CD featuring seven different versions of *This Charming Man* was issued by WEA in limited numbers in 1990. It featured the withdrawn Manchester, London, New York Vocal (the most popular dance club version) and New York Instrumental mixes along with a version recorded for John Peel's show, a remix of the single and the original version.

bittersweet agonies of life and love in song far outdistanced the attempts of his contemporaries. His Bowie-esque flirts with homosexual imagery didn't seem to hurt, either. On the contrary, any gay references only seemed to reinforce the mystique of this new group. Meanwhile, the ringing and jangling of Johnny Marr's guitar was ever-present, propelling the songs forward with a fresh playing style that didn't seem rooted in any definable influence. Praise by critics and purchases by the ever-growing cadre of worshippers pushed THE SMITHS to No. 2 in the UK.

Reaction to the first album was so strong that Rough Trade decided they'd better release a swift follow-up in order to capitalize on the band's momentum while buying time for the Smiths to record a proper second album. Geoff Travis cobbled together HATFUL OF HOLLOW, a sixteen track collection of singles, B-sides and radio sessions and released it on November 13, 1984. Offered at a price lower than a regular album, HOLLOW was an immediate hit with the Smiths' faithful, especially the tremolo-heavy tension and art-rock dance beat of How Soon is Now.[3] It now seems remarkable that the Smiths weren't too keen on that song. Had it not been necessary to fill space on HATFUL OF HOLLOW, it's possible that the song may have never been released.

The Smiths third album (and second proper studio recording), MEAT IS MURDER, was issued on Valentine's Day, 1985, and entered the UK charts at No. 1 the following week, kicking Bruce Springsteen's BORN IN THE USA out of the top spot. Although some were turned off by the self-righteous vegetarian preaching of the title track,[4] the album received generally good reviews. At the same time, it failed to provide the group with any kind of major hit single. The best MEAT could muster was the No. 23 showing of The Boy With the Thorn in His Side in October. Those who took the time to buy the album were entertained by stories of sadistic schoolteachers (The Headmaster's Ritual) and child abusers (Barbarism Begins At Home) as well as anti-Thatcherite tirades.

Morrissey was also becoming more outspoken during interviews. Holding forth on everything from politics to sex to the evils of meat, he was also not adverse to bad-mouthing some of his musical contemporaries (Robert Smith of the Cure was a frequent target.) While this forthrightness and often contrary opinions endeared him to the Smiths faithful and turned the Smiths into media sensations — Morrissey was always good for an outrageous quote — it didn't make him any new friends in the music industry.

As 1985 drew to a close — and after the group's first tour of North America — things started to get strange and uncomfortable.[5] Andy Rourke's longtime heroin habit had grown to difficult proportions. Even though he was on methadone, his playing was sometimes erratic and sloppy, something the perfectionist Morrissey found impossible to tolerate. After an Irish tour in February 1986, Rourke was told to leave the band with the proviso that he would be re-admitted once he had successfully kicked his addiction.[6] In the interim, the group hired Craig Gannon, a rhythm guitarist ex of Aztec Camera, on June 21, 1986. Rourke, eventually forgiven for his chemical indiscretions, was allowed to return later in the year.

Personnel problems were the last thing the Smiths needed at this point. Just as they were on the verge of becoming a major international act, the group teetered on the brink of several disasters. Fans accustomed to seeing their heroes in clubs were becoming alarmed that their group was now taking on the trappings of stadium rockers. Morrissey was still feeling the fallout from his pointed comments critical of Live Aid the previous summer. Management troubles had plagued the band through 1985,

---

3. One record company called How Soon is Now the " Stairway to Heaven of the 1980s." Legend has it that while the guitar tracks were monstrously complicated to sync up, Morrissey's vocal take was done in just one or two passes. The studio was bathed in red light at the time in order to achieve the right atmosphere. The song peaked at only No. 24 on the singles charts, probably because HATFUL had such a cheap retail price that few fans bothered to buy the single, opting instead to purchase the whole album.
4. Listen carefully to the title track and you'll hear the hoof-beats of cattle heading off to the slaughterhouse. MEAT arrived at about the same time Morrissey began to get more vocal about his views on vegetarianism and animal rights.
5. This North American tour was rather successful from a hype perspective. People magazine ran a feature on Morrissey on June 24 under the title 'Roll Over Bob Dylan and Tell Madonna the News: The Smiths' Morrissey Is Pop's Latest Messiah.'
6. More legend: It's been told that while Marr tried to be a good friend to Rourke, Morrissey delivered the news of his sacking by placing a note on the window of Rourke's car: "Andy, you have left the Smiths. Good-bye." Morrissey's defenders say this was simply another case of him trying to avoid a personal confrontation with a junkie. They also point out that when Rourke was arrested for possession several weeks after his firing, Morrissey immediately came to his aid. By spring, he was back in the band and together with Gannon, the Smiths began operating as a quintet.

The Smiths

resulting in much bad blood and a somewhat poisonous atmosphere as Morrissey and Marr began to renegotiate their contract with Rough Trade (EMI was reportedly lurking in the shadows with offers of a deal.) There was also much dithering over whether the new album should be recorded in England or if the band should relocate New York. Delays stretched from weeks to months.

Despite the awkwardness between management, the label and themselves (no to mention the criticisms coming from fans and the press), the Smiths answered with what has become a classic of the alt-rock genre. THE QUEEN IS DEAD (released in June 1986) showed the Smiths at their peak. Never had Morrissey's lyrics been so interesting and open-hearted, and never had Marr's playing and arranging been so sharp. The album yielded three important singles — Big Mouth Strikes Again (featuring Morrissey's sped up vocals at the end, No. 26), the scathing indictment of radio DJs, Panic (No. 11.)[1]

Although the band continued to be lavished with critical praise and worshipped by a large and loyal audience, Morrissey and Marr were still consternated by the Smiths inability to conquer the UK charts. One of the main problems — or so they felt — was Rough Trade. As 1986 drew to a close, two decisions were made. The first declared that Craig Gannon had outlasted his usefulness and was not long for the band. The second involved a jump to EMI once the Rough Trade contract ran out. Perhaps they could help the Smiths achieve some chart glory.

All of this must have seemed insignificant on the morning of November 12, 1986. Johnny Marr had spent the previous evening drinking tequila and wine with Mike Joyce and they had made the stupid decision to drive themselves home. Less than a quarter mile from the house, Marr pushed his new BMW a little too hard around a corner in the driving rain and lost control. The car bounced between stone walls on either side of the road, crushing it into a heap of metal. Extracting himself from the wreckage, he ran home, hoping to distance himself from the accident before anyone in authority showed up. When morning came, he was admitted to hospital with pains in his neck and legs. To everyone's relief, the damage appeared to be minor. Investigators who examined the BMW were amazed that Marr hadn't lost his legs, and had escaped from the crushed passenger compartment.[2]

If 1986 had been a difficult year in the Smiths' existence, 1987 was even worse. The split from Rough Trade was acrimonious and the appearance of EMI had Smiths purists thinking in terms of sellout. It was also becoming apparent that Morrissey and Marr didn't like each other very much anymore. Caught in a constant battle over musical direction and wedged apart by the new record deal, their working relationship became strained and then began to break down. Marr was tired of Morrissey's self-absorption and dictatorial stand on matters involving the group. Another change in management introduced policies and plans that Morrissey refused to endorse. Marr, meanwhile, was only too happy to entertain new career ideas. He wanted to tour and to do press, just like any other professional pop band. Morrissey wanted no part of such a pedestrian rock and roll existence. It wasn't long before the band cleaved into two factions, Morrissey vs. Marr, suffocating everyone in the process.

The rift between Morrissey and Marr had grown into a chasm by the time the sessions for STRANGEWAYS, HERE WE COME wrapped up on May 19, 1987. A burned-out and bummed-out Marr flew off to Los Angeles, leaving Morrissey at home in England to deny all the breakup rumors being fanned by the music press. In truth, the band had probably ceased to exist the moment Marr left the studio for the last time, although everything was kept quiet through the early part of the summer. After a damning story appeared in the press in August — and following some fancy spin-doctoring by Morrissey, Marr and EMI — the real truth came out on September 12 — the Smiths were dead. Even with the hype, weeping and gnashing of teeth surrounding their demise, it wasn't enough to give the band the major chart victory they so desperately wanted. Sixteen days after the official breakup, STRANGEWAYS was released and debuted at No. 2, second only to Michael Jackson's BAD. A fine start to be sure, but none of the singles from the album made it higher than No. 13 (Girlfriend in a Coma.) It was the same old story. Under the guise of a solo Morrissey show, the Smiths — Morrissey backed up by Joyce, Gannon and Rourke — played an impromptu farewell to their fans on December 22, 1988, at Wolverhampton Civic Hall.

---

1. The DJ in question was Steve Wright who was heard by Morrissey as be worked on BBC Radio 1 on April 26, 1986. After making an announcement that the Chernobyl reactors had just begun spewing radioactivity all over eastern Europe, Wright segued into I'm Your Man by Wham. Thinking that he had trivialized the severity of a nuclear meltdown by following up such a grave news story with a piece of fluff, Morrissey is said to have uttered "Hang the DJ!"
2. One version of the story says that the cops were told that Angie Marr had been driving. Why? Because not only was Johnny most likely drunk at the time of the accident, he also didn't have a valid drivers' license.

Much has happened in the years since the Smiths imploded. While he's had his moments, Morrissey's attempts at becoming a major solo artist have not fared as well as he'd hoped. A succession of highly anticipated but slow-selling albums on a variety of record labels has hurt his marketability and his reputation among alt-rock fans. Meanwhile, music moved on and the delicate introspective poetry that made the Smiths so fervently admired no longer has the same effect on young record buyers. Johnny Marr has soldiered on as a rock and roll journeyman, working as a session player and sideman and as part of Electronic, a successful "supergroup" formed with New Order singer Bernard Sumner.[3]

Mike Joyce took a job with the Buzzcocks to help pay the bills before he discovered that he had perhaps been cheated out of a fair share of the Smiths profits. Doing a little digging, he found that both Morrissey and Marr had each taken a 40% cut of the proceeds, leaving him and Andy Rourke to share the remaining 20%. After a long legal battle that saw Joyce sued both Morrissey and Marr over unfair business practices, a judge declared that Morrissey did in fact owe Joyce about £1 million.[4] An appeal by Morrissey (Morrissey said the ruling was in part an unfair attack on his character; Marr did not participate in the appeal) to three senior High Court judges was unsuccessful. Morrissey was forced to pay Joyce close to £1 million plus hundreds of thousands of pounds in court costs.[5] Joyce has used some of his winnings to explore possibilities of forming a new band with former Stone Roses guitarist Aziz Ibrahim. He's also appeared in Sinead O'Connor's backup band.

Although they were around for just four years, the Smiths succeeded in becoming the definitive British indie band of the 1980's. Not only did they help hurry the death of the techno-pop frenzy that dominated the early part of the 80's, they also set the stage for the basic guitar pop that would eventually take over the English scene in the late 80's and early 90's. While they were together, the Morrissey-Marr alliance was one of alt-rock's finest song writing combinations, reintroducing the simple pleasures of three minute pop songs that were played on traditional rock and roll instruments. While DIY punk attitudes were very much a part of their makeup, they also recognized the value in everything from Elvis Presley to the girl groups of the 1960's. Morrissey's strangely charismatic persona and penchant for drama, and the forlorn, doomed romanticism of his poetry only made the combination all that more appealing. Like Depeche Mode and the Cure, the Smiths gave troubled music fans something to hang on to. No matter how badly they felt, they came to realize that Morrissey not only understood their pain but could also articulate it in a way few could.

Will the Smiths every reunite as the periodic rumors say? It's doubtful, especially given the legal ruckuses that have wracked the band since the firing of Craig Gannon. The Smiths were a rite of passage for a whole generation of alt-rock fans in the 80's. Any attempt to recreate that would just spoil memories of a righteous bad mood.

Fast Facts

o Peter Morrissey (Morrissey's father), named his son after Patrick Steven Morrissey, a brother who died as an infant.

o After leaving the Nosebleeds (a gig that lasted about seven weeks), Morrissey auditioned for Slaughter and the Dogs.

o Along with being a rabid New York Dolls fan, Morrissey was also so infatuated with James Dean that he wrote a book on him in the late 70's. *James Dead Is Not Dead* was published by Manchester's Babylon Books.

o The first drummer for the Smiths was Simon Wolstencroft, a holdover from Johnny Marr's old group, Freaky Party. Wolstencroft had already quit a band called English Rose — a group that eventually morphed into the Stone Roses. He quit the Smiths because he felt the band didn't have what it took to make it big. Wolstencroft eventually found steady work with Mark E. Smith in the Fall.

o The tradition of flowers (especially gladioli) at Smiths gigs was a nod to the horticultural preferences of Oscar Wilde (1854-1900), the flamboyant Irish novelist, poet and playwright who died in prison

---

3. Marr has worked with or for Billy Bragg, The The, Bryan Ferry, the Pretenders, Paul McCartney, Talking Heads and Kirsty MacColl, to name but a few.

4. Andy Rourke didn't take part in the suit because he reached an out of court settlement with Morrissey and Marr amounting to £83,000. Yes, he probably wishes he had thrown his hat in with Mike Joyce, especially after declaring bankruptcy in February 1999.

5. In the original ruling, a High Court judge described Morrissey as "devious, truculent and unreliable."

following a scandalous trial where he was prosecuted and imprisoned for his homosexuality.

o The working title of the first album was *The Hand That Rocks The Cradle*. Despite the praise that the Smiths received for that album, Marr, Rourke and Joyce were only too aware of Morrissey's limited vocal range. They forced him to take singing lessons.

o The cover artwork of *The Smiths* is a still shot of actor Joe Dellasandro from an Andy Warhol film called *Flesh*. The cover of *Hatful of Hollow* features playwright Joe Orton. *Meat is Murder* is another movie still. Taken from a 1969 anti-Vietnam war movie entitled *In the Year of the Pig*, the original inscription on the soldier's helmet ("Make Love Not War") was erased and replaced with the title of the album. On the *Queen is Dead*, we see French actor Alain Delon.

o Like many artists of their era, the Smiths liked to etch cryptic messages into the run-off grooves of their vinyl releases. For example, the original 7-inch release of *This Charming Man* features this note: "Slap me on the patio." Morrissey continued the tradition after going solo.

o Johnny Marr married his girlfriend, Angela Brown, on June 20, 1985.

o The Smiths often made strange demands on their contract riders. In 1985, one such rider read "The Promoter shall provide on stage at no charge to the artiste [sic] a live tree with a minimum height of three feet and a maximum height of five feet, species and type to be agreed by the tour manager at least fifteen days before the performance."

o Morrissey's anti-meat stance became the stuff of legends. While the group was together, he claimed that all the members were vegetarians. Although that wasn't true, he decreed that no one in the band was ever to be photographed eating meat. Later, as a solo artist, Morrissey had it written into his concert contracts that any venue in which he performed could not sell meat at the snack bars. Hot dogs, therefore, were banned from Morrissey shows. Imagine the embarrassment of a Scottish promoter who tried to make a little extra money by selling advertising space on the back of tickets to his shows. He sold the space to McDonalds, who invited concert-goers to redeem their Morrissey ticket stubs for two McChicken sandwiches.

o The Smiths hated doing videos. The odd clip for *How Soon Is Now* was put together by the Smiths' US label just so they could offer MTV something. Commissioning some English film students in 1985, Sire told them to put together something appropriately conceptual. The identity of the woman in the video is not known. The only other video of consequence was for *Girlfriend in a Coma* (1986) which featured a solo Morrissey.

o The last reliable estimate puts Johnny Marr's worth at £2 million. Before his disastrous court ruling, Morrissey had a fortune worth about £8 million.

o Canadian author Douglas Coupland's 1998 novel *Girlfriend in a Coma* was inspired by the Smiths song of the same name. He's always been a big fan of the band. During signing sessions for the book, he'd often ask that Smiths music be played in the background.

Recommended Listening

o THE SMITHS (Rough Trade / Sire, 1984)

o HATFUL OF HOLLOW (Rough Trade / Sire, 1984)

o MEAT IS MURDER (Rough Trade / Sire, 1985)

o THE QUEEN IS DEAD (Rough Trade / Sire, 1986)

o If you're looking for compilations, your best bet is probably SINGLES (Sire, 1995.) Another possibility is the two part set BEST ... 1 AND BEST ... 2 (Sire, 1992.)

o THE WORLD WON'T LISTEN is a UK release featuring singles and various obscurities from 1985 and 1986. The North American LOUDER THAN BOMBS is somewhat similar, although it deletes any references to THE QUEEN IS DEAD and includes a few tracks that date back as early as 1983.

Internet Resources

o http://moz.pair.com

o www.cam.org/~wsd/index.html

o www.geocities.com/SunsetStrip/Underground/2360/main.html

o www.geocities.com/SunsetStrip/Lounge/3438/

° www.q-net.net.au/~bauhaus/homepage_new.html

Recommended Reading

° Bret, David. *Morrissey: Landscapes of the Mind*. London: Robson Books, Ltd.: 1994.
° Rogan, Johnny. *Morrissey & Marr: The Severed Alliance*. London: Omnibus Press, 1992.
° Rogan, Johnny. *The Smiths: A Visual Documentary*. London: Omnibus Press, 1994.

Related Listening

The Cure, R.E.M., Suede, David Bowie, The Sundays, New Order, Depeche Mode, Roxy Music, the New York Dolls, T-Rex, Electronic, James, the La's, the Cranberries, Morrissey's solo work.

The Story Thus Far . . .

By picking up the ambisexual thread of David Bowie's Ziggy Stardust years and combining it with the poetic sensibilities of Patti Smith, Morrissey eventually evolved into one of the most important lyricists of the 80's. Johnny Marr's ringing guitar style (vaguely reminiscent of the English pop acts of the 60's) held form the foundations of what would eventually be called Britpop.

~ 19 ~
THE PIXIES
Music from the Planet of Sound

Back in the 19th century, a German naturalist and scientist named Alexander von Humboldt described the three stages of attitude that a society assumes towards a great discovery. At first, von Humboldt declared, everyone doubts that the discovery even exists. Once its existence is proven, society tends to deny the importance of the discovery. Finally, by the time everyone realizes what is going on, credit for the discovery is inevitably given to the wrong person.

This model can be applied to music. When it comes to breaking new musical ground, the people on the front lines — the true pioneers — rarely get the credit they deserve. For example, once people realized that grunge was happening, most of the world was quick to give all the credit to Nirvana. Thankfully, most alt-rock fans know the truth. While Nirvana certainly was the major force behind grunge and the whole alt-rock explosion that followed in the early 90's, they most definitely did not invent this music. Nirvana picked up threads left by the many unsung bands who came before them. The Pixies were one of those groups.

The Pixies must be ranked up there with the Founding Fathers and Mothers of modern alt-rock. Although they were criminally under-appreciated while they existed, they are now the subjects of much hindsight praise. They were one of the Kurt Cobain's favorites. Dave Grohl still loves them. Gavin Rossdale of Bush believes that they were one of the greatest bands of all time. Billy Corgan admits to patterning much of the Smashing Pumpkins' dynamic range on the Pixies. U2 thought they were brilliant. It's even possible that the entire Lollapalooza concert was inspired by one particular Pixies performance.

But if they were so good and so influential, why didn't they sell any damn records? They had no hit singles, no platinum albums. Why did they fail to capture the attention of the general public? Probably because their sound was so far ahead of its time. And frankly — like Sonic Youth, Jonathan Richman and the Velvet Underground before them — the group was somewhat of an acquired taste. Those without patience wrote them off as just a bunch of amateurish college kids who couldn't play their instruments and got off by making a big noise. But had they listened closely instead of being so blithely dismissive, these people might have heard something new and exciting. Only pumped-up, super-enthusiastic music fans could find *those* chords and make *those* sounds. Sometimes the best music comes from those who don't realize that rock and roll has rules. And if you don't know any better, who knows what you might do?

The Pixies were founded in 1986 while Charles Michael Kittridge Thompson IV (born April 4?,1965) was an economics major at the University of Massachusetts in Boston.[1] When he wasn't studying — which was often — he was off in Puerto Rico, ostensibly learning how to speak Spanish as part of a class at school. Instead, he was often found at the beach or drinking beer or reading books on space and UFOs. His U-Mass roommate was Joey Santiago (born June 10, 1965), a Philippines-born English student who carried a pocket dictionary wherever he went. Although Joey's family was quite wealthy and well connected politically, some relatives began to disappear under mysterious circumstances when the Marcos regime began to crumble. Joey's father (a doctor) thought it best that his son spend his university years in the relative safety of Boston.

By the time Charles returned from the Caribbean, he had decided that he wasn't cut out for a career in anthropology. When a trip to New Zealand for the fly-by of Halley's Comet turned out to be too expensive, he told Joey that he was going to follow his dreams of being a rock star. After two weeks of constant nagging, Joey — much to the chagrin of Dr. Santiago — also dropped out of university to tag along with Charles.

They really had no idea what they were doing because neither one of them could play guitar that well nor did they know the first thing about song writing. However, by applying time-honored empirical research methods (which, in this case, consisted of going to clubs and timing the sets played by other groups in order to determine exactly how much material they'd need), they established a basic game plan. Crossing their fingers, they placed an ad in a couple of local papers, hoping to attract a bass player and a drummer who were into both Peter, Paul and Mary and Hüsker Du.

The phone rang just once. The caller was Kim Deal (a.k.a. Mrs. John Murphy, born June 10, 1961), an ex-cheerleader from Dayton, Ohio who was bored with going to football games every Friday and Saturday. When she heard that the guys were also looking for a drummer, she suggested that she bring along her twin sister Kelly. At first, Charles liked the idea twin sisters in his band and even contributed fifty dollars towards a plane ticket — but when he realized that Kelly was even more of a novice on drums than he was on guitar, he rescinded the offer.[2] Deal then suggested her new friend, Boston native David Lovering (born December 6, 1961), an ex-member of bands with names like Riff Raff and Iz Wizard. Deal remembered meeting him at her wedding reception.

Once everyone convened in Boston and began rehearsing in Lovering's father's garage, it was time to come up with a name. It was Joey Santiago who found something appropriate in his ever-present pocket dictionary. He thought that "pixie" was a cool word, especially when one took Charles' rotundity into consideration (Charles as a "mischievous little elf?" Er, okay.) He was also enamored with "panoply," which describes a full suit of armour. He therefore suggested that the group be named "Pixies in Panoply" before he being overruled in favor of just "the Pixies."[3]

By the fall of 1986, the Pixies were making the circuit of the dozens of live music clubs that go hand-in-hand with Boston's university culture: The Rat, Green Street Station, T.T. The Bear's. Those who saw them at the time really didn't know what to make of this new band. Although the rhythm section seemed rock solid, the singer seemed, well, a little manic. Songs would begin fairly traditionally. Then suddenly, like a Porsche going from 0-60, the music would careen from quiet, almost folky verses to a loud explosion of sound in chorus with the singer often screaming in Spanish about alien abductions and born-again Pentecostals.[4] On the other side of the stage, the guitarist seemed to be inventing new chords on the spot. Compared to the mainstream rock and roll of the day (think of bands with poodle haircuts and spandex pants), this just wasn't normal.

---

1. Some sources insist he was studying anthropology.
2. Don't cry for Kelly. She eventually ended up in The Breeders with her sister.
3. A word about names. Kim Deal went by "Mrs. John Murphy" until her divorce came through in 1988 and she was able to revert to her maiden name. Charles Michael Kittridge Thompson IV adopted the name "Black Francis" towards the beginning of 1987. He loved cheesy stage names like "Iggy Pop" and "Billy Idol" and thought he should have one. After a talk with his father (a big fan of old-style westerns), they came up with Black Francis. It somehow sounded appropriately theatrical and menacing. Another version of the story suggests that Charles Thompson III wanted his next son to be named Black Francis. Because no new child appeared forthcoming, Charles IV got that handle.
4. Much of Black Francis' anti-religious tirades can be traced to the severe, uncompromising fundamentalist leanings of his parents.

After a particularly blistering gig supporting local Boston scenesters the Throwing Muses, Gary Smith, a producer from Roxbury's Fort Apache studios offered to help the Pixies record some demos. Recorded over three days in March 1987 (and financed by a thousand dollar loan from Black Francis' father), the seventeen song demo became known as THE PURPLE TAPE and began making the rounds of record labels. Predictably, no one in America was much interested in taking a chance on what they considered to be nothing more than experimental, nonsensical noise. One person, however, got what the Pixies were all about.

When Ivo Watts-Russell, head honcho for England's ultra-cool 4AD label, heard THE PURPLE TAPE, he immediately recognized that the Pixies were trying something new. Since his label was already in the business of releasing avant-garde rock music, he was willing to take a chance on the band. Six songs were extracted directly from the demo and combined with two new tracks as COME ON PILGRIM (released October 1987), making the Pixies just the second American group to appear on 4AD.[5] It was immediate college radio hit, especially with campus DJs who had grown bored with carefully constructed song writing of R.E.M.

The Pixies (left to right): Kim, Black Francis, David and Joey

The Pixies assault on the senses continued on March 21, 1988, with the release of SURFA ROSA, the group's wonderfully abrasive, beautifully unpredictable debut album. Filled with shrieks, psychotic screams and unimaginable guitar chords, the songs took the listener on a roller coaster ride of dynamics (quiet-LOUD-quiet-EVEN LOUDER) and featured a style of boy-girl harmonies that would eventually become commonplace in alt-rock. Producer Steve Albini (he prefers the term "recorder") encouraged the band to go over the top with every song, allowing chaos to mingle freely with pop sensibilities, creating an oddly exhilarating effect. As alternative music went, SURFA ROSA was an art-rock statement equal to anything in the Sonic Youth catalogue.[6] Its barely contained calculated sloppiness made it a formidable rock album.

While the album was a hit with aficionados of underground rock in America, mainstream rock remained more concerned with the hair-metal bands of the day. Britain, however, was a different matter altogether. The UK music press loved the Pixies, requiring the band to make two trips across the Atlantic in 1988. It was only after SURFA ROSA topped the UK indie charts and the band played a series of sold out shows that American labels started to take notice.

Thanks to inroads made by R.E.M. via the college radio circuit, the large labels were beginning to consider

---

5. Throwing Muses were the first. Francis took the title of the EP from a song called *Come On Pilgrim* by Larry Norman, a Christian folk singer who was much admired by his fundamentalist parents.
6. SURFA ROSA also contains the eight tracks from COME ON PILGRIM.

---

how they might be able to exploit this so-called "alternative music." As the Pixies' rep grew on both sides of the Atlantic, it was soon painfully obvious that they were a band who had got away. Bewildered A&R staff all wondered the same thing: How did we allow this *American* band to sign with a *British* label? A minor bidding war broke out with Elektra emerging as the eventual winner in the United States while Mercury / Polydor (through their association with 4AD) snagged the band for Canada.

In late 1988, the Pixies returned to the studio with British producer Gil Norton to work on an album that they planned to entitle WHORE.[1] When the record finally appeared in the stores on April 29, 1989, it was called DOOLITTLE. While markedly more polished and cleaner-sounding than SURFA ROSA, Norton made sure not to mess with the Pixies now-trademark schizophrenic sense of musical dynamics. Lyrically, the album walked another fine line between innovation and ultra-surreal weirdness, carefully picking the proper moments to indulge in a few edgy excesses. The album even contained two singles: the environmental rant *Monkey Gone to Heaven* and *Here Comes Your Man*, an oddly catchy pop song. Beneath all the shrieking and strange chords was the rock solid rhythm section of Deal and Lovering. DOOLITTLE was truly a remarkable record that was nearly alone in a musical universe dominated by flaccid and declawed corporate rock.

The album was a huge hit in the UK, making the Top Ten and resulting in dozens of high-profile gigs including a major headlining slot at the1990 Reading Festival. At the end of the year, the Pixies achieved a rare hat trick as all three UK weeklies — NME, *Melody Maker* and *Sounds* — voted *Monkey Gone to Heaven* as the best single of the year. In North America, it was a different story as the album stalled at No. 98 on *Billboard*. Locked in the era of hair-and-spandex rock, most of North America didn't get what the Pixies were trying to do. Despite all the positive press — *Rolling Stone* was effusive in its praise of the band — the marketplace just wasn't ready to embrace something as radical as the Pixies just yet. Instead, the band would alter the course of alt-rock in the most indirect of ways.

When the Pixies appeared on the main stage at Reading on August 26, 1990, the crowd went crazy. By the time the band launched into *Debaser*, more than 30,000 people were singing and screaming along with Black Francis.[2] It was an impressive and encouraging sight, seeing all those kids truly appreciate a band as fresh and innovative as the Pixies. It just so happened that this whole scene was witnessed by Perry Farrell of Jane's Addiction, another band at that year's festival. Although he was thoroughly enjoying the vibe of the weekend, he kept coming back to the same troubling questions. Why couldn't there be something like this in America? With 300 million people on the continent, why couldn't there be an annual festival that featured nothing but cool, new bands? The defining moment appears to have been that set by the Pixies. When Farrell saw 30,000 people singing *Debaser*, he knew then in his heart that his concept would work. When he returned home, Farrell began to work on his festival, something he would eventually call "Lollapalooza."

The third Pixies album was once again produced by Gil Norton and was ready in time for the band to fly to Reading. More atmospheric than the first two albums and featuring more of Black Francis' interest in surf-rock sounds, BOSSANOVA (released August 7, 1990) veered into strange sci-fi territory. With its tales of time travel, aliens in Las Vegas, the flying saucer crash in Roswell, New Mexico, and the legend of the Lemurians (cousins of the inhabitants of Atlantis), the album was weird even by Pixies standards. Although the reviews were somewhat mixed, the album was another big hit in the UK where it reached No. 3 on the indie charts. Meanwhile, at home in America, it was the same old story. BOSSANOVA quickly became a college radio favorite but, as usual, that somehow failed to translate into meaningful record sales. The album stalled at No. 70 despite a successful North American tour that saw the band sell out 2,000-seaters across the continent.

All was not well within the band, either. Tensions between Black Francis and Kim Deal continued to build, especially after none of Deal's songs were included on BOSSANOVA. A planned North American tour was canceled with the official excuse being "exhaustion." Something was definitely wrong.[3]

---

1. Apparently, some record executives felt that WHORE was pushing things a bit. Gil Norton (Echo and the Bunnymen, Wet Wet Wet) is another producer who cut his teeth on the Pixies. Based on his work with the band, he would later receive a ton of work from bands like the Foo Fighters. Dave Grohl still considers DOOLITTLE to be the finest rock album ever made.
2. A word about *Debaser*. The song is based on a movie entitled *Un Chien Andalou* which was directed by Salvador Dali and Louis Brunuel. It's very, *very* weird.
3. Was there ever. At the end of 1989, the members of the group took at much-needed rest from each other. Joey went to

After a brief break where all four members spent time away from each other, the Pixies began work on another album with producer Gil Norton at Master Control Studios in Los Angeles. Enlisting the aid of former Pere Ubu keyboardist Eric Drew Feldman, the group turned their attention back to the loud, abrasive style of the first two albums.[4] When it was released on October 8, 1991, received some good reviews but fans couldn't help notice that Kim Deal had once again been shut out. Not only did none of her songs make the record, but her vocal contributions had been drastically scaled back. Another great concern was the Breeders, a band that was looking more and more like valuable backup plan. When POD sold in encouraging numbers in 1990, Deal began to think that this "Bangles from Hell" project might have more long-term potential than the Pixies. Meanwhile, TROMPE LE MONDE followed the all too familiar story line. It was a huge hit in the UK but barely registered on America's radar.

Just as the Breeders fueled the breakup rumors by releasing an EP called SAFARI, the Pixies got a call from U2. Bono and the Edge were both big fans of the group and wanted the Pixies to open a number of dates on the North American leg of their monstrous Zoo TV tour. Black Francis was thrilled, thinking perhaps that this would be the band's big break, the event that would finally take the Pixies to the next level in America. In fact, the result was just the opposite.

The story goes that Spin magazine desperately wanted an interview with U2 for an upcoming issue. Stymied by refusals from U2's management, Spin writer Jim Greer grew determined to get some kind of inside scoop on the tour. His ace in the hole — or so he thought — was the fact that he was going out with Kim Deal at the time. Accompanying Deal to a series of shows, Greer collected some behind-the-scenes dirt and inter-band gossip which culminated in an unflattering article on how U2 treated their opening acts with specific emphasis on the Pixies. When U2's management got wind of the article, they went ballistic and almost kicked the Pixies off the tour. For Black Francis, this was a nightmare. A tour with U2 was a dream come true. How dare Deal sabotage everything? By the time the tour wrapped up, it was a foregone conclusion that the Pixies were finished. The final Pixies show took place at the Commodore Ballroom in Vancouver on April 24, 1992. On December 31, Black Francis faxed a note to the group's manager declaring that the Pixies were over. He offered the first public confirmation of the split during a BBC 5 radio interview on January 14, 1993.

All four ex-Pixies have remained very active since the breakup. Kim Deal has been the most successful, scoring a multi-platinum hit with the Breeders' LAST SPLASH album (released August 31, 1993.) Since then, however, the Breeders have stalled, hurt by internal squabblings and the much-publicized drug bust of Kelly Deal. Another project, the Amps, lasted only one album. Black Francis changed his name to Frank Black and continues to make a decent living as a cult hero. Joey Santiago continues to work with Frank and has also been hired as a session player by a variety of acts, including Canadian chanteuse Holly McNarland. David Lovering also remains busy having worked with Nitzer Ebb, Cracker and Tanya Donnelly. He also appeared with Joey and Linda Santiago in a short-lived post-Pixies group called the Martinis.

The Pixies influence, however, remains alive and well. Using SURFA ROSA and DOOLITTLE as templates, many young alt-rock bands began to incorporate the Pixies' sense of dynamics into their song writing.[5] At the same time, the list of performers who profess undying admiration for the band is almost endless: Kurt Cobain, Dave Grohl, Billy Corgan, David Bowie and Gavin Rossdale are but a few.

For some, it was the guitar influence. For others, it was just the way the Pixies looked. Black Francis proved that you didn't have to be in one of those spandex-and-hair bands to be cool; being short, fat and balding was perfectly acceptable. That alone — this proof that anyone could make exciting music, no matter how they looked — was enough to inspire people. It may sound superficial, but it's true. The Pixies' influence has even extended beyond music. Chris Carter, the creator of both The X Files and Millennium for Fox TV, remains a huge Pixies fan. Why do you think the lead character in Millennium is named "Frank

---

visit the Grand Canyon while David rested on a beach in Jamaica. Black Francis bought a bad-ass yellow Cadillac and drove coast-to-coast, playing solo gigs for gas money along the way. The band's "Fuck or Fight" tour definitely included more of the latter. One hundred-plus dates frayed nerves until they broke. There were drunken confrontations between Francis and Deal while Santiago was prone to equipment-smashing fits of rage. Deal also managed to crash a moped while in Greece. Meanwhile, Francis developed a severe flying phobia and insisted on traveling everywhere by car.

4. They later joked that TROMPE LE MONDE was loud and raucous because Ozzy Osbourne was working on an album in the next studio. Sessions at the California studio were also interrupted by the Northridge earthquake.

5. The Smashing Pumpkins, with their quiet verses and explosive choruses, are an excellent example.

Black?"

Along with groups like the Velvet Underground, Iggy Pop, the Ramones and Sonic Youth, the Pixies did some serious trailblazing for music fans everywhere. Maybe they were never rewarded in a financial way for what they did. Perhaps they were vastly under-appreciated during the five-and-a-half years of their existence. But one thing's for sure: music as a whole is better because of what they accomplished.

Fast Facts

o Black Francis believed in what he called the "90 second rule." He believed that the meat of the song should be piled into the first 90 seconds. Anything beyond that is the outro of the song (e.g. a repeated chorus.)

o Steve Albini is an ex-music critic from Chicago who had gone into music. While still with Big Black, the Pixies' SURFA ROSA was his first major success as a producer. Based on what he did with the Pixies, Albini would later get producing gigs with the Smashing Pumpkins, Nirvana and Bush.

o Kim Deal and Tanya Donnelly of the Throwing Muses have been friends since the days both bands were playing the Boston college circuit. They started making demos for what they jokingly called the "ultimate disco album" as far back as 1988.

o Deal met Josephine Wiggs during the Pixies' first UK tour when Wiggs' band, Perfect Disaster, supported the Pixies at the Mean Fiddler on April 8, 1988. They kept in touch and eventually joined forces in the Breeders when the Pixies went on hiatus in early 1990. Their debut album, POD (produced by Steve Albini at a studio in Edinburgh, Scotland, over just twenty-one days and interrupted briefly when the roof of the studio caved in), was issued that spring and was an immediate hit in the UK, peaking at No. 22. In some parts of the world, POD outsold BOSSANOVA, something that caused Black Francis great consternation.

o The name "Breeders" was taken from a folky duo Deal had formed with her sister Kelly when they were teenagers. According to the sisters, that version of the group "played a lot of truck stops" and died a natural death when Kim moved to join the Pixies in Boston.

o The GIGANTIC EP was released on August 22, 1988 to coincide with a triumphant tour of Britain. With all four songs sung by Kim Deal, this was the band's first experience with British producer Gil Norton.

o Once Elektra won the right to sign the Pixies in 1988, they issued a promo-only live album (PR8127.) It remains a coveted collector's item.

o The Pixies liked to mess with their audiences a bit. Sometimes they'd perform their set in alphabetical order. On other occasions, they'd leave the stage after the first song only to return to play and encore of fifteen songs.

o DOOLITTLE was finally certified gold (sales of 500,000 copies in the US) on November 10, 1995, six years after it was released. Most of those sales came in 1994 after Kurt Cobain was quoted in *Rolling Stone* as saying that "Smells Like Teen Spirit" was little more than his attempt at trying to write a Pixies song.

Recommended Listening

o SURFA ROSA (4AD, 1988)

o DOOLITTLE (4AD / Elektra, 1989)

o DEATH TO THE PIXIES (Elektra, 1997) is a fine collection of the band's best work. The limited edition two CD version of the album contains a second disc of featuring twenty-one live tracks.

Internet Resources

o www.pixies.com/uk/

o www.multimania.com/alec

o www.ozemail.com.au/~hehird

o www.evo.org/html/group/pixies.html

o http://dag.life.be/debaser

Recommended Reading

o Sadly, no one has seen fit to publish a proper Pixies biography. A disappointing oversight, to be sure.

Related Listening

Nirvana, Hüsker Du / Sugar / Bob Mould, Dinosaur Jr., the Fall, My Bloody Valentine, Sonic Youth, the Lemonheads, Belly, the Breeders, Frank Black's solo work.

The Story Thus Far ...

Emerging out of the incredibly vibrant Boston scene, the Pixies alternately whisper and shriek themselves to cult-rock stardom by sticking to the tried and true DIY model. Along with R.E.M. and Sonic Youth, they become college radio darlings and help spread the gospel of alt-rock to a new generation of music fans.

~ 20 ~
BRIAN ENO

Musician, Producer, Artist, Philosopher, Oblique Strategies

You would be forgiven if you first mistook the man as an accountant or a postal clerk. A second glance may cause you to speculate that he might be a university professor with tenure at a prestigious school such as Oxford or Cambridge. A more wild guess may be that the man is an artist of some sort — a writer perhaps. Now we're getting closer to the truth.

It takes Brian Eno a long time to explain what he does for a living. His *curriculum vitae* is surely one of the most colorful you will ever see: glam-rocker, multimedia artist, record producer, world traveler, philosopher, thinker, artistic foil, computer scientist, musical visionary, futurist and all-round egghead. Although his own recordings are hardly what you'd call best-sellers, his methods and theories have influenced music through three decades. From his position in the background as a record producer, Eno has helped others — David Bowie, the Talking Heads, U2 — move mountains. His innovative studio practices have had a massive effect on everything from how music is composed to how it can be perceived. As a musician himself, flirting on the outer fringes of the rock universe, he broke some of the original ground for much of today's ambient, techno and even New Age music. All this from a man who prefers to describe himself as a "bald and grumpy non-musician."

Brian Peter George St. John le Baptiste de la Salle Eno was born May 15, 1948 in Woodbridge, England, the descendent of three generations of postmen. As a child, he became fascinated with the music played on American Armed Forces Radio. This "Martian music" — so-called because the otherworldly sounds of American doo-wop and R&B seemed to come directly from space to the sedate English countryside — steered young Brian into the world of art school. At the Winchester School of Art (where he eventually became president of the Students' Union), he discovered the work of such avant-garde musicians as La Monte Young, John Cage, Terry Riley and, eventually, the Velvet Underground. Between 1964 and 1969, Eno studied music along with conceptual painting and something that became known as "sound sculpture." One of his favorite pursuits was experimenting with reel-to-reel tape recorders — making what we would call "tape loops" today — using the machines to treat and shape common sounds into something totally new. One of his first projects was a recording of a metal lampshade being struck and then overdubbed with a poetry reading.

Eno's first attempt at forming a band seems to have been in 1964 when he was part of a group called the Black Acres. This was followed by a stint in a performance art troupe called Merchant Taylor's Simultaneous Cabinet. At around the same time, he joined Maxwell Demon, an improvisational rock band that featured Eno on vocals and "signal generator." In 1969, he became a member of Cardew's Scratch Orchestra before playing clarinet in the somewhat infamous Portsmouth Sinfonia.[1]

---

1. Cardew's released an album in 1971 entitled THE GREAT LEARNING. The Sinfonia was an avant-garde outfit made up of musicians with widely disparate abilities and skills.

Through his old art-school chum Andy Mackay, Eno was invited to participate in the start-up of a new art-rock / glam-rock outfit called Roxy Music. Along with serving as an eccentric visual centerpiece for the band's live performances — it wasn't unusual to see Eno in full makeup and wearing feather boas — it became his duty to electronically treat the sounds made by the conventional instruments in the group. This arrangement lasted for two albums (ROXY MUSIC in 1972 and 1973's FOR YOUR PLEASURE) before the constant personality clashes with singer Bryan Ferry drove Eno into a solo career by July 1973.[1]

Eno's first post-Roxy album was issued in November 1973 and was a collaboration with King Crimson leader and guitar supremo, Robert Fripp. NO PUSSYFOOTING featured the debut of an Eno-designed tape-delay system he called "Frippertronics." Consisting of tying two reel-to-reel machines together to create a looped delay, Eno's careful manipulation of delay, echo and signal degeneration demonstrated how studio equipment could be used as effective tools for composing music.[2] Eno's first solo release was HERE COME THE WARM JETS (released late 1973), an album that listed his contributions as "simplistic keyboards, snake guitar, electric larynx and synthesizer." Despite being pretty experimental and weird, the album did managed to make the Top 30 in the UK, partly on the strength of a single entitled *Seven Deadly Finns*.

Joining a group called the Winkies in early 1974, Eno's health took a turn for the worse. He was hospitalized with a collapsed lung just five days into the band's English tour. Part of his convalescence included a trip to San Francisco where he found his next musical inspiration in the form of Chinese opera. The resulting stream-of-consciousness TAKING TIGER MOUNTAIN (BY STRATEGY) — the title is taken from a Chairman Mao-era revolutionary opera — was in the stores by the fall. Further study of Chinese culture and I Ching philosophy eventually led to the creation of Eno's "oblique strategies" approach (see Fast Facts.)

Eno's bad luck with his health continued in 1975 when a car accident left him bedridden for several months. As painful as the experience was, it led him down a path of discovery involving the subtle use of music in the creation of an environment. Because he was unable to move and incapable of even adjusting the volume on his stereo after a visitor put on some quiet harp music, Eno came to the conclusion that music could been seen to have the same properties as color or light. Careful blending of music with visual input could create a harmonious and balanced sensory experience. Unlike the cold, harsh electronic world of Kraftwerk, Eno's synthesizers had soft edges. The compositions unfolded slowly, mesmerizing the listener with gentile, flowing repetition. This music tinted the atmosphere and, when done correctly, produced a self-regulating and very pleasing environment. These weren't songs that needed to be heard; they were soundscapes that needed to be experienced. It was the birth of a new genre that Eno called "ambient music."

Eno's first attempt at creating music for this purpose was ANOTHER GREEN WORLD (1975) but DISCREET MUSIC (also 1975) was his first full-flown ambient recording. Side one featured various synthesizer loops meandering through a series of movements while the second side contained variations of Pachebel's *Canon in D Minor*. DISCREET MUSIC became the first release in a ten-album series of experimental recordings on his new label, Obscure.

While Eno continued with his ambient and left-brain pop experiments with BEFORE AND AFTER SCIENCE (1977), MUSIC FOR FILMS (his first true ambient record, 1978) and MUSIC FOR AIRPORTS (1979), he was also being sought as a collaborator and producer. Having already worked with a variety of people (Robert Fripp, John Cale, Nico, and an atmospheric German band called Cluster, among others), Eno found himself genuinely enjoying the artistic and intellectual challenge presented by these projects. Even though Eno's methods had earned him some notoriety (especially with those on the fringes of rock and roll), the phone call from David Bowie came as a surprise.

---

1. There were other reasons, too. Eno was exhausted after ten months of touring and was still recovering from injuries sustained when he was hit by a car. When he was in the hospital, Eno realized that he'd lost interest in Roxy Music's approach to rock.
2. It worked like this: A signal was recorded on a reel of tape on Machine One. After passing over the recording heads of Machine One, the tape was guided to Machine Two where it passed across the record/playback heads to the take-up reel of Machine Two. This allowed the signal to be simultaneously played back on Machine Two and re-routed electronically to Machine One, creating an adjustable delay effect. Frippertronics was applied mainly to guitar and synthesizers. Compare this method to the present-day hip hop practice of delivering raps over looped background tracks.

In the mid-70's, Bowie was one of the biggest stars in the world. His music, his shape-shifting personas and ultra-theatrical tours had already lifted him to near mythical status. But by the time 1976 came to a close, Bowie realized that after a six-year run of success, he had hit a creative wall. His inability to think of what to do next was further addled by the soul-sucking coke-and-booze excesses of his adopted Los Angeles home. Determined to clean up and move on, Bowie decided to isolate himself in Berlin — and he wanted Eno to help him with his next album. Bowie was a great admirer of the textures and sound manipulations of ANOTHER GREEN WORLD and asked Eno if he could show him how to take his music in a similar direction. Eno — who quite enjoyed Bowie's last album, STATION TO STATION — accepted the challenge.

In the end, Eno produced three albums for Bowie, the so-called Berlin Trilogy that revitalized his flagging creative energies: LOW (1977), HEROES (1978) and LODGER (1979.) As an active collaborator on much of the material, Eno was able to push Bowie into new territory. Using new synthesizers, new outboard studio effects and the ever-present Oblique Strategies cards as guides, Eno helped Bowie not only to break of his slump, but to reformulate his outlook on music in general.

Eno's late-70's production credits extended far beyond working with David Bowie in Berlin. On May 13, 1977, Eno was in the audience when one of his favorite new American art-punk bands, the Talking Heads, played the Rock Garden in London. Impressed with the Heads' combination of quirkiness and intelligence, he invited the band back to his house to discuss the possibilities of some kind of future alliance. When he moved to New York in 1978 to further immerse himself in the underground Manhattan music scene, he offered to produce the Heads' second album. He ended up producing three records for the band, guiding them through their metamorphosis from Bowery New Wave bar band to one of the most progressive and radical-sounding groups of the 1980's.

Working as an unofficial fifth member of the group (feel free to make comparisons with George Martin and the Beatles), Eno encouraged the Talking Heads to take more chances with rhythm and electronic processing. Through the three albums featuring Eno's touch — MORE SONGS ABOUT BUILDINGS AND FOOD (1978), FEAR OF MUSIC (1979) and REMAIN IN LIGHT (1980) — the Heads developed a unique style underpinned by complicated non-Western rhythms and percussive effects that often involved subtle studio trickery. At the same time, the melodies and chord changes that floated over this pulse were simplified. The result was a sound that was both complex and clean, a fresh and invigorating fusion of rock and African-inspired dance rhythms. It was an approach that helped the Talking Heads sell millions of records.

With each project he took on, the demand for Eno's studio expertise only increased. Impressed with his work on LOW, Ultravox asked him to oversee the production of their debut album, ULTRAVOX! (1977.) Devo enlisted him to help organize the quirkiness of Q: ARE WE NOT MEN? A: WE ARE DEVO! (1978.) Eno was also instrumental in organizing NO NEW YORK (1978), the definitive collection that documented New York's short-lived but highly influential No Wave scene of the late 1970's.[3]

Despite his busy schedule as a producer, Eno wasn't about to let anything get in the way of his solo work and his explorations of ambient music. Two albums were released in 1980: POSSIBLE MUSICS (an ethno-musicological exercise with Canadian trumpet player, Jon Hassell) and THE PLATEAUX OF MIRROR (with minimalist composer Harold Budd.) African rhythms were explored with David Byrne in 1981 on the critically-acclaimed MY LIFE IN THE BUSH OF GHOSTS, an album inspired by a book of the same name by Nigerian novelist Amos Tutuola.[4] Two more albums of ambient material appeared, ON LAND (1982) and MUSIC FOR FILMS, VOLUME 2 (1983) and were followed by a collaboration with his brother Roger and Canadian engineer Daniel Lanois on APOLLO ATMOSPHERES, a soundtrack to a NASA documentary.

In early 1984, Eno once again picked up the phone only to find a major rock star on the other end asking for help. Bono, acting on a suggestion by drummer Larry Mullen, was wondering if Eno would help U2 take their sound to the next level in much the same fashion as he did with David Bowie and the Talking Heads. Once again accepting the challenge, Eno and Daniel Lanois encouraged U2 to experiment with song writing methods as THE UNFORGETTABLE FIRE (1984) slowly came together. When it was finally

---

3. For more on this album and its fallout, see the Chapter 16 on Sonic Youth.
4. The book tells the metaphorical story of a young man who leaves the conventions and traditions of his village in favor of an uncertain life in the mysterious bush country.

---

released, many U2 fans were shocked by the obviously creative leap forward from WAR. Even more pronounced was the genius of THE JOSHUA TREE (another Eno-Lanois project, 1987), an album that won a fistful of Grammy Awards.[1] Two more successful U2 albums followed: ACHTUNG BABY (1991) and ZOOROPA (1993.) Through this association with U2, both Eno and Lanois became recognized as two of the best producers and back room innovators in all of music. Few production teams have helped sell so many records.

Eno continued working on a variety of projects throughout the 90's. He participated in various ways on albums with John Cale, Jah Wobble, Michael Brook, Brian Ferry and Peter Gabriel as well as producing James for two successful releases (the more conventional LAID and the experimental WAH-WAH.) His expertise has also been sought by everyone from Depeche Mode and Slowdive to Laurie Anderson and "video painter" Christine Alcino. He also reunited with U2 on a MUSIC FOR FILMS-type project called ORIGINAL SOUNDTRACKS 1 (1995) that was released under the name the Passengers. Originally envisioned as an experimental album featuring scores to non-existent movies (just like Eno's MUSIC FOR FILMS albums), it was ultimately considered too weird to be issued as an official U2 album. Meanwhile, he continued to conduct further musical experiments with NERVE NET (1991), THE SHUTOV ASSEMBLY (1992), NEROLI (1993) and the oddly numbered BRIAN ENO collection (1993 and 1994.)[2] Eno has also flirted with publishing, multimedia art installations, and music-driven computer screen savers. He also moved to St. Petersburg, Russia, for six months in 1997.

While not a star in the traditional sense, Brian Eno is nonetheless one of the most important alt-rock figures of all time. Although he has made some valuable musical innovations, Eno's most important contribution has been how he has changed the way other composers and performers *think* about music. Through Eno's work as both a performer and a producer, the rock universe has become much more cerebral and thus has expanded far beyond its original natural boundaries. A thousand keyboard bands — ambient, electronic and techno, ranging from the Orb and Underworld on up — all owe a debt to Eno's non-rock electronic futurist experiments of the 1970's and 80's. Eno helped Bowie break out of a serious slump and forever altered his approach not only to music but to all art. Eno was instrumental in collecting together the best of the No Wave movement on an album that inspired the birth of Sonic Youth and countless other noise practitioners. Third-world sounds — such as the African and Latin rhythms used by the Talking Heads and David Byrne — have become more prevalent. And who knows if U2 would have become mega-superstars had Eno not guided and pushed them through the of creative minefields that resulted in the best albums of their career.

The scope of Professor Eno's activities and influences in nothing short of mind-boggling. In the end, it all comes down to *thinking*. Eno's strength lies with his ability to creatively and constructively combine seemingly unconnected ideas. Had it not been for his influence, today's rock and roll — all of it, not just the alt-rock variety — would sound *very* different.

Fast Facts

o The title of the album HERE COME THE WARM JETS is allegedly an allusion to urinating.

o Eno's Oblique Strategies evolved out of a series of happy accidents in the recording studio. Designed to encourage outside-the-box thinking, OS consists of a series of thought-provoking and often cryptic phrases on tarot-like flash cards that force musicians to look at their music in non-linear and more organic ways. Examples of these aphorisms include: "Don't be afraid of things because they're easy to do", "Don't break the silence," "Only a part, not a whole" and "Go slowly all the way round from the outside."

o The track Qu'ran (Koran) was left off some editions of MY LIFE IN THE BUSH OF GHOSTS for fear that it may offend certain quarters of the Islamic community because it contained some ritual chanting. It was replaced by *Very Very Hungry* on those editions.

---

1. Eno's crack-the-whip methods during the sessions for these two albums are legendary. Although he was not beyond having a little fun (a entire day's worth of recording for FIRE was done in the nude), he was a stern taskmaster, often pushing the band (especially Bono) to their creative and emotional limits. One of the things that makes Eno such an successful producer is that he will not stand for mediocrity, no matter who you might be. Who knows where U2 might be today if Eno had refused Bono's plea to produce the band? For more details on Eno's relationship with U2 (and with a description of some of the studio methods that worked with the band, both on a musical and psychological level), see Bill Flanagan's excellent *U2 At The End Of The World* (Delacorte Press, 1995.)
2. BRIAN ENO II was released a year before BRIAN ENO I.

○ In the early 80's, Eno created an art installation entitled *Mistaken Memories of Medieval Manhattan*, which consisted mainly of images broadcast through televisions that had been turned on their sides. Eno called this "vertical-format video."

○ Through the mid-80's, Eno thought about creating "Quiet Clubs," permanent art installations combining ambient music, light and color where people might retire to think. He abandoned the concept when he couldn't raise the necessary financing. Today's clubs and raves often have such areas.

○ Eno has a permanent video art installation at the Swarovski Museum in Austria.

○ In 1989, Eno was commissioned to create music for the opening of a Shinto shrine in Japan.

○ Using his home studio in Suffolk as a base for all his experiments, Eno has become somewhat of an expert in perfumes. In the early 90's, Eno reportedly worked on a scent that acted as a male aphrodisiac. The album NEROLI was named after one of Eno's scent experiments.

○ The SHUTOV ASSEMBLY, a collection of ambient works, was released after Russian painter Sergei Shutov complained that not enough of Eno's music was available in Russia.

○ Eno likes his porn. He's admitted to having a large collection of pornographic playing cards.

○ There were plans to build and amusement park with Peter Gabriel and Laurie Anderson in Barcelona. Problems with financing doomed the project.

○ According to sources within the computer industry, Eno was apparently paid $35,000 by Microsoft to compose the musical flourish that plays when Windows 95 boots up. Not a bad payday for a piece of music that has a running time of 3.25 seconds. (Eno submitted eighty-four short pieces in all; only one was chosen.)

○ Eno has provided music for several TV commercials for companies ranging from BMW to Microsoft.

○ Eno has an honorary Doctorate of Technology from the University of Plymouth. He also a Visiting Professor at the Royal College of Art in London.

Recommended Listening

○ HERE COME THE WARM JETS (Island, 1973)

○ ANOTHER GREEN WORLD (Island, 1975)

○ BEFORE AND AFTER SCIENCE (Island, 1978)

○ MUSIC FOR AIRPORTS (PVC, 1979 / E.G., 1982)

○ MY LIFE IN THE BUSH OF GHOSTS (with David Byrne, Sire 1981)

○ NERVE NET (Opal, 1992)

○ If the budget allows it, try locating the boxed set entitled BRIAN ENO I: INSTRUMENTALS (Virgin, 1994.) WORKING BACKWARDS 1973-1983 (E.G., 1984) is a good collection of some of Eno's early work.

○ For an idea of how much impact Eno has a producer, compare the Talking Heads debut with the albums featuring Eno's hand. The same goes for the leap U2 made from WAR to THE UNFORGETTABLE FIRE through to ZOOROPA.

Internet Resources

○ http://metalab.unc.edu/mal/MO/eno/

○ www.dream.com/Oblique.html

○ www.hyperreal.org/music/artists/brian_eno/

○ www.sseyo.com/genmus1.html

○ www.spies.com/Eno/Enohome.html

Recommended Reading

○ Eno, Brian. *A Year With Swollen Appendices*. London: Faber and Faber, 1996.

○ Eno, Brian and Mills, Russell. *More Dark Than Shark*. London: Faber and Faber, 1986.

○ Tamm, Eric. *Brian Eno: His Music and the Vertical Color of Sound*. New York: Da Capo Press, 1995.

Related Listening
David Bowie, Talking Heads, U2, James, Michael Brook, the Orb, Aphex Twin, Laurie Anderson.

The Story Thus Far ...
Eno's experiments in soundscapes give birth to a million keyboard bands while his outside-the-box thinking helps turn around the career of David Bowie (adding years of productive life to his career) and transforms the Talking Heads and U2 into superstars.

THE 1990'S

~ 21 ~
THE BEASTIE BOYS
Three MCs and One DJ

For more than a decade after funk and disco gave birth to them on the streets of New York, most of the world viewed rap and hip-hop almost exclusively as a Black Thing. As vibrant and innovative as this music was, it was virtually ignored by most of the rock and roll establishment. Incredible as it may seem today, MTV barely touched *any* black music until Michael Jackson forced their hand with *Billie Jean* in January 1983. The funkiness of Prince made some gains before Run-DMC (thanks in large part to the fact that Aerosmith, favorites of white, suburbanite rockers everywhere, appeared on the recording and in the video) broke through with *Walk This Way* in 1986. This should have set the stage for some talented and deserving black performer to bust it wide open for rap and hip-hop in mainstream music — but it didn't. Prejudices and biased attitudes dictated that there had to be at least one more intermediate step. That step came in the form of three snotty kids who just wanted to drink beer and meet chicks.

The Beastie Boys didn't start out as a rap band nor did they have any designs on taking hip-hop to the suburbs — and they certainly didn't expect to find themselves running a record label, a line of clothing or petitioning China to stop their oppression of Tibet. Yet in the years since they were first formed, they've done all this and more. Thanks to the Beasties, not only has the color barrier surrounding rap and hip-hop continued to fall (allowing this music to become one of the dominant pop music genres on the planet), they are also one of the genre's premiere practitioners.

It's ironic that a style of music invented in the ghettos and streets should be advanced by three affluent kids from Manhattan. Mike Diamond (born November 20, 1965) was the spiky-haired drummer son of a couple of art dealers from the Upper West Side. Adam Yauch (born August 15, 1964) was the son of an architect who was often see at the same Bad Brains gigs as Mike. Finally, there's Adam Horowitz (born October 31, 1966), son of respected playwright Israel Horowitz, a kid who preferred to slum with the punks than behave in the company of his parents' Broadway insiders.

Mike was the first to form a band. The Young Aborigines — consisting of Mike, John Berry (birth date unknown) and Kate Schellanchach (born January 5, 1966) — were just awful and mercifully broke up after playing just two gigs, both of which were conveniently scheduled on the same night. Almost immediately, the Aborigines were recycled into a new four-piece band that included their Number One Fan, Adam Yauch. He was handed a bass guitar and told to do the best he could.

The group's original manifesto was simple: do what was necessary to annoy other members of the immediate punk crowd. They officially dubbed themselves **B**oys **E**ntering **A**narchistic **S**tates **T**owards **I**nternal **E**xcellence — "Beastie Boys" for short. History records that their first show took place at John Berry's loft at 100th and Broadway in Manhattan on August 15, 1981 — Adam's seventeenth birthday party. It was also the first time Adam ever got drunk.

The party proved that the Beastie Boys somehow seemed more viable than the Young Aborigines and they set about getting themselves some gigs in hardcore-friendly venues around the city including CBGB, Max's and A7.

After a few disappointing and lackluster shows, it was decided that the Beasties should break up. Just then, a friend named Dave Parsons intervened with a proposition. He already owned a record store in the East Village called Rat Cage and was thinking of expanding the enterprise into a record label. Parsons got the joke the Beasties were trying to perpetuate and wondered if they would be interested in being the first band on his new label. There was a hasty reformation and everyone gathered outside a studio called 171A. With just two days available (the studio was going broke and the landlord was threatening to sell all the equipment in order to collect some back rent), the Beasties managed to put eight songs on tape. Then they broke up again.[1]

As the sheriff's department was repossessing all the studio's gear, an engineer named Scott Jarvis managed to rescue a tape machine and the Beasties' master tape. Mixing four of those tracks in his bedroom, he gave Parsons the tape who then released POLLYWOG STEW, a four-track 7-inch EP, on Parsons fledgling Rat Cage Records in November 1982. When the EP actually started to sell a few copies at Parsons' store, the Beasties reunited yet again. This time, however, they brought along a new member. Guitarist Adam Horowitz was available now that the Young and the Useless had broken up (their drummer had been sent to military school.) The band was once again a going concern.

Over the next twelve months, the Beastie Boys gigged when they could and attended a mix of hardcore and rap shows when they couldn't. Rap was starting to spread throughout New York as DJs like Grandmaster Flash and Afrika Bambaataa brought the sounds of Queens, the Bronx and Brooklyn to Manhattan dance clubs. On the subway, boom boxes boomed with homemade and bootleg tapes of MC battles that were taped in the streets and at house parties. Conspicuous by its absence on the radio (with the exception of *Rapture*, the No. 1 hit by Blondie), rap dwelled underground, *in* and *of* the streets. With the 70's New York CBGB scene now dead and with New Wave going nowhere, rap was New York's new punk rock. Rather than segregating it away from rock and roll, some people — like the Beastie Boys — chose to treat rap as part of a larger post-punk underground music scene.

Given the Beasties enthusiasm for this new music, it was inevitable that they began to explore the possibilities of fusing punk with rap and the break dance culture of the time. Armed with a few dollars, they decided to get one of these new ideas down on tape. The concept was very simple. First, they made a prank phone call to a local Carvel ice cream store, ostensibly to order a cake called a "Cookie Puss." Once the tape of that phone call was spiced up with some bits — samples — from a Steve Martin comedy album, some basic break dance beats were added underneath. As unique as *Cookie Puss* was in the context of the hardcore / rap / hip-hop scene of the day, it was still just a novelty record. The B-side, however, was a different story.

Cookie Puss was issued as the A-side of a 12-inch single on Rat Cage in August 1983. The other side of the record featured a reggae-ish song entitled *Beastie Revolution*. Although the truth seems to be lost forever, it's a fact that this song financed much of the Beastie Boys' musical pursuits over the next few years. Somehow — and no one is really sure how a major European airline came into possession of a novelty single by an unknown New York indie act — a bite of *Beastie Revolution* ended up in a commercial for British Airways. Because they did so without the band's permission, the Beasties sued the airline. According to legend, British Airways acknowledged the gaffe and paid the group an out-of-court settlement totaling $40,000. Taking their winnings, all four Beasties moved to a small rat-infested Chinatown apartment above a Korean brothel. The apartment became Beastie HQ as *Cookie Puss* continued to create a minor buzz in New York's hip-hop community.

It soon became obvious that if they were going to compete on an equal level with some of the other performers on the scene, sooner or later, they were going to have to find themselves a DJ. At the very least, they needed someone who knew how to add beats to their live rendition of *Cookie Puss*. Enter Rick Rubin.

---

1. Once again, they believed that the group had run its course. Meanwhile, John Berry had a bit of a crystal meth problem, which didn't help things much.

Rubin — who preferred to go by the name "DJ Double R" — was a film student at NYU who moonlighted as a DJ. Once he joined the group (he was the Beasties' only choice; they didn't know anyone else with equipment), Rubin began to encourage the band to move further into the realm of rap and hip-hop and further from their hardcore punk leanings. Because Rubin had fast hands on his turntables, the Beasties were also able to lose their instruments and thus concentrate more on their rapping and rhyming. Rubin also convinced the group to start dressing more like MCs with matching Adidas track outfits, backwards-facing baseball caps and chunky gold chains. Everyone adopted hip-hop handles: Mike Diamond became Mike D; Adam Yauch went with MCA (Master of Ceremonies Adam); and Adam Horowitz was reborn as the King Ad Rock. Rubin also managed to force Kate Schellenbach out of the group.[1]

As the months passed, the Beastie Boys completed their transition from hardcore punks to full-fledged hip-hoppers. Through Rubin's connections with promoter and entrepreneur Russell Simmons (brother of Joseph Simmons, a.k.a. Run from Run-DMC), the group was able to secure gigs with black artists such as Kurtis Blow. Some of these shows were pretty interesting. After all, who had ever heard of a rap group featuring three *white* MCs? Meanwhile, Simmons craftily concluded a bait-and-switch routine with Madonna when she asked if he could provide an opening act for her Like A Virgin tour. Promising her one thing, he instead delivered the Beastie Boys. The contrast between the Beasties in-your-face antics and the expectations of the teen Madonna wannabes in the audience made for an interesting tour.

By November 1984, Rubin and Simmons had founded Def Jam, a record label designed to promote rap and hip-hop. The company's first release was in October 1984, a single entitled *I Need a Beat* by a Queens teenager who called himself LL Cool J.[2] Def Jam's second release (November 1984) was the mythological *Rock Hard* single from the Beastie Boys, a 12-inch that was quickly withdrawn when AC/DC discovered that the group had sampled elements of *Back in Black* without asking. A year later, a single called *She's On It* (released in 1986), managed to find its way onto the soundtrack of a film entitled *Krush Groove*.

By the time Def Jam was ready to send the Beastie Boys into the studio to record their first album, the group was displaying a knack for annoying people. Even if you were really into their music, it was still all too easy to hate the Beastie Boys and their ultra-obnoxious drunken frat-boy antics. This love-hate relationship extended from the people who went to their shows all the way to the British music press. Some of that animosity, however, abruptly turned into respect.

When LICENSED TO ILL appeared in November 1986, it fell into a yawning gap in the rap canyon. The songs weren't of the same street-level MC banter best exemplified by Run-DMC and the ever-bragging LL Cool J. Nor did the record sound anything like rap forefathers such as Grandmaster Flash who were still chained to their turntables and mixers. Instead, LICENSED TO ILL arrived with all the subtlety of a brick to the head. Half rap, half rock and all attitude, the album took the rock world totally by surprise. With its heavy beats, occasional blasts of blistering guitar and well-chosen Led Zeppelin samples, the album's appeal also lay in the snotty references to beer, girls and being dumb. Even though *(You Gotta) Fight for Your Right (to Party)* had One Hit Wonder written all over it (or so it seemed at first glance), the rest of the album was just too powerful — and fun — to ignore. It was as if KISS had mated with Run-DMC while listening to both NEVER MIND THE BOLLOCKS and LED ZEPPELIN II while *Animal House* was running on the VCR.

LICENSED TO ILL was a massive record for the Beastie Boys and Def Jam. This new fusion of rock, rap and hip-hop proved to be almost universally appealing, cutting across all the usual musical boundaries. The album was played in white clubs, black clubs, on black radio, college radio, alternative radio and mainstream rock radio. It reached across the social and culture gap between black and white, bringing two groups closer together than anything had in years. Doors opened between rock and rap — and things have never been the same since.

Commercially, LICENSED TO ILL also broke down barriers. It quickly became one of the fastest-selling debut albums in history as more than four million copies were sold by December 1987. The album sailed

---

1. The resignation/firing of Kate Schellenbach opened a rift that did not heal for many years. She maintains that Rick Rubin created such a powerfully sexist atmosphere that she couldn't possibly stay in the group. She later emerged as an important part of Luscious Jackson.
2. A Beastie legend says that Rubin might never been alerted to LL Cool J's talents had Ad Rock not discovered his demo tape among the litter on the floor of Rubin's dorm room.

to No. 1 on the album chart, becoming the first ever rap record to reach that height.[3] It stayed there for seven weeks while *Fight for Your Right* reached No. 2 on *Billboard's* Hot 100 singles chart. But let's pause long enough to consider this: how might this album have sold if the Beasties had been allowed to go with their choice for a title? They really wanted this record to be called DON'T BE A FAGGOT.

While the Beasties Boys found millions of new fans with LICENSED TO ILL, they also managed to make millions of new enemies. Perceived through their flip comments as misogynists and homophobes — and unable to comprehend what appeal British teens found in the foul, primitive sounds of rap — the group was the subject of a series of attacks by the British press. Once the tabloids picked up on the story, they were merciless. *The Daily Mirror* carried a front page headline on May 14, 1987, that read "DEPRAVED" and proceeded to relate a fabricated story that detailed how the group had laughed at and taunted a group of kids with terminal leukemia. By the time fans rushed to the group's defense — including some of the kids in that hospital group — the damage had been done.

At the same time, the band didn't do themselves any favors. Shows were raucous affairs, featuring scantily-clad dancing girls in cages and the group's now-infamous hydraulic penis prop. At a gig in Liverpool on May 30, 1987, a bunch of football thugs intent on teaching the trio a lesson started throwing cans and bottles at the band. The Beasties responded by returning the missiles using baseball bats. In the resulting melee, a girl was hit in the eye and Ad Rock was arrested for assault.[4] At the same time, fans, seeking to construct their own Beastie Boys jewelry, were causing havoc across the country. Volkswagen owners returned to find that the "VW" emblems had been pried off their cars and turned into medallions. No wonder a faction of MP's wanted the group banned from the UK for life.

By the time the tour supporting LICENSED TO ILL came to a close, all three Beasties were burned out and surly. Deciding that they needed a long rest (otherwise they'd kill each other), the three members of the group scattered to follow individual pursuits. Ad Rock was probably the most active. He bolted for Hollywood to spend time with then-girlfriend Molly Ringwald. While he was on the coast, he managed to start an acting career, appearing in an episode of the TV series *The Equalizer* and in two films, *The Santa Ana Project* and *Lost Angels*.

Meanwhile, there were problems brewing with Def Jam. Russell Simmons wanted another album right away so the label could capitalize on the momentum the Beasties had built up over the previous twelve months. The band, tired and spent, refused, saying that they needed time to regenerate. In retaliation, Def Jam refused to pay the band any of the royalties they were owed, saying that by not providing the label with a new album, Beasties were failing to live up to the terms of their contract. The group's counter-charge was that if they weren't being paid, then Def Jam was negligent in their duties as a record label and therefore in breach of contract. Lawsuits and counter-suits were filed and within a few short weeks, both sides had become entrenched and unwilling to budge. It was one of those peculiar entertainment industry standoffs.

Then the band made a bold move. Declaring that Def Jam had forfeited all rights to future Beastie Boy material by not paying the group their rightful share of royalties, the band put themselves on the open market while technically still under contract to Def Jam. After consulting their battery of lawyers, Capitol won a fierce bidding war, reportedly offering upwards of $3 million to sign the group. While the Capitol legal department promised to clean up the group's awkward departure from Def Jam, the A&R department promised that the group would have complete creative control over their next project — whenever they chose to start work on it.

When the Beastie Boys delivered PAUL'S BOUTIQUE in July 1989, the executives at Capitol were taken aback. They were under the belief that their $3 million was guaranteed them another LICENSED TO ILL. What they got was a bill for sixteen months of studio time and an album that sounded like nothing else in the world.

In the two years that elapsed between LICENSED TO ILL and PAUL'S BOUTIQUE, the Beasties' skill at using the recording studio as a compositional tool had leaped light-years ahead. Using a production team

---

3. Cynics will bitterly point out (with some justification) that it took a bunch of white MCs to take a black musical art form into the mainstream. The good news is at least the Beastie Boys did help rap break through, paving the way for future widespread acceptance of all rap, whether its origins be white or black.
4. He spent the weekend in jail and was eventually released on £10,000 bail.

---

known as the Dust Brothers (John King and Mike Simpson a.k.a. King Gizmo and EZ Mike), the band's new sound was far more polished and mature than anything they had accomplished to that point. Critics loved the record for its incredibly complex pastiche of sounds and samples, many of which had been pillaged from the 1970's. Beats and rhythms were mixed and matched with an untold variety of diverse musical elements, resulting in a crazy-quilt design that was all somehow seamlessly stitched together. Even *Time* ran a positive review, urging readers to pay attention to the myriad of cultural references.

The hip-hop community was totally blown away by the album, marveling at the amount of information the group was able to jam into each track. Up until this point in rap history, budgetary and technological considerations dictated that most records have a rough-hewn sound to them. The production on PAUL'S BOUTIQUE, while still having the essential feel, was super-smooth and contained more samples than an entire rack of rap records put together. At the same time, all three members had become accomplished MCs, dropping rhymes that were often clever and fun but also occasionally serious and thought-provoking. It was a refreshing change to macho boasting found on many other rap records. Perhaps these three white rappers weren't a big joke after all.

The general public, however, wasn't so sure. People were expecting more frat-boy goofball stuff and wanted an album full of songs that they could like right away. But because PAUL'S BOUTIQUE was an experiment that challenged the listener, most people didn't bother to take the time. The first single, *Hey Ladies* died at No. 36 on the *Billboard* charts. Even though the album managed to move 800,000 copies, that paled in comparison to the numbers generated by LICENSED TO ILL. Capitol Records heard a great sucking sound: it was their $3 million investment being flushed away. In the boardroom, many heads rolled over the Beastie Boy fiasco. Even the president was fired for allowing a dog like this to be signed in the first place.[1]

The one positive that came out of the experience was that it destroyed all preconceptions and notions of who the Beastie Boys were; they were now truly free to re-define themselves again without having to deal with outside expectations. They also vowed to take the business aspect of what they were doing more seriously.

Moving west with the remainder if Capitol's $3 million advance, the Beasties Boys built a studio in the Atwater Village of Los Angeles. Dubbing it G-Son, the studio was equipped with the latest digital gear as well as a basketball court and a skateboard ramp. Surrounding themselves with a group of trusted collaborators and advisers (including a new management team from the same company that looked after Nirvana), the guys settled down to work on their third album. Relaxed and isolated from the pressures of the outside world, CHECK YOUR HEAD slowly took shape.

For the first time since their early hardcore days, the Beasties grabbed their real guitars, turned up the amplifiers and rolled tape as they wailed away. Some four hundred hours of jamming later, these real guitars and real drums were mixed with the usual bewildering array of samples and loops and beats. Vocals were recorded using old, junky microphones, making the performances oddly distorted and adding a certain edginess to the proceedings. A further fresh twist came with the addition of Money Mark Nishita on keyboards.[2] The final result was as different from PAUL'S BOUTIQUE as that album had been from LICENSED TO ILL.

When CHECK YOUR HEAD was released on April 21, 1992, the executives at Capitol really didn't give it much thought. After the disaster of the last album, they were content to let the Beastie Boys play in their new studio just as long as they didn't cause any trouble. No one — not even the band — expected the album to debut at No. 10 on the American charts.

Suddenly, the Beasties Boys were back. In the years following PAUL'S BOUTIQUE, the influence of rap and hip-hop has spread further into the white community. Although many white suburban kids were into the hard gangsta rap of Public Enemy, Ice-T and NWA by the beginning of 1992, they had not abandoned

---

1. Another theory regarding the initial under-performance of PAUL'S BOUTIQUE is that it arrived too late to compete with a hip-hop classic: De La Soul's 3 FEET DEEP AND RISING.
2. A carpenter by trade, he met the Beastie Boys after Mike D drove his car through a fence at what was slowly becoming the G-Son compound. Mark and the guys got to talking, which lead to a job constructing the cabinetry in the studio (check the references on *Finger Lickin' Good*.) After hanging out with the guys for a while, he was invited in as a contributing member of the Beasties' musical entourage.

rock entirely. Then along came the Beastie Boys with what amounted to a new "alt-rap" sound. Not only did the real guitars and distortion attract rap fans that were looking for something new, but the music also appealed to alternative rock fans, people who were into grunge, industrial and high-intensity lo-fi indie rock. It was the right combination at the right time — and the fact that the album didn't feature a single Top 40 hit only enhanced the group's street cred.

As the album continued to sell (and as they crept back into Capitol's good graces), the Beastie Boys spent most 1992 and 1993 growing in different

Beastie Boys, 1998

directions. Mike D morphed into a savvy businessman, spending more time on Grand Royal, the Beasties personal record label. Not only did Mike pursue other groups for the label (such as Luscious Jackson and later Sean Lennon, Scottish indie group Bis, Atari Teenage Riot and the John Spencer Blues Explosion), he expanded the company's activities to include a magazine and a mailing list. A line of hip-hop / skate clothing called "X-Large" was created with Mike acting as one of the principle investors. Adam Yauch, in a new quest for personal spiritual satisfaction, took a trip to Tibet that changed his life.[3] First becoming a Buddhist, he then began to get involved in a series of pro-Tibet / anti-China causes. Horowitz also married actress Ione Skye (daughter of 60's legend Donovan) in July 1992 while Mike D married director Tamra Davis. The frat-boys from New York were growing up.[4]

Work on the fourth album started in New York in May 1993. With the Cult of Beastie growing both larger and impatient, the group wisely decided to concentrate on making a record that was a logical follow-up to CHECK YOUR HEAD rather than attempt to reinvent the wheel a fourth time. ILL COMMUNICATION took shape as an obvious extension of CHECK YOUR HEAD right from the beginning. The move back to New York was also deliberate; the group needed to get away from the growing distractions at G-Son. Using the now-familiar selection of real instruments, cheap microphones again and high-tech digital gear, the album coalesced from hours of tape with elements of jazz sneaking in here and there.

The album was pretty well completed when Mike D decided to write one more track. Although the final product sounded a little out of place when compared to the rest of the album, it gave the band something they hadn't had since LICENSED TO ILL: a massive, across-the-board hit single. Throughout the summer of 1994, *Sabotage* was all over radio and the video channels plus it was one of the most-requested tracks in all kinds of dance clubs. As silly as the lyrics were (they really *don't* make much sense), *Sabotage* was pure fun, just what the band needed to kick things to the next level.[5]

With ILL COMMUNICATION, the Beastie Boys officially became alt-rock heroes. Now that Kurt Cobain was dead and grunge was starting to lose its grip on the alt-rock nation, the Beastie Boys were in a position to step into the breach in order to fill a quickly developing void. The album was released May 31, 1994. Ten days later, it debuted at No. 1 on *Billboard*. After years in the wilderness, the Beastie Boys' comeback was complete.

A main stage appearance on the 1994 Lollapalooza Festival injected a much-needed sense of humor into

---

3. This 1992 trip was his second. He had first visited the country in 1990.
4. Adam Yauch is married to a woman named Dechen Wangdu.
5. The *Sabotage* video was directed by Spike Jonez, a former pro skateboarder. Before the shoot, he instructed the band to grow hair and beards. Mike D, however, finds it hard to grow any facial hair. With deadlines looming, it was decided that everyone would use bad wigs and fake glue-on mustaches and beards. At first, the Beasties were quite concerned that this would make things look too cheesy. In the end, however, it's this cheesiness that made the clip work so well.

a music scene that was starting to sink under the weight of years of accumulated gloom. Once Lollapalooza was over, the Beasties embarked on their Quadrophonic Joystick Action Tour, a sold-out road trip that saw every single seat at Madison Square Gardens snapped up in less than thirty minutes.

When he wasn't performing or recording with his bandmates, Adam Yauch was thinking about the situation in Tibet. Back in May 1994, he and an American student named Erin Potts had established the Milarepa Fund, a foundation designed to raise money for pro-Tibet causes. From fairly humble beginnings (donating royalties from two songs that used Tibetan monk samples on ILL COMMUNICATION), the Fund slowly began to get involved in other projects, such as sponsoring Tibetan children through North American schools. As 1995 drew to a close, Yauch, taking a page of Bob Geldof's Live Aid playbook, began work on benefit concert that would not only raise money for Tibetan causes but also awareness of the Tibetan peoples' plight under China.

It took some heavy organizing, but he pulled it off. More than 100,000 people paid thirty dollars each to attend the first annual Tibetan Freedom Festival at Golden Gate Park in San Francisco on July 15, 1996. The lineup included the Beastie Boys, the Smashing Pumpkins, Sonic Youth, Björk, the Red Hot Chili Peppers and Rage Against the Machine. The event was so successful that a two day event was held at RFK Stadium on June 13 and 14, 1998. Although the lineup was again impressive and the crowds were enthusiastic (more than 120,00 tickets were sold), the first day was marred by bad weather and a bolt of lightning that sent one woman to hospital (she survived.)[1] The 1999 edition of the festival was one of the most impressive concerts ever staged: four shows on four continents (Amsterdam; East Troy, Wisconsin; Tokyo and Sydney) creating an event that lasted more than twenty-four hours.

The fifth Beastie Boys record was cobbled together while all three members were involved in remixing songs and producing albums for other people. For the first time since PAUL'S BOUTIQUE, the cheap, distorting microphones were left at home as the guys opted for a cleaner, less spittle-ridden vocal sound. Rhymes were worked out at each other's apartments and over many Grande Cappucinos at Starbucks. Extra help was brought in as necessary: Jill Cuniff of Luscious Jackson, Miho from Cibo Matto and the legendary dub master, Lee "Scratch" Perry. Hardcore tracks that might have made an album earlier in the decade had already been spun off onto a separate CD, leaving the group to concentrate on other things.[2] The group even got into the late-night infomercial business, plugging the new record in some cities across America (It was a great parody TV pitch, featuring juicers, screaming physical fitness freaks, psychics and get-rich-fast money guys.) The attention to detail paid off once again. When HELLO NASTY hit the stores on August 25, 1998, more than 700,000 copies were sold in North America in the first seven days, giving the Beastie Boys their second consecutive debut at No. 1 on the albums charts. By the end of the second week, the album was just 2,000 copies short of being declared platinum. The tour that followed — ultimately culminating with the aforementioned 1999 Tibetan Freedom Festival — was also a massive success.[3]

The Beasties Boys were also becoming more interested in the possibilities of expanding their presence on the Internet. Grand Royal already had an interactive web site but the boys were also intrigued by the potential the Internet held for distributing music directly to fans. The Beasties soon became one of the first groups to offer exclusive non-album songs through their own web sites using special Microsoft encryption software as well as offering straight MP3 downloads through an agreement with mp3.com. Grand Royal even maintains an Internet radio station.

As the century drew to a close, the Beastie Boys announced that they were going to take a long break. With so many avenues now open to all three members, they decided that they'd like to pursue some of these new interests so that they may continue to grow as musicians, businessmen, activists and adults.

Thanks in large part to the Beastie Boys, hip-hop has grown beyond its original urban fanbase, reaching into the hearts of white kids in the suburbs. This widespread acceptance of a formerly exclusively black art form has already had an immensely positive impact on music as styles and trends blend in new,

---

1. Lysa Selton, 25, of Lancaster, Pennsylvania, was hospitalized in serious condition with burns when she was struck by lightning inside RFK Stadium. She was among 11 people injured Saturday as a result of the bad weather. Most were not seriously hurt, although three others were taken to hospital for a check up. Selton eventually made a full recovery.
2. AGLIO E OILO (Italian for Garlic and Oil, released in 1995) featured eight hardcore songs in just eleven minutes.
3. Things would have been perfect had it not been for the Adam Horowitz's marital trouble with Ione Skye. After being separated for several months, she filed for divorce on May 29, 1999, citing irreconcilable differences.

colorblind ways. The lines between hip-hop and rock have now blurred to the point where it's often impossible to tell where one genre ends and the other begins. At the same time, the Beastie Boys have demonstrated that it's possible to make new music out of old. Their cut-and-paste cultural piracy has shown many a rapper how to re-energize a sound that can occasionally get bogged down in bad habit and old ideas.

For a group once written off as a one-hit-wonder publicity stunt that was doing nothing more than pillaging the music of the black community, the Beastie Boys have matured into an act that has sent significant ripples through pop culture. Rock and roll is a far better thing thanks to these three guys. And like all good rock, it started out as nothing more than attempt to meet chicks and maybe get some free beer.

Fast Facts

o The Young and the Useless recorded one long-lost single: *Real Men Don't Use Floss*.

o After leaving the Beastie Boys, John Berry went on to form a band called Thwig.

o Much of the band's early material — including the infamous *Cookie Puss* — was gathered together on SOME OLD BULLSHIT in 1994.

o LICENSED TO ILL remains one of the best-selling back catalogue albums in the world. Although the album came out in late 1986, it still sells hundreds of thousands of copies each year.

o *Brass Monkey* can be two things: (1) A rather foul but cheap alcoholic beverage sold in liquor stores or (2) A concoction consisting of ½ vodka, ½ light rum and orange juice.

o BBC-TV banned the *Fight for Your Right* video. Even that didn't stop the single from reaching No. 11 in the UK.

o Perhaps the video should have been banned in Washington, DC. In August 1987, $350,000 damage was done to a home when five teenagers tried to recreate scenes from the video. The house ended up burning to the ground.

o The cover of PAUL'S BOUTIQUE requires some explaining. While it is true that the album was named after a thrift shop / used clothing store in Brooklyn, it's NOT the store we see on the cover. That photo was taken at Ludlow and Rivington Streets in Manhattan. Despite the sign that identifies it at Paul's Boutique, the store shown is actually Lee's Sportswear. Paul's Boutique had gone out of business before anyone had a chance to shoot the cover. The sign was added later.

o The Dust Brothers got their big start by producing the debut record for Tone Loc. Based on the sound they had achieved with tracks like *Funky Cold Medina*, the Beastie Boys actively sought out the Dust Brothers in February 1988.

o The rift between the Beastie Boys and Kate Schellanbach began to close when they met at the funeral of a friend in 1990. Afterwards, they got to talking about past regrets and slowly became friends again. Luscious Jackson was one of the first bands to sign to the Beasties' Grand Royal label.

o The Beasties took the name of their label, Grand Royal, from a favorite phrase ("Grand royal — guaranteed fresh!") of their friend, rapper Biz Markie.

o Despite claims that Nathaniel Hornblower is Adam Yauch's uncle, don't believe it. Underneath all that fake hair, he looks suspiciously like Adam himself.

o There's a story behind the title HELLO NASTY. The name of the Beastie Boys' publicity company is Nasty Little Man. Toco, the Japanese woman who answers the phone at the office, greets callers with "Hello, Nasty!"

o There are several Internet resources that detail the originals of the samples used on Beastie Boys records. Start with this site: www.csulb.edu/~bsb/beastieboys/samples/paulsboutique.html

Recommended Listening

o LICENSED TO ILL (Def Jam, 1986)

o PAUL'S BOUTIQUE (Capitol, 1989)

o CHECK YOUR HEAD (Capitol, 1992)

o ILL COMMUNICATION (Grand Royal / Capitol, 1994)

o HELLO NASTY (Grand Royal / Capitol, 1998)

○ The Japanese editions of these albums generally come with extra tracks. For a special insight into the Beastie Boys' creative process, you might want to look for THE IN SOUND FROM WAY OUT (Grand Royal / Capitol, 1996), a collection of instrumentals used in the construction of both CHECK YOUR HEAD and ILL COMMUNICATION. SCIENTISTS OF SOUND (Grand Royal / Capitol, 1999) is fine collection of 12-inch remixes. A proper greatest hits CD was scheduled to be released in November 1999.

Internet Resources

○ www.beastieboys.com

○ www.grandroyal.com

○ www.grandroyaldirect.com

○ www.milarepa.org

○ www.musicfanclubs.org/beastieboys/

Recommended Reading

○ Bately, Angus. *Rhyming and Stealing: A History of the Beastie Boys.* London: Independent Music Press, 1998.

Related Listening

Run-DMC, Money Mark, Public Enemy, De La Soul, Wu-Tang Clan, Consolidated, Stereo MCs, Disposable Heroes of Hiphoprisy, Beck, G. Love and Special Sauce, Rage Against the Machine, Limp Bizkit, Korn.

The Story Thus Far ...

Powered by punk principles and inspired by the music from the streets of New York, the Beastie Boys create a new rock-rap hybrid that makes a serious dent the hip-hop color barrier. By the time the 1990's begin, this rock / rap / hip-hop sound has spread to the suburbs and beyond, setting the stage for a brand new flavor of alt-rock. And don't forget the impact of those great videos.

~ 22 ~
NINE INCH NAILS
Anger is an (industrial) energy

Anger, violence, self-obsession, self-destruction. In some quarters of the rock and roll universe, these elements are as essential to life as air and water. The music that's come from this dark corner has arrived wearing many different shades of black: heavy metal, goth, industrial. Although each approach has its appeal, only a few manage to break into the collective consciousness of the mainstream. But what if someone found a way to combine all those sounds in a manner that was louder, more obnoxious and above all, darker than all the rest? What if there was a way to integrate the primal energy of metal with the glorious gloominess of goth and the thunderous tribal dance beat practiced by the best industrial masters? There was — and it took a Pennsylvania farm boy to show how it could be done.

With just two albums and one EP over five years, the despair-driven, Macintosh-powered rage of Trent Reznor forever altered the alt-rock landscape. Reznor's portrait-of-an-artist-as-a-torture-victim turned him into something of an anti-hero, someone who produced anthems detailing such isolation and pain that listeners were sucked into his pit and forced to face demons of their own. For many Gen Xers, frightened by AIDs, recession and a terribly uncertain future, Nine Inch Nails offered both a cathartic outlet and a place to commiserate. Unlike the cartoonish nightmares offered up by Alice Cooper and KISS, the bad dreams summoned by the ultra-charismatic Reznor were all too personal and therefore far more real and far more frightening.

But there's more to Nine Inch Nails than Reznor's personal problems. As an artist, Reznor has managed to achieve and maintain an envious level of integrity and credibility as he pushes the edge of the envelope with music, video and stage performances, all of which are legendary for their violent intensity and disturbing imagery. His technical expertise in the studio is such that he's always been hunted down by others in hopes that he will hook up as a collaborator, producer or remixer. Meanwhile, his records (and many of those that bear his fingerprints) sell in the millions. In short, Trent Reznor is one unlikely pop star.

Mercer, Pennsylvania is a quiet town of just over 2,500 people about halfway between Erie and Pittsburgh on Route 19 in the western part of the state.[1] It's a pretty conservative place, surrounded by corn fields farmed by the kind of people who instinctively understand the term "family values." It's also a gentle part of the world. It wasn't all that long ago that town fathers suspended all criminal trials over the Christmas season, concerned that juries might become a little too caught up in the Christmas spirit and end up being too soft on the accused in the witness box. On the other hand, there were no cool record stores, no college radio stations or even MTV on cable. About the only intrusions from the outside world were the McDonalds and the chain stores at the Shenango Valley Mall. One almost expected to see Andy and Opie walking with fishing poles down Main Street.

The Reznor family has deep roots in this part of the state. Two generations ago, a Mr. Reznor founded a heating company called Reznor Heaters. Michael Reznor was a student at the local high school when he met Nancy Clarke and by 1964, with both of them still in their teens, they were married. Love had something to do with it, although one shouldn't discount the fact that Nancy was pregnant at the wedding. Michael Trent Reznor was born just a few months later: 7:30AM, May 17, 1965.

Soon after Trent was joined by a baby sister named Tera in 1971, the family began to disintegrate. Michael and Nancy's marriage broke up and, with neither parent financially able to look after the children, Trent fell under the care of his maternal grandparents while Nancy looked after Tera.

Shortly after he moved in with Grandma and Grandpa, Trent began to take piano lessons. His teacher, Rita Beglin, immediately recognized Trent as a natural musician and encouraged him to pursue more difficult classical studies. This suited him fine because, as somewhat of a loner (his parents' divorce had left a permanent mark on his psyche), he often sought solace at the piano. Still, despite his awkward shyness, he was well liked and managed to make a number of friends, especially after he got involved with the school band where he learned to play the tuba and saxophone. In high school, he appeared in a couple of school musicals, playing the lead role in The Music Man and the part of Judas in Jesus Christ Superstar — and was even voted "best in drama" by fellow students.

"It wasn't cool to play music where I was from," Trent told Rolling Stone. "You had to be an athlete, or else a fucking turd in a football uniform. The teachers at my school were shitty for the most part, and I got a pretty bad education because I had a bad attitude. If I wanted to get good grades, I could. Stuff I'd like to know now, at the time, I thought was irrelevant: typical teenage stupidity."

"I hated school," he said in a separate confession in Musician, "I fucking hated it. The fact that it revolved around something you didn't have access to. If you weren't on the football team, if you were in the band, you were a leper. When people say those were the best years of our lives, I want to scream. But my parents allowed me to do things that my friends weren't allowed to. I smoked pot with my dad for the first time [at age 14.] I didn't have to be in by midnight. It was an open environment . . . at least I had that liberal, questioning environment."

At home, Trent spent more and more time at the piano. When he wasn't practicing, he was off listening to KISS albums like DESTROYER and ALIVE. Although he loved the way the piano could be used to express feelings of angst and sadness, he realized the inherent limitations of sticking with minor key classical pieces. Sure, Beethoven was majestic — but Gene Simmons was cool, not to mention the fact that he probably got lots of chicks.[2]

From the evil power of KISS, Trent branched out to Supertramp's CRIME OF THE CENTURY (a natural choice for any kid interested in the piano) as well as THE WALL from Pink Floyd. He soon developed a

---

1. This chapter is a condensation of the author's previous work, The Making of Pretty Hate Machine and The Downward Spiral (Collector's Guide Publishing, 1996.)
2. Even years later, Trent remembered what KISS meant to him. "They were the coolest," he told Spin. "Fucking demonic, monster-loud rock band. They were super-heroes to me. We are always having God of Thunder yardstick concerts. I was Gene Simmons in the Halloween parade, aluminum foil on my shows. I was fucking styling."

Trent Reznor, saxophone player

morbid fascination with science fiction, comic books and A-grade horror movies. In an interview with *Details* magazine, Trent says *The Omen* scared him so much that he became convinced that *he* was the Antichrist. For weeks after seeing the movie, he'd search through his hair just before bed, looking for the telltale "666" mark, just like Gregory Peck had done with little Damien in *The Exorcist*. He also remembers licking the metal tools in his grandfather's garage, just to see what they tasted like.

Michael Reznor, looking to repair some of the damage caused by the divorce, encouraged his son's growing interest in rock music. In addition to working as an interior designer and graphic artist, he was also an amateur bluegrass musician who ran a small music shop that sold a variety of acoustic instruments and guitars. In his spare moments, he taught Trent the basics of the guitar and later managed to procure Trent an electric piano. It wasn't long before Trent and some of his friends began jamming together in the small room at the back of the shop. Once techno-pop hit, Trent immersed himself into that culture, fascinated by groups such as the Human League whose music was generated entirely by machines. As he later told *Spin* magazine, "The excitement of hearing a Human League track and thinking, that's all machines, there's no drummer. That was my calling. It wasn't the Sex Pistols." Successfully lobbying his parents for cash, he purchased a cheap Moog synthesizer and set about trying to create the same sounds he heard Greg Hawkes play on all those Cars records.

Although there have been some attempts to revise Trent Reznor's musical background over the years, Nine Inch Nails was by no means his first musical project. By the time high school graduation came around, Trent had formed at least one band, an outfit called Option 30. About one-third of their material was original with the rest consisting of covers by Wang Chung, Elvis Costello and other new wave stuff from the early 80's.[1]

As music took up more and more time, Trent came to the realization that this may be his ticket out of Mercer. Enrolling in a computer engineering course at Allegheny College in nearby Meadville, Pennsylvania (pop. 15,000), his initial hope was that a degree might lead to a career in synthesizer design with a big company like Moog or Sequential. Discovering that designing electronic keyboards was more about math than it was about music, he dropped out after his first year.

Trent spent the next year living with his father out in the woods somewhere near Mercer, planning how he would ultimately make his escape to Cleveland, 200 miles to the north. To Trent, Cleveland was a different planet. There you could hear the latest new music on the radio, browse through stacks of cool new albums at record stores and actually meet other people who thought and felt the same way he did. After bidding his father farewell, Trent packed up whatever gear he had and moved to Cleveland, determined to explore music made by machines.

---

1. Much to his chagrin, demos and recording during the Option 30 days are now available through Shriek Records (www.shriekrecords.com.) The CD features a radio interview with Trent along with some wonderful covers of New Wave classics like Falco's *Der Kommissar* and *Lies* by the Thompson Twins. I highly recommend the CD to NIN completists.

Techno-pop was on the cutting edge of music in the early 80's. Pop bands like OMD, Depeche Mode, the Human League, New Order and Howard Jones were doing wonderful things with keyboards and sequencers that allowed a single person to create fantastic sonic landscapes with just the touch of a button. Then there was the cold, dispassionate, robotic approach favored by Fad Gadget, the Normal, Gary Numan and Kraftwerk. The more Trent explored this computer-driven music, the more it enveloped him. Before long, he was listening to highly experimental groups like Die Krupps, Cabaret Voltaire, Throbbing Gristle, Skinny Puppy and Einsturzende Neubauten — groups who specialized in a sound that some people were calling "industrial."[2]

Slowly but surely, the anvils, hammers and pipes favored by the original industrial bands were replaced by aggressive-sounding keyboards pro-pelled by powerful sequencers and Macintosh computers. Although the music remained hard and heavy, it also began to acquire a dance beat. Sometimes the rhythm was carried by metallic clanking; other times, it was a beat that hit you like a rapid series of shotgun blasts. Soon, the sounds that were once heard only on the factory floor started having an effect on the dance floor. And although most of industrial music's early appeal was in Europe (especially in Germany and Belgium), it did find a small cadre of fans in North America — and that included Trent Reznor.

"When I started to hang around better colleges," he reported to *Rolling Stone*, "I realized, Jesus Christ, there's a lot of music I'd never heard. It was like a musical awakening — from Test Dept. to XTC, all these bands I never knew existed. All those classic one-hit-wonder synth bands were permeating the airwaves — and it was kind of interesting just to see Devo and Human League briefly edge out Bruce Springsteen. That was about when synthesizers were becoming relatively affordable, and sequencers for home computers were just coming out. And when I stumbled into all that harder-edge music that incorporated electronic elements, it pretty much fit with things that were already in my head. Suddenly, music started to make sense."

Taking a job as a keyboard salesperson at a Cleveland music store called Pi Cooperation, Trent spent eight hours a day demonstrating all the latest electronic gear to curious customers. This meant that he had to know everything about every piece of gear in the store, even if it meant taking home a keyboard or two just so he could experiment with its capabilities. It was only good business.

Trent found a cheap apartment with his friend, Chris "Podboy" Vrenna, another musician (mainly drums) originally from Erie, Pennsylvania. Trent and Chris became brothers in poverty, surviving on the standard struggling musicians' diet of wieners and beans, corndogs and peanut butter sandwiches, and resorted to trading albums and video game cartridges for food and gas. Days were spent at the music store while nights were reserved for rehearsals and gigs with a variety of local bands. Any spare time was spent listening to the latest industrial music from Europe or old records from the Velvet Underground, Iggy Pop and David Bowie.

Shortly after he and Chris moved in together, Trent joined a band called the Innocent. Like hundreds of other groups at the time, they were forced to play Loverboy / Foreigner-style AOR crap if they wanted to get any work around town. The group did issue at least one album entitled LIVIN' IN THE STREETS (Red Label, 1985.)[3] When they folded, Trent sang and played keyboards for a group called the Urge.[4] Like the Innocent, they were a band typical of the era, specializing in cover versions of well-known songs. The Urge actually got a lot of work because they were very good at imitating ZZ Top, Van Halen, Styx and Journey. Up to a to a thousand people a night would pack into some of Ohio's biggest bars, just to see the Urge regurgitate current FM radio play lists. It wasn't all that gratifying from an artistic point of view, but it paid the rent, allowed Trent to play and sing — and it brought in a fair amount of cash that was immediately re-invested into new keyboard equipment.

---

2. Several years earlier, San Francisco performance artist Monte Cazzaza had coined the phrase "industrial music for industrial people" to describe the world of his friends in Throbbing Gristle. They had been working on a harsh, angry style of music that was half punk and half performance art since about 1975. No subject was taboo for them: death, war, sex, drugs and the occult were all fair game. The music was often deliberately unpleasant and sounded an awful lot like the noise that would result from a fifteen car pile-up on the floor of a steel foundry. Meanwhile, groups like Einsturzende Neubauten took it even further, using hammers, lead pipes and anvils as "instruments." It was extreme stuff that appealed to extreme people.

3. Trent claims he didn't play a note on this long-deleted record. However, despite what he may say these days, the liner notes on the album clearly read "Trent Reznor — keyboards." His picture is also on the cover.

4. Not to be confused with the St. Louis band of the same name.

After the Urge broke up, Trent joined a synth-pop band called The Exotic Birds. Originally a trio formed by three percussion majors from the Cleveland Institute of Art, they hired Trent to play keyboards when they expanded to a quintet. They, too, became a decent draw around Cleveland, gaining a reputation as being one of the finest techno-pop dance bands in the city. Things went so well that they released a five-song EP in 1986 entitled L'OISEAU on a local label called Pleasureland. That album proved to be the high point for the band as they broke up over creative differences soon after the EP hit the stores.

Trent's next gig was in a Michael J. Fox movie. When the studio began scouting for locations in Cleveland for *Light of Day*, a call went out for musicians who would be willing to act as extras. Trent and two members of the Exotic Birds were cast as members of a fictional band called The Problems. Trent was the perfect accouterment to the film: a reasonably photogenic musician who just happened to own tons of equally photogenic equipment. In the movie, The Problems are dismissed by just about every character (Michael J. Fox disparagingly refers to them as "A Flock of Seagulls") and don't even get a proper chance to play in the film. Their only contribution is a cover of Buddy Holly's *True Love Ways* — and you can't even hear most of it because most of the performance is obscured by dialogue. The song didn't even make the official movie soundtrack when it was released in 1987.

Once the movie gig wrapped up, Trent began looking for more work. He hung out with drummer Martin Atkins (PiL, Killing Joke, Pigface) and his band, Brian Brain, an association which resulted in Trent playing live with Brian Brain a couple of times.[1] His next stop was another dance-y Cleveland band called Slam Bam Boo where Trent played a few keyboard parts on a 1988 single entitled *White Lies / Cry Like a Baby* (Slack.) That same year, he was asked to perform on an EP by Lucky Pierre called COMMUNIQUÉ (Banana.)[2] Finally, Trent appeared on a 1990 song called *Warm Jets* by Hot Tin Roof, a band formed by an old roommate named Ed Lash. The song appeared on a Cleveland indie compilation entitled KILLER BLOW (Blue Bus Records.)

Despite the succession of dead ends, Trent was beginning to acquire the confidence to write his own material. At first, it felt awkward and weird; his musical ideas seemed to be completely at odds with what everyone was doing. There might be money in writing danceable pop songs, but Trent couldn't shake the feeling that this music was vacuous, dull and totally unsatisfying. He made an attempt to write political material in the style of the Clash, but when he couldn't figure out how to sing without sounding insincere and phony, he gave up. By the end of 1988, he was having a serious crisis in confidence regarding his abilities as a musician.

Then it hit him. One of the first rules any artist learns is that they should write about things that they know about. Since Trent was well-acquainted with fear, insecurity, frustration and anger, he started to write about those subjects, drawing on what he felt inside. It was then only natural for Trent to gravitate further towards the heavy, aggressive guitars-and-machines approach of Skinny Puppy, Ministry, Front 242, Test Dept. and KMFDM. With intense electronic effects and vocals that were somewhere between a shriek and a primal scream, they were nothing but noise to most people. To Trent, however, it was beautiful.

He had also stumbled across the perfect day job. Right Track Studios (now called Midtown Recording at 2108 Payne, Suite 406), a local recording facility hired Trent to cover everything from engineering sessions to acting as a studio musician to cleaning the toilets — all for about $100 a week. As reward for the long hours and low pay, Bart Koster, the owner of The Right Track, allowed Trent to use the studio after all the paying customers had gone home. Trent began by using the equipment he knew; he taught himself how to use the rest. And because he kept weird hours (usually 2 to 8 am), he worked alone.

Along with his accumulated arsenal of keyboards, the studio became Trent's instrument. Scraps of lyrics, often taken from his personal journal, were recorded over rhythm tracks provided by a drum machine. Once that was down on tape, synthesizer lines would be layered on top. And just to make things a little more different, Trent added some guitar similar to the way Al Jourgensen had spiced up Ministry's A MIND IS A TERRIBLE THING TO TASTE. Trent now freely admits that he often he didn't know what he was doing, especially when it came to playing guitar. But then again, if you have no preconceptions about what an instrument can do, chances are that you seldom end up obeying its limits. The same thing goes with

---

1. Instead of keyboards, Trent played trumpet.
2. Kevin McMahon would later sign to Trent's Nothing Records and record under the name Prick.

electronics. If you just *go for it* without following any of the rules, who knows what you may end up with?

Sometimes Trent liked the results of his all-night sessions enough to keep them around on a demo reel; other sessions were erased twelve hours after they were finished. The first track Trent remembers finishing is a suicide fantasy he called *Down In It*. He described as a "total rip-off" of *Dig It*, Trent's favorite Skinny Puppy track and allegedly inspired by a soured relationship with a woman only known as "Chrissie." Other products of these first attempts at recording included *Twist* (a song that was eventually renamed *Ringfinger*) and *Head Like a Hole*.

When he wasn't working on music, Trent was trying to come up with a name.[3] Over the years, Trent had accumulated about two hundred

Option 30, One of Reznor's pre-NIN bands

possibilities subjecting each one to what he called his "two week rule." The concept was simple: if he still liked the name after two weeks, it would make the cut. The only name to survive the entire two weeks in the history of this exercise was Nine Inch Nails. Although it has no literal meaning, it had a cool, tough and somewhat frightening sound to it. And along with looking great in print, it could be both easily abbreviated and offered interesting logo possibilities. "Nine Inch Nails" it was.

Trent worked on his composing and recording through the winter of 1987-88 and by the following summer he had three songs that he thought were good enough to be released. He talked it over with John Malm (his old manager from his days with the Exotic Birds) who suggested that the material should be submitted to several small, independent labels, all of whom might be interested in releasing one or more of the songs as 12" singles. A three song demo tape was sent to ten small labels, most of which were based in Europe, the key market for industrial music.

Much to Trent and John's surprise, all ten labels expressed interest in doing a deal. Perhaps Trent had underestimated the strength of his material and he should rethink his strategy. Several larger independent companies were approached, including Vancouver's Nettwerk Records. Unfortunately for Nettwerk, they had just blown a big wad of cash on signing a deal with Front 242 and were having what was politely referred to as a "cash-flow problem." They desperately wanted to sign Nine Inch Nails, but only if Trent could hang on until more money started coming in — six months, tops. And to show that they were honestly interested, Nettwerk slipped Trent a few bucks and arranged for Nine Inch Nails to open for Skinny Puppy on their upcoming tour.

The whole venture was a disaster. Since most of the songs were written and arranged exclusively for the studio, they really didn't lend themselves to live performance. To make matters worse, the hastily-assembled live version of Nine Inch Nails didn't gel and most performances were completely substandard. Ten dates into the tour, they were asked to leave.

---

3. There are lots of rumors about where the name "Nine Inch Nails" came from. Here are three of the best: (1) Some people insist that it was inspired by the idea that the nails on the Statue of Liberty are nine inches long. (2) The nails used to seal a coffin are allegedly nine inches long. (3) Christ was crucified using nine inch nails. Nice theories; it's just too bad that none of them are true. "Nine Inch Nails" was actually the product of some mindless doodling. Coming up with a name for a band is one of the most difficult things a musician has to do. The name has to be unique, memorable, project an image, be easy to spell, lend itself to good graphic design and most of all, capture the essence of your music. To make things even more frustrating, a name that might sound really cool to you one night may hit you as crazy and stupid in the morning.

One label that was not dissuaded by the fiasco was TVT. TVT stood for "Tee Vee Toons" because up until a rep saw Nine Inch Nails play with Skinny Puppy, their bread-and-butter was releasing albums filled with old TV theme songs. Knowing full well that the market for digital copies of the theme from *Gilligan's Island* was only so big, TVT president Steve Gottlieb was interested in signing some proper bands to his label. He wanted Trent to be one of the first.

When Gottlieb first heard the Nine Inch Nail demo tape, he was thrilled; in fact he wanted to release them just the way they were. It was danceable pop music with an edge, just the kind of the thing that could get plenty of radio airplay, not to mention big exposure on MTV. Gottlieb saw Nine Inch Nails as the band that was going to make his label a lot of money. Trent, however, had other ideas. He believed that the demos were only a starting point, not a completed work. Trent knew that he was onto something: taming the rage and aggressiveness of industrial music with pop song sensibilities. He had the melodies and the song structures together but he wasn't sure the music was hard enough.[1] Trent insisted on looking for a producer who could show him how to add the necessary edge to his material.

Several people were approached. There was Flood, the Englishman who had worked with Nitzer Ebb, Erasure and Depeche Mode. Then there was John Fryer, who had also worked with Depeche Mode along with Wire, the Cocteau Twins, Xymox and Love and Rockets. And then there was Adrian Sherwood and Keith Le Blanc. Sherwood had been a big part of Ministry's evolution from a quasi-goth band into a full-blown industrial monster when he produced their 1986 album TWITCH. He also ran On-U Sound, a label specializing in experimental dub music that featured artists such as Gary Clail and Tackhead.

Since *Down In It* was the first song Trent had completed, it was also the first song to be given the producer's treatment. In its earliest form, the song was about half the speed of the finished product that Trent handed to Adrian Sherwood. He molded *Down In It* into three mixes: the "Skin," the "Shred," and the "Singe." When all the mixes were complete, they were issued in three forms by TVT in 1989. There was a 12-inch single (which was commercially available), a 12-inch promo-only single and a promo-only 3-inch CD single (the regular 5-inch CD wasn't available to the general public until 1990.) Collectively, these releases became known as "Halo One" — the first official item in the Nine Inch Nails catalogue.

Once pre-production was finished at Right Track in Cleveland, Trent flew to Blackwing Studios in London where he was given one month to complete the album with John Fryer. Unfortunately, Reznor quickly found himself at odds with Fryer's methods. To make things even more complicated, Trent was dealing with relationship problems involving an ex-girlfriend he refers to simply as "Patti." Just before he left for England to work on the album, the two of them had re-connected. Trent spent much of his free time thinking about her and how to firmly rekindle things once the record was done. But after John Malm let it slip that Patti was pregnant and getting married, Trent was crushed. Much of that heartbreak appeared as gut-wrenching lyrics in songs like *Sanctified* and *Something I Can Never Have*. As for the rest of the album, Trent played virtually all the parts himself (that's why the liner notes read "Nine Inch Nails is Trent Reznor"), although Chris Vrenna proved to be an invaluable assistant, especially when it came to finding and isolating samples for several songs.[2]

While Trent and John Fryer were working on material together, Flood had been messing with two other tracks, *Head Like a Hole* and *Terrible Lie*. Trent was very satisfied with the way those two songs turned out, but the products of the Fryer sessions were less satisfying. Keith Le Blanc was called in to remix a good portion of Fryer's work.

When all the producers had completed their work, Trent and Chris Vrenna spent hours with the material, editing and sequencing everything into a finished album. They went through fifteen different

---

1. This is painfully obvious to anyone who hears some of the unreleased studio tracks from the WELCOME TO THE HATE MACHINE bootleg on Rain Records. There's a real mid-80s Depeche Mode feel to much of the material.

2. For example, it was Chris who found the sample that comes up at the end of *Sanctified* (a song inspired by a relationship with a cocaine pipe.) The whispering sounds like it could be Trent but it's not; it's the main character of the 1975 movie *Midnight Express* reading a letter that he has written to his parents. Other samples, sounds and ideas were lifted from everyone from Jane's Addiction (listen for the half-second sample in *Ringfinger*) and This Mortal Coil (the source for the piano and background sounds for *Something I Can Never Have*) to Prince and Public Enemy. If you can't hear those bits, don't worry. Most samples on PRETTY HATE MACHINE were rendered totally unrecognizable by the Mac. One particular Public Enemy bit was looped into a two-second sample, turned upside down by the computer and modulated through the Turbosynth with an oscillator tuned to the pitch of the song. The net result was a strange flanging effect in *Ringfinger* that's in key with the rest of the song. Every single drum fill on *Terrible Lie* was lifted intact from six songs on six different finished albums.

versions of each song, cutting them down and splicing them together until everything sounded right. Special edits were made at the ends and beginnings of songs in order to make the record flow properly (for example, check out the segue between tracks one and two.) Ten songs made the final cut. The record opened with *Head Like a Hole*, an angry, defiant masterpiece and ended about forty-nine minutes later with *Ringfinger*. There are few actual breaks in the album; Trent and Chris meant for it to be listened to as a whole. Finally, it was done. The album was stamped "Halo Two" and given the title PRETTY HATE MACHINE.

The Innocent, another forgotten pre-NIN band

When PRETTY HATE MACHINE was delivered to TVT in mid-1989, Trent Reznor was confident that he had turned in a good album. It had been an intensely personal experience, both in terms of Trent as a musician and Trent as a human being. Since most of the lyrics were adapted from his journals, the record acted like a window to his soul. He also found that exposing those deep negative feelings served a purpose; Trent felt cleansed.

Unfortunately, Steve Gottlieb of TVT records wasn't impressed at all. After Trent handed in the finished product, he heard nothing from Gottlieb for two whole weeks. Finally, there was a phone call. Gottlieb hated the record, calling it "an abortion" and accusing Trent of messing up some perfectly good pop songs by making them too hard and heavy. He boldly predicted that MTV and radio would avoid the record like the plague and as a result, the label would be lucky to sell 20,000 copies.

TVT nevertheless issued the album on November 29, 1989, and first, Gottlieb's prediction seemed accurate. To a majority of radio programmers, industrial music was equated with ratings suicide. The music was just too heavy and too weird to get any kind of regular airplay. MTV concurred; industrial artists and fans were out on the fringe; there weren't enough of them to justify giving PRETTY HATE MACHINE any real attention.

But out on the fringe, things were changing. Thanks to bands like Front 242 and Ministry, the music was evolving into something more sophisticated and accessible. Gone were the days of Einsturzende Neubauten's hammer-on-anvil recordings and KMFDM's symphonies of vacuum cleaners. The new industrial music of the late 80's was buffed up, carefully constructed and spiked with a new type of rage and negativity. Guitar snarls now meshed seamlessly with carefully programmed synth lines and samples as distorted vocals drifted in and out, making the music even more threatening and apocalyptic. It was a sound that expertly straddled the lines between punk, metal, dance and experimental electronic music.

When PRETTY HATE MACHINE was unleashed into the industrial community, just about everyone was blown away. The music was a techno-terrorist assault without being too "performance art" and too out of control. From the first listen, it was obvious that Trent had done the impossible: he had hacked himself a new niche in music, a brilliant blend of pop song structures and industrial beats.

What's even more important was that fans began to identify with Trent as a human being, noting that when he sang about pain and anguish, Trent always sang in the first person. Not only did industrial fans comprehend the music, but for the first time they could identify with the *person* singing it. Reznor's raw, naked and sometimes psychosexual lyrics took you inside his head, making the music more human and more emotional than ever before.

By now, some of the cooler dance clubs were all over the 12-inch single that had been pulled from the album and were clamoring for more. Trent knew that this meant he was going to have to take his act on the road once again. The new band consisted of long-time pal Chris Vrenna on drums, ex-Exotic Bird (and now member of Filter) Richard Patrick on guitar and keyboardist David Hames. In January 1990, they hit the road with the Jesus and Mary Chain. Several of these shows began to turn up as highly collectible bootlegs, the earliest being a cassette copy of a gig at California Theater on February 2, 1990.

On March 16, in Boulder, Colorado, NIN switched tours and began opening for Peter Murphy, who was out promoting his excellent DEEP album. It was during the Murphy tour that Nine Inch Nails acquired a reputation of staging loud and violent shows that more-or-less pummeled the crowd into submission. Trent would often throw himself across the stage, body-checking anyone or anything that just happened to be in his way. Drum kits were knocked over, keyboards were ripped from their stands and smashed and guitars were pounded to pieces on the floor. Sometimes he'd wrap the mic chord around his neck in a mock attempt at self-strangulation; other times he seemed intent on permanently maiming everyone on stage. Bandmates and roadies had never worked so hard for their money.

The physical nature of the shows weren't really calculated; Trent's violence was mainly a manifestation of his frustration in not being able to have any impact on the pseudo-goth crowds NIN was forced to face. Sometimes he and the band would throw flour or cornstarch on the crowd as a way of poking fun at the deathly pallor of the young vampire kids who had come out to see Murphy. Strangely enough, the more they were abused and the more violent and extreme the performances became, the more audiences got into the music. It wasn't long before word-of-mouth began to spread about this frenzied kid and his new band. Mosh pits full of leather-bound pierced kids began to form even before NIN hit the stage. And when the music started, an outside observer gazing down at the stage and the audience might think he was witnessing a scene straight out of hell. Very quietly and mainly through word of mouth generated by these shows, PRETTY HATE MACHINE started to sell.

By the end of 1990, more than 150,000 people had bought a copy of the album plus Down In It had made No. 1 on Rolling Stone's dance club chart as well as cracking the Top 20 of Billboard's club chart. Although Steve Gottlieb had been proven wrong, he wasn't about to give up control — and Trent was getting a more than a little pissed off at the unsupportive attitude he was getting from his label. If TVT wasn't going to get behind Nine Inch Nails a little more and leave Trent to worry about the music, he wanted out of his contract. Lawyers were called in and Trent quickly found himself under a pile of very expensive legal bills.

Trent tried to keep his hand in making records by moonlighting with other industrial groups like Pigface, the Revolting Cocks and 1000 Homo DJs. Although it was a nice distraction, it just wasn't the same as making his own records. The guys in those bands were having so much fun, mainly because they all had complete creative control over their music. That realization made Trent even more aware of his miserable situation with TVT.

A timely invitation from the organizers of the first Lollapalooza tour provided some much-needed cash. Earning $12,000 per show, the gig helped pay off a portion of the mounting legal bills — plus it turned on thousands of kids to Nine Inch Nails. By the time the tour ended, NIN had thousands of new fans and enough cash to maintain his vow of never recording for TVT again. Gottlieb, however, was not backing down. TVT was constantly getting offers from other labels who were willing to buy out Trent's contract, Steve Gottlieb refused them all. It was a no-win situation on both sides.[1]

The TVT dispute paralyzed Reznor for two full years. Well, almost paralyzed him. Because the label legally owned everything associated with the name Nine Inch Nails, Trent had to resort to making music without Steve Gottlieb knowing about it. Taking some of the money left over from Lollapalooza, Trent began checking into studios under fake names like "The Stunt Popes." Astonished that he had forgotten how to compose a song on a synthesizer and desperate to get back into any kind of song writing groove, Trent decided to take another approach: he picked up a guitar.

Maybe it was the accumulated result of all that frustrating time on the sidelines. Perhaps he just wanted

---

1. When Gottlieb found out that Trent had contributed vocals to a recording of Supernaut (the Black Sabbath song) for a Ministry side-project called 1000 Homo DJs, he went to court to prevent that version from being released. As a result, Al Jourgensen had to re-record the vocals if he ever wanted the song to see the light of day. The Trent version eventually turned up as part of the Wax Trax BLACK BOX set.

to prove something to Steve Gottlieb. Or maybe, deep down, he needed to prove something to himself. Whatever the case, everything Trent felt inside was poured into these sessions.[2]

All you really have to do is look at the song titles: *Happiness In Slavery, Help Me I Am In Hell, Gave Up* — the fear, the self-loathing, the rage, the frustration and the pain came out in huge waves, manifesting themselves in one of the hardest industrial albums ever conceived. The music was faster and the beats were heavier than anything Trent had done before. The vocals little more than howling screams that are sometimes hard to make out. In a few cases, that's because Trent had reduced himself to tears, barely able to remember the words, let alone pronounce them properly. In interviews, he referred to the project as an "ultra-fast chunk of death." When the EP was finally finished, it was marked "Halo Five" and given the title BROKEN.

Unknown to Trent, Jimmy Iovine from Interscope Records (a former producer who used to make records with Tom Petty and the Heartbreakers) had decided that he had to have NIN for his label. Very quietly, he and Steve Gottlieb had been working on a deal whereby TVT would continue to receive a steady cash flow from the group in exchange for waiving all control over any future NIN project. In effect, TVT retreated to the background as little more than a silent partner. It wasn't the prettiest of compromises, but at least both parties could live with it. Meanwhile, there were plums waiting for Trent. He received written assurance that he was to have complete creative control over all future NIN projects. Even more interesting was that he and John Malm were given permission to set up their own label (called Nothing) within the Interscope family that they would manage and control. It was an arrangement that featured practically everything any recording artist could ever dream of. The only catch was that along with the Interscope and Nothing logos, the TVT mark had to continue to appear on all future NIN product. In retrospect, it seemed like a small compromise to make in order to end two years of litigation.

Once all the contract kinks were worked out, Trent handed the completed BROKEN tapes over to Interscope who released Halo Five on September 16, 1992. It was a beautiful digi-pack package, complete with lyrics and credits written on three wings that folded out from the center. Steve Gottlieb must have cringed when he saw the note that read "No thanks: you know who you fucking are."

BROKEN was issued in several different forms, including four versions of the CD. A promo-only CD5 featured the six new Reznor compositions. Meanwhile, the public was treated to six NIN tracks and two covers: *Suck* from Pigface and *Physical* by Adam Ant. The first pressing of BROKEN featured all eight tracks. A second pressing had the six NIN songs on a CD5 with the covers exiled to a bonus CD3. The third version of the EP had the Reznor songs on tracks one through six followed by ninety-one blank tracks that clicked by at the rate of one per second. You don't hear *Suck* or *Physical* until the CD counter got to tracks 97 and 98. Meanwhile, people who bought the cassette found the new NIN songs on side one and the covers on side two. And as if fans weren't confused enough, BROKEN was also made available as a one-sided 12-inch EP (with all six songs on side one) that came with the two covers on a bonus 7-inch.

Anyone who was expecting PRETTY HATE MACHINE PART 2 was in for a rude shock right from the beginning. BROKEN was so angry, so hard and so noisy that most people would take one listen and come to the conclusion that Trent was performing commercial hara-kiri. If Steve Gottlieb thought the first album was uncommercial, BROKEN must have given him a heart attack.

But the demand for any new NIN product was so great by this time that BROKEN debuted at No. 7 on *Billboard's* album charts the week after it was released, eclipsing all chart success by PRETTY HATE MACHINE. BROKEN went platinum at supersonic speed and even won a Grammy for "best metal performance with vocal."[3] Critics were fell all over themselves praising the EP and other musicians — including, allegedly, Prince — started calling up, asking if Trent would like to collaborate with them.

Then there was the matter of the videos for BROKEN. The clip for *Happiness in Slavery* featured performance artist / professional masochist Bob Flanagan being fed naked into a machine that make

---

2. Two songs seemed to take direct aim at Steve Gottlieb. Deep at the end of the EP, Trent seems to whisper "Eat your heart out, Steve" about thirty seconds into the bonus track, *Physical*.
3. Trent likes to make a joke of that award, once suggesting that his epitaph should "Reznor. Died. Said 'fist fuck.' Won a Grammy."

---

human hamburger — a visual essay on how ecstasy can be achieved through torture and total submission. There are a few scenes involving penis and testicle clamping that are not for the squeamish (and yes, those shots *are* real.) It took about two seconds for MTV to ban it.

But this was just the beginning. The original concept was to film a video for every song on BROKEN that would then be released as a video companion to the EP. But the further the project progressed, the more extreme and twisted the visuals became. The footage of *Happiness, Wish* and *Pinion* (with its infamous banned-by-MTV "toilet dive" scene) was pretty sick by any measure. Coil's Peter Christopherson was called in to help with *Gave Up* and to come up with a way to tie all the clips together. The result *was* straight out of the mind of a serial killer. Centered on a victim being forced to watch NIN videos while being tortured with devices straight out of *Henry: Portrait of a Serial Killer,* the final product was too much, even for Trent. It was never released. Few people apart from his close circle of friends have ever seen it. A bootleg copy (and precious few exist) is probably the rarest NIN collectible out there. Trent admits that the entire BROKEN video experience makes *Happiness In Slavery* "look like a Disney movie."

BROKEN did end up with a companion: a remix album entitled, appropriately enough, FIXED (released on February 28, 1994.) Contacting a series of artists he admired, Trent requested that they submit a remix or two of tracks from BROKEN. Unfortunately, things didn't turn out quite as expected. Only about half the submitted remixes were usable, and even then, most NIN fans found the new versions to be too radical for their liking. As a result, FIXED turned out to be a bit of a stiff. Because it was released in limited quantities (probably about 50,000 copies were issued), Halo Six is now available mainly as an import in North America.

On July 4, 1992, Trent moved out to Los Angeles with plans to start working on a second full album. The plan sounded simple. Instead of setting up in a formal recording studio, he wanted a house where he could build his own custom studio; that way, he could work on his own time and at his own pace.

After being shown through about fifteen houses in one day, Trent settled on a house in Bel Air at 10050 Cielo Drive. It was perfect. Cielo Drive is a narrow, hard to find, uphill cul-de-sac high above the smog in the Hollywood Hills off Benedict Canyon Road. The main house was more than a hundred feet behind a big gate and hidden from the road by a large number of trees. The nearest neighbor was more than a hundred yards away. To make things even more inviting, the rooms were huge (the main house was over 3,200 square feet) and there was a large free-form swimming pool off the master bedroom. If any guests dropped by, they could be put up in the 2,000 square foot cottage towards the back of the property. It was quiet and secluded yet accessible to the rest of the city, exactly the kind of place where a musician could work in comfort.

Although the house had been up for sale for a couple of months, owner Al Weintraub had been unable to move the property. Trent probably assumed that it had to do with the $4.9 million price tag. But if it was so expensive to buy, why was it so relatively cheap to rent? Perhaps someone should have told him about the history of 10050 Cielo Drive. It was world famous as a human slaughterhouse: the location of the first Manson murders.

Just after midnight on Saturday, August 9, 1969, three women and one man, all members of Charles Manson's "Family," cut the phone wires, scaled the embankment off the road and crept across the yard. Stephen Parent was shot in the driveway. Coffee heiress Abigail Folger was chased out onto the lawn and stabbed so many times that her white nightgown appeared red. A short distance away was the body of her Polish lover Voytek Frykowski. He had been shot twice, bludgeoned over the head with a gun butt thirteen times and stabbed fifty-one times. Back in the large central room of the house, actress Sharon Tate (who was eight months pregnant) was left stabbed, mutilated and bloody on the floor, wearing nothing more than bra and panties. Around her neck was a white nylon rope which was pulled over a rafter and then down around the neck of Jay Sebring, an internationally known hair stylist. He had been shot. Pools of blood were everywhere, especially on the front porch and walk where Frykowski had tried to escape. And on the front screen door, in big letters written in Sharon Tate's own blood, Family member Susan Atkins had carefully printed the word "PIG."

After investigations into the infamous Tate-Labianca murders were over (and the owners hired a shaman to drive out the evil spirits), 10050 Cielo Drive slowly slipped into obscurity, although it did become a macabre tourist site for those fascinated by the Charles Manson mystique. The owner, agent Rudi Altobelli, held onto the property until 1991 when he sold it to Al Weintraub. Unable to sell it himself, he rented it to Trent.

Trent claims that he knew nothing about the history of the house and that none of the his realty agents mentioned anything about what had taken place there. In fact, he didn't know where he was moving until he mentioned his new address to a friend who immediately showed Trent a copy of the *Helter Skelter*, the Vincent Bugliosi book on the Manson murders. Initially freaked out by the news, Trent went back to New Orleans to check on one of the house he had been looking at, but it had been sold. So, with nowhere else to go, Trent and his gear moved into 10050 Cielo Drive in July. The studio was immediately christened "Le Pig." A couple of voodoo candles were brought in and the Grammy was put on the fireplace mantle, overlooking the spot on the floor where Jay Sebring died.

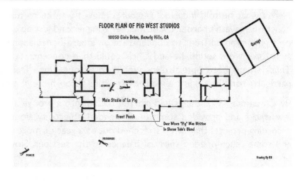

FLOOR PLAN OF PIG WEST STUDIOS
10050 Cielo Drive, Beverly Hills, CA

It took more than three months for all the equipment to be installed, right in the middle of the great room where Sharon Tate and Jay Sebring were found. Part of the delay involved getting all the gear to work properly. Especially frustrating was a crucial piece of machinery called a Timeline Micro-lynx synchronizer, which was supposed to sync up two Studer tape machines with Digidesign Pro Tools. Whenever the Micro-Lynx went down (which was up to a dozen times a day), it would have to be turned off and every cable would have to be disconnected and then reconnected. Trent lost count of the number of times a service guy had to be called into look at the problem. Another big hassle was with the automation programs on the Amek mixing console; it would often just stop working. Everyone in the house quickly learned about the major downside of having your own studio: when something stops working, you either have to drop whatever you're doing and fix it or you have to call in technical help and then wait around for the guy to show up. Meanwhile, you lose whatever creative momentum you have. Most big commercial studios have help available around the clock with no waiting.

Looking back on the project, it wasn't the most efficient way to make an album. Before getting down to the business of writing and recording some songs; a house had to be found; equipment had to be purchased and installed; a technician was called in to tune the studio acoustically; then Trent had spend months learning how to operate all the new gear. For a while, it seemed as if Trent and Chris Vrenna were just going in circles, not knowing how or where to focus their attention or their energies. Some days were spent on installation problems. Others were spent experimenting with the new equipment. Sometime they just did nothing, totally frustrated by equipment problems. For example, Trent might spend hours sculpting a section of a certain track, only to find out that a glitch in the system had somehow caused all the vocals to be out of sync and in the wrong pitch.

When the studio was working properly, weeks would go by when the only thing they did was sample sounds. Chris ended up listening to more than 3,000 movies for interesting sounds — no dialogue, just *sounds*. He found some unusual stuff (ranging from a swarm of bees to a selection of screams to some random electronic noise) which he then downloaded onto DAT. Whenever he got the chance, Trent would review the tapes, cut the samples up into short segments, process them through a Turbosynth and then set everything aside on an optical disc. Before long, they had dozens of gigabytes worth of ready-to-use samples, stretching over ten discs.

That was great — but there were still no new songs. Writing, recording and engineering a new album at the time using new and unfamiliar equipment was almost too much. Those old doubts of fear and self-loathing were starting to come back.

Fed up by the constant equipment glitches and unable to use his arsenal of electronics for hours and even days at a time, Trent was forced to start writing on the three guitars he had brought with him: a white Gibson Les Paul, a Fender Strat and an Ovation steel string acoustic. A great deal of the initial song structures were written using those guitars — which actually ended up being a good thing because it forced Trent to look at his music in a new light.

Here's what he told *Industrial Nation*: "I knew I wanted to make a broader scope type of record that consciously wasn't harder, faster, meaner, tougher, and just boxing myself into a corner that way." Writing on a guitar forced Trent to concentrate on a bare-bones approach to the new material. Once the song structures were sound, he and Chris could then concentrate on adding the appropriate atmospherics. That's when those optical discs would come out. Once Trent and Chris determined the mood of a particular song, it was just a matter of sorting through the library of samples for something appropriate.

By Christmas 1992, things had started to slip into a groove. Flood had been called in to co-produce a few tracks and provided some much needed objectivity along the way. Having dealt with complicated recording projects that often stretched out to a year or more, he was able to provide technical guidance and some much-needed spiritual balance to the sessions. Slowly but surely, everyone started to make progress.

As the songs began to come together, it became more and more obvious that they were chronicling one man's dark journey through self-examination, desolation and loss. A very loose narrative seemed to thread its way through all the tracks, culminating in complete despair. There's a constant focus on decay, self-destruction and the reoccurring mantra of "Nothing can stop me now" that can be interpreted as both a threat and as a vow. More than one person began to point out the similarities between the emerging album and what Roger Waters and Pink Floyd did with THE WALL. Trent took that as a compliment.

The album became an exercise in sonic architecture. Almost a year was spend at Le Pig, meticulously layering and sculpturing every second of its sixty-five minutes. In fact, there are more sounds on THE DOWNWARD SPIRAL than the human ear could possibly distinguish at any one time.

Describing the technical aspects of THE DOWNWARD SPIRAL is like writing a textbook on recording engineering. The techniques used to create and capture the sounds that eventually made up the album were so much more complex, so much more esoteric than what is normally required for a typical platinum-selling record that even experienced musicians and programmers have a hard time grasping everything that went into its construction. It's an album built by robots and programmed by some very clever humans.

Almost the entire album was recorded to hard disk; almost no tape was used at all. Regular instruments like vocals, guitar and bass were dumped directly into a computer equipped with Digidesign Sound Tools software. The Mac was the ideal place to store and manipulate material with the trusty Turbosynth and other outboard effects.

"I played stuff right into the board and then into the computer, and then manipulated it with programs that don't work in real time," he explained to *Musician*. "Once it's in there, you can do things to it that have no equivalent in the real world. Like analyze the frequency and flip it upside-down. It takes maybe ten minutes for the Macintosh to process that cut, and you wind up with sounds that are different from anything you could get otherwise. I like the idea that there are guitar players out there trying to figure them out. Hopefully, that'll cause some misery."

One other guitarist was brought in to add some spice. Adrian Belew is best known for his studio and touring work for everyone from David Bowie and the Talking Heads to King Crimson and Frank Zappa (not to mention his own band, The Bears.) And while most of the songs were complete, both Trent and Flood were discussing how certain tracks needed a "kick in the ass," Adrian's name came up and it just so happened that he was in Los Angeles at the time working with Paul Simon. Songs featuring samples of Belew's playing include *Mr. Self-Destruct* and *The Becoming*.

Virtually all the drum tracks were programmed. Experimenting with two PZM microphones, Chris Vrenna's drum kit was set up in about two dozen different rooms, ranging from bathrooms to garages to the live rooms at A&M Studios in Hollywood. Trent and Chris would set up the two microphones the same distance away from the drums in each setting (nothing was close-miked) and then hit each of the drums with varying degrees of force. Every shot was recorded on a DAT machine and then sampled in stereo using one of Trent's two Akai S100 samplers. Those sounds were then downloaded onto disks and fed into a Roland TR 808 drum machine which was then programmed as required for each song.

One notable exception was the rhythm track of *Closer*. The fat bass-and-snare sound was lifted directly from the introduction of Iggy Pop's *Nightclubbing* from his 1977 album THE IDIOT. After mangling it a bit with the computer and outboard gear, the samples were loaded into a Roland R-70 to in order to give it that mechanical, drum machine feel. Some of the only real live drumming on the album can be heard towards the end of *Piggy*. As an experiment, Trent put on hair of headphones and began wailing away along with the music just to see what it would sound like. He was completely out of sync with what was going on — but in the end, he decided that it sounded cool, so his drum part made the final cut. Stephen Perkins (ex-Jane's Addiction) and Tommy Lee (Motley Crue) also helped out with some percussion parts and drum loops on a couple of songs.

There were other happy accidents. A great example is the quiet piano section in *March of the Pigs*. Originally just some goofy part on the demo, Trent later realized that it was a perfect counterpoint to the violence of the rest of the song. The guitar solo in *Ruiner* was also destined to be deleted until Trent decided that it was just too cheesy and funny not to keep. Trent says the spirit of Pink Floyd and *Comfortably Numb* entered his body and was responsible for playing that part.

Finally, it was over. THE DOWNWARD SPIRAL was labeled Halo 8 and released to the public on June 29, 1994. The following week, it entered the *Billboard* album charts at No. 2. It was a massive critical and commercial success. It was praised by fans and critics for striking that impossible balance of being both uncompromising and accessible at the same time. Musicians marveled at its complex textures and skillful programming. Fans loved it for the way Trent Reznor vocalized the rage of an entire generation.

In the years since the album's release, Trent Reznor has become acknowledged as one of the most important artists of the 90's. Not only has he expanded his own fanbase, but he has also drawn millions more people into the now-exploding world of "alternative" music and its conquest of the mainstream. It was a pretty safe bet that the album was a sure-fire platinum hit (it sold close to five million copies around the word, but who would have guessed that *Closer*, complete with its chorus of "I want to fuck you like an animal," would have become a Top 40 hit?

Trent continued to make one right move after another, especially when it came to the inevitable series of live dates that followed the release of SPIRAL. The club dates and warm-up slots were a thing of the past; now NIN was headlining stadium gigs all over the world. The culmination of all those shows was a spectacular set at Woodstock on Saturday, August 13, 1994. Covered in mud, Nine Inch Nails delivered an explosive set which, by all accounts, was *the* highlight of the festival. That one mud-caked performance went a long way towards pushing NIN into the realm of super-stardom. Trent also earned $250,000 for that one appearance.

After SPIRAL ran its course, Trent all but disappeared for close to five years, surfacing just three times. In March 1994, NIN appeared on *The Crow* soundtrack, performing Joy Division's *Dead Souls*. On August 13, 1994, the soundtrack of Oliver Stone's *Natural Born Killers* was released, featuring a series of songs expertly stitched together by Reznor. He was heard from again on May 13, 1997, when he issued *The Perfect Drug*, a single from the David Lynch Film, *Lost Highway*. Beyond that, Reznor busied himself with remixes, producing records, composing music for video games (most notably, *Quake*) and scouting for talent for Nothing. Apart from a tour with David Bowie, Trent remained largely outside the public eye. He moved to New Orleans, bought a former mortuary in the Garden District, and renovated it into both a home and a state-of-the-art recording studio. Months were spent in the new digs working with his new Nothing charges, Marilyn Manson.

But what of Nine Inch Nails? Rumors of a new album were met with deafening silence. There were stories of writer's block, dead ends, trashed tapes and false starts. There were cryptic magazine ads, Internet chatter and odd postcards sent to radio stations and record stores. The death of his grandmother (the person who raised him as a child) at age eighty-five in 1997 took its toll. Taking a suggestion from producer Rick Rubin, Reznor when into isolation for ten weeks in Big Sur, California, in hopes of breaking through the creative logjam.[1] That didn't work, and, at the same time, another crisis in confidence loomed: his relationship with Marilyn Manson began to collapse. The long silence finally broke on July 20, 1999, when a single entitled *The Day the World Went Away* (Halo 13) appeared in stores.[2]

---

1. Only one song, *Le Mer*, survived from what Reznor calls his "Billy Joel phase."
2. Consumer response to the new CD single was overwhelming. In its first week, *The Day the World Went Away* sold 71,150 copies, making the third-highest selling single of the week. In Canada, *World* debuted at No. 1, outselling its nearest competitor, Will Smith and *Wild Wild West* by a margin of 8 to 1.

A third album, the sprawling double set entitled THE FRAGILE, was released on September 21, 1999, more than five years after the release of THE DOWNWARD SPIRAL. To the surprise of absolutely no one, it debuted at No. 1 on the Billboard album charts, selling 228,746 copies in its first week. In Canada, the album debuted at No. 2 (behind Our Lady Peace), moving 36,865 units. A world tour was scheduled to start in Europe in November.

There's no question that Trent will continue to develop as an artist. He's obsessively self-critical and is constantly looking to push the edge of his own personal envelope. Then there's the matter of Trent the Businessman. Not only does he finally have control of his own destiny, but together with manager John Malm, he runs his own label, Nothing Records. Now that he can call the shots, he's allowing other bands to get a break by allowing them learn from his experience.

Looking back on Trent's career, there's an odd bit of irony. He began as a solitary artist, working alone at night because he couldn't find anyone who was willing to put in the same hours. That was fine, because those quiet recording sessions allowed him to explore his own psyche with music and to express some deep, negative feelings about the world. More than anything, it was good therapy. But that private anguish is no longer private; it has since made him one of the most successful musicians on the planet — which, in turn, has made him vulnerable to criticism and scorn from those who believe he has "sold out," an undeserving epithet for someone who has been a remarkably consistent innovator. Music made with this much skill and honesty deserves our respect. And our gratitude.

Fast Facts

o Each official NIN project is given a "Halo" number much in the same way Factory Records gave FAC numbers to its releases.

Halo 1:	Down in It (single)
Halo 2:	PRETTY HATE MACHINE
Halo 3:	Head Like a Hole (single)
Halo 4:	Sin (single)
Halo 5:	BROKEN
Halo 6:	FIXED
Halo 7:	March of the Pigs (single)
Halo 8:	THE DOWNWARD SPIRAL
Halo 9:	Close to God (single)
Halo 10:	FURTHER DOWN THE SPIRAL
Halo 11:	The Perfect Drug (single)
Halo 12:	CLOSURE (VHS tape)
Halo 13:	The Day the World Went Away (single)
Halo 14:	THE FRAGILE

o Gary Talpas at Föhn Design was commissioned to come up with something appropriately menacing for the cover of PRETTY HATE MACHINE. He submitted a treated photo of some turbine blades that were stretched vertically to look like the bones of a ribcage.

o Many of the lyrics included with PRETTY HATE MACHINE are not sung on the album. According Trent, these were phrases he had written but couldn't fit into the songs because they just didn't work when it came combining them with the arrangements. So why include them in the liner notes? No special reason. Trent just thought it would make for cool discoveries for the people who took the time to both listen to the album carefully and to read the lyric sheets. Some fans swear if you string all the lyrics that were printed but not sung, you'll end up with a separate and distinct poem.

o During the filming of a clip for Down In It, one particular aerial shot required that a video camera be tied to a helium balloon. Unfortunately, a gust of wind broke the balloon's tether and both it and the camera floated off into the sky. A few days later, it was found lying in a field by a farmer who promptly turned everything over to the police. When they viewed what was on the tape, the cops thought they were seeing an actual "snuff film" and turned everything over to the FBI who immediately launched a murder investigation. Six months was spent trying to track down both the murderer and the victim. Needless to say when they discovered the truth, the boys at the Bureau were a little embarrassed, especially when the whole story turned up on the tabloid news show, Hard Copy.

o During an opening slot for Guns N'Roses in front of 65,000 people in Germany, only three people were moved to buy a NIN T-shirt.

o A warning in bright, red letters cautions that BROKEN was "not for use with mono devices." According to Trent, this was to let everyone know that certain parts of the sound will disappear entirely if the recording is played back in mono. This is because some elements on BROKEN were deliberately mixed out of phase so that they would stand out in a strange way — but the only way for the listener to hear this effect is if the songs are played back in stereo. It's simple to experiment with the phase properties of the EP. Just hit the mono button on any stereo and listen to the snare drum disappear for most of *Happiness in Slavery*.

o The sample at the beginning of *Get Down Make Love* was apparently lifted from an old cable access program called *Video Psychotherapy*. The moaning is courtesy of Al Jourgensen who found it on a Japanese porn film.

o Trent commissioned an artist named Russell Mills to take care of all the artwork for THE DOWNWARD SPIRAL. Trent was familiar with the work Russell had done for Brian Eno and David Sylvian and was looking for something strange and unique. Russell was given some simple instructions: don't make it look like any previous NIN work and keep in mind that THE DOWNWARD SPIRAL has a very decaying organic quality to it. If he could capture those aspects in three or four paintings, he had a sale. In the end, Trent was so pleased with the work Russell did that he was commissioned for a serious of treatments on the NIN logo. Once Russell was finished, everything was assembled into a special multi-piece package.

o The house at 10050 Cielo Drive was destroyed in an earthquake in January 1994. The debris was removed that May and a new house was built on the lot.

o At the 1994 Woodstock Festival, there were a few tense moments when a live high-voltage power line fell over the NIN bus. The power was shut off and the line was removed without incident.

o NIN's Self-Destruct tour was interrupted when Maise, Reznor's beloved golden retriever, died after jumping off a third floor balcony at a venue in Columbus, Ohio. Shows were canceled as Trent went off to grieve.

o *Playgirl* once named Trent Reznor as one of the ten sexiest men in rock.

o Trent's acupuncturist recommends he drink an herbal pick-me-up (consisting mainly of ginseng and echinacea) before each show. Even still, roadies keep oxygen at the ready just in case the performance gets extra-physical.

o The video game *Super Mario World* features a character named "Reznor."

Recommended Listening

o PRETTY HATE MACHINE (TVT, 1989)

o BROKEN (Nothing / TVT / Interscope, 1992)

o THE DOWNWARD SPIRAL (TVT / Interscope, 1994)

o THE FRAGILE (Nothing / Interscope, 1999)

o There are a variety of EP's and bonus track-laden singles available, such as SIN (featuring the excellent cover of Queen's *Get Down Make Love*, TVT, 1991), FURTHER DOWN THE SPIRAL (Nothing / TVT / Interscope, 1995) and MARCH OF THE PIG (Nothing / TVT / Interscope, 1994.) There are several collections of these releases, included FISTED. As mentioned earlier, the reissued self-titled Option 30 disc is a scream. Look for it at www.shriekrecords.com.

Internet Resources

o www.nin.com

o www.seemslikesalvation.com

o www.nin.net

o www.nineinchnails.net

o http://members.xoom.com/Nin/index.html

Recommended Reading

o Cross, Alan. *The Making of* Pretty Hate Machine *and* The Downward Spiral. Burlington, Ontario: Collector's Guide Publishing, 1996.

- Huxley, Martin. *Nine Inch Nails.* New York, New York: St. Martin's Griffin, 1997.
- Remington, Tuck. *Nine Inch Nails.* London: Omnibus Press, 1995.

Related Listening
Ministry, Skinny Puppy, KMFDM, Front 242, Consolidated, Filter, White Zombie, Rob Zombie

The Story Thus Far . . .
Taking the thread left by the techno-pop masters (Depeche Mode, Human League) and combining it with punk nihilism and Bowie-esque surrealism, Trent Reznor redefined industrial music, taking from the fringe and forcing down the throats of the mainstream.

~ 23 ~
NIRVANA
The vital link of the 90's

Rock and roll can be as volatile as a truck full of diesel fuel and fertilizer or a house with a gas leak in the basement. All it takes is one spark and in less time than it takes for the brain to register what the eye is seeing, the landscape changes forever. Predicting these explosions is all but impossible. At least you can sweep for land mines.

Until the early 1990's, post-punk alternative music occupied its own little corner of the rock universe. For the better part of a decade, it had been left to evolve on its own, like some mold in a forgotten petri dish. This was the stuff of indie labels, cramped clubs, weird little record stores and goofy college radio programs. There were occasions where the occasional indie band bubbled up into the mainstream — R.E.M. was the best example — but for the most part, this music was largely ignored by the big labels and the general public. If one of the majors did happen to sign an alternative group, chances are they were just looking for a tax write-off.

That all changed when a band from a tiny logging town in Washington released their second album. Not only was Nirvana the spark for the explosion, they were a catalyst that set a variety of events in motion that would ultimately change the entire complexion of the entire rock and roll universe. A new generation of music fans was suddenly and unexpectedly swept up in a cultural sea of change, as a new type of rock took hold, creating a new world in which the old rules no longer applied. By the time we heard the terrible news on April 8, 1994, the momentum of the new alt-rock attitude had grown far beyond the effect of just one album. The spirit of indie rock was now calling the shots.

Kurt Donald Cobain was born on February 20, 1967, in Aberdeen, Washington, a small logging center at the end of Route 8, about 100 miles southwest of Seattle — a town that had the dubious distinction of having one of the highest suicide rates in the United States. Kurt's father, Donald, was a mechanic at the local Chevron gas station while his mother, Wendy, tried to be a good stay-at-home mom.

Kurt was a weird little kid. He had an imaginary friend named "Boddah" who was so real to Kurt that he often demanded a place be set for Boddah at the dinner table.[1] He was hyperactive to the point where his energy had to be cranked down with Ritalin several times a week. One area where his attention disorder was conspicuously absent was music. Aunt Mary first introduced Kurt to the Beatles and then to the guitar, teaching him his first chords.

When Kurt was 8, Wendy and Donald were divorced, an event that destroyed a part of Kurt's soul. Turning inward, he began to use music as a means of escape. When his father thought Kurt was old enough to go through his record collection, Kurt immediately gravitated towards Led Zeppelin, Aerosmith and Black Sabbath. The B52s also became a big favorite after Kurt watched them on *Saturday Night Live* in 1980. Seeing that his nephew had a serious interest in rock, Wendy's brother Chuck bought

---

1. Note that Kurt's suicide note was address to Boddah.

Kurt his first guitar for his fourteenth birthday, a beat-up secondhand model from Sears.[2]

It was a local punker named Buzz Osbourne who had the greatest effect on Kurt's musical outlook. Buzz headed up a local band called the Melvins and would sometimes let Kurt act as a volunteer roadie. He would also slip Kurt the occasional cassette of some of his favorite bands: the Sex Pistols, Black Flag, Husker Du, the Dead Kennedys, Sonic Youth. Up until he heard those tapes, Kurt's knowledge of punk consisted mainly of what he read in Creem magazine and his prized copy of the Clash's SANDINISTA!

With his only interests being rock, art and drugs (Kurt was quite the stoner in school), Kurt set about forming his first bands. The first appears to have been Fecal Matter, followed by Brown Towel (sometimes mis-reported as "Brown Cow".) Then he met Krist Novoselic (born May 16, 1965), a lanky six-foot-seven kid he kept bumping into at Melvins shows. Their first band went by a variety of names: Skid Row, Ted Ed Fred, Throat Oyster, Pen Cap Chew, Windowpane. There was also a short-lived Melvins spin-off group called the Stiff Woodies and a CCR cover band called the Sellouts. "Nirvana" was eventually the winner when Kurt decided that he didn't want a typical angry or stupid-sounding name for his punk band.

On January 23, 1988, using the Melvins' Dale Crover on drums,[3] Nirvana had their first-ever recording session. With Kurt paying the freight from his salary as a janitor, they spent $152.44 for six hours at Reciprocal Recording in Seattle, a studio known for its indie-friendly atmosphere. The completed tape featuring ten songs was sent out to indie labels across the country and received exactly one response. A tiny, perpetually broke company in Seattle called Sub Pop said they might be interested in what Nirvana had to offer.[4]

On June 11, 1988, Nirvana recorded their first official single. Love Buzz was an obscure cover, originally recorded by a Dutch band called Shocking Blue. Sub Pop issued one thousand hand-numbered 7-inch singles in October 1988 and letter included it as one of the first installments in their new Sub Pop Singles Club. A second song, Spank Thru, was recorded on September 27 and eventually included as part of SUB POP 200, a compilation of bands on the roster.

Through the rest of 1988, Nirvana played gig after gig, honing their new sound and burning through drummers faster than Spinal Tap (more on that later.) By Christmas, they had saved enough money to begin recording what was originally envisioned as an EP. Hopped up on codeine cough syrup, the first sessions were held on December 24. A little more was done on the 29th, followed by a final session on January 24, 1989. The band was so pleased with just about everything that they'd put down on tape that the decision was made to expand the EP into a full album. It was called BLEACH.[5]

When the album was released in June 1989, Kurt Cobain found that he didn't like it has much as he had six months earlier. It didn't sound as big or as heavy as he'd first thought — plus he was a little embarrassed that he hadn't spent a little more time working on melodies. Sub Pop, however, didn't seem to notice; it was common knowledge around the office that good punk songs didn't have melodies. Nevertheless, Kurt quietly began to incorporate more pop into his punk. Elements of this change in direction started showing up through the rest of 1989, especially during a successful spin through the UK and Europe. When the group recorded the BLEW EP late in the summer of 1989 (released in December 1989), some of the stylistic changes were already evident.

It's now time to talk about drummers. From the very beginning, Kurt and Krist had a hard time finding someone with ability and ambition to match their own. Aaron Burckhard was Nirvana's first drummer, but his desire to party overwhelmed his need to rehearse and he was terminated. Dale Crover of the Melvins was always a welcome fill-in, but when Buzz Osbourne moved the band to San Francisco, Nirvana's backup drummer was no longer available. A metalhead friend of the Melvins, Dave Foster, had filled in for a few months in 1988, but the chemistry wasn't right. He was fired after going to jail for

---

2. Kurt's first proper amplifier was purchased in May 1984 with the proceeds obtained by pawning his stepfather's guns. His mother had thrown Pat O'Connor's gun collection into the Wishkah River after a big fight. Kurt, observing the scene from his bedroom window, later fished them out of the river and sold them.

3. The group's regular drummer at the time was a fellow stoner named Aaron Burckhard, a kid who lived down the street from Kurt. He and Krist had lost touch with him during the period they were planning to record their first demo tape.

4. The call from Sub Pop was a big surprise considering that Kurt hadn't sent them a tape in the first place; he didn't know their mailing address. It was Jack Endino, producer of the demo sessions at Reciprocal, who, impressed with the quality of Kurt's voice, made a dub of the demo and passed it onto his buddy, Jonathan Poneman at Sub Pop.

5. The total cost of this recording — which has grossed millions of dollars — is the now-famous sum of $606.17.

assaulting a rival for his girlfriend's affections. Chad Channing joined in time to appear on most of BLEACH (Dale Crover appeared on three tracks) but he eventually ran afoul of Kurt and was squeezed out. Channing's spot was temporarily filled by Dan Peters of Mudhoney who played exactly one show with Nirvana on September 22, 1990.

About a year before the band jumped from Sub Pop to DGC — this would be April 1990 — Nirvana began work on a series of demos for their second album. Chad Channing was the drummer when the group made their first trip to Butch Vig's Smart Studios in Madison, Wisconsin. In May, after they returned home, Kurt fired Channing. Losing a drummer at such a crucial time — what with a new album and Sub Pop's problems and all — might have been disastrous had it not been for fortuitous appearance of David Eric Grohl (born January 14, 1969) at that one-and-only gig featuring Dan Peters.

Grohl was an ex-member of a pretty solid DC punk band called Scream who first met Kurt and Krist backstage at a Melvins show in San Francisco in 1990. When Scream broke up shortly thereafter, Grohl found himself stranded in Los Angeles with no band and no money. A phone call to Buzz Osbourne put him in touch with Nirvana who, predictably, were going through yet another drummer crisis. Within a few weeks, Dave — one of the hardest-hitting drummers Kurt and Krist had ever seen — was a full-fledged member of Nirvana. It was the fall of 1990.

The fatal financial crunch for Sub Pop had come that summer. The company bank account was in the red and all the staff was laid off; just being able to keep the lights on for another month was considered a great victory. As a matter of self-preservation, Nirvana covertly started searching for another label to call home. At the same time, Sub Pop was offering to sell off some of their best groups to a major in exchange for some quick cash. After much negotiation with Capitol, Charisma, Slash, Island, MCA and Columbia, Nirvana became the property of DGC, a newly created subsidiary of Geffen Records. At first, making the jump from an indie to a major was greeted with much suspicion, but because Sonic Youth — the ultimate American indie band of the 1980's — had decided that DGC was good enough for them, then Kurt Cobain believed that it was good enough for Nirvana.[1] The contracts were formalized on April 30, 1991, and Nirvana was issued an advance of $287,000. For their trouble, Sub Pop was paid $75,000 and promised a two per cent royalty on all future Nirvana albums.[2]

Now armed with a solid recording contract and a management deal with a powerful L.A. firm called Gold Mountain, Nirvana moved to Sound City Studios in Van Nuys to begin work on their second album. At the helm was Butch Vig, a producer with impeccable indie credentials (Killdozer, Smashing Pumpkins, Laughing Hyenas, Tad.) The sessions lasted through May and June 1991 — twelve hours a day, six days a week. When DGC heard the master tapes, they brought in Andy Wallace to remix things somewhat in order to give the album a fine pop sheen.[3] Total cost of the project? A very reasonable $130,000.

NEVERMIND was officially released on September 24, 1991. Exactly 46,251 copies were pressed up and sent to record stores around the world. Everyone associated with the project hoped that it would sell at least as well as the last Sonic Youth record. At best, that meant selling 200,000 copies. Five months later — January 11, 1992, the same day Nirvana appeared on *Saturday Night Live* — NEVERMIND knocked Michael Jackson out of the No. 1 spot on *Billboard*. It was selling 300,000 copies *a week*.

Led by *Smells Like Teen Spirit*, NEVERMIND became a genuine phenomenon. With its fusion of punk power and pop sensibilities, Nirvana somehow managed to bridge the gulf between the alternative world and mainstream rock and roll. The songs were powerful and uncompromising yet accessible and appealing. At the same time, Cobain was somehow able to reach a large, disenfranchised and alienated group of music fans who were hungry for a music to call their own. The galvanizing force of NEVERMIND was formidable. The rage and emptiness expressed on the album became a unifying force among the newly categorized group of kids known as Generation X. After years of enduring recycled classic rock and spandex-and-hair bands playing one too many power ballads, Nirvana was the first rock band in a long time that meant something. It was a long overdue triumph of substance over style. Indie rock had begun to bring together

---

1. Kim Gordon of Sonic Youth reportedly phoned Kurt almost every day during the negotiating period, assuring him that DGC would allow Nirvana complete creative control over their material. Since Kurt revered Sonic Youth's DIY punk ethics, he eventually decided to sign with DGC.
2. Nirvana decided to take a smaller advance against a greater share of royalties. Smart move. Very smart.
3. Kurt hated the final sound of NEVERMIND. He thought Wallace smoothed out too many of the rough edges, turning the album into "a Motley Crue record."

a new generation who had been looking for a way to rebel through music.

Within a matter of months, the entire rock and roll universe shifted on its foundations. Record companies, long known for giving lip service to few alternative acts on their rosters, suddenly woke up to the fact that they had been ignoring a huge pool of new and exciting music. Beginning mainly with grunge bands[4] (i.e. Nirvana sound-alikes), a vigorous emphasis was placed on finding and promoting alternative acts. Commercial radio stations, once fearful of alt-rock acts destroying their ratings, jumped on a bandwagon and began playing not only Nirvana but Soundgarden, Pearl Jam, Alice in Chains, Nine Inch Nails, Jane's Addiction and a host of other former untouchables. The music that once prided itself on being an "alternative" to the mainstream had quickly become the mainstream. It was one of the most remarkable "out with the old, in with the new" housecleanings in the history of rock music. Grunge had become the 90's version of Beatlemania.

A young, happy Kurt Cobain

Not only had the stunning commercial and cultural success of NEVERMIND surprised everyone, it really scared Kurt Cobain. He was bewildered that people were now clamoring to hear this intensely personal music. The sudden stardom began to eat at him as he fretted that Nirvana might be perceived as a sellout. He was also worried that Nirvana was now attracting the wrong kinds of fans — people who bought into the alternative mindset for the wrong reasons. No wonder the drug use escalated.

Kurt had always been into drugs. Back in Aberdeen, he had a reputation as one of the town's biggest stoners, a grade 9 student who smoked pot every day. By the time he had dropped out in grade 11, he had tried just about everything: hash, coke, solvents, glue, aerosols, Percodan and, of course, lots and lots of alcohol. He tried heroin for the first time when he was 22, partly because he was curious to see what his hero, Iggy Pop, found so fascinating about the drug. Meanwhile, there were the now-infamous stomach problems, which, by Christmas 1991, kept him in pain twenty-four hours a day. The drugs became an escape.

Another distraction had appeared in the form of Courtney Love, a bit actress, one-time stripper and leader of a punk outfit called Hole. She and Kurt had first crossed paths in 1990 when Nirvana played the Satyricon Club in Portland, Oregon. In May 1991, they met again in Los Angeles at a Butthole Surfers

---

4. Nirvana was not the first grunge band nor did they invent the term. Writer Lester Bangs once used the term to describe the sound of 70's bands like KISS. Mark Arm of Mudhoney is generally regarded as the first person to use the word "grunge" to describe the sludgy, distorted sound of some of the bands in Seattle. The first recorded use of this word vis a vis the Seattle scene seems to have been in the first edition of a local weekly called *Desperate Times* in 1980. A letter to the editor (written by Mark Arm, later of Mudhoney, under the pseudonym Mark McLaughlin) insisted that the most overrated Seattle band was a fictional outfit called Mr. Epp and the Calculation. McLaughlin/Arm described their music as "pure grunge." Arm later lent the term to Sup Pop founder Bruce Pavitt at the same time Mudhoney released the "ultra sludge, grungy, glacial, heavily spatial, dirty punk" of *Touch Me, I'm Sick*.

/ Redd Kross / L7 triple bill. By the end of the year, they were inseparable, often spending days together injecting heroin, eliciting snide comparisons to Sid Vicious and Nancy Spungen. The faster NEVERMIND sold, the more heroin they did.

Shortly after Nirvana hit No. I in January 1992, Courtney discovered that she was pregnant. Fearful of what the chemicals might do to the fetus, they both entered a detox program before flying to Hawaii to get married. The date was February 24, 1992.[1]

Back in Los Angeles, Kurt ditched his methadone prescription and went back to a $400 a day heroin habit. Between the fights with Krist and Dave over his health, Courtney, money and the future of the band, he began to write material for the next album. There were also two more attempts at detox before the infamous Vanity Fair story appeared. The Lynn Hirschberg article painted an unflattering picture of Kurt and Courtney, portraying them as drug addicts who didn't seem to care what the chemicals were doing to their unborn child. Two weeks after Frances Bean Cobain was born on August 18, 1992, (with her father passed out on the delivery room floor, suffering from withdrawal), California child welfare officials took custody of the child. It took Kurt and Courtney over a month to convince a judge that they were fit parents and more than a year to settle any outstanding legal issues and regained full custody of their daughter. The toll this took on Kurt was frightening. Depressed to the verge of suicide, he sometimes laid his collection of handguns on the floor, deciding which one he might use.

In an interview in the Los Angeles Times on September 21, 1992, Kurt came clean about his addictions in hopes that honesty would stop at least some of the rumor-mongering. However, the bad press continued as the couple became a constant source of material for supermarket tabloids, especially after it was revealed that Courtney blew up at a couple of British writers (Britt Collins and Victoria Clarke) who were trying to cobble together a biography of Nirvana. Transcripts of the threatening messages by both Kurt and Courtney left on the writers' answering machine eventually ended up in the press, leading to another PR disaster.

Despite the personal hell, Nirvana continued to look and sound good. After some blazing performances in the UK, the group returned to Los Angeles in time to make an appearance at the MTV Video Music Awards.[2] DGC, anxious to keep the Nirvana juggernaut rolling as long as possible, decided to issue a history lesson in the form of INCESTICIDE (released December 15, 1992), a collection of pre-Teen Spirit material culled from demos, the BLEW and DIVE EP's, a Japanese / Australian-issue EP called HORMOANING, outtakes and BBC recordings. Less polished and far more punk than NEVERMIND, the album was an interesting reminder that the band had been around long before the word "grunge" started appearing in the mainstream press. INCESTICIDE did what it was supposed to: it held the crowds at bay long enough (a la HATFUL OF HOLLOW for the Smiths) for the band to record a proper follow-up to NEVERMIND.

Early in 1993, it seemed that Kurt had his drug problems under control, saying that the experience of being a father had forced him to grow up. He seemed positive and optimistic, someone who was enjoying the security of a stable family unit for the first time in decades. This new-found domestic bliss might have continued indefinitely had it not been for those stomach pains.

In the first few months of 1993, Kurt consulted nine different specialists, none of who seemed to render the proper diagnosis. The best guess was that Kurt had a pinched spinal nerve, which could explain why only powerful opiates (Percodan, Dilaudid, morphine and, yes, heroin) were able to dull the pain. Physical therapy helped some, as did a drug called Buprenex.

Pain or not, Nirvana moved to Pachyderm Studios in Minneapolis to begin work on the follow-up to NEVERMIND with Steve Albini, a producer with an even more impressive set of punk credentials (Big Black, Rapeman, Scratch Acid, the Pixies) than Butch Vig. Isolated from both the media and any record company meddling, Nirvana and Albini set about making a record that was deliberately less glossy than its predecessor, perhaps in hopes of redeeming Nirvana in the indie punk community. Most the songs had been written over the previous twelve months while Kurt and Courtney lived in their Hollywood

1. The bride wore a lace dress once worn by actress Frances Farmer. The groom wore green flannel pajamas.
2. That performance (September 8, 1992) was quite interesting. During a rendition of Lithium, Krist Novoselic managed to hit himself in the head with his bass (he had thrown it up in the air) and was rendered unconscious. Backstage, Kurt got into a huge argument with Axl Rose.

apartment on North Spaulding Street. Although the material was conceived during periods of both heavy drug use and personal crisis, the songs weren't of typical junkie quality. Even as a serious smack user, Kurt Cobain proved himself to be an excellent songwriter. Within two weeks of rendezvousing with Albini, the album — jokingly called I HATE MYSELF AND I WANT TO DIE — was done.[3]

When DGC and Gold Mountain were finally able to hear samples of the new album, they were aghast. To them, it appeared that the biggest band of the 1990's was trying to commit commercial suicide by turning in an album that would alienate a good portion of the millions of fans who had purchased NEVERMIND. Kurt, meanwhile, didn't understand what the problem was. Hadn't he turned a $130,000 investment into an album that grossed more than $50 million just two years earlier? DGC, although uncomfortable with second-guessing the tastes of their most profitable property, nevertheless called in R.E.M. producer Scott Litt to perform a little surgery on the master tape. Rumors of this ugly tug-of-war between Nirvana, the label and Albini were dutifully reported by a bemused media.

Kurt Cobain's suicide note

IN UTERO — its title taken from Kurt's fascinating with babies, dolls and the female reproductive system — was released on September 21, 1993. The lead single, Heart-Shaped Box, was inspired by Courtney's large collection of heart-shaped candy boxes. Although the album debuted at No. 1, reviews were decidedly mixed. DGC became resigned that this album would be lucky to sell half the units that NEVERMIND did.

Deeper behind the scenes, the happy domesticity in the Cobain household was beginning to crack. The long, slow denouement was already underway.

o **May 2, 1993:** Kurt was admitted to hospital and then a rehab center following a minor overdose at a party.

o **June 2, 1993:** Courtney called police to the house, complaining that Kurt had assaulted her. He was arrested and then released on $950 bail. Police also confiscated a number of guns.

o **July 23, 1993:** Kurt overdosed in the bathroom of his New York hotel room, forcing the cancellation of a show that night.

o **March 1, 1994:** Nirvana played their last concert together at Terminal Endz in Munich, Germany.

o **March 5, 1994:** The date of Kurt's strange suicide attempt in room 541 of the Excelsior Hotel in

---

3. Another working title was VERSE CHORUS VERSE. A song with that title ended up as a hidden bonus track on a 1993 compilation entitled NO ALTERNATIVE while a track entitled I Hate Myself and I Want to Die turned up on THE BEAVIS AND BUTTHEAD EXPERIENCE.

Rome. After reaching the hospital barely alive, a mixture of champagne and a powerful tranquilizer called Rohypnol was pumped from his stomach. Although initially written off as an accident (if washing fifty pills down with have a magnum of champagne can be considered an "accident"), it was later confirmed that something resembling a suicide note was found in the room.

o **March 18, 1994:** Police were called to the new Cobain residence at 171 Lake Washington Boulevard East in Seattle after a despondent Kurt locked himself in a room with his gun collection.

o **March 25, 1994:** Courtney and some close friends organized an intervention for Kurt. Faced with enormous pressure to clean up his act, Kurt agreed to check into rehab.

o **Wednesday, March 30, 1994:** Kurt and his good friend Dylan Carlson purchased a Remington 20 gauge shotgun from Stan Baker Sports on Lake City Way in Seattle for $308.37. Later that day, Kurt made good on his promise to seek help and flew to the Exodus Recovery Center in Marina Del Rey, California.

o **Good Friday, April 1, 1994:** Less than forty-eight hours into his treatment program, Kurt left the rehab center by scaling a wall in the garden. By the following morning, he was back in Seattle.

o **8:54am, Saturday, April 2, 1994:** Although Kurt tried to reach Courtney's room at the Peninsula Hotel in Los Angeles (she was doing pre-release press for Hole's LIVE THROUGH THIS), he failed to get through nor did Courtney apparently get his message.

o **Easter Sunday, April 3, 1994:** Kurt was spotted by a number of people in Seattle. At the same time he was seen around town, Courtney, worried about her husband, hired a Beverly Hills detective named Tom Grant to trace Kurt's whereabouts using credit card transactions.

o **Monday, April 4:** Concerned about her son, Wendy Cobain filed a missing persons report with the Seattle police. Near the house on Lake Washington Boulevard, Kurt is spotted one last time. An investment counselor from Michigan named Brad Barnett ran into Kurt in the small park next door. He may have been the last person to see him alive.

o **Tuesday, April 5, 1994:** After writing a suicide note that talked of "burning out and fading away" and injecting a massive dose of heroin Kurt Cobain died of a shotgun blast to the head.

o **2:15am, Wednesday, April 6, 1994:** Still trying to locate Kurt, Tom Grant and Dylan Carlson searched through the Cobain house. They didn't think of checking the room over the garage out back.

o **Thursday, April 7, 1994:** A search of Kurt's usual Seattle hangouts came up empty.

o **8:40am, Friday, April 8, 1994:** Gary Smith, an electrician from Veca Electric, pulled up to the house to install a new alarm system. When no one answered the doorbell at the house, he walked over to the garage. Peering through the window in the room upstairs, he saw what he first thought was a mannequin. He called his boss, a local radio station and then the police. By noon that day, the whole world was buzzing over the suicide of Kurt Cobain.

The days immediately following the news passed by in a blur. On Saturday, April 9th, the New York Times ran a front page obituary. By noon that day, at least two stores in Greenwich Village were selling memorial T-shirts with the obit silk-screened on the front for fifteen dollars apiece. As tacky as that was, it pales in comparison to the studio executive who allegedly called up Nirvana's management company offering to buy the film rights to Kurt's story. Meanwhile, Sub Pop received a surprise order for 30,000 copies of BLEACH. Sales of IN UTERO doubled while INCESTICIDE began to sell at four times the usual clip. NEVERMIND jumped from No. 167 to No. 56 on the Billboard album chart in a matter of days.

On Sunday the 10th, Courtney Love and 200 guests attended a private memorial ceremony at the Unity Church of Seattle. Later that night, more than 5,000 people attended a candlelight vigil at the Seattle Flag Pavilion. One of the last things Courtney did was distributed some of Kurt's old clothes to the faithful. Although his body was cremated on the 14th, the exact location of his ashes remains a mystery.[1]

After Kurt's death, the principle players in the Nirvana drama began to scatter. Dave Grohl displayed

---

1. One story had Courtney hauling around a good portion of those ashes in a teddy bear-shaped backpack as she traipsed across the country. Other sources say that some ashes were buried under a weeping willow in the back yard of the house on Lake Washington Boulevard with the remainder interred at a public cemetery in Seattle, three Buddhist shrines and sprinkled on the banks of the Wishkah River in Aberdeen.

unexpected versatility as leader of the Foo Fighters, proving that he was much more than Kurt Cobain's timekeeper. Krist Novoselic started writing a novel — it still hasn't been published — before becoming involved in a number of music-related activist groups, including the Joint Artists and Music Promotions Political Action Committee (JAMPAC), an organization that fights against music censorship. Krist also dipped back into music with a group called Sweet 75 who released a debut album in 1997. Courtney Love has gone forward with a successful scandal-ridden career, both as the front person with Hole and as an actress of some acclaim.

There were some notable posthumous releases. The first post-suicide release came in June 1994 when *Pay to Play*, the original demo version of *Something in the Way* from NEVERMIND, appeared on a compilation CD entitled DGC RARITIES, VOLUME 1. On November 1, 1994, DGC issued UNPLUGGED IN NEW YORK, featuring Nirvana's stirring acoustic performance for

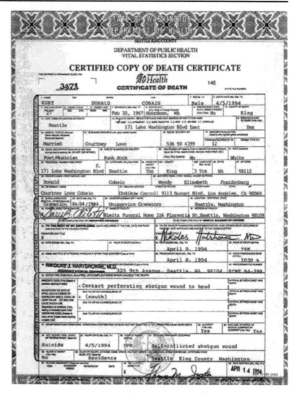

Kurt Cobain's death certificate

MTV.[2] A video, LIVE! TONIGHT! SOLD OUT!, quickly sold 100,000 copies after it was released on November 15, 1994. After being put on hold for close to two years, a live album, FROM THE MUDDY BANKS FOR THE WISHKAH, was released on October 1, 1996.

As a band, Nirvana had probably ceased to exist even before the trigger was pulled. There are indications that the group had broken up sometime in late March after Kurt staunchly refused to accept an offer (rumored to be worth up to $10 million) to headline that summer's Lollapalooza tour. There were also fights with Dave and Krist about how the royalties were being divided. And then there were the constant specter of drugs and his discomfort having to deal with the obligations that came with fame and money. In other words, even had Kurt Cobain not taken his life, the chances of Nirvana surviving another year were very slim.

The legend of Nirvana, however, will not die. On one hand, we're left with the intriguing (some would say distasteful) Kurt-was-murdered conspiracy theories propagated by Tom Grant and others.[3] On the other, we have the Nirvana's musical legacy, something that goes far, far beyond the songs that they recorded. The period between 1991 and 1993 was one of the most exciting times for rock and roll in more than a decade. Alternative music, indie rock, new rock, college rock — whatever you want to call

---

2. All fourteen songs were recorded in one take each. Kurt also chose to stay away from Nirvana's big hits, preferring to concentrate on more obscure material as well as songs by David Bowie, blues legend Leadbelly and the Meat Puppets.

3. The suspicious and paranoid, take note: there are some very real unanswered questions surrounding Cobain's death. How could he have shot himself with so much heroin in his system? How did his drug paraphernalia end up neatly put away when the dosage would have incapacitated him almost immediately? Why were there three rounds in the shotgun? Did he write all of the suicide note? Who was using his credit card in the hours *after* he died? These JFK-like avenues are explored in the fascinating and controversial book *Who Killed Kurt Cobain? The Mysterious Death of an Icon* (Birch Lane Press, 1998.) By the way, the author who is mentioned in regards to a live TV debate that took place on Canada's *Jane Hawtin Live?* That was me. I just wish they had got the name of my first book right. It's not *The Encyclopedia of Alternative Music*; it's *The Alternative Music Almanac* (Collector's Guide Publishing, 1995.)

it — finally broke through. It was a sound that was every bit as real as what was heard in the streets of London in 1976 and as generation-defining as of the Summer of Love in 1967. Thanks to the Nirvana, boring corporate rock and pretentious hair metal was swept aside for a few years. Rock and roll — mainstream rock music! — was *dangerous* again.

But if you're going to run this hot, it's only a matter of time before you burn out. Grunge was on already on life support when Kurt Cobain died. Once Nirvana provided the bridge between the alternative universe and the mainstream world, it was inevitable that the major labels would eventually beat grunge (and all things alternative) to death. Soon after, the world's fascination with alt-rock reached a peak before beginning to cycle downward. The Gen Xers who fueled the alt-rock surge grew older, got jobs in an improving economy and moved on. They were supplanted by a new group of music fans who wanted happy, mindless pop music like the Spice Girls and the Backstreet Boys. Others, all too aware that guitar-based rock music is in large part their *parents'* music, set themselves apart by embracing hip-hop and rap, a form of music that parents tend to hate.

Quoting Neil Young in his suicide note, Kurt wrote that it was "better to burn out than to fade away." Kurt himself may have burned out, but it will be a long time before his memory and music fades away. And one day, when the conditions are right, Kurt Cobain's successor will emerge and the world will change again.

Fast Facts

o An English group named Nirvana owned the original rights to that name (they were formed in 1965.) In May 1984, they launched an infringement suit against the Aberdeen Nirvana. The matter was eventually settled out of court.

o The original *Love Buzz* 7-inch will now fetch in excess of $700 from collectors. Beware, however, that many counterfeits exist. There are many ways to tell the original from a fake, but the easiest is to look at the run-off grooves for the etching — "SP-23-A Why don't you trade these guitars for shovels?" — If it's not there, you're holding a fake. True copies also feature the names ALICE WHEELER and SUZANNE SASIC on the picture sleeve.

o Bassist Novoselic originally spelled his first name "Chris." By the time IN UTERO was released, he had changed that to "Krist" in order to better reflect his Croatian heritage.

o Jason Everman was the person who paid the $606.17 bill for BLEACH. A part time commercial fisherman who made good money during the summer working of the coast of Alaska, he began hanging out with the band in late 1988. After Nirvana finished recording BLEACH (Everman was rewarded with a credit on the album even though he never played a note) he joined the band on guitar for Nirvana's first national tour (June 22 to July 18, 1989) before leaving the group for good.

o In the days before the band became famous, Kurt would often experiment with various spellings of his name. For example, the liner notes of BLEACH list him as "Kurdt Kobain."

o The original working title of NEVERMIND was SHEEP. The first official name of the hidden track on the album (a track accidentally left off the first editions of the record) was *The Noise Jam*. It later became known as *Endless, Nameless*.

o During the NEVERMIND sessions, Novoselic was arrested and jailed for sixteen hours on a drunk driving charge.

o The baby on the cover of NEVERMIND is five month-old Spencer Eldon of Eagle Rock, California. He was paid $200 for that shot. The fish hook and the dollar bill (Kurt's idea) was added later. There was also some controversy over the blatant display of Spencer's penis. DGC went so far as to prepare a cover with the offending naughty bit airbrushed out.

o *Smells Like Teen Spirit* was inspired by a bit of graffiti Bikini Kill's Kathleen Hanna spray-painted on the wall of Kurt's apartment after a night of drinking. Kurt thought the statement ("Kurt smells like Teen Spirit") was a compliment, something to do with his DIY punk esthetics. Hanna actually meant that she smelled light and fruity, just like the scent of a girls' deodorant called "Teen Spirit." When he wrote the song, Kurt was trying to write in the style of the Pixies. In the end, he was a little disappointed with his effort, believing that he had instead come up with a punk rip-off of Boston's *More Than a Feeling*. And while we're on the subject, *Teen Spirit* wasn't projected to do all that well. DGC envisioned the song simply to be a pre-cursor to the *really* big song from the album, *Come As You Are*.

o   Kurt sang all of Nirvana's songs, right? Wrong. Dave Grohl is featured on one song, *Marigold*, which turned up as a bonus track on the *Heart-Shaped Box* CD single.

o   The 20 gauge shotgun recovered from the suicide scene was donated to a group called Mothers Against Violence in America. They had it melted down.

o   More than a dozen artists have written about Kurt Cobain since his death. They include Patti Smith (*About a Boy*), the Squirrels (*Mighty K.C.*), Imperial Teen (*You're One*) and perhaps Pearl Jam (there's still some dispute over the origin of *Last Exit*.)

o   Tom Grant is not the only person who believes that there may be more to Kurt's death. Lee Remington, a cable access host in Seattle, has been pursuing what he called "the Cobain matter" since April 13, 1994.

o   A surreal story involving the El Duce (real name: Eldon Hoke), lead singer of the L.A. hardcore band the Mentors, suggests that Courtney allegedly asked him to assassinate Kurt in exchange for $50,000. He was later decapitated in a strange railway accident.

o   Courtney Love sold the house at on Lake Washington Boulevard years ago. The mansion — originally built in 1902 — has been extensively renovated by the new owner. The garage at the back has been torn down.

o   There is some debate about how much music Kurt left behind. After a show in Toronto on September 1, 1994, Courtney told MTV that Kurt recorded three songs as demos just before he died. The first, *Talk to Me* was apparently presented to Iggy Pop. Another, entitled *Opinion* was given to Mark Lanegan of the Screaming Trees. The ultimate destination of a third song, provisionally titled *Do-Re-And-Me*, has yet to be determined. A final Cobain composition, *You Got No Right* was performed by Hole during their MTV UNPLUGGED appearance.

Recommended Listening

o   BLEACH (Sub Pop, 1989)

o   NEVERMIND (DGC, 1991)

o   IN UTERO (DGC, 1993)

o   If you're into bootlegs, the five volume OUTCESTIDE series on Blue Moon Records is absolutely wonderful. Loaded with outtakes, demos and live tracks, the CD's offer an insight on Kurt Cobain and Nirvana not available through their official releases. Highly recommended.

Internet Resources

o   www.geffen.com/nirvana/

o   www.geocities.com/~dperle/ms/

o   www.geocities.com/SunsetStrip/3105/index.html

o   www.tiac.net/users/tobya

o   http://t-indie.simplenet.com/stain/stain.html

Recommended Reading

o   Arnold, Gina. *Route 666: On the Road to Nirvana*. New York, New York: St. Martin's Press, 1991.

o   Azerrad, Michael. *Come As You Are: The Story of Nirvana*. New York: Main Street Books / Doubleday, 1993, 1994.

o   Black, Suzie. *Nirvana Tribute*. London: Omnibus, 1994.

o   Crisafulli, Chuck. *Teen Spirit: The Stories Behind Every Nirvana Song*. New York, New York: Fireside / Carlton, 1996.

o   Halperin, Ian and Wallace, Max. *Who Killed Kurt Cobain? The Mysterious Death of an Icon*. Secaucus, New Jersey: Birch Lane Press, 1998.

o   Humphrey, Clark. *Loser: The Real Seattle Music Story*. Portland, Oregon: Feral House, 1995.

o   Morrell, Brad. *Nirvana and the Sound of Seattle*. London: Omnibus Press, 1993.

o   Rocco, John. *The Nirvana Companion: Two Decades of Commentary*. New York, New York: Schirmer Books, 1998.

o   Sanford, Christopher. *Kurt Cobain*. London: Victor Gollancz, 1995.

° Thompson, Dave. *Never Fade Away: The Kurt Cobain Story*. New York, New York: St. Martin's Mass Market Paper, 1994.

Related Listening
The Melvins, Sonic Youth, the Vaselines, Hole, Tad, Mudhoney, Green River, Stone Temple Pilots, Bush, Smashing Pumpkins, Pearl Jam, Garbage, Creed.

The Story Thus Far ...
As a fan of the Beatles, Bowie, old-school metal (Black Sabbath, KISS) and punk (ranging from the Sex Pistols to Black Flag and, of course, the Melvins), Kurt Cobain and Nirvana produce near-perfect synthesis of punk and pop. They accidentally launch a musical revolution that changes the course of rock for the rest of the decade.

~ 24 ~
PEARL JAM
Anti-stars from Seattle

No band in the 90's has been adored, analyzed, written about, followed around and bootlegged more than Pearl Jam. They've taken on Big Business, embraced a host of political and social causes, worked to preserve the environment, championed the underdog, encouraged fans to tape their shows, commandeered satellites for private radio broadcasts, eschewed making videos, survived the hype (and death) of grunge and — until 1999, anyway — steadfastly refused to make themselves available for interviews. Yet despite all this (or more likely, because of it), Pearl Jam has amassed a worldwide fanbase that extends to virtually every corner of the planet.

Principled and humble almost to a fault, Pearl Jam became the anti-stars of the 1990's. Led by the still-enigmatic Eddie Vedder, the group has made a second career of trying to prove to everyone that they're just regular people who just happen to have been extraordinarily lucky. On one hand, this approach has served them well, endearing the group to a legion of fans who hate typical rock star hype and the phony posturing in which too many other groups indulge. On the other, these same fans are sometimes frustrated by the fact that their heroes refused to be behave like, well, *heroes*. Underlying this odd duality is the fact that the quality of Pearl Jam's musical output has been remarkably consistent, balancing growth and maturity with the primal need to turn all the amplifiers up to eleven.

The birth Pearl Jam began with the death of a Seattle singer named Andrew Wood. Andrew's band was Mother Love Bone, a group of some local renown and obvious potential. MLB also featured guitarist Stone Gossard[1] (born July 20, 1965), a veteran of such forgotten bands as March of Crimes and the Ducky Boys. On bass was Montana native Jeff Ament (born March 10, 1963), ex of a group called Deranged Diction. Stone and Jeff had first teamed up in Green River, a proto-grunge outfit that lasted for a couple of records before they split in two in October 1987. Singer Mark Arm left to form Mudhoney while Stone and Jeff regrouped with Wood, guitarist Jeff Fairweather and drummer Greg Gilmore in Mother Love Bone, taking their name from a line in a song called *Capricorn Sister*.[2]

Andrew Wood was prone to extreme behavior, especially when it came to pumping his body full of chemicals. He picked up a serious heroin habit several years earlier while fronting a Seattle glam-punk group called Malfunkshun. Andrew first got into cocaine and smack in high school, simply because it was the rock star thing to do. He also loved to wear big fur coasts, spandex pants and flashy red scarves. His idol was Freddie Mercury of Queen; anything Freddie was into was okay by Andrew.

Shortly after the group began circulating some demos, they were discovered by KISS bassist Gene Simmons whose support was instrumental in getting MLB a major record deal. As exciting as that was,

---

1. "Stone" is his real name. He has a sister named Star.
2. Their first choice for a name was Lords of the Wasteland.

the group had other things to think about, namely the health of their singer. Wood's penchant for excess had begun to consume him, especially after Polydor came through with a big advance. By November 1990, Wood was so out of control that he was sent to dry out for a month at a rehab center in California. When he rejoined the group, he managed to stay clean during the time it took MLB to record their debut album.

Two weeks before APPLE was to be released, Wood was found in a deep heroin coma at his girlfriend's apartment. He never woke up. With the drug damage too severe to offer any hope of recovery, his family ordered doctors to shut down the life support machines on March 19, 1990. On March 24th, more than a thousand music fans turned out to his memorial at Seattle's Paramount Theater, the site of Mother Love Bone's last gig.

The surviving members split into two camps. Fairweather and Gilmore formed Blind Horse while Stone and Jeff, tired and disillusioned, opted to drop out of the music scene altogether. That retirement lasted until the end of the year when, bored with their day jobs, they both decided to give music another try. Their re-entry into the Seattle music scene came via Luv Co., a group that featured guitarist Mike McCready (born April 5, 1964), ex of a parade of local bands with names like Shadow and Love Chile. Finding a drummer proved to be a bit of a problem. Soundgarden's Matt Cameron filled in part-time in the beginning with the position eventually going to Dave Krusen, a member of a group called the Boibs. He had been recommended by another early part-timer, Matt Chamberlain.

Within a few weeks, Luv Co. had recorded a quick demo tape featuring a series of muscular guitar instrumentals. A copy of the tape was given to Jack Irons, the former drummer with the Red Hot Chili Peppers. Knowing that Stone and Jeff were looking for someone who was the exact opposite of Andrew Wood, he promised to pass the tape along to a kid he sometimes played basketball with down in San Diego.

From the moment Edward Louis Severson III was born on December 23, 1964, things began to get complicated. The short, difficult marriage between Eddie's mom, Karen, and his biological father, Edward II, ended in divorce shortly after he was born. There were stories of physical abuse and to this day, Karen suspects that Ed was bisexual or perhaps even gay. On November 5, 1966, about two months shy of Eddie's second birthday, Karen married Peter Mueller, a lawyer with a boy and a girl from a previous marriage, creating a *Brady Bunch*-like brood with Eddie and his two siblings, Jason and Chris. When the adoptions came through, Eddie Severson became Eddie Mueller. All this happened so early in Eddie's life that as far as he knew, Peter Mueller was his biological father.

Young Eddie had thriving show business career by the time he was five. He worked as a clothing model for a couple of department store catalogues, amassing a bulging portfolio of photos entitled "Edward Mueller, professional model." This work led to TV commercials, including an appearance in an ad for Hallmark Christmas cards, Chuckles candy and a national spot for "Big Wheels" in the early 1970's. He even managed to wrangle a much-coveted spot on *Bozo the Clown*, one of the most popular children's shows of all time.

The Muellers moved from Chicago to San Diego when Eddie was eight. Eight years after that — sometime around February 1983 — the marriage between Karen and Peter collapsed. During the ugly divorce proceedings that followed, Karen told her son the truth about his father: his real father was the man named Ed, the family friend who often came around to the house when the Muellers were still living in Illinois. Unable to do much because he was suffering from multiple sclerosis, he and Eddie often watched TV together, enjoying each other's company.[3] However, the disease eventual got the best of Ed and he died in January 1981. The whole time Eddie had no clue that this man was his real father.

After Peter and Karen split up, Karen's intention was to move the kids back to the Chicago area. Eddie would have none of this. Angry about the charade regarding his father's true identity, he made it clear that he was staying in San Diego. At first, he tried to stay with Peter, but when the feuding became too much, he found an apartment of his own on Lake Murray Boulevard in the suburb of La Mesa. Now on his own, he was determined to make a clean break by changing his last name to something that had no link to either of his fathers. Adopting his mother's maiden name, Edward Mueller became Eddie Vedder.

---

3. Ed and Karen stopped fighting when he became ill.

Eddie established a routine in San Diego. In the morning, he'd go surfing followed by some pick-up basketball in the afternoon. At night, he worked as a pumper at a Chevron storage depot, filling big tanker trucks with gas for delivery to local service stations. On the weekend, he got involved in the local music scene, thanks to his live-in girlfriend, Beth Liebling. She was the talent booker for a couple of clubs including Bachanal, the same place where Eddie occasionally worked as a house roadie, helping bands load in and out. When he wasn't carrying someone else's gear, he played in a couple of groups, including Surf and Destroy, the Butts and, most notably, Bad Radio.

One afternoon during his usual round of three-on-three basketball, Jack Irons (an acquaintance from Bachanal) slipped Eddie the Luv Co. cassette, telling him that the group was still looking for a singer. Listening to the instrumentals over and over again during his shifts at the tank farm, Eddie took it upon himself to write lyrics to three of the five tracks on the tape. Together, they formed a semi-autobiographical mini-opera. The first track, tentatively entitled *Dollar Short* (later to be known as *Alive*) was the one that he liked the most. It's first-person tale of a teenager who finds out that the man he thought was his father was actually his stepfather and that his real father has just died. Dubbing his voice over the three instrumentals, he entitled the new cassette MAMASAN and sent it up to Seattle. Luv Co. was impressed enough with Eddie's initiative that he was invited to join the band. He was so excited that he sketched out some lyrics to another song on the original cassette (something called *E Ballad*) on the plane, calling it *Black*.[1]

Arriving in Seattle, Eddie was drafted to sing backup for a temporary band known as Temple of the Dog. Soundgarden's Chris Cornell, Andrew Wood's old roommate, had written two songs in memory of his friend. Neither song was suitable to Soundgarden, so it was decided that these tracks would become part of a special memorial album dedicated to Andrew. Various members of the Seattle music community (including Jeff, Stone and Mike) were recruited for Temple of Dog and spent several weekends in the fall of 1990 recording tracks from the album. As the new kid in town, Eddie's participation in the project was his first introduction to what was going on in the Pacific northwest.

In between sessions for Temple of the Dog, Eddie, Stone, Jeff Mike and Dave Krusen began to work on their own material in the basement of a Seattle art gallery called "The Galleria Potatohead." In five days, they had eleven songs. One day six, they played their first gig: October 22, 1990, at The Off Ramp Café. The 299 people in attendance saw a group called Mookie Blaylock play eight songs.[2]

Mookie Blaylock played exactly fourteen shows before the real Mookie had his lawyers demanded that this freaky, long-haired Seattle band stop using his name. Mookie was actually a little flattered, but because his name was tied to some endorsements and trademark issues, use of the name "Mookie Blaylock" by anyone else created some difficult legal issues. It was in everyone's best interests that the band find another name.[3]

The first suggestion was Reenik Roink, which was dismissed almost immediately as too silly. Then Eddie came up with "Pearl Jam," a name he said was derived from an old family recipe for preserves. According to Eddie, Great Grandmother Pearl had been married to a very spiritual Native American who liked getting high on peyote. The resourceful Grandma Pearl found a way to include peyote in her favorite jam, creating a hallucinogen that was not only powerful but tasted good on toast. It was a story that made for good press (Epic seized the story for use their official bio release) but it was completely untrue. While Eddie's great grandmother was, in fact, named Pearl Hazel Howard — a nice Scottish-Irish woman — she had been married to a circus contortionist from Denmark. This little-known genealogical fact seems to throw water on any claims Eddie may have made about having any Native American blood. Regardless of the little white lie behind the origins of the name, Mookie Blaylock became Pearl Jam by

---

1. For the record, the other two songs in Eddie's semi-biographical mini-opera were entitled *Once* (which showed up on TEN) and *Footsteps* (later to appear on the *Jeremy* CD single.)
2. This name requires explanation. According to legend, an NBA basketball card featuring the New Jersey Nets point guard somehow found its way into the box that contained the new band's first demo recordings. Taking this as some kind of omen, the group decided to co-opt his name.
3. What, for example, if Mookie Blaylock — the basketball player — got a shoe deal with Nike? If Mookie Blaylock — the band — trademarked the name "Mookie Blaylock" first, it would mean that Mookie — the basketball player — would have the pay the band a royalty for the privilege of being able to use his own name. Of course, the same thing could happen in reverse. So, rather than deal with the complicated issue of copyright and trademarks, Mookie Blaylock — the band — decided to look for another name.

the end of May 1991.

The first half of 1991 was very busy for the new group. Not only had Eddie, Stone and Jeff appeared in a Cameron Crowe film called Singles (watch for them as members of Matt Dillion's backup band, Citizen Dick), the group recorded their debut album. With a new deal from Epic in hand, the record started taking shape in March and took less than a month to complete. Once the record was done, Dave Krusen quit, reputedly because of the pressures of having a new baby daughter and an escalating drinking problem. After one final gig on May 25th — the Singles wrap party — he was replaced by Matt Chamberlain, ex of a Texas band called Edie Brickell and New Bohemians, and the guy who had originally recommended Krusen for the job.[4]

While the official release of TEN was set for August 27th, it was preceded by two separate releases of Alive. The first appearance of the song was on one of a series of compilation tapes available by buying packs of Coke, Diet Coke and Sprite early that summer.[5] A proper release followed in August, just before TEN hit the stores — and just as Matt Chamberlain bolted to take a job in the house band for Saturday Night Live. His tenure with Pearl Jam lasted from the beginning of June through to the filming of the Alive video on August 3rd. Several weeks earlier, when he gave his notice, he also recommended a possible replacement: another Texas boy named Dave Abbruzzese (born May 17, 1968.) His addition to the lineup provided some long-sought — albeit temporary, as it turned out — stability.

At first, TEN sold just moderately well but as word of the band's energetic live shows spread, sales began to pick up drastically. During a support slot on a Red Hot Chili Peppers / Nirvana tour (several shows were also played with a new group from Chicago called the Smashing Pumpkins) through the fall and early winter, radio airplay began to increase as stations from coast to coast were flooded with requests. By the time, the group left for a European tour in February 1992, TEN had hit the one million mark and was still climbing.

The rest of the year featured a series of triumphs. The crowds kept getting bigger and bigger, leading to an invitation to appear on the twenty-four date Lollapalooza tour that summer. During the festival, Eddie became more outspoken and more of a character. On stage, he pushed himself to exhaustion, often diving into the mosh pit, sometimes to rescue a fan in trouble. Many a set was interrupted when Eddie stopped in mid-song when he saw a mosher in trouble. There was a very public war of words over music principles with Kurt Cobain.[6] Eddie began railing against music videos and launched an internal crusade against Epic when they tried to release Black as a single. Eddie refused to allow that simply because he didn't want the song to be a single. He launched further attacks on Epic when he believed the marketing campaign for TEN became too cheesy and too corporate.

Pearl Jam fans loved Eddie for all this. They saw him as a man of principles, an icon of integrity — and they showed their appreciation by buying more albums and more concert tickets. They even appreciated Eddie's reluctant messiah persona and his attempts to keep fame at bay. Pearl Jam may have been selling millions of albums, but they at least gave the impression that they were trying to stay small.

After more than a year of touring, Pearl Jam finally found time to record a second album in March 1993 with producer Brendan O'Brien. With most of the songs written in the studio in order to preserve a looseness and feeling of impro-visation, the twelve tracks that emerged from the sessions were still hard but without the old-style rock pomp of Alive or Evenflow. Once recording was complete, Pearl Jam headed out on the road again, stopping only long enough to pick up an MTV Video Award for Jeremy in September.

On the surface, all seemed well. Those close to the band knew the truth. Eddie's tortured anti-rock star act was starting to wear a little thin not only with the press but with the other members of the band. This was complicated by a new arrangement regarding how royalties were now being divided unevenly among the group (instead of everyone being entitled to 20% each, Eddie was now going to get a 36% cut while everyone else had to make do with 16%.) There was another crisis when Mike McCready went through a bout of heavy drinking, something that almost got him fired.

---

4. Krusen later reappeared in Hovercraft, an experimental group fronted by Eddie's wife, Beth.
5. The tape was ROCK CASSETTE VOLUME 1.
6. There's a persistent story that Eddie and Kurt actually came to blows backstage during the Chili Peppers tour. The story says that Cobain got the best of Eddie with a swift kick to the groin.

Edward Mueller, Professional Model

Meanwhile, demand for new Pearl Jam product was reaching a fever pitch. Plans were drawn up to release the new album in September 1993, but when it was discovered that Nirvana was planning to release the follow-up to NEVERMIND that same month, the new record was delayed until October. As the wait was extended, confusion swirled surrounding the title of the second Pearl Jam album. In the beginning, the band wanted to make a solidarity statement by calling it FIVE AGAINST ONE. Mike disagreed, suggesting that they go with A SHARK IN BLOOD WATERS while Jeff was keen on PAUL'S DEAD. Eddie's first idea was to called it AL after Aleister Crowley. As the release date approached, rumors circulated that the album was going to be called FIVE, as in "half of TEN." Things became more confusing when the Roman numeral for five —V — was apparently substituted. A final decision wasn't made until September when the band unanimously chose Vs., a title that allowed for many different interpretations.

There was also a battle with Epic. They wanted a CD-only release; the band, still fond of vinyl and always willing to monkey with the music industry's plans to force everyone to change over to CD's, insisted that there be at least a limited LP release. As a compromise, a vinyl edition of Vs. was released on October 11, 1993. All 30,000 copies disappeared immediately. A week later — October 19, 1993 — Pearl Jam set an all-time sales record. In the first week the CD's and cassettes were in the stores, 950,378 copies were sold, shattering a two year-old record established by Guns N'Roses' USE YOUR ILLUSION II by almost 200,000 units. By way of comparison, Nirvana's IN UTERO — the follow-up to one of the most important records of all time — managed to sell just 180,000 copies in its first week. Just as impressive was the fact that TEN continued to sell at a clip of 40,000 copies every seven days. Eddie appeared on the cover of *Time* while both *People* and *CNN* ran features on the group. In the space of less than two years, Pearl Jam had become one of the biggest bands in the world.

After another bout of relentless touring that extended well into 1994, there were two more changes in Pearl Jam. The first was a union, a wedding, as Eddie and Beth were married in a quick private ceremony in Italy on June 3, 1994. The second was a split as Dave Abbruzzese was suddenly fired almost three years to the day from when he first joined the band. The reasons for his dismissal are still somewhat murky, but most chalk it up to the fact that he and Eddie never really managed to click. As president of the corporation that is Pearl Jam, it was up to Stone to fire Dave, the employee. His replacement was Jack Irons, ex of the Chili Peppers and Eleven (born July 18, 1962) — and the guy who contacted Eddie on behalf of Stone and Jeff back in 1990.[1]

There were other problems, too. Following a show at the New York's Palladium on April 17, 1994, Pearl Jam announced that they were canceling their summer tour. At the source of the cancellation was a dispute over what the band believed were excessively high services charges levied by Ticketmaster on concert tickets. They told fans that until they could find a ticket agent who would agree to charge no more than 10% of the face value of the ticket, the band would remain on the sidelines in protest.

---

1. It's quite possible that Eddie had been lobbying to have Jack join the band as early as 1992.

The fight got really nasty a month later when the group filed a complaint with the U.S. Justice Department, accusing Ticketmaster of threatening to sue promoters who work with Pearl Jam on setting up an alternative tour featuring lower ticket prices and service charges. After subpoenaing the financial records of Ticketmaster in June, a House of Representatives anti-trust subcommittee asked Stone Gossard to testify in Washington. During his appearance, Stone alleged that it was impossible for a group to launch a large scale tour of North America without using Ticketmaster, explaining the intricacies of the exclusive contracts signed between the ticket agency and large promoters. As the investigation dragged on and as more complaints were filed by Pearl Jam, all touring activity came to a grinding halt.

Pearl Jam's stance against the Establishment only cemented their reputation as anti-stars in the eyes of their fans. Like Vs., Pearl Jam's third album was released in two stages. The vinyl version hit the stores on November 22, 1994, while anyone who wanted the CD or cassette was forced to wait until December 6th. During that second week of December, 877,000 people bought a copy of VITALOGY.

Still unable to tour because of the Ticketmaster fiasco, Pearl Jam had to find alternate means of reaching their fans. On a Sunday night in January 1995, Pearl Jam purchased some satellite time and invited radio stations to pick up a broadcast they called "Self-Pollution Radio." For close to six hours, listeners were treated to live performances by Pearl Jam, Soundgarden, Mudhoney, Mike's new side project called Mad Season, the Fastbacks, Layne Staley from Alice in Chains and host of other Seattle friends. Between the music, Eddie served as a rambling, mumbling DJ, playing a clip of *This is a Call* from a demo tape of Dave Grohl's new still unnamed solo project. Krist Novoselic also appeared in a non-musical capacity, electing to read from his uncompleted novel.[2]

Meanwhile, the service charge crisis lumbered on. In the spring of 1995, Pearl Jam thought that they had come up with a solution: a tour conducted with the help of a new computerized ticket distribution company called ETM. Although Pearl Jam's plans were announced with much fanfare, the hassles began long before the tour did. Problems with ETM's contract, difficulties in finding non-Ticketmaster venues and confrontations with local law enforcement officials over concert security eventually spelled doom for the road trip. After Eddie was forced to leave the stage in San Francisco suffering from food poisoning on June 24th, everything began to unravel at light speed. By the end of the month, the rest of the tour had been postponed. On July 5, 1995, the Justice Department dropped its investigation against Ticketmaster. The war had been lost.[3]

While the remainder of 1995 was spent licking wounds and recovering from the tour disaster, the first half of 1996 saw everyone working solo. Eddie appeared with Pakistani singer Nusrat Fateh Ali Khan on the soundtrack to a Tim Robbins film entitled *Dead Man Walking*. Mike worked with an outfit called Bumrush before joining Peter Buck of R.E.M. in the jazzy Tuatara. Ever the businessman, Stone Gossard tended to Loosegroove, his new record label as well as jamming with Brad and a new project called Three Fish.

Despite these diversions, everyone was quite happy to reconvene to record another Pearl Jam album that spring. The result was NO CODE (released August 27, 1996.) By this time, grunge had died away and it was generally acknowledged that the interest in alt-rock that had swept the world in the first half of the decade was definitely on the wane. With segments of the industry desperately depending on Pearl Jam to rekindle interest in new rock, observers and critics were quick to point out that NO CODE only managed to sell 350,000 copies in its first week, less than half the first week totals of its predecessor. Any illusions of the album selling 900,000 copies in seven days were unrealistic; after all, Pearl Jam hadn't toured properly in years — and there was still the matter of the embargo on music videos. As good as the album was — the exotic rhythms of drummer Jack Irons added a nice touch — it wasn't enough to re-launch the spirit of 1991.

Over the next six months, Pearl Jam engaged in some serious soul-searching. One possible avenue was that the group could continue to work as a large cult act, playing only for themselves and their still-substantial following. As appealing as this might have seemed, it probably would have eventually spelled

---

2. As interesting as this broadcast sometimes was, many radio stations dumped the feed an hour or two into the show. By most measures, the program was indeed very self-indulgent.
3. The ETM scheme worked well enough for the first several shows before the complaints started. In the end, though, the battle against Ticketmaster turned out to be more trouble that it was worth.

---

the end of the group as preaching to no one but the converted inevitably leads to creative stagnation. The other possibility was a concerted effort to cast aside the "reluctant heroes" thing, carefully embracing the concept that they were rock stars and, to a certain point, it was okay to behave like rock stars. Although this meant doing interviews, making videos and yes, facing the facts with Ticketmaster, it was at least a way towards growth and survival.

Through the first ten months of 1997, Pearl Jam slowly re-engineered their image, growing it beyond the anti-star legend that had served them well in the past. When it was announced that a new album would be released in early 1998, much was made of the fact that the title was YIELD. It was a subtle message that Pearl Jam was going to stop fighting who they were and what fans expected of them. It was declaration that they were willing to play the music industry game — yielding to the necessary demands of a band in their position — but not without imposing some limits. The important thing was that the music be allowed to get out there. YIELD made its appearance on February 3, 1998, and despite criticisms over similarities between the first single *Given to Fly* and Led Zeppelin's *Going to California*, reviews were generally good.

Then, just as things seemed to be going in the right direction, Jack Irons excused himself from the drummer's job for health reasons. Jack has long suffered from manic depression, a mental condition that can be exacerbated by lack of sleep and stress. Although the condition can be controlled by drugs, the side effects can sometimes be worrisome especially for someone who depends on emotion and creative energy to make a living. Having already left the Chili Peppers and Eleven because of his problem, Jack was eager to make an attempt at touring with Pearl Jam, but after the South Pacific leg of the 1998 world tour, the strain proved to be too much. When Pearl Jam's North American tour began in Missoula, Montana, on June 20, the band's new timekeeper was once again Matt Cameron (born November 28, 1962.) Things had come full circle; Matt was one of the drummers who, on loan from Soundgarden, appeared on the original Luv Co. demo that Jack Irons gave to Eddie Vedder on that basketball court.[1]

The rest of the 1998 world tour went off without a hitch. Most shows were complete sellouts and reviews were uniformly excellent. Things went so well that a live album, LIVE ON TWO LEGS (released November 24, 1998), was culled from all the DAT tapes Eddie insisted be made every night. A photo book, *Place / Date*, also emerged from the tour.

There was one final story to be told as the 90's drew to a close. For most of the decade, Pearl Jam has rewarded the loyalty of their official fan club with a special single release each Christmas. The material varies from year to year, ranging from rare live performances to oddball seasonal numbers. These 7-inch singles are never sold to the general public and have become valuable collector's items over the years (see Fast Facts for the complete list of Christmas singles.)

In 1998, the annual Ten Club release featured two covers. One was an old Arthur Alexander song from the early 60's entitled *Soldier of Love*, a song often performed by the Beatles in the first years of their existence. The other was a 1964 hit by J. Frank Wilson and the Cavaliers called *Last Kiss*. It was Eddie who found that one, buying the original single for ninety-nine cents at a Seattle flea market. The band liked it enough to use the song as a sound check exercise during the 1998 world tour. When Pearl Jam was setting up for a Voters for Choice benefit in Washington, DC, on September 19, 1998, the tapes were rolling and a loose version of *Last Kiss* — the second run-through of the track — was recorded for posterity.[2] This became the source of Side A of the 1998 fan club single. Side B, *Soldier of Love*, was performed as part of the regular set that night. All told, five or six hours went into rehearsing, performing and mixing the two tracks.

In early 1999, several radio stations managed to get hold of a copy of *Last Kiss* and began playing it regularly. As the request lines lit up, more and more fans began searching for their own copy of the song. By early spring, reaction to the song had been so strong, so positive and so widespread that Pearl Jam did something they had never done before: they made a fan club-only song available to the public. But there was a catch. Pearl jam would agree to a public release of *Last Kiss* if their proceeds were donated to a variety of relief agencies dealing the tragedy in Kosovo. When Epic agreed, official copies were

---

1. Jack's last live gig with the band was on March 20, 1998, in Perth, Australia. Matt's first outing with the group was an appearance on *The Late Show with David Letterman* on May 1st.
2. The first instance of a performance in front of an audience seems to be on August 20, 1998, when the band played the Molson Centre in Montreal.

distributed to radio stations on May 3rd and a single appeared in stores June 8th. More than 140,000 copies were sold in the first week and a further 110,000 copies in the second — mind-boggling numbers for a single in the era of the album and the Internet download. By the end of June, Last Kiss had risen to No. 2 on the Billboard singles charts, making it the most successful Pearl Jam single ever. At the very minimum, the song raised $1 million for Doctors Without Borders, OXFAM and CARE.[3]

Of all the megabands in the world, Pearl Jam probably most deserves their reputation as a group who never takes the easy way out. They actually go beyond being mere "the-show-must-go-on" troupers. They have often made life difficult for themselves by deliberately choosing the bumpy road in a never-ending effort to prove that they deserve their crowns as paragons of integrity and rock and roll virtue. You may criticize their methods, but you can't argue with their results; out of all the bands to emerge from the Seattle Scene of the early 90's, they are the only superstar act left standing.

As groups go, Pearl Jam has few peers. Not only do they continue to sell millions of records, but they have the rare ability of making a majestic arena performance seem as intimate as a gig in a small club. Add to the fact that group has taken on the burden of being at least the part-time conscience of the rock community, taking a strong leadership role in everything from abortion rights and cleaning up beaches to registering voters and lobbying for fair treatment of Tibet. It will be a tough slog for as long as the band continues to exist. Then again, somebody has to take care of this stuff.

Fast Facts

o Jeremy almost didn't make the TEN album. Inspired by the true story of Jeremy Delle of Richardson, Texas — a kid who shot himself with a .357 magnum in front of his English class on January 8, 1991 — the song was almost cut from the record before Eddie re-did the vocals and cellos were added to the mix. Eddie says the lyrics were also partly inspired by a kid he knew from his school days that once brought a sawed-off shotgun to class.

o During the TEN sessions, Eddie spent most nights in the guest room at manager Kelly Curtis' house. Another frequent guest was Jerry Cantrell of Alice in Chains.

o The beloved stick figure — most often referred to as Stickman — that adorns the Alive CD single was drawn by Jeff in the summer of 1991. When the band started seeing more and more fans with Stickman tattoos during their first tours, they knew that something was up.

o Although Yellow Ledbetter (a leftover from the TEN sessions) is an all-time Pearl Jam favorite, it's never appeared on any album. The best place to find it is on the CD single for Jeremy. And don't bother trying to decipher the words. Because he tends to change them all the time, even Eddie doesn't know what the proper lyrics are — and he wrote the damn song! Any transcripts you may uncover should be treated as nothing more than rough approximations. By the way, the song seems to have been written as a tribute to Tim Ledbetter, an old friend of Eddie's from Chicago.

o For his role in the movie Singles, most of Matt Dillion's wardrobe was taken directly from Pearl Jam's closets.

o Why the long ban on videos? Eddie was never comfortable with the concept of video clips. To him, they just reeked of "rock star." In the beginning, he went along with Epic's wishes because he realized it was just something every new band had to do. But then he ran into Mark Eitzel of American Music Club in mid-1993. Since Eddie respected Mark's opinions on just about everything, he really took it to heart when Mark told him that he hated the (acclaimed) Jeremy video, saying that it was too artsy. After that conversation, Eddie got it into his head that for Pearl Jam to become credible again, they had to stop doing videos. For the longest time, there were just four clips: Alive, Jeremy, Evenflow and Oceans. The video embargo was lifted slightly in time for the YIELD album, resulting in the Todd McFarlane clip for Do the Evolution.

o Like the crisis U2 endured nine years earlier when someone stole Bono's notebook full of lyrical ideas, Eddie suffered a similar fate on June 25, 1992 in Stockholm when the band's dressing room was looted. Rumors say that pages from Eddie's two journals were later seen on sale in Greenwich Village for $50 each.

o The title Elderly Woman Behind the Counter in a Small Town was chosen as a joke. The overly-long title

---

3. Both Last Kiss and Soldier of Love appear on the NO BOUNDARIES benefit CD (Sony, 1999.)

---

was a poke at the fact that most Pearl Jam songs carried one word titles.

o If you listen carefully to the very end of *Rearviewmirror* on Vs., you'll hear Dave Abbruzzese throw his drumsticks in frustration after a confrontation with producer Brendan O'Brien. He also put his fist through his snare drum and then tossed the whole thing over a cliff.

o The first pressings of Vs. don't include the title because the band had yet to decide on what to call the album. There are also at least three different cover shots for the album.

o When Dave Abbruzzese was fired, there was a rumor that Dave Grohl (now unemployed following the death of Kurt Cobain) was going to join the group. This rumor seems to have originated with an Internet posting by Courtney Love.

o VITALOGY took its name from an 1899 medical advice book written by E.H. Ruddock, a nineteenth century specialist in clean, healthy living. Parts of the book were used in the very elaborate liner notes for the album.

o One of the worst crises in Pearl Jam history was Eddie's failure to complete the set at the Polo Grounds in San Francisco on June 24, 1995. With 50,000 fans in attendance, Eddie left the stage after just seven songs, his place taken by Neil Young. The previous night, he had been treated for a suspected case of food poisoning after a bad tuna sandwich. According to some sources, the bad vibe surrounding the tour and that show in particular almost led to the breakup of the band.

o Stone has used some of his Pearl Jam profits to build Litho Studios, a popular recording facility in Seattle. The studios are also the headquarters of Loosegroove Records.

o Jeff Ament is a pretty fair basketball player. For a time, he played for the Grizzlies at the University of Montana in Missoula where he was studying art.

o Pearl Jam does allow taping of their shows providing that the tapes are traded and never sold. Despite this unspoken agreement, Pearl Jam has become one of the most-bootlegged bands on the planet. With a little searching, it's possible to find a recording of virtually ever live set Pearl Jam has ever played. The most treasured bootleg is probably the five-CD boxed set entitled HALLUCINOGENIC RECIPE which contains material dating back to 1989, including recordings from Eddie's Bad Radio days in San Diego.

o Speaking of Bad Radio, *Betterman* began life as a Bad Radio song entitled *Stand By*.

o Here's a list of the Pearl Jam Christmas singles
   1992: *Let Me Sleep (Christmas Time)* / *Ramblings*
   1993: *Sonic Reducer* / *Ramblings continued (Who Killed Rudolph?)*
   1994: *Angel* / *Ramblings (Fuck me in my brain)*
   1995: *History Never Repeats* (live) and *Sonic Reducer* (live) / *Swallow My Pride* (live) and *My Way* (live)
   1996: *Olympic Palladium* / *Smile* (live)
   1997: A split single with R.E.M. Pearl Jam's contribution was *Happy When I'm Crying* while the R.E.M. song is called *Live for Today*
   1998: *Last Kiss* / *Soldier of Love*

Recommended Listening

o TEN (Epic, 1991)

o Vs. (Epic, 1993)

o VITALOGY (Epic, 1994)

o NO CODE (Epic, 1996)

o YIELD (Epic, 1998)

o LIVE ON TWO LEGS (Epic, 1998)

o If you still need more, try and track down the CD single for *Jeremy* if only to have a studio recording of *Yellow Ledbetter*. It also appears on the Japanese issue of *Daughter*. Most other EP's are filled with non-album material.

Internet Resources

o www.fivehorizons.com

o www.sonymusic.com/artists/PearlJam/

○ www.release.org/index.shtml

Recommended Reading
- ○ Clarke, Martin. *Pearl Jam and Eddie Vedder: None Too Fragile*. London: Plexus Publishing, 1998.
- ○ Morrell, Brad. *The Story of Pearl Jam*. London: Omnibus Press, 1997.
- ○ Neely, Kim. *Five Against One: The Pearl Jam Story*. New York, New York: Penguin, 1998.
- ○ Mercer, Lance and Peterson, Charles, photographers. *Pearl Jam: Place / Date*. Universe Publishing, 1999.
- ○ Power, Martin. *Pearl Jam: Dark Corners*. London: Omnibus Press, 1998.
- ○ Ruddock, E.H. *Vitalogy: An Encyclopedia of Health and Home*. Applewood Books, 1995 (originally published in 1899.)
- ○ Wall, Mick. *Pearl Jam*. London: Sidgwick and Jackson, 1994.

Related Listening
Alice in Chains, Soundgarden, Green River, Mudhoney, Mother Love Bone, Temple of the Dog, Stone Temple Pilots, Nirvana, Bush, Silverchair.

The Story Thus Far ...
Pearl Jam tries to resurrect the DIY ethics of the original punk bands of the 70's and the anti-star attitudes of American indie rock groups of the early 80's. They do all right.

~ 25 ~
SMASHING PUMPKINS
Corgan's Heroes

When Kurt Cobain died in 1994, panicked alt-rock fans rushed to crown a new Voice of a Generation. The list of potential successors was quickly whittled down to just two potential candidates. The first person on the list, Eddie Vedder, was disqualified almost immediately on the grounds that he appeared to be almost as unstable as Kurt. These people had a point; in 1994, Eddie was the odds-on favorite in the rock and roll death pool. Besides, while Pearl Jam did have impeccable alt-rock credentials, their music and lyrical output were occasionally a little too, well, *happy*. The job was therefore handed to Bachelor Number Two, Chicago angst-meister Billy Corgan and his band, the Smashing Pumpkins.

Since then, Corgan and the Pumpkins have been top-of-mind whenever we've need a fix of unhappy post-punk fuzz-rock. With a dynamic range as great as that of the Pixies and with a twin guitar attack thicker and more dense that Nirvana and Pearl Jam combined, the Pumpkins have been quite consistent in their ability to churn out material that veers from delicate ballads to crunching arena anthems. Behind it all is the not-so-benevolent dictatorship of Mr. Corgan, the maker and enforcer of all rules and policies within the band. But few will dare complain. Under his iron fist, the Pumpkins have sold tens of millions of albums by successfully articulating a generation's rat-in-a-cage rage.

The Pumpkins began — and will ultimately end — with William Patrick Corgan. Born on March 17, 1967 (just twenty-five days after Kurt Cobain), his early home life was not exactly what you'd call normal. Billy Sr. was a professional musician, a guitar player, who often spent weeks on the road and away from home. He was once even up for a gig with a band called the Amboy Dukes, but the job eventually went to a crazy guitarist from Detroit named Ted Nugent. Martha Corgan was a flight attendant who also found herself away from home more than she liked.

Billy Sr. and Martha split when Billy Jr. was still very young. After the divorce, he first went to live with his grandmother and great-grandmother. Shortly after he turned five, Billy and his brother Ricky went to live with Dad and his new wife, Penelope. Billy's stepmother soon gave birth to Jesse, a son with a serious genetic disorder that made him unable to walk, talk and or function normally. From the day he was born (when Billy was about ten), Jesse has required constant attention — a responsibility that often fell to

The first Indie cassette

young Billy Jr. Watching the struggles of his stepbrother soon had a major effect on Billy and his general outlook on life.[1]

The rest of Billy's childhood could best be described as "confused." When his father and Penelope split up, Billy and Jesse stayed under the care of Penelope, who eventually married a man named Anderson and soon bore him a son named Andrew. The whole time, Billy and Ricky lived within an hour's drive of both natural parents. It was enough to give a person a complex.

And it gets weirder still. The revolving cast of fathers and constantly shifting living arrangements took serious psychic toll on Billy. His problems only intensified when Penelope insisted that he see a therapist in order that he may be cured of what she saw as a persecution complex. The therapist, a good, dear friend of Billy's stepmother, attacked Billy's case from the perspective that Penelope wasn't the problem; it was *Billy* who was being irrational.

Seeking an escape, Billy sought refuge in music. His first exposure to rock was through his father's record collection. His favorites became the Beatles, Led Zeppelin, Black Sabbath, KISS and Judas Priest.[2] At first, Billy was content just to listen. He might have picked up a guitar earlier had Billy Sr. displayed any interest in giving him lessons. However, his father believed that Billy Jr. was the *smart* child; he was going to college to be a lawyer and not waste his life being an itinerant rock and roller. Billy's introduction to the guitar had to wait until he was fourteen when a friend showed him his new Gibson Flying V, just like the kind Michael Schenker (of UFO, one of Billy's favorite English metal bands) played. From that moment, Billy decided that he'd rather play music than just listen to it. In an effort to learn more about the instrument, Billy's collection of KISS and Judas Priest records soon included albums by U2, Iggy Pop, David Bowie and R.E.M.

By the time he reached his eighteenth birthday — this would be about 1985 — Billy was back living with his biological father and had become a fairly accomplished guitarist. When he graduated from Glenbard North High School in Coral Stream, Illinois, he formed Hexen, his first band. They rather quickly evolved into a group known as the Marked, a name inspired by the fact both Billy and the drummer had rather prominent birthmarks. The Marked was into a really gloomy, pseudo-goth, quasi-satanic, death-metal headspace. Since the Chicago market was saturated with similar groups in the mid-80's, the Marked moved to St. Petersburg, Florida, which, despite the large number of retirement homes, is also known as the one of the death-metal capitals of the world. However, the Florida adventure soon turned into failure and nine months later, a dejected Billy found himself back in Chicago.

1. Jesse would later become the inspiration for the song *Spaceboy* on SIAMESE DREAM.
2. An interesting re-evaluation of 70's rock can be traced at least in part to the Smashing Pumpkins. Before the Pumpkins came along, professing their love for groups such as Judas Priest and KISS, it was considered the height of uncool to admit to liking such music. When Billy Corgan bravely declared his admiration for these bands, it marked the beginning of a general attitude change towards 70's rock. Many kids were introduced to KISS and Black Sabbath after hearing Billy talk about them.

Shortly after he moved north, Billy met James Jonas Iha (born March 26, 1968), a graphic arts student at Loyola. Hitting it off, they talked about forming a group together and even worked on a couple of songs before James' duties with a group called Snake Train took precedence. Fortunately for Billy, Snake Train met with the same fate as the Marked a few months later, prompting James to give Billy a call. Pooling a few ideas, they came up with a few geeky, gloomy art-rock songs that were good enough to nab them some low-key shows in some of the Polish bars around the Chicago area. Their first live performance — just Billy, James and a drum machine — took place on July 9, 1988, opening for a band called StillLife at a bar called Chicago 21.

Things took a turn for the better when Billy and James decided to check out a band called the Dan Reed Network at the Avalon Ballroom, one of Chicago's better music venues. After the show, they were loudly critical of the DRN's performance, provoking a fight on the sidewalk with a fan of the band. Her name was D'Arcy Elizabeth Wretzky.

D'Arcy (born May 1, 1968) was a classically trained musician, proficient on both the oboe and violin. She had just returned from Europe where, as a foreign exchange student, she had been kicked out of the house by her sponsor family. When her plane landed at O'Hare, she was unable to reach her parents in South Haven, Michigan, to tell them that she was back in the country and needed a ride home. D'Arcy's second call was to a friend in Chicago who offered to put her up for a while. A few days later, D'Arcy decided to stay in Chicago and found work in a bakery.

The argument on the sidewalk with Billy and James soon turned into a useful discussion of music. D'Arcy ended up at Billy's house where he gave her a tape of fifty songs he had written. "Learn these songs," he said, "and you can be in our band." Within a week, the new group — now dubbed the Smashing Pumpkins — had a new member.[3]

Backed by that temperamental drum machine, the Pumpkins recorded a quick demo that was then used as a calling card at clubs around town. Appropriately enough, the first bar to give them a shot was the aforementioned Aragon and the Pumpkins appeared in front of fifty people on August 10, 1988. Cover charge for the night was one dollar.

In the crowd that night was Joe Shanahan, owner of the Cabaret Metro, Chicago's biggest and most prestigious music club. Although he acknowledged that the band's playing was a little rough, he told the Pumpkins that he saw potential in their approach and offered them an opening slot for Jane's Addiction — if they promised to ditch the drum machine and hire a real, live timekeeper. To make it easy, Shanahan recommended that they contact a guy from Joliet named Jimmy Chamberlain.

At first, the fit with Jimmy (born June 10, 1964) seemed awkward. He was a big band drummer by training and had been earning a decent living first with Eddie Karosa's Polka Party and then with JP and the Cats, a ten-piece outfit that played Tommy Dorsey and Benny Goodman in Holiday Inn lounges from Cleveland to Las Vegas. Jimmy admittedly wasn't much of a rocker; he believed the most radical band in the world was Squeeze. Jimmy also wasn't crazy about the Pumpkins' lack of virtuosity. As a big band player in the style of Gene Krupa and Louis Bellson, Jimmy was quick to admire talent and equally quick to sneer at amateurs. About the only thing he did like about the Pumpkins were Billy's musical ideas. He especially liked Billy's sense of phrasing and dynamics that, as he pointed out, were essential elements of classic big band songs. Another attractive point with the Pumpkins was Billy's determination to make his band *huge*. After thinking it over for a while, Jimmy opted out of JP and the Cats and joined the Pumpkins in time for their third-ever show, October 5, 1988, at the Cabaret Metro followed by a second gig at the Avalon on October 29. The band had taken flight.

By April 1989, the Pumpkins began to sell homemade indie cassettes at their shows. There were three separate cassettes that year, all with pink hand-drawn labels and produced in lots of 500 copies.[4] One

---

3. A word on the origin of the name "Smashing Pumpkins." The group went through dozens of names before finally settling on a moniker. There are many stories behind the origin of the name — a dream involving Joe Strummer, a snippet of an overheard conversation at a friend's party — but the most likely scenario is that it was a case of free association. Billy wanted to use the word "smashing" and when it was nonsensically mated with the word "pumpkins," everyone seemed to agree that the combination worked.

4. The cassettes were SMASHING PUMPKINS (six songs), MOON (eight songs) and EYE (nine songs.) The latter two releases featured an early version of *Rhinoceros*.

---

tape eventually fell into the hands of the owner of a small Chicago label called Limited Potential who offered to release one thousand 7-inch copies of I Am One (backed with Not Worth Asking) in May 1990. This single attracted the attention of another small label, Sub Pop, who agreed to release the band's next recording. Seven thousand, five hundred copies of Tristessa (backed with La Dolly Vita and produced by Butch Vig) appeared on colored vinyl in December.[1]

The Pumpkins' relationship with Sub Pop started off well enough with Billy all set to have the company release the band's first album. Now that they were one of the hottest unsigned bands in the country and the subject of a bidding war, Billy was prepared to follow his punk instincts and allow the perpetually broke indie label issue the record. But then he heard something that disturbed him. He discovered that the Afghan Whigs — the first non Seattle band on the Sub Pop roster — weren't being given complete creative control over their album artwork. Since Billy was determined to call the shots on everything his band did, negotiations with Sub Pop broke down and talks began with other companies.[2]

Thanks to some quick work by the Pumpkins' new management team (the same people who were handling Love and Rockets), the group picked up a deal with Caroline Records, a subsidiary of Virgin (and later, a sister company to a British label called Hut.) Once the contracts were signed, rehearsals began in their small practice space in Chicago. About the only witness was Stumpy, a three-legged cat that liked to hang around. Once the songs were ready, the band drove up I-90 to Madison, Wisconsin, in December 1990 to begin work at Butch Vig's Smart Studios.

The problems started almost immediately. Except for one song, all the material was written entirely by Billy. James, D'Arcy and Jimmy had known that Billy was something of a control freak, but even they were surprised by his inflexibility during the recording process. His perfectionist tendencies took over, extending the recording sessions to four months plus an additional eight weeks for mixing. When it was finally completed, the album featured re-recordings of both I Am One and Tristessa along with several songs from the old indie cassettes, including Rhinoceros. As a surprise to anyone who bothered to listen all the way through, an unlisted mystery track (later identified as I'm Going Crazy) was tacked on at the end. The album was entitled GISH after the silent film star Lillian Gish, a favorite of Billy's grandmother and was released on May 28, 1990.

Reviews were generally good, although the media and some fans took to lumping the Pumpkins in with the grunge movement. Then again, many of the signs were there. They had released a single on Sub Pop; their guitar sound was big and sort of grungy; they appeared on the soundtrack of Singles, the Cameron Crowe film about life in Seattle; and Billy was seen dating someone who was becoming more and more associated with the music scene in the Pacific Northwest: a woman named Courtney Love. As annoying as it was to be categorized as part of a specific sound — let alone be mis-categorized — the association with grunge proved to be rather beneficial. The more attention Nirvana, Pearl Jam, Alice in Chains and Soundgarden received, the more attention people paid to the Smashing Pumpkins.

The Pumpkins also found themselves unexpectedly popular in the UK. With a new void created by the end of the "Madchester" era, the vacuum was temporarily filled with heavy American guitar bands. (This fascination with things American ended with the onset of the Britpop era, a time in English music created as a reaction to American musical imperialism.) Both the Pumpkins and Nirvana found themselves playing to large crowds in Britain and on various BBC programs that September. Once the Pumpkins returned home, they jumped on a tour with the Red Hot Chili Peppers, sharing the opening slot with Pearl Jam.

Caroline Records had expected GISH to sell about 30,000 copies. By the end of 1991, more than 100,000 people had bought a copy and sales continued strong thanks to non-stop touring through 1992. But by the time the Pumpkins were finally allowed to go home in the fall of '92 after eighteen months on the road, all was not well. James and D'Arcy, who had began the tour as a couple, had broken up and weren't talking to each other. Jimmy's addictive personality took over, leading to bouts of drinking and his not-so-secret heroin habit. Meanwhile, Billy was slowly going insane. His relationship with Courtney Love was over. His longtime girlfriend, Chris Fabian (a museum worker and artist), had split, leaving Billy without a

---

1. The appearance on grunge's favorite label soon resulted in the Pumpkins being lumped in with the plethora of sludgy groups from the Pacific Northwest.
2. While Sub Pop made history with Nirvana, it should be noted that they let both the Smashing Pumpkins and Soundgarden slip through their fingers.

---

place to live. And to make the crisis complete, Virgin let it be known that they expected the Pumpkins to go right back into the studio to record a new album. Billy, however, was so stressed out that he had not written a single new song.

The first Moon cassette

It was a complete and perfect case of writer's block. Try as he might to compose new material, Billy continually came up empty. He was gripped with depression, unable to do little more than eat and sleep. His weight ballooned and the odd suicidal thought danced through his head, requiring another trip to a therapist. It was not a very good time to be a Pumpkin.

The breakthrough came when Billy was at his lowest point. He wrote a song about how things couldn't possibly get any worse, starting it with the ironic words "Today is the greatest day I've ever known." That song, *Today*, broke Billy's creative logjam and several new songs (*Disarm* and *Rocket*) were written in short order. The new material, meager as it was, provided enough of a foundation for him to start work on the new album.

Those terrible months had produced at least one positive result. Billy had come to the realization that if this whole enterprise was going to succeed, then the Pumpkins had to be *his* band, one hundred per cent. No democracy, no discussions, no arguments. This ultimatum was presented to the group in simple language: do it my way or get out. In retrospect, Billy was a jerk about it, a real tyrant, but at the time, it was the only way things were going to be accomplished.

Butch Vig was hired to produce the record at Triclops Sounds in Atlanta.[3] With pressure mounting to deliver some new material to Virgin (and with Jimmy Chamberlain suffering a breakdown five days into the sessions), Billy took the unprecedented move of electing to do everything himself. Since Virgin expected a brilliant new album (and not a mere re-run of GISH), the song writing and arrangements had to show growth and maturity. That

The Limited Potential version of *I Am One*

meant that the drum sounds had to be bigger, the guitars had to be fatter and the performances had to be top-notch. Unable to trust anyone but himself, Billy played all the parts (except drums) himself.[4] As the sessions dragged on, the Pumpkins fell eight weeks behind schedule and more than a quarter million dollars over budget. When the master tapes were complete — thirteen album tracks, twelve potential B-sides and another fifteen or so song fragments — James and D'Arcy still weren't speaking and Jimmy was still battling his addictions. But at least Virgin had their album. A first single, *Cherub Rock*, was released on July 7, 1993.

Expectations were running high. GISH had far exceeded projections, ringing up sales of more than 300,000 copies. Even so, few predicted that SIAMESE DREAM (released July 27, 1993) would debut at No.

---

3. There are several explanations regarding the sudden move south. The most common theory is that Jimmy would have a harder time getting heroin if he wasn't in Chicago. He had already spent twenty-eight days in detox.
4. Writing lyrics were another challenge although Billy's formula was simple in the end. Whenever he wrote something that made him cringe, those are the words he would use.

The Sub Pop issue of *Tristessa*

10 on the *Billboard* album chart before peaking at No. 4. Pumpkin madness only escalated after a sold out tour and an ultra-successful appearance on *Saturday Night Live* (performing *Cherub Rock* and *Today*) that immediately translated into a 22% increase in album sales. In the next six months, the Pumpkins sold more than two million albums and were even nominated for a Grammy. Things even improved on a personal level. James and D'Arcy learned to get along while Jimmy dried out and straightened up — at least temporarily. Even Billy and Chris got back together, eventually marrying that summer and buying a nice house on the north side of Chicago.

Then came the suicide of Kurt Cobain in April 1994.

Cobain's death hit Billy very hard. They had been fairly regular acquaintances, having played together many times, and although Billy and Courtney Love were no longer dating, she remained a bridge between the two men. The professional fallout of Kurt's death was just as difficult. With Cobain gone, Billy and the Pumpkins were automatically nominated to take Nirvana's place at the top of the alt-rock world. These expectations even extended to the 1994 Lollapalooza Festival when the Pumpkins were suddenly promoted to headliner in lieu of a now-defunct Nirvana.[1] Annoying as it was to be given top billing by default, the Pumpkins made the best of things and rode out the tour to somewhat mixed reviews. Once the band was home, Virgin released an album of B-sides and rarities entitled PISCES ISCARIOT on October 4, 1994.

As 1994 drew to a close, it was generally acknowledged that the Pumpkins were one of the most important alt-rock bands in the world. GISH and PISCES ISCARIOT had both gone platinum while SIAMESE DREAM was well on its way triple platinum. A home video, VIEUPHORIA (released October 4, 1994), was also selling briskly and *Spin* magazine had declared the Pumpkins "Artist of the Year." Even so, more than a few people thought Billy was crazy when he started dropping hints that the next Pumpkins project would be a double album.

The first indication that Billy had a grand vision for the band's third proper studio album appeared in *Musician* magazine in the summer of 1994 and was underscored that fall in an interview in *Guitar Player*. Knowing that the first two Pumpkins albums were full-blown guitar productions, Billy felt that maybe that approach was getting a little old. Maybe it was time to take things to the next level. At the same time, Kurt Cobain's death got Billy to thinking about his lyric-writing style. Perhaps the dysfunctional schematics that underlay the Pumpkins' songs needed to be re-evaluated as well.

After a short post-Lollapalooza break, Billy went on a tear, working on new material six days a week. Some songs were written on guitar (as usual) while close to half were written sitting at a piano. When they entered the studio in February 1995 with producer Flood[2] (a favorite of Billy's ever since he heard what he had done with Depeche Mode and U2), the pace increased with many days stretching to sixteen hours or more as the band worked on fifty new Corgan compositions and another dozen or so by James. The old writer's block bugaboo was definitely history.

After months of recording and re-recording, mixing and remixing, the new record was finally ready —

---

1. The original plans had Nirvana going on last with the Pumpkins appearing second-last.
2. Flood's real name is Mark Price.

and, as promised, it was a sprawling double album that was more varied, more textured and more ambitious than anything the Pumpkins had ever attempted. Clocking in at more than 140 minutes, MELLON COLLIE AND THE INFINITE SADNESS was divided into two parts.[3] The first CD, subtitled DAWN TO DUSK, started quietly enough with the album's instrumental title track before picking up momentum with *Tonight, Tonight, Jellybelly, Zero,* and the first single, *Bullet With Butterfly Wings.* The second CD (TWILIGHT TO STARLIGHT), somewhat more varied in sound, contained two major hit singles, *Thirty-Three* (accompanied by a brilliant video) and *1979* (a song that evolved out of a demo called *Strolling.*) MELLON

James, D'Arcy and Billy.
D'Arcy's departure was made official on September 9,1999

COLLIE was released on October 24, 1995, and promptly sold 240,000 copies in its first week, an impressive number for a single album and downright astounding for a double set. Within five months, sales would approach three million.[4]

As the Pumpkins started their massive world tour at the Phoenix in Toronto on January 2, 1996, things looked great. Sales were strong, reviews were excellent and the general buzz about the band had never been better. But as usual, disaster was lurking just around the corner.

The first seven weeks of the tour went quite well before things started to disintegrate into madness. On February 29, Jimmy Chamberlain and touring keyboardist Jonathan Melvoin OD'd on heroin while the band was in Bangkok, Thailand. Three weeks later, shows in New Zealand and Australia had to be canceled when Chamberlain's father died. There was an even scarier OD event in Lisbon, Portugal on May 2nd when both Jimmy and Jonathan were found unconscious outside the Pumpkins hotel. Rushed to the hospital, they were both revived with *Pulp Fiction*-like adrenaline needles to the heart. On May 11th, a seventeen year-old fan named Bernadette O'Brien was crushed to death during an energetic performance of *Bullet With Butterfly Wings* at the Point Theater in Dublin. In June, there were more mosh pit injuries at a show in San Francisco leading to a ban on Pumpkins concerts by the city of Cincinnati. And more was still to come.

Jimmy Chamberlain's substance abuse problems went way back to the days before SIAMESE DREAM. Although he had sought help in the past, relapses were frequent and often destructive. After the overdose in Thailand, Jimmy promised the band that it was an isolated incident and that it would never happen again. The Lisbon incident had been a last straw of sorts. Jimmy was put on notice that the next slip-up would see him thrown out of the band. Jonathan Melvoin was fired outright but was asked to help the Pumpkins finish the tour.

On July 11, 1996 — just hours before the Pumpkins were scheduled to play two sold-out shows at Madison Square Garden in New York — Jimmy and Jonathan left the Regency Hotel and traveled to a seedy part of the East Village to score some heroin. Purchasing some a very potent brand of smack known as Red Rum, they went back to the hotel. By 4:00 the next morning, Jonathan was dead. Jimmy, who had managed to awake from his stupor long enough to call 911, tried to revive Melvoin by sticking him in a cold shower — but it was too late. Within hours, everyone was down at the 19th Precinct giving

---

3. MC&IS was also released as a three-LP vinyl set.
4. There's much confusion over the sales figures generated by MC&IS. Because it was a double album, each sale was counted as two units by the Recording Industry Association of America, the official counter of these things. Therefore, if you read that the album sold six million copies, it really means that three million sets of MC&IS were sold.

statements. Melvoin's funeral was on July 15th. No one from the band was invited.[1]

The official statement was released on July 17:

> Today we are very sorry to tell you that we have decided to sever our relationship with our friend and drummer, Jimmy Chamberlain. This may come as a shock to some, to others, not, but to us, it is devastating.
>
> For nine years, we have battled with Jimmy's struggles with the insidious disease of drug and alcohol addiction. It nearly destroyed everything we are and stand for.
>
> We have decided to carry on without him, and we wish him the very best we have to offer. We would like to thank everyone for their well-wishes and support in this very tragic week.

Following some super-secret auditions for a drummer who could help the Pumpkins finish their tour, the group decided on ex-Filter member Matt Walker. Melvoin's keyboard parts were played by Dennis Flemion, on loan from a Milwaukee band called the Frogs. The tour resumed in Las Vegas on August 27th. Back in Manhattan, Jimmy Chamberlain appeared in a Manhattan court on charges of drug possession on October 8th. The judge allowed him to enroll in a drug rehabilitation program instead sending him to jail for fifteen days.

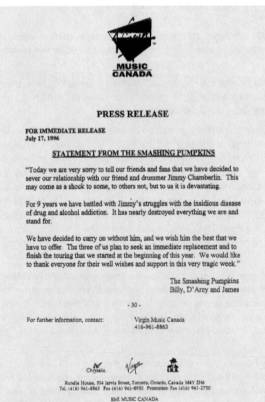

PRESS RELEASE

FOR IMMEDIATE RELEASE
July 17, 1996

STATEMENT FROM THE SMASHING PUMPKINS

"Today we are very sorry to tell our friends and fans that we have decided to sever our relationship with our friend and drummer Jimmy Chamberlin. This may come as a shock to some, to others not, but to us it is devastating.

For 9 years we have battled with Jimmy's struggles with the insidious disease of drug and alcohol addiction. It has nearly destroyed everything we are and stand for.

We have decided to carry on without him, and we wish him the best that we have to offer. The three of us plan to seek an immediate replacement and to finish the touring that we started at the beginning of this year. We would like to thank everyone for their well wishes and support in this very tragic week."

The Smashing Pumpkins
Billy, D'Arcy and James

- 30 -

For further information, contact: Virgin Music Canada
                                         416-961-8863

Rundle House, 514 Jarvis Street, Toronto, Ontario, Canada M4Y 2H6
Tel. (416) 961-8863 Fax (416) 961-8950 Promotion Fax (416) 961-2750

EMI MUSIC CANADA

If all this wasn't enough, Billy had more difficult issues with his family. His mother, Martha, was diagnosed with terminal cancer. She would die within five months. Another blow came on December 29th when Billy's wife, Chris, filed divorce papers in Chicago after a six month trial separation. It had been a truly horrible year.

The MC&IS tour continued through the first few months of 1997 until, after 165 shows over a difficult fourteen months, the band was finally allowed to go home. Unable to sit still, Billy immediately began work on the next Pumpkins album, promising that the next batch of songs would once again take the group in an entirely new direction. Fans were alarmed when the band became embroiled in a lawsuit with Chrysalis, their music publishing company in January (it was settled rather quickly) and then annoyed when an Internet prankster fooled everyone with a series of official-looking Virgin Records postings about the Pumpkins' recording plans.

The Pumpkins played sporadically throughout the year, often taking the opportunity to road test new material. In December, Matt Walker announced that he was leaving his temp position as drummer, leading to another round of super-secret auditions before the band moved to Los Angeles to start recording what would become known as ADORE.

---

1. It's ironic that Melvoin was trained as an emergency medical technician. His widow later sued the Pumpkins, accusing them of not doing everything in their power to keep him away from heroin. The case was settled out of court.

When the album was finally issued on June 2, 1998 (debuting at No. 2 on *Billboard*), longtime Pumpkins fans weren't sure what to make of the group's new sound. Recording without a full-time drummer for the first time (live drums were contributed by several musicians, including Matt Walker, Matt Cameron of Soundgarden and Joey Waronker of Beck's band), the songs were much more electronic, filled with loops and samples.[2] Reviews were quite mixed and some fans openly wondered where Billy's edge had disappeared. A tour (using drummer Kenny Arnoff, a journeyman player whose resume includes John Mellancamp, Melissa Etheridge and John Fogerty) helped boost sales — a fourteen-show benefit tour that raised over $2.5 million for charities was a nice touch — but it was generally agreed that for the first time, a Pumpkins album failed to meet expectations.

Billy was disappointed and hurt by the reaction to ADORE. After a little grousing in the press of the "why won't they let me change" variety, he set about making more drastic changes. The first involved the firing of Q Prime, the band's powerful Manhattan-based management company, in November 1998. In mid-January 1999, fans began to hear fantastic and outrageous rumors regarding the imminent return of Jimmy Chamberlain. *Rolling Stone* reported the first hints that something was up, and *Spin* picked up the thread in February. On February 16th, the on-line music magazine *Sonicnet* confirmed that Chamberlain had indeed been rehired and was working with the band in the studio. Within a few weeks, an eight-date club tour had been booked with Jimmy making an official return to the stage at St. Andrew's Place in Detroit on April 10, 1999, an event that was broadcast through the official Pumpkins web site.

However, this return to the original four-piece lineup was temporary. Without warning or explanation, D'Arcy quit the band sometime in late August. On September 9, 1999, a statement confirmed her departure to be official. As things were wrapping up with this book, no replacement had been hired, although Hole's Melissa Auf Der Maur (a longtime Corgan buddy) keeps being named as a possibility. As 1999 drew to a close, Billy Corgan continued to multitask (this guy once had *writer's block*?), working on both a new Pumpkins album and the score of a film called *Stigmata*. With the group returned to its original four-piece lineup, fans are expecting the Pumpkins to return to the hard and thick guitar sound of the past with a new studio album in February 2000.

Whatever the outcome and whatever new tribulations the group may face, their obstinate resilience to adversity seems to suggest that the Pumpkins will no doubt bear fruit for years to come.

Fast Facts

o While in high school, Billy worked as a dishwasher in a Chinese restaurant. After he discovered the guitar, he quit in order to save his fingers from the ravages of soap and broken china. He also worked in a record store and as a pizza delivery driver.

o Before Snake Train, James was in a group called the Feds.

o Although the Pumpkins homemade indie cassettes are valuable to collectors (prices of $100 each aren't uncommon), the most valuable collectible from the early days remains the red vinyl test pressing of *Tristessa* on Sub Pop. Only five ever existed. Prices start at $400. A flexi-disc of that song handed out at the first Pumpkins show in the UK might be worth even more.

o The name of the dog that appears in the GISH liner notes is Bugg. James inherited the husky / lab / Weimaraner cross from an old roommate who could not longer take care of him.

o The original Caroline issue of GISH is slightly different from Virgin's 1994 reissue. The easiest way to tell them apart is to look at the CD itself. If the cover image is mirrored on the CD, that's the Caroline edition.

o Billy and James have been known to use more than twenty different guitars and up to forty different effects pedals over the course of one album, all in the name of finding just the right sound. On

---

2. Here's something else to consider about the sound of ADORE. When the Pumpkins were a four-piece, one favorite song writing method involved everyone getting into a room, turn up all the amps, flicking on a tape machine and just jamming away. Afterwards, the band would listen to the tape to see if any good ideas came out of that free-form rehearsal. When you write songs this way, most of the new material tends to be focused around guitar riffs; once you find a cool riff you can build a song from there. But when you don't have a drummer, it makes it tougher to jam like this. No jams, few guitar riffs. This means it changes the way you write songs, forcing you to perhaps concentrate more on writing with an acoustic guitar or at the piano. It also may mean learning to use drum loops, samplers and computers in new ways. All of this will inevitably lead to a new sound.

Rhinoceros, Billy layered seventeen tracks of feedback to make up the latter half of the song.

o In late 1994, D'Arcy and James founded Scratchie, an indie label that's home to the Frogs, Fountains of Wayne, Chainsaw Kittens and others. For more, see www.scratchie.com.

o D'Arcy is married to Kerry Brown, drummer for an Illinois indie band called Catherine. Her correct name is "D'Arcy Wretzky-Brown." Following his divorce from Chris, Billy began dating photographer Yelena Yemchuk.

o The famous "rat in a cage" lyric from *Bullet With Butterfly Wings* was inspired by some bad memories of being on stage during Lollapalooza '94.

o Like the Ramones, the Red Hot Chili Peppers and Aerosmith before them, the Pumpkins made a guest appearance on *The Simpsons*. They appeared with Sonic Youth, Cypress Hill and Peter Frampton in the infamous "Homerpalooza" episode which first aired on May 19, 1995.

o There was a big breach in security when an acquaintance of D'Arcy's stole some demo tapes from her house in late 1995. Several bootlegs resulted from the theft.

o That's one of D'Arcy's two sisters on the cover of the *Today* single.

o Between the time he was banished and rehired, Jimmy Chamberlain briefly appeared in a group called the Last Hard Men with Kim Deal of the Breeders, Jimmy Flemion of the Frogs and Sebastian Bach, ex of Skid Row. One recording, *School's Out*, appeared on the soundtrack of the film *Scream*.

o When the Pumpkins played a free show in Minneapolis on July 17, 1998, a murderer was in the audience. Pamela Keary was such a Pumpkins fan that she escaped from prison in order to see the show. She was eventually arrested and returned to her cell to continue her twelve year sentence for murder.

o Starchildren is an on-again, off-again Billy Corgan side project. The best place to find a recording by them is on the Joy Division tribute CD, MEANS TO AN END. They do a fine version of *Isolation*.

o James has done some runway modeling for designer Anna Sui.

Recommended Listening

o GISH (Caroline / Virgin, 1991)

o SIAMESE DREAM (Virgin, 1993)

o MELLON COLLIE AND THE INFINITE SADNESS (Virgin, 1995)

o Since Billy Corgan beat his writer's block in late 1992 / early 1993, he's written more songs than will fit on Pumpkins albums — even double sets. Most of the overflow has been taken up by a series of EP's. Five such discs were collected together in a boxed set called THE AEROPLANE FLIES HIGH (Virgin, 1996.) Of all the Pumpkins EP's, one of the most interesting is ZERO which features a twenty-minute-plus collage of ideas stitched together from innumerable jams.

o James Iha released a 1996 solo album on Virgin entitled LET IT COME DOWN.

Internet Resources

o www.smashingpumpkins.com/

o www.smashing-pumpkins.net

o www.spfc.org/main.html

o www.starla.org

Recommended Reading

o Stapleton, Jim. *Smashing Pumpkins*. London: Carlton Books, 1994.

o Wise, Nick. *Smashing Pumpkins*. New York, New York: Omnibus Press, 1994.

Related Listening

The Pixies, Judas Priest, Black Sabbath, Cheap Trick, Soundgarden, Nirvana, Bush, Sponge, Silverchair.

The Story Thus Far ...

Blending Billy Corgan's alterna-rock passions of his youth (lots of Cure with a good helping of Joy Division and Siouxsie and the Banshees) with his father's record collection of 70's metal, the Smashing Pumpkins create a radio-friendly sound that's as big as the Pixies but with arena-rock appeal.

~ APPENDIX ONE: ~
HOPE FOR THE FUTURE

Rock and roll has continued to grow because each successive generation manages to build on the accomplishments and successes of the previous one. Given a little more time, it's very possible that anyone on this list may one day be included among the all-time greats.

Beck: Alt-rock, alt-folk, alt-everything. One of the most innovative solo performers to come along in years. A loser? Hardly.

Bjork: Wonderfully quirky and with talents that extend beyond just music, Bjork never appears restrained by any rock and roll conventions.

Blur: Always teetering between wild success and terminal disaster, Blur keeps fans guessing with a style that shifts from album to album. Second only to Oasis in the race for Biggest British Band of the 90's.

Garbage: The guys in the band are getting a little long in the tooth but Shirley Manson has become a role model for women worldwide. One of the best female-fronted bands of the 90's.

P.J. Harvey: Alternately slinky, sexy and freaky disturbing, few performers are able to create musical tension like Polly Jean.

Hole: Say what you will about Hole's music, but Courtney Love is a star in every showbiz sense of the word. Hard-headed and ambitious, she's determined to mold music and movies in her own image.

Manic Street Preachers: The UK believes that they're one of the best bands on the planet. Who else can write a song about the Spanish civil war (*If You Tolerate This, Your Children Will be Next*) and get away with it?

Marilyn Manson: As ambitious and intelligent as Courtney Love, you get the idea that a band might be just a step towards Mr. Manson's goal of world domination.

Oasis: The biggest British band of the 90's and, along with Blur, the engine behind Britpop. With Noel Gallagher calling the shots (and Liam providing tabloid fodder), who knows how many more albums they might sell?

Offspring: After SMASH, they were called one-hit-wonders. After AMERICANA — an album that was supposed to flop after the public's fascination with alt-rock died in the late 90's — they are properly addressed as "sir."

Pavement: Although the band seems to be perpetually on the verge of breaking up, their sometimes sloppy lo-fi approach has had repercussions throughout the entire industry. Had it not been for SLANTED AND ENCHANTED, Damon Albarn would have never made millions of dollars by going "Woo-Hoo!" in *Song 2*.

Prodigy: Liam Howlett is one of the best electronica practitioners in the world right now. How far can he take things on his own?

Radiohead: All their albums have been both critical and commercial successes. With oodles of talent to spare and with a reputation as an astonishing live act, there's no reason to suspect that Radiohead won't be with us for years to come.

~ APPENDIX TWO: ~
HONORABLE MENTIONS

The performers profiled in the preceding twenty-five chapters are like the steel girders of a skyscraper; through their music, they created the basic foundations and structure for alt-rock. The following list consists of acts who have provided the necessary nuances and subtle shadings that has helped create a wonderfully diverse and seemingly infinite musical universe.

Tori Amos: Spiritual descendent of Kate Bush.

Bad Religion: Legendary San Fernando punkers and founders of Epitaph Records.

The Bauhaus Family (including Tones on Tail, Love and Rockets and Peter Murphy): Where would goth be without them?

Captain Beefheart: An early favorite of those who liked disagreeable-sounding music. Johnny Rotten used to clear out parties whenever he put TROUT MASK REPLICA on the turntable.

B52s: Goofy band that put Athens, Georgia, on the map before R.E.M. The prototypical American New Wave party band.

Black Flag: Mighty Orange County hardcore pioneers and founders of SST, one of America's first punk DIY labels.

Blondie: The band that bridged the gap between punk, pop and disco in the early 80's. The archetype for all American New Wave bands. And don't discount the powerful role model established by Deborah Harry.

Kate Bush: The original dream pop queen who established a lineage that extends down through Tori Amos, Sarah McLachlan and Alanis Morissette.

Elvis Costello: One of the best pure songwriters of the last half of the twentieth century.

Cranberries: Although often pilloried in the press, the Cranberries are heirs to some of the attitudes and sounds first put forth by the Smiths.

Devo: People forget that they were formed in 1974. Their quirky electro-pop added fuel to the rise of New Wave in the late 70's.

Duran Duran: Pretty New Romantic popsters who almost single-handedly made MTV a profitable enterprise.

English Beat: Together with Madness and the Specials, the Beat revived 1950's ska for a new generation. Kids have been skankin' ever since.

Perry Farrell: Founder of both Jane's Addiction (brilliant pre-Nirvana alternative rock) and Lollapalooza (cultural institution — at least for a while.) 'Nuff said.

Fugazi: Name another punk band with this much street cred.

Bob Geldof: A singer from a mid-level Irish band who proved that rock and roll could change the world for the better. And that's "Sir Bob" to you, buddy.

Green Day: Punk pop from the Bay Area that introduced Ramones-style music to the Lollapalooza generation.

Happy Mondays: Part of the original Madchester Triumvirate with the Stone Roses and the Inspiral Carpets.

Richard Hell: Not only did he come up with the term "blank generation," his tattered wardrobe was the fashion inspiration for thousands of punks.

Hüsker Du: Part of the Twin Cities Indie Rock Trinity with the Replacements and Soul Asylum.

Inspiral Carpets: Progenitors of the Madchester sound — and the band that gave Noel Gallagher a break by hiring him as a guitar roadie.

Jam: Mod revivalists that set the scene for much of the British pop of the 1980's.

Madness: Ska legends and one of the most successful singles bands in the history of the UK charts.

Bob Marley: By exporting reggae to the world, we all became richer.

MC5: More political and far more angry than Iggy Pop and the Stooges, who knows what damage they might have done had they been able to stay out of jail?

Malcolm McLaren: Svengali-esque manager and promoter that not only introduced the torn-T-shirt-and-safety-pin look to London's new punk scene, he also accidentally changed history when he decided to form the Sex Pistols.

Massive Attack: Trip-hop and all its fallout began in Bristol with these people.

Dr. Bob Moog: Inventor of the portable and affordable keyboard synthesizer.

Alanis Morissette: Pop tart turns alternative (i.e. sings about blow jobs in movie theaters) and sells 30 million records.

Mudhoney: Precursors to most of the Seattle scene. Singer Mark Arm credited with first applying the word "grunge" to a particular type of music from the Pacific Northwest.

My Bloody Valentine: Although LOVELESS nearly destroyed the finances of Creation Records, it went on to become a landmark album of the 1990's.

New York Dolls: Campy, sloppy and the first band to wear spandex on stage, the Dolls were essential participants in New York proto-punk scene of the early 1970's. The carnage they created inspired Malcolm McLaren to get into band management.

"Nuggets" bands: Once Patti Smith guitarist Lenny Kaye gathered together some of his favorite sloppy American garage bands of the 60's on one album (NUGGETS, now on Rhino), like-minded people began to take notice. The Nugget list includes the Standells, the Kingsmen, Count 5, ? and the Mysterians, the Barbarians and the Seeds.

Gary Numan: Creator of cold Kraftwerk-inspired sci-fi rock that took New Wave in an unexpected direction.

Pere Ubu: First appearing in Cleveland in 1975, they quickly became pioneers on the American indie scene. *Thirty Seconds Over Tokyo* (Heathen) could be characterized as the first modern indie-rock single in the U.S.

Police: Originally categorized as falling in the gap between punk and New Wave in the late 70's, their love of reggae and superior musicianship set new standards in the early 80's.

Portishead: By having a worldwide hit with DUMMY, trip-hop was exported to the four corners of globe, making it one of the most important British dance records of the 90's.

Pretenders: Like Deborah Harry of Blondie, Chrissie Hynde broke through the rock and roll gender gap and proved that a woman could front a band as well as a man. The Pretenders also built important bridges between punk, New Wave and pop.

Public Enemy: Politically controversial and musically intense, the Bomb Squad-produced PE specialized in a noisy, multi-layered hip-hop sound that still reverberates in hundreds of alt-rock bands.

Public Image Limited: While most people focus on what Johnny Lydon did in the Sex Pistols, his contributions with PiL (especially in the early years) have been largely forgotten, especially when it comes to the evolution of industrial music.

Red Hot Chili Peppers: Along with Fishbone, one of the originators of funk-rock.

Replacements: Bad-ass boys from Minneapolis who, along with Soul Asylum and Hüsker Du, specialized in DIY indie rock that offered no compromises.

Siouxsie and the Banshees: Although later disowned by serious goth fans for being too pop, there's no disputing that Siouxsie lent the movement a serious sense of style.

Honorable Mentions

Soundgarden: One of the most successful of all the bands to emerge from Seattle in the early 1990's.

Specials: Founders of Two Tone, the label that brought ska back to life in the post-punk years.

Stone Roses: Kings of Madchester and harbingers of Brtipop. Their self-titled debut album is still one of the best ever.

Talking Heads: Smart art-punk that took the CBGB scene to a higher level. Perhaps they should have had their own chapter in this book.

Television: Who knows where we might be had they not convinced CBGB owner Hilly Kristal to open his club to new rock acts in 1974?

Johnny Thunders: Sure, he took self-destruction to its logical conclusion — but man, he could play guitar.

Underworld: Club culture and electronica was never quite the same after *Born Slippy*.

Verve: Brilliant songwriters and musicians who, when combined for too long, proved to be far too unstable.

Wire: Simple chords and text presented in interesting ways.

XTC: Pop tunesmiths in the Beatles tradition.

Neil Young: His propensity for sloppy, obnoxiously overdriven guitar made him the undisputed Godfather of Grunge.

ABOUT THE AUTHOR

Alan Cross is a broadcaster and writer based in Toronto, Canada. By day, he works the afternoon shift at Edge 102, one of the longest-serving commercial new rock stations in North America. Along with hosting the long-running weekly alt-rock documentary series, *The Ongoing History of New Music*, he writes liner notes for CD collections, produces the odd bit of syndicated radio programming and does a two hour inflight audio program for Air Canada. Together with his wife and Strange Little Dog, he spends far too many evenings drinking non-fat lattes at Starbucks. This is his fourth book on alternative music and new rock.

More books by Alan Cross:

○ *The Alternative Music Almanac*
   Collector's Guide Publishing, 1995
   ISBN 1-896522-14-9

○ *The Making of* Pretty Hate Machine *and* The Downward Spiral
   Collector's Guide Publishing, 1996
   ISBN 1-896522-31-9

○ *Over the Edge: The Revolution and Evolution of New Rock*
   Prentice Hall Canada, 1997
   ISBN 0-13-778309-4

○ CD collections featuring Alan's detailed liner notes:
   Retro 80's, Volume 1: Retro Mix (EMI Canada, E2-72434-94887-2-4, 1998)
   Retro 80's, Volume 2: Rare & Brilliant (EMI Canada E2-72434-97801-2-5, 1998)
   Retro 80's, Volume 3: 2-Tone (A Look at Ska) (EMI Canada, E2-71434-97802-2-4, 1998)
   Retro 80's, Volume 4: Retro Dance (EMI Canada, E2-72434-20021-2-2, 1999)
   Retro 80's, Volume 5: Spiked (A Punk Overview) (EMI Canada, E2-72434-20022-2-1, 1999)
   Retro 80's, Volume 6: Pure Canadian (EMI Canada) (EMI Canada, E2-72434-20023-2-0, 1999)
   The Ongoing History of New Music, Volume 1 (EMI Canada, 7243-8-37559-2-9, 1996, deleted)
   The Ongoing History of New Music, Volume 2 (WEA, WTVD 35995, 1997)
   Spirit of the Edge, Volume 2 (Mercury / Polydor, 314 535 487-2)

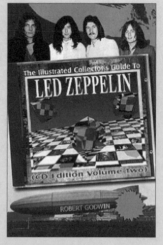
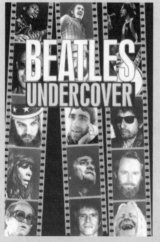
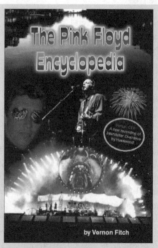